Time for a Model Change

The automotive industry ranks among the most significant business phenomena of the twentieth century and remains vitally important today, accounting for almost 11 per cent of the GDP of North America, Europe and Japan and one in nine jobs. In economic and social terms alike, its products have had a fundamental impact on modern society – for better or for worse. Yet the industry has found it hard to adjust to recent challenges and is no longer much valued by the capital markets. It has become riven with internal contradictions that inhibit reform, and now faces a stark choice between years of strife or radical change. This book is a wake-up call for those who work in the automotive business. It highlights the challenges and opportunities that exist for managers, legislators, financial institutions and potential industry entrants. Most of all, it gives us all cause to reflect on the value of our mobility, today and tomorrow.

Graeme P. Maxton is Programme Director, Economist Conferences; Contributing Editor, Economist Intelligence Unit (EIU), and a Director of *auto*POLIS Strategy Consultants. He contributes regularly to a variety of Economist Newspaper Group publications and is author of the EIU's *World Car Forecasts, The Emerging Markets of Asia–Pacific* and *Asia–Pacific: After the Crisis*. He is also co-author (with John Wormald) of the best-selling *Driving Over a Cliff? Business Lessons from the World's Car Industry, 1994.*

John Wormald is a Director of *auto*POLIS Strategy Consultants and works throughout the automotive industry. He regularly contributes to the business and automotive press and is the co-author (with Graeme P. Maxton) of the best-selling *Driving Over a Cliff? Business Lessons from the World's Car Industry,* 1994.

With very few exceptions, the world's leading car manufacturers have become notorious in recent years for destroying shareholder value, and their future prospects look bleak. How they got into this situation, and how they might escape from it, are the themes of this timely and important book.

The authors bring their long experience of the industry to bear on the key challenges that it is now grappling with – market saturation in the advanced countries, uncertain growth prospects in the developing world, unstable relations with suppliers and distributors – and they conclude that nothing short of a radical make-over is necessary. Traditional business models, including the quest for global scale and an ever-widening range of models, have run into the sand. Companies need to look afresh at what they are good at, decide which part of the value chain they should concentrate on, and organise themselves accordingly.

Manufacturers need to unbundle and reconstitute themselves in order to achieve the optimal balance between size and diversity. If they follow this course, the authors persuasively argue, they could lift themselves into a new era of prosperity, providing a better service for customers and higher returns for investors. The stark choice is between 'graceless degradation' and 'planned revolution'.

The authors have produced both a powerful diagnosis and an imaginative blueprint for reform. The industry and everyone who depends on it would do well to take notice.

Sir Geoffrey Owen, former editor of the Financial Times and currently Senior Fellow at the Institute of Management at the London School of Economics

This is the book to read if you want to know – in plain English – where global car-making is and where it should be going. Graeme Maxton and John Wormald distil their encyclopaedic knowledge of the industry and the world economy into an authoritative, comprehensive and lucid analysis on which they base their recommendation for a thorough reorganisation of the automobile sector.

The authors demolish mirage solutions to the current chronic oversupply: the boundless China and India markets, the standardised 'world car', the proliferation of different models and over-reliance on brand image. They then document the damage perpetrated by motor vehicles and balance this against the contribution of the motor industry to economic growth and to the quality of life. Governments, they predict, will take a more active role in adopting more road pricing, restrict vehicle use within cities and toughen laws on safety and emissions. And oil reserves are finite.

So how can car-making survive? What is needed, say the authors, is a 'fourth automotive revolution' involving the 'unbundling' of automotive business to enable manufacturers to differentiate roles appropriately. This would allow a radical redesign of engines and bodies, a change in corporate culture, the emergence of new manufacturers and the development of real competition in dealerships and servicing. The result? Cheaper and better cars for consumers and bigger profits for car-makers.

Ken Davies, Senior Economist, Investment Division, OECD

Time for a Model Change

Re-engineering the Global Automotive Industry

Graeme P. Maxton and
John Wormald

PUBLISHED BY THE PRESS SYNDICATE OF THE UNIVERSITY OF CAMBRIDGE
The Pitt Building, Trumpington Street, Cambridge, United Kingdom

CAMBRIDGE UNIVERSITY PRESS
The Edinburgh Building, Cambridge, CB2 2RU, UK
40 West 20th Street, New York, NY 10011–4211, USA
477 Williamstown Road, Port Melbourne, VIC 3207, Australia
Ruiz de Alarcón 13, 28014 Madrid, Spain
Dock House, The Waterfront, Cape Town 8001, South Africa

http://www.cambridge.org

First published 2004

Printed in the United Kingdom at the University Press, Cambridge

Typefaces Swift 9/12 pt., and Formata Condence   *System* LATEX 2ε   [TB]

A catalogue record for this book is available from the British Library

Library of Congress cataloguing in publication data

Maxton, Graeme P.
Time for a Model Change: Re-engineering the Global Automotive Industry / Graeme P. Maxton
and John Wormald.
     p.   cm.
Includes bibliographical references and index.
ISBN 0 521 83715 4
1. Automobile industry and trade.   2. Automobile industry and trade – Management.   3. Reengineering
(Management).   4. Competition, International.   I. Wormald, John.   II. Title.
HD9710.A2M3863   2004
338.4′7629222 – dc22   2004045634

ISBN 0 521 83715 4 hardback

Contents

Figures

Foreword

The automotive sector is a critically important and complex one. Other than the vehicles themselves, and the roads and fuel needed to run them, the business is intricately tied to the manufacture of a wide range of components and the extraction of precious raw materials. It is linked closely to the policies of governments, the earnings of banks. Indirectly, it brings us road congestion, too many fatalities and a wave of other environmental troubles. In many ways, the automotive sector offers an almost endless stream of social, political and economic inter-connections which affect us all in some way. As you read their exciting book you realise how much the authors know about this world and how compellingly they express their knowledge to build yours. The shock comes when you wake up to the questions they pose.

Readers of their first book, *Driving Over a Cliff* published a decade ago, will see a continuing progression in the ruinous steps which have forced the industry into a socio-politico-economic corner. Whether this slide is related to flat demand or to the industry's creation of an ever-wider range of vehicles that many buyers seem to care little about, there is a problem. As with most ageing systems, problem descriptions are difficult because we like to hear problems defined in terms of potential solutions. Yet none are evident – or at least none that will be easy for the protagonists to apply.

Those working in the industry typically have five- or ten-year strategies. They can no longer survive with these. Business leaders need to generate a font of new visions which can be developed into constructive action. Only then can there be solutions. The future lies in the abilities of companies to continuously and creatively tear-down and recreate themselves, to meet customers' demands. Since few companies dominate their value-chains from start to finish, the future of competition will no longer be limited to that between individual companies, but between changing segments of the supply and distribution chains. Companies have to unbundle and reconstruct to survive. Can we believe that such strategies are on their drafting tables in this industry today?

It looks unlikely. Indeed, how can there be any *recreations* in an industry populated, as the authors note, by self-importance, lack of trust in partners, compulsive command-and-control behaviour, reluctance to relinquish territory, contempt for legal authority, squandering of resources and on, and on. Whatever the system of relationships in the industry, the banking fraternity is on the far side of being wary. Other industry watchers must ask if it can really be so bad . . . isn't it just temporary, aren't these monoliths too large and too important to fail? Perhaps not.

Maxton and Wormald develop all we can reasonably know about this great part of our personal and business lives, looking at its history and progression, the excitements and the love affair we've had with the automobile and how deeply this system affects us all. They then set the industry between the devil and the deep blue sea – it either faces a *graceless degradation* or must rejuvenate itself, through a revolution in the way companies are constituted and how they operate. The changes required are unsubtle and urgent, forcing us to hear a call for radical change, or else. After a large portion of my life spent working in the automotive industry and now engaged in teaching a broad-scale set of graduate courses in management and automotive systems, I'm convinced that a revolution will come, perhaps one affecting several industries and not just automotive. This book is now forcing my guesses as to when this will be as it should force those of our manufacturing giants and banks and unions and governments.

No change in one part of a system leaves any other part untouched. Something profound will happen. This will be influenced by the people who share the analysis presented here.

Professor G. Fredric Bolling
University of Michigan

Acknowledgements

There are a great many people we would like to thank for their help, their insight and their support. Many are in the auto industry, many are not. In no particular order we would like to say thank you to the following people. Fred Bolling at the University of Michigan who was instrumental in encouraging us to write this book. Anthony Millington of ACEA in Tokyo for his endless wisdom and kindness. The delightful Qing Pan of DaimlerChrysler in Singapore for his thoughts. Jay Kunkel for his friendship and advice on any number of subjects. The many people in the Economist Group who have supported and cajoled – but especially Andrew Vine, Carolyn Meier, Daniel Franklin and Iain Carson. Kai-Uwe Seidenfuss, lately of Mitsubishi Motors in Japan, for many stimulating discussions. Lee Brandsetter at Columbia University. Martina Tichy for her Panta Rei *Weltanschauung*. Ken Davies of the OECD in Paris for many years of good ideas. Bloomberg Tokyo – especially Peter Hannam, Kae Inoue and Lindsay Whipp. John Monk of *auto*POLIS in Detroit, Patrick Guiraud in Paris, Vicky Gardner in London, Kim Rennick in Sydney. David Andrea, previously of CAR, in Ann Arbor, Michigan. Mukund Rajan of Tata in Mumbai, particularly for the trip to the company's steel plant in Jamshedpur. Alexina, Robin, Pamela, June and Jocelyne. Jeff Ng of Citigroup in New York. Glenn Mercer of McKinsey in Cleveland for his thoughts, ideas and an endless sense of irony. John Coneybeare at the University of Iowa. Mark Critz of Visteon (and Sue) in Ann Arbor. Oliver Brinkmann of Deutsche Bank in Singapore. Marsha Stopa in Detroit for her boundless enthusiasm. Dr Amir Albadvi of Iran Khodro in Tehran. Gérard Gastaut, formerly of Renault, and many of his colleagues there for numerous stimulating discussions. Eric van Ginderachter and his team in the Directorate General for Competition of the European Commission. Phil Evans, the trenchant and persuasive economist who led the UK Consumer Association's efforts on car pricing and distribution, and on the European Block Exemption Regulation. Our many clients in the components industry and the aftermarket in Europe. Gabriel de Bérard and Patrick Joubert of FEDA, the French aftermarket distributors' federation. Hartmut Röhl and Sylvia Gotzen of its European equivalent, FIGIEFA. Peter Upton of the FAPM and all our friends in the industry and government in Australia. Arjab Basu in India, John Evans in Bangkok and China, Caroline and Michael Berkeley in London, Gerry Ambrose in Singapore and everyone else who has helped and supported and guided us over these years whom we have rashly neglected to mention.

Glossary

4WD	Four-wheel drive
ACEA	Association des Constructeurs Européens d'Automobiles
AFTA	Asian Free Trade Area
aftermarket	the downstream service and repair sector of the industry
ASEAN	Association of South-East Asian Nations
bbl	barrel
BEUC	Bureau Européen des Unions de Consommateurs (the European Consumers' Organisation)
BMW	includes Rover from the beginning of 1994 to 2000
CAD	computer-aided design
CAFE	corporate average fuel economy
CAGR	compound annual growth rate
CAM	computer-aided manufacturing
CAR	Center for Automotive Research
CARB	California Air Resources Board
CBU	completely built up
CECRA	Conseil Européen du Commerce et de la Réparation Automobiles
CFC	chlorofluorocarbon
CKD	completely knocked down (a kit of the vehicle)
CNC	computer numerically controlled
CNG	compressed natural gas
CO	carbon monoxide
CO_2	carbon dioxide
CV	commercial vehicle
DI	direct injection
EBIT	earnings before interest and tax
EC	European Community
EDI	electronic data interchange
EEA	European Economic Area
EFI	electronic fuel injection
EFTA	European Free Trade Association
ERM	Exchange Rate Mechanism, in Europe
EU	European Union

EV	electric vehicle	NHTSA	National Highway Traffic Safety Administration
FAW	First Auto Works (China)		
FIGIEFA	Fédération Internationale des Grossistes, Importateurs et Exportateurs en Fournitures Automobiles (International Federation of Automotive Aftermarket Distributors)	NIC	newly industrialising country
		NOx	oxides of nitrogen
		OECD	Organisation for Economic Cooperation and Development
		OEM	original equipment manufacturer
GDP	gross domestic product	OES	original equipment supplier
GM	General Motors	OPEC	Organisation of Petroleum Exporting Countries
GNP	gross national product		
HC	hydrocarbon	parc	the number of cars in use
HEV	hybrid electric vehicle	PM	particulate matter (soot)
IAM	independent aftermarket	PSA	Peugeot SA (Peugeot-Citroën)
IDI	indirect injection	RAC	Royal Automobile Club
IIHS	Insurance Institute for Highway Safety	SAIC	Shanghai Auto Industry Corporation
IMF	International Monetary Fund	SKD	semi-knocked-down (vehicle)
IMVP	International Motor Vehicle Programme	SUV	sports utility vehicle
		Toyota	includes Lexus
JIT	just-in-time	TTI	Texas Transportation Institute
LCV	light commercial vehicle		
LDC	less-developed country	UAW	United Auto Workers Union
LEV	low-emission vehicle	ULEV	ultra-low-emissions vehicle
LPG	liquid petroleum gas	UN	United Nations
M&A	mergers and aquisitions	VAT	value-added tax
MPV	multipurpose vehicle	VM	vehicle manufacturer
n/a	not available	VW	Volkswagen
NAFTA	North American Free Trade Agreement	WD	warehouse distributors
		WTO	World Trade Organisation
		ZEV	zero emissions vehicle

Introduction

The world's automotive industry affects almost all of us in some way. It employs millions of people directly, tens of millions indirectly. Its products have transformed society, bringing undreamed-of levels of mobility, changing the ways we live and work. For much of the developed world, and increasingly for the developing world, it is a pillar industry, a flag of economic progress. Without an automotive industry it is impossible to develop an efficient steel business, a plastics industry or a glass sector – other central foundations of economic progress. The automotive industry has been a core industry, a unique economic phenomenon, which has dominated the twentieth century.

What can we expect of it in the twenty-first century? Not the same, for sure. The automotive industry now suffers from a series of structural schisms. It has become riddled with contradictions and economic discontinuities. For the capital markets and the finance sector it has lost a lot of its significance, as a result of ever declining profits and stagnant sales. The proliferation of products means that it has become hopelessly wasteful of economic resources. There is now a divided world of over-motorised countries like those in Europe, the US and Japan, and hungry aspirants almost everywhere else. Motorising these markets to the same extent is simply not possible soon. So there is a growth problem too.

In our view, many of these problems and their implications are self-inflicted – the industry suffers from a lack of systemic thinking: brand proliferation at the expense of rational resource allocation and profit; oligopolistic power without the expected returns;

unreasonable pressures placed on suppliers, bully-boy behaviour to manage them, as well as distributors, dealers and governments; micromanagement rather than real leadership.

While all this sounds like a very gloomy assessment of such a vast economic phenomenon, we are not in the end despondent. A different future is possible for the industry, and a highly desirable one. We map out two options. The first we have called Graceless Degradation. This is what we think will happen to the industry if it does not change. The other, the Fourth Revolution, looks at the potential for sustained growth if it does.

The main themes we will develop in this book are as follows.

- The automotive industry is the world's greatest industry, unique in its combination of manufacturing some of the most significant consumer durables, and the home of some of the greatest brands, and the source of a vast array of technologies, unmatched as a manufacturing organisation, on a truly global scale.
- It has made enormous contributions to human welfare and to economic development but the societal and environmental challenges to it continue to increase.
- The level and diversity of technologies that it must deploy are increasing, which imposes both new investment burdens and new uncertainties and risks.
- All this is taking place within a fast-maturing world market. The developed markets are full. The emerging markets will bring only limited growth for another

decade and are not necessarily easy to access.

- The revolution in the supplier industry, begun twenty to twenty-five years ago, has not fully run its course. Relationships with this sector are still very one-sided. There is a danger of excessive pressure on it killing the geese that increasingly lay the golden eggs of innovation.
- The parallel revolution that ultimately has to take place in the downstream (distribution and service) sector has barely begun. The longer-term implications of what took place in Europe around the time of new Block Exemption Regulation are only very dimly perceived but they raise profound questions about the future balance of power in this part of the business.
- The financial performance of the industry has been dismal, with a few exceptions. The capital markets take an increasingly jaundiced view of it, as a destroyer of value. There is clearly something wrong with its economic model.
- On its present course, things seem unlikely to improve. We are concerned about the poor quality of the industry's relationships. We believe that the obsessive proliferation of products does little for growth, inflates development costs, poisons attitudes and potentially threatens investment in needed future technologies.
- There is an alternative future, involving a complete unbundling of the business, more open co-operation and a more rational division of roles and responsibilities. This would lead to a better-balanced, more responsive and less defensive industry, and one with a sounder economic and financial basis.

The interpretation presented here is our own, except where specifically attributed to others. Some will applaud our ideas, others will find them uncomfortable, even alien. We have tried to be as accurate as possible and have used as wide a variety of sources as possible to corroborate our hypotheses. We are, quite deliberately, trying to shake this industry out of some of its introspection and complacency. At the same time we want to stimulate the minds of those who lead the business, to let them see that there is a better way. We want to provide legislators with some ideas and financial institutions with some support, and give society at large some cause to think about the value of our mobility today and in the future. Again, some will enjoy that, others will not. Blandness is not our style.

We are particularly grateful to all those in and around the industry for whom we have had the privilege to work in the last fifteen years, even to those with whom we have occasionally crossed swords.

This industry remains a very great one. It deserves well-informed analysis, commentary and debate. Our motivation, at the very least, is to have contributed to that.

From automania to maturity – in the main markets at least

Out of gas – and nowhere else to go

In the time it takes you to count to five, ten new cars and trucks will have been built and sold somewhere across the world: all day, every week, throughout the year. In the same time, almost as many vehicles will have been wrecked beyond repair or scrapped and hundreds will have been damaged in other ways. In the next 15 minutes, thirty-four people will have been killed as a result of motor vehicle accidents. Hundreds will have been hospitalised.

The automotive industry works on a scale so awesome and has an influence so vast that it is often difficult to see. Roughly a million new cars and trucks are built around the world each week – they are easily the most complex products of their kind to be mass-produced in such volumes. The industry uses manufacturing technology that is at the cutting edge of science. It uses 15 per cent of the world's steel, 40 per cent of the world's rubber and 25 per cent of the world's glass. The vehicles themselves, these emotive icons of success, use a staggering 40 per cent of the world's annual oil output.

The motor industry is the world's largest single manufacturing activity. In 2002, the industry's most recent peak, it produced almost 58 million vehicles worldwide. Each contained up to 8,000 individual parts of widely varying materials, made in highly specialised factories across the world. Every year, almost 460 billion parts are needed just to manufacture new vehicles. Massive capacity is also dedicated to the production of replacement parts, for when originally fitted parts wear out or are damaged. There is a range of businesses that focus on vehicle distribution, sales and the service and repair aftermarket too, as well as a massive network of industries involved in the supply of fuel, financing and insurance. The automotive industry is a huge consumer of energy and raw materials. It is also a vast source of employment.

For most of its existence the motor industry has been a model of industrial and social discipline and control. It is not just that the auto sector offers a 'pillar' of industrial development; it also offers something else. Mussolini described the automobile as 'a powerful and delicate machine, which brings together titanic rhythms in its steel heart', which neatly sums up its immense emotional appeal. The Fascist regimes in Europe used the promise of mass motorisation as a means of satisfying individual aspirations without political concessions – although they never delivered on the promise. The industry has provided opportunities for spectacular demonstrations of technical prowess through racing, and for grandiose public works projects starting with the German *Autobahnen* and culminating in the vast US interstate highway network. As coal and the steam engine were to the nineteenth century, so the automobile and oil were to the twentieth. A few have tried to oppose the trend: Nikita Khrushchev rejected mass motorisation for the USSR; some Communist Party officials in China reportedly have doubts. These exceptions apart, the industry has in many ways been a mirror of our societies and our values over the last hundred years.

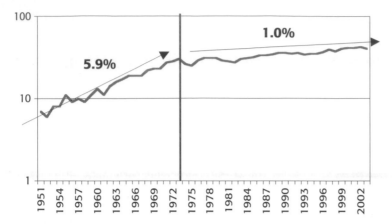

Source: autoPOLIS, Economic Intelligence Unit

Fig. 1.1 Slowing world production (millions of vehicles per year)

In this book we look at the impact and influence of the car and the automobile industry. We also look at the discontinuities that have built up in this massive business sector which have to be resolved. It may be a colossal industrial sector, and it may be critically important to millions of us for many reasons, but it is also full of structural schisms that will need to be fixed in a variety of good and not so good ways over the next decade. Like most things that are a hundred years old, the industry is in need of an overhaul. Throughout its history, it has been growth that has been the fuel that has kept the motor industry's engine running; that has kept it on the road. Unfortunately, however, that engine has now stalled. The industry experienced a compound annual growth rate of 8 per cent a year for most of its first century. But the pace has been slowing steadily. Figure 1.1 shows the history of world car production volumes since 1950. The logarithmic scale on the y-axis is used to show ratios instead of absolute numbers. We have illustrated it this way to make the changes in growth rates clearer. There is a very visible break in 1973, the year of the first oil shock. Before that, from 1950 to 1973, world vehicle production grew at almost 6 per cent per year. Between 1973 and the mid-1990s, it slowed down to 1 per cent a year, on average.

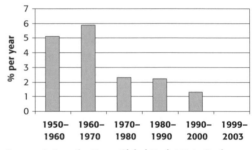

Source: *Automotive News, Global Market Data Book,* June 2003 and previous years

Fig. 1.2 Coming to a halt: compound annual growth in world production volumes

Between 1999 and the end of 2003 it came to a halt.

The obvious temptation in looking at the figure is to blame the oil shocks for this change in pace. In fact they had only a temporary effect, with less of a downturn in 1974 and 1975 than might have been feared. After that, the OPEC oil producers were paid in dollars rapidly devalued by inflation, so that the real (constant currency value) price of oil quickly returned to where it had been. But vehicle production did not return to the old growth curve. In retrospect, 1973 merely signalled the end of the post-World War II phase of reconstruction. It heralded the beginning of a new phase for the auto industry. This

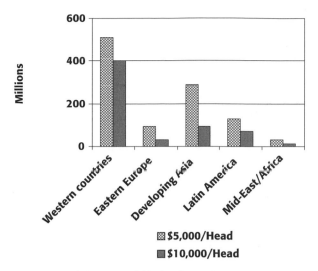

$\boxtimes$ **$5,000/Head**

$\blacksquare$ **$10,000/Head**

Source: UN statistics (not available for all countries)

Notes: Western countries: France, Germany, UK, Italy, Spain, United States

Eastern Europe: Turkey, Poland, Hungary, Russia

Developing Asia: China, India, Indonesia, Pakistan, Philippines, Thailand, South Korea, Malaysia

Latin America: Brazil, Mexico, Columbia, Argentina, Venezuela, Chile

Mid-East/Africa: Nigeria, Egypt, Algeria, Morocco, Ivory Coast, Tunisia

Fig. 1.3 Number of people over purchasing power parity disposable income thresholds, 2000

was the point at which the developed-country markets almost reached saturation. Growth for the world's automotive industry began to slow (see figure 1.2). As we shall see, this is a problem which has become progressively more serious. Over the last thirty years it has affected much of the industry's investment, its behaviour and its performance. Curiously, however, it is a problem that few in the industry seem formally to recognise or even to be aware of.

Throughout most of the twentieth century the motor industry expanded rapidly, moving in parallel with the development of the biggest economies in North America, Europe and Japan. As people became wealthier they aspired to owning a car and the industry made that possible through lowering the costs and prices of vehicles as volumes grew. Yet, even today, the industry and the vehicles themselves remain a feature of life only for the

world's rich. More than 70 per cent of all cars and trucks are still sold in the developed world.

The level of car ownership in any country is driven almost entirely by two factors: the percentage of the population who have crossed the threshold of minimum income needed to be able to afford their own vehicle; and population growth. In other words, and perhaps unsurprisingly, the industry's development is mainly a factor of economic development. There are some exceptions, especially in the short term where markets can be boosted or cut for other reasons. We shall explore those more later. As a rule of thumb, though, it is economic development which fuels the industry.

Cars are expensive to own and run – they consume up to a quarter of household budgets in many wealthy countries. You need, on average, US$10,000 of personal disposable

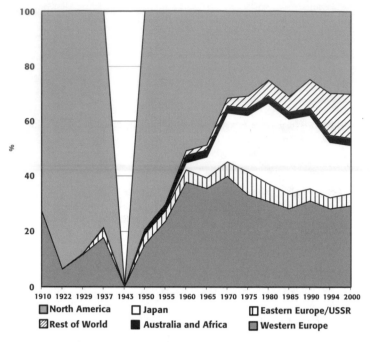

Sources: MVMA data, quoted in Gerald Bloomfield, *The World Automotive Industry,* Newton Abbot: David and Charles, 1978; *auto*POLIS

Fig. 1.4 The first 100 years – production by region

income a year to afford a conventional car, although efforts are underway to produce more affordable, so-called entry-level, cars for emerging markets such as the Renault Logan. Figure 1.3 shows that the population with this level of income is overwhelmingly in the OECD countries.

In 2003 there were a little fewer than 600 million vehicles on the world's roads, roughly one for every ten people. Nearly 80 per cent of these were in three regions – North America, Japan and Western Europe. Almost the same proportion were produced there. Moreover, almost every vehicle innovation, every design and almost every idea affecting the business came from these three places too.

So, in its first century, the automotive industry was a developed-country business, as you can see in figure 1.4. Born in Europe, it first grew up in the United States, extending back to Europe and then to Japan, with the rest of the world trailing far behind. Newspapers

may be filled with stories about the spectacular opportunities in countries like China and India today, yet the volumes in these newer markets remain marginal. In 2002, just over a million cars were sold in China, roughly the same number as are sold every *week* in the rest of the world.

There is a critical question behind the end of this growth trend, of course, which the industry needs to ask itself. Is this slowing in the industry merely cyclical (as many like to think) or is it structural?

The answer is that it is both. In many of the developed markets it is structural. The reasons are twofold. First, it is simply a question of demographics. The population in the countries of Western Europe is mostly stable (see figure 1.5), as it is in Japan, while the number of people in the US will grow only slowly, and mostly as a result of immigration, in the next fifty years (figure 1.6). In fact, in many European countries and in Japan, populations will begin to decline and so the demand for cars will begin to shrink. Add to that the rising costs of car ownership and the growing pressures from environmentalists in some places to cut car use and this drop-off in demand could be pronounced in some countries.

Moreover, the population of Japan and of Western Europe is set to start declining fairly soon (see figure 1.7). This will cause enormous problems of age dependency, with too few young earners to support a swelling proportion of retirees. The strain on European retirement funds is being felt already. It will also affect the auto industry by cutting disposable incomes and changing spending priorities.

So the problems in Europe and Japan are structural. There will be some growth in the US but it will be comparatively small, will take time to come and may not compensate for the drop-off in the other developed markets. So, in the world's largest markets, the overall outlook in terms of demographics – and so vehicle sales growth – is not too good.

The second structural reason for the gloomy growth prospects in the developed countries is market saturation. In most of the major markets there are simply enough cars on the roads already to satisfy most people's needs for individual motorised transport – which is why demand has become flat in Japan and mostly flat in Europe. Worse, congestion, especially in urban areas and at peak travel times, is starting to put a lid on the growth in the use of cars. There is neither the money, the space nor – increasingly – the inclination to build more roads to accommodate traffic. We shall never again see schemes such as those that put expressways along the banks of the river Seine in the heart of Paris in the 1970s.

But surely the developing world has a huge unsatisfied demand for cars? Will this not make up the shortfall? If they reach the levels of motorisation of the developed world, the demand for cars will continue to grow healthily, will it not? After all, if China alone had the level of motorisation of the US, world demand would double. (See figure 1.8 for how

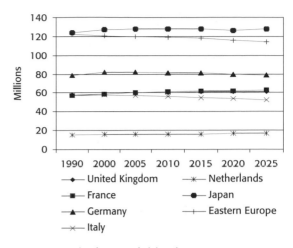

Source: International Energy Administration

Fig. 1.5 Population trends in European countries

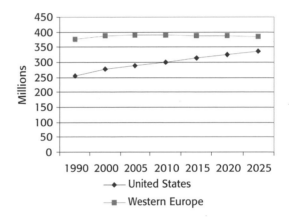

Source: International Energy Administration

Fig. 1.6 Population, US versus Europe

many cars there are per thousand people in countries that are part of different world regions.)

Certainly, it is not population or population growth that is lacking. The UN's forecast in figure 1.9 makes clear the contrast between the demographic stagnation of the developed world and the continued growth in developing regions. The constraint, of course, is income levels, shown in figure 1.3. Until these new countries reach equivalent levels of income, they will not see any Western-style mass motorisation. And that will take,

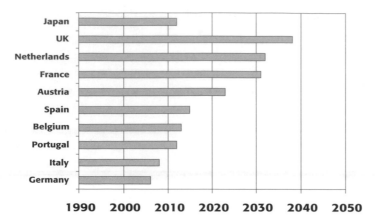

Sources: US Census Bureau, *Financial Times,* 7 June 2003, University of Utrecht Library

Fig. 1.7 Fewer future car buyers: year in which population starts to decline

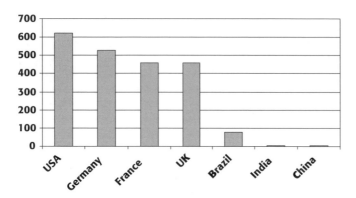

Source: Economic Intelligence Unit

Fig. 1.8 Car parc per thousand population, 2003

in many cases, more than a decade. China's GDP per head is a tenth of the level needed for motorisation; India's is less than half that.

So while everyone might talk about markets like China and India having masses of potential because of their large populations, rapid rates of economic growth and comparatively few cars today, such thinking is naïve. The reason most people in China and India do not have cars is simply that they cannot afford them. The sales opportunities in these markets – even ten years from now – are far too small to compensate for the stagnation in the biggest markets.

So the growth problem facing the industry is mostly structural. In the long term, a decade or more from now, the growth will return as these developing markets motorise – and so there is a longer-term cycle which will play back in the industry's favour. This is why we have said that the ending of the growth experienced by the industry is also cyclical. Eventually, once the emerging markets are large enough, high rates of growth might be possible for the industry again. There is a longer-term global cycle which might come into play again in another decade or so. But it is the next ten years that are the problem.

In addition, the growth in the emerging markets may prove illusory. It should not be counted on. Figure 1.10 shows what happened

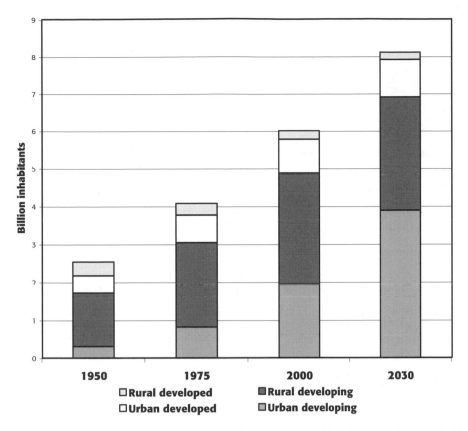

Source: UN, *Demographic Yearbook,* New York: United Nations, 2000; World Business Council for Sustainable Development, *Mobility 2001,* Geneva: WBCSD, reproduced with permission

Fig. 1.9 World population growth 1950–2030 (billions of people)

in the car markets of the major emerging regions between 1995 and 2003. This was the time when they were seen as the 'next big thing', when they were flooded with new automotive capacity and were seen as the great hope for sales volumes.

Demand in South America boomed for a while and then collapsed. The region has gone nowhere. By far the largest market there is in Brazil, a country that never ceases to disappoint by not achieving its vast potential. Car sales there in the early 2000s were less than in the 1990s. Argentina, the second-largest market, which is economically and socially very different, a formerly wealthy semi-European country, fell on desperately hard times. Sales collapsed there too. Our pet theory on Argentina, inciden-

tally, is that its wealth was transitory, earned through agricultural exports in the time after Lenin and Stalin wrecked Russian agriculture, which had previously been a considerable exporter.

Central and Eastern Europe have not lived up to expectations either. Instead of having a vast emerging market after the collapse of the Soviet system, the area has been troublesome and volatile. Today, it broadly divides into two groups: the countries that acceded to the European Union in 2004; and Russia and many of the remaining Eastern European countries, which are locked in poverty and corruption. The former were already surprisingly well motorised under Communist rule and have merely shifted their purchasing to Western European vehicles. The latter will not

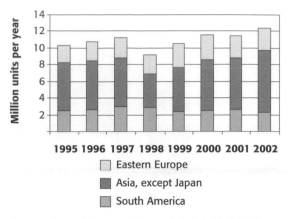

Source: *autopolis, Automotive News, Global Market Data Book.*

Fig. 1.10 Recent performance of emerging region markets

take off soon, leaving Russia as a market of huge unrealised potential.

Asia (outside Japan) held enormous hope for the industry in the 1990s too, but most of this came to a halt when the all too predictable (we certainly predicted it) economic crisis hit the 'Asian Tigers' in 1997–8. The region also failed to live up to many expectations because China was still very poor, with a car market that was still largely confined to higher members of the Party, at least in the early and mid-1990s. That, of course, has begun to change – indeed we are optimistic about demand in China. We believe it will be very volatile but also that it will overtake Japan by 2020 (see figure 1.11). We will explore this more in chapter 4.

So the emerging markets have not lived up to expectations so far. But let us brush aside such scepticism and assume that they will grow as many hope in the future. Let us assume that they help make up at least a little of the overall growth shortfall. Even then, there is another problem. There is another assumption about these places that may be over-optimistic.

The world's carmakers look at places like China and India and hope they will generate a surge in sales. Their sales. As we have shown, it has not happened as they planned so far. But even if it did, would they benefit? Perhaps surprisingly, there is growing doubt over whether

or not the traditional carmakers in the industry – those in Europe, the US and Japan – will be the ones to benefit from the next wave of growth. The newly developing markets already have other ideas.

Let us look long term. By 2020, we think China will have grown to become one of the world's largest automotive markets, making Asia the world's dominant automotive region (see figure 1.12). India is likely to play an increasingly important role by then too. Yet foreign carmakers entering the market in China have already found the going tough. They have found that their technology has been acquired by rivals and that there has been too much competition, leading to a vast array of products and few economies of scale. There have even been counterfeits of complete cars – an issue we shall come back to later. But there has also been one more troublesome issue in China which most foreign firms have been conveniently ignoring. It is the fact that it is an explicit policy of the Chinese government that foreign firms will not be allowed to end up in control of the country's auto sector. Few of those clamouring for a share of this seemingly attractive market have remembered to mention this when they tout their apparent successes.

China remains a centrally planned economy in some important respects. Beijing has made its plans very clear. The automotive industry policy document issued by the State Planning Committee in 1994 and subsequent amendments lay out exactly how many Chinese firms will dominate which sectors of the market by when. It specifies which technologies will be developed over which timeframes and in which sequence. It specifically states that the industry will become an 'independent' one, free from foreign control. A draft policy document published in 2003 made the policy clearer still, specifically suggesting that the government wanted to curtail the ability of foreign automakers and suppliers to protect their proprietary technology and intellectual property in China. It stated that, by 2010, half the vehicle market should be in the hands of 100 per cent Chinese firms using their own

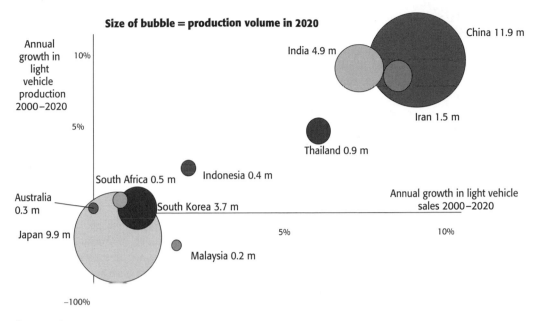

Source: *auto*POLIS

Fig. 1.11 China, the engine of future growth in Asia

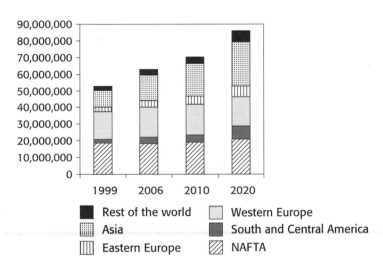

Source: *auto*POLIS

Fig. 1.12 Asia finally takes off – forecast market volumes to 2020

technology. Few foreign investors seem to have paid this much attention.

Similarly, although India is not quite as determined as China to build its own automotive sector, it proved extremely difficult for most foreigners to establish anything other

than minor positions in the market during the 1990s. The only exception was Hyundai, which managed to achieve a creditable share of the car market. This time the failure of most firms was more for cultural reasons but also because of the strength of

Maruti and Tata, two long-entrenched local manufacturers.

So while it may be true that Asia will have the fastest growth for the world's auto industry over the next twenty years, that does not mean that much of it will be up for grabs by Western and Japanese carmakers. Asia will not solve the problems of lack of growth facing the world's biggest carmakers today.

In fact, in growth terms, the developed world's automotive industry is in something of a pickle. Sales are stagnant in its traditional main markets and the others are too small, too fragmented or too difficult to penetrate successfully. The established industry is approaching a sustained period of low growth, which will affect the largest, most established manufacturers most. This may all be part of a normal industry lifecycle, but it is especially troubling for an industry so fixated on achieving economies of scale and so used to the rapid expansion of past decades. It is a discontinuity that will ultimately change the nature of the business.

Failing to add value elsewhere – the illusion of the world car

If developed market demand is stagnant and emerging markets are both small and likely to be troublesome, can the product itself be changed? Can more value be added through the introduction of different models or designs, so that customers will pay more for them? Alternatively, can the product be more standardised: made more universal, to lower costs, so that prices can be reduced and demand stimulated? Can the growth problem – and the damaging impact this has on the returns the industry can generate – be addressed in one of these ways?

Unfortunately, the answer is no. In fact, a look at how the market for cars was segmented in the developed markets in the late 1990s and early 2000s suggests the opposite is the case. Instead of there being an opportunity to add more value to cars or offer additional

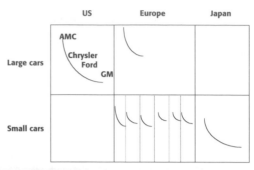

*Source: auto*POLIS

Fig. 1.13 The good old times

new products, changes in market segmentation mean that there are already far too many products on offer. Costs have been rising while prices and margins have been falling. We shall look at the option of adding more models and more variations in detail in the next chapter. But what of the other alternative – standardisation? Is it possible to sell a standardised product into a mature market and lower costs? Can we develop a world car?

Let us go back for a moment to the good old times of forty years ago, when roads were uncrowded, you could drive as fast as you liked in most of Europe, and gasoline cost as little as 10 cents a gallon in some parts of the US; when cars were called Rambler or Borgward or Wolseley. Figure 1.13 summarises the world order then. In each box the vertical axis is each manufacturer's average unit cost for new vehicles, while the horizontal bar is their production volume. The world was neatly segmented, so that manufacturers did not have to do anything as uncouth as competing with each other excessively.

Americans drove around in large rear-wheel-drive cars, with nice big low-stressed lazy engines. Competitively, there was something like a national scale curve. GM (General Motors) had about 50 per cent of the market, the highest level of integration (how much of the car it made itself as opposed to buying in parts and materials) and the presumed lowest cost. Ford had around 25 per cent and was less integrated. Then there was Chrysler at 15 per cent or so. It was less integrated still. Finally, there was AMC (remember them?) hanging onto the lower fringes. There were also a few imports, notably the old Beetle. The US market was a stable, self-regulating oligarchy. If GM raised its prices too much, it lost market share. If it cut them too much it risked pushing AMC over the edge, and then the Justice Department might go after it for predatory pricing.

Europe ran small cars. Each national market and each national industry was to a large extent distinct, with little interpenetration of markets. Italian car manufacturers dominated Italy, French ones France. The European Common Market was still less than ten years old at the time, and it was intended to pool coal, steel and nuclear power at first, rather than consumer goods. So competitors within each country operated on a distinct scale curve. Somewhere above this sat the European upline players – such as Mercedes – who were the first to go international.

Japan sat in its own box too, on the bottom right of our figure, building small cars that were not much noticed by anyone else as yet. The only significant intercontinental flow of cars was of Volkswagen Beetles from Wolfsburg to the United States, where they had started to create a cult following within a fairly distinct segment of the population, mainly college students.

This was all fine, until the system was subjected to some strong exterior forces, symbolically associated with the names of a few well-known individuals.

In the 1960s, Ralph Nader in the United States, through his book *Unsafe at Any Speed*, launched the idea that government safety standards should be imposed on the industry as part of an essentially political process – an idea which then spread to Europe and Japan. We shall return to the whole issue of industry–government relationships in chapter 2. But this initiative was important because it brought about fundamental changes in the way cars were designed and built. Across the world, it created more uniformity in the approach taken by car manufacturers to the market.

Following the first oil shock in 1973, OPEC – headed by Sheik Yamani – imposed a major increase in crude oil prices on importing countries. This resulted in long lines of cars at gasoline stations in the US and car-free days in some European countries. Children were able to roller-skate on empty expressways in the Netherlands. All this came as a profound shock, not least in the United States, which suddenly became extremely conscious of its dangerous dependency on imported oil. It led the US government – which for political reasons could not reduce fuel consumption through higher fuel taxes – to force the CAFE (corporate average fuel economy) consumption standards on its domestic car industry. A massive programme of downsizing was then undertaken, which drove the US to much smaller, mainly front-wheel-drive cars. The results – for cars at least – are still very visible today. Gone are the massive gas guzzlers. But the policy also opened the door of the US to an assault by Japanese manufacturers: an unintended consequence, as one so often gets from well-intentioned sweeping legislative measures.

Over a longer timescale, Jean Monnet and others started a movement designed to prevent Europe inflicting on itself and others the horrors of any more European civil wars. This was the creation of the European Union, which has so far resulted in faster economic than political integration. It has also had a substantial effect on the automotive industry, triggering the interpenetration of European markets. Cross-border sales of cars are now common – with Volkswagen selling cars not predominantly in Germany as it once did, but in France, Italy and Spain, and all the other markets too. The creation of a more open regional market also accelerated an integration and rationalisation of the components industry, although this still remains incomplete (we shall return to this subject later).

These changes and others seemed to point towards that idea so fashionable in the 1990s –

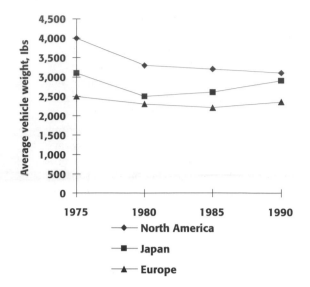

Source: Graeme P. Maxton and John Wormald, *Driving Over a Cliff? Business Lessons from the World's Car Industry,* Harlow: Addison Wesley Longman, 1994.

Fig. 1.14 Convergence of vehicle weights

globalisation – as the logical next step. Thinking in the auto industry – and so many others – was that we were inexorably heading for a global market and a global industry, with no place for the weak or sub-scale to hide from the fierce tides of global competition. Some indicators suggested that this would indeed be so. It really looked for a while as though vehicles throughout the world were converging to common standards of architecture, size and weight (see figure 1.14) for an illustration). We fell for it too – the figure is taken from our earlier book.

Ten years on, we have to face the truth: there is no such thing as a 'world car', a standard global passenger vehicle, even although some carmakers have tried to build one. The VW Beetle was a 'world car' in its time, in the sense that it was widely exported. So was and is the Toyota Camry or the Honda Accord, which are also extensively built outside their home territory, notably in the United States. At the other end of the scale, one could say the same of the Mercedes S-Class. They, too, are exported worldwide, but into niche market segments. But no vehicle has yet managed

to set the common standard across the major automotive regions of the world. Ford once tried this with the Escort, but the European and US, versions eventually ended up so different that they reportedly had only three parts in common.

In fact the uses made by car owners of their cars still vary enormously from country to country, creating different market structures in different parts of the world. Light trucks are far more popular in the US, for example, accounting for half the market, while tiny 660 cc cars are very popular in Japan. How these segments change from year to year determines what carmakers can sell and what they have to produce – mainly locally. As we have said, for political reasons, the US government could not face the obvious solution to restraining fuel consumption in the 1970s by taxing fuel more heavily. So it put the squeeze on the supply side: on the manufacturers, through the CAFE standards. Americans were forced into smaller cars, while their fuel prices remained abnormally low by world standards. But the government left a loophole in the form of looser consumption standards for light vehicles other than passenger cars, probably not wishing to take on the powerful farming lobby by forcing them to downsize their pick-up trucks. The regulations meant that the big-car genie was temporarily squeezed into the bottle, forcing Americans to drive smaller cars. But eventually it got out again. American drivers wanted bigger vehicles. They got them by an alternative route – light trucks. The demand for light trucks – RVs (recreational vehicles), MPVs (multipurpose vehicles), and SUVs (sports utility vehicles, i.e. 4 × 4s) – then grew massively, as shown in figure 1.15. By 2003, these vehicles accounted for more than half the passenger vehicle market, up from less than a quarter twenty years before. Light trucks have accounted for all the growth of the US market and then some during the last twenty years.

This growth in light trucks in the US is clearly attributable to the only partly applied

CAFE standards and to the contradiction between them and low fuel taxes – but also to fashion and because the Big Three manufacturers in the US (GM, Ford and Chrysler) needed to develop the sector to survive. For the Big Three these vehicles were highly profitable, which cars were not. Competition was also negligible, as the invading Japanese remained focused on the car market, certainly until very recently. (The competitive dynamics of the industry and battles between the different manufacturers are addressed in chapter 4.)

This shift towards light trucks used as substitutes for large cars was, and remains, a North American one, although there are also some signs of it in Australia, with its similar pattern of living and relatively low fuel prices. As we shall see later, the future of the segment is now under threat, as concerns about oil use and the environmental damage caused by such massive fuel wasters grow. The fat profits that attracted the Big Three to the business are also under assault. Japanese and European competitors, seeing the margins on offer, belatedly attacked the US light truck market during the late 1990s and early 2000s, with the result that the high margins started to decline. In chapter 7 we look at the financial implications of this change and at the benefits the Big Three derived from dominating the sector for so long.

In a way, then, we are back where we began, with quite different regional markets, except that the major Japanese manufacturers are now so firmly ashore in the US that they are virtually regarded as domestic. Their success in transplanting their manufacturing operations to America also encouraged them to do the same in Europe. But the fundamental fact about markets remains: although people everywhere aspire to personal motorised mobility, they buy different cars in different parts of the world because they have different patterns of living and working – and different levels of wealth. We only need to look at some basic transport statistics to demonstrate their different transportation needs. Figure 1.16 shows the modal mix, the techni-

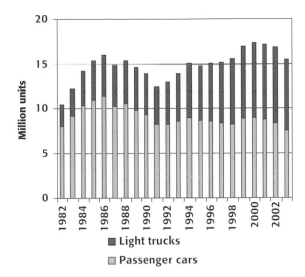

Source: vehicle manufacturers, *Automotive News, Global Market Data Book, auto*POLIS

Fig. 1.15 US market for light vehicles, 1982–2003

cal term for the mix in means of travel used by people in different world regions.

The world as a whole relies on the car (or light trucks as car substitutes) for about 55 per cent of passenger transport. Buses play the next largest role. But they are still the dominant mode in the developing world, which is why some of the world's largest bus markets are in China, India and Brazil. Cars dominate in the developed world, notably North America and Western Europe, with Eastern Europe and Latin America following. But note the anomaly for the region denoted as PAO in figure 1.16, covering Australia, Japan and New Zealand, but dominated by Japan, where the railways keep a large share. This is not because of a preference for rail imposed by the state, as in the former Soviet Union (FSU), or poverty plus the British legacy of massive nineteenth-century railway construction, as in the SAS region (the Indian sub-continent). The Japanese are wealthy but they live in a very crowded environment. They typically do not drive to work in the way everyone in the developed West has got used to doing. So their modal mix is different. Incidentally, Australia, and to a lesser extent New

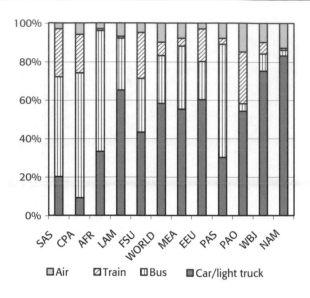

Key:
CPA   China and other Centrally Planned Asia
SAS   Bangladesh, India, Pakistan
PAS   Pacific Asia
AFR   Kenya, Nigeria, South Africa, Zimbabwe and
      other Sub-Saharan Africa
FSU   Former Soviet Union
PAO   Australia, Japan and New Zealand

MEA   Middle East and North Africa
EEU   Eastern Europe
LAM   Latin America and Central America
WEU   European Community, Norway, Switzerland
      and Turkey
NAM   Canada and United States

Source: WBCSD, *Mobility 2001,* reproduced with permission

Fig. 1.16 Modal split of passenger travel in
different world regions

Zealand, should clearly not have been lumped in with Japan in this analysis. They are closer to the North American pattern of travel. Americans use their cars twice as intensively as Europeans, who use theirs twice as intensively as the Japanese (see figure 1.17).

Just as the need to travel varies between world regions as a function of local conditions, so does the pattern of vehicle types sold. One can also see it in the kind of features customers require in their vehicles. In Japan, the emphasis is on vehicle features such as navigation systems – an obvious requirement in the Japanese urban environment. In the US, the accent is on comfort items such as air conditioning, automatic transmissions and the boulevard ride. In Europe, drivers are most interested in taut handling and vehicle dynamics.

The simplest first cut at this is to distinguish between passenger cars and light trucks, or

light commercial vehicles as many of them are called in Europe, which is shown in figure 1.18. Light trucks form half the light vehicle market in the US. Australia is similar to the US, although the distorting incentives in fact work in opposite ways. The US light truck market has been protected – notably from Japanese import competition – by a higher tariff than on passenger cars. The Australian farm work vehicles sector is covered by a lower tariff, which differentially favours imports of these vehicles.

Asian markets also have a high proportion of light trucks but for different reasons. Sales of light trucks are higher because of lower incomes and the need to use the same vehicles to shift people, animals and goods. Latin America is more like Asia, in that light trucks are mainly utility vehicles. Their penetration in Europe is mainly limited to commercial uses. There has been growth in their use as

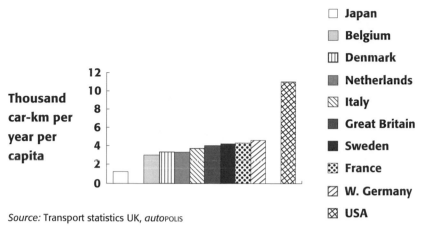

Source: Transport statistics UK, *auto*POLIS

Fig. 1.17 Comparative intensity of car use

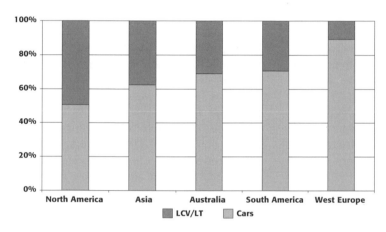

Source: *auto*POLIS

Fig. 1.18 Structure of light vehicle markets

substitutes for passenger cars but in quite small volumes. The big recent successes have been in building minivan-type vehicles on passenger car platforms, i.e. more to European size requirements.

Across the world, the markets for cars are remarkably dissimilar. Figure 1.19 shows a breakdown by size class for the major markets, using conventional European size class categories. Each class is denoted by a letter. A is the mini segment for very small cars like the Fiat Seicento. The B segment is the supermini, with cars like the Volkswa-

gen Polo, Opel Corsa or Renault Clio. The C segment is small saloons such as the Volkswagen Golf, Ford Focus or Honda Civic. The D class is for medium saloons such as the Ford Mondeo, Honda Accord or Opel Vectra. Finally, the E segment is for large saloon cars like the Renault VelSatis, Opel Omega or Peugeot 607. Beyond these categories are other specialist groupings for multipurpose vehicles (MPVs), recreational vehicles (RVs), sports utility vehicles (SUVs) and sports and luxury cars.

North America, on the left, still has a fair proportion of large cars but nowhere near as

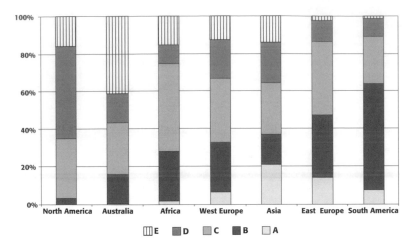

Source: As figure 1.18

Fig. 1.19 Car markets by size class

many as it used to have in the age of tailfins. The segment of the car market selling large cars has been creamed off by light trucks. Interestingly, that leaves Australia with the largest proportion of large cars in its car market. These are still designed to a very American kind of formula. A Commodore 3.8 litre sedan, for example, is not that different from a Pontiac or a Chevy. But it is very different from, say, a Mercedes-Benz 380 SL.

As we move across to the right, the proportion of small cars steadily increases. In Latin America, which is dominated by Brazil, the standard car today is a European B-class. If there is a world car class at all, it is probably that. The US Big Three are really not in the world car market, except through their European subsidiaries – which Chrysler mostly lacks. Even Latin America is no longer their backyard. Asia – including Japan – has a large proportion of A- or even sub-A-class cars. In the case of Japan, the minicars are favoured by legislation in that, unlike full-sized cars, they do not require a mandatory parking space to be registered. All that is, once again, a clear reflection of Japan's very dense urbanisation – replicated in all the major cities of Asia.

There is really no such thing as a world light truck market either – see figure 1.20. In descending order the labels stand for:

SUV, sports utility vehicle (a Range Rover or Jeep Cherokee, for example); PUP, pick-up truck (Ford F-150, Nissan Armada); MVAN medium-size commercial van (Ford Transit, Mercedes Sprinter); MPV (Chrysler Voyager in the large size, Renault Scenic in the small size); MIC (micro-vehicles, of multiple models and brand); HVAN, heavy commercial van; CDV, car-derived van (a car with sheet metal in the place of rear side window glass, tax-advantaged in Europe). While the US, Australian and Latin American markets are dominated by sports utilities and pick-ups, this is not the case in Europe or Asia. There, we see a completely different mix, with medium-sized commercial vans, multipurpose vehicles, micro-cars and vans, heavy commercial vans and car-derived vans preponderant. Two-thirds of the Chinese market consists of a plethora of different light commercial vehicles, used for both passenger and goods transport, and produced by a huge variety of local firms.

So the picture is clear. There is no such thing as a global car or light vehicle market, or a world car or world light truck or light commercial vehicle. There are similar market segments across different world regions but they occur in quite different proportions according to where you look. There are some largely region-specific market segments,

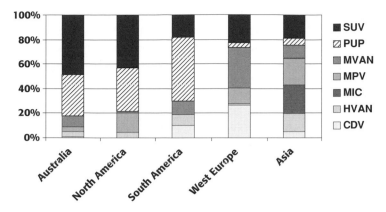

Source: As figure 1.18

Fig. 1.20 Structure of LCV/LT markets

notably US light trucks at the large vehicle end of the scale and Asian micro-vehicles at the other.

The idea of trying to counter the growth through some sort of scale-driven standardisation of vehicles on a global scale is not, then, realistic. The industry will still have to meet the needs of different markets. That has an implication for costs and so for revenues. What of the other alternative, though: the idea of adding more product: more variations, more models and more features to cars? Why not add more value to raise revenues? That is the subject of the next section.

Excess supply, changing demand – piling on the products

The problem of the lack of growth in the auto market cannot be tackled by any mass standardisation programme. There are simply too many differing demands across the globe. So the option of cutting costs and improving returns this way is closed. Is there another option? Is it possible to increase the range of vehicles offered, to increase the line-up, to add value that way? Could that solve the growth problem? Unfortunately not. It has already been tried. It is exactly the strategy that has been adopted for the last thirty years, after

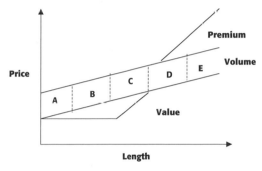

*Source: auto*POLIS

Fig. 1.21 Size and price range of European vehicle classes, circa 1980

the global demand started to slow. The trouble now is that it has been pushed too far. The range of models on offer is already so vast that instead of providing a revenue fillip, the strategy has become a source of financial woe.

In Europe, and in much of the rest of the world, cars were traditionally segmented according to size. This continuum of vehicle classes stretched across a wide range of sizes and prices, as shown in figure 1.21, illustrating the traditional European product segmentation pattern. The vertical axis is the new-car price. The horizontal axis is length, used here as a simple surrogate for the size classes, which are based on a more complicated formula, which assigns relative weights to a number of size- and performance-related parameters. The approximation is good enough for our discussion.

The A- to E-class vehicles sat in a continuum, with price broadly increasing with size. This was the volume car market – the home of the European volume Big Six: Fiat, Ford of Europe, GM-Europe (Opel and Vauxhall), PSA (Peugeot-Citroën), Renault and VW. There were also some marginal former volume players left on the fringes, notably British Leyland, later renamed Rover (and now known as MG Rover, having been first bought and then disposed of by BMW).

Above the A- to E-class vehicles sat a wedge-shaped area of upline, executive, luxury and speciality cars such as the larger BMW and Mercedes-Benz cars. Traditionally, these deviated from the volume market in terms of their price-to-size ratio. They were typically larger and more expensive. Yet there was never anything exceptional about the fundamental design or functionality of the vehicles made by these companies. Many had rear-wheel drive, but this was simply a packaging option that made relatively more sense in larger cars anyway. They were traditionally distinguished from volume cars by having more features, higher-quality components, more investment in development and particularly strong branding. This allowed them, and still allows many of them, to command substantial price premiums.

Below the continuum was a value segment, i.e. cars that were inexpensive in relation to their size. This notably included the Citroën 2CV, the Renault 4, the VW Beetle – all left-overs from the earlier era of single-product mass motorisation and unrepeatable because of non-conformity with crash safety requirements – but also subsidised East European exports, notably Skoda, Lada and Polski Fiat, the last two being outdated versions of Fiat cars. Even though these cars have long since disappeared from the market, the value or entry-level sector still exists. It was and still is mainly satisfied by used cars. Korean manufacturers, notably Hyundai and Daewoo, have made an entry into it in more recent years.

A similar pattern existed in the car sector in the United States, although, with many fewer small cars, the American car market's segmentation pattern would sit a few notches further to the right on the figure. Prices were not higher; in fact they were generally lower, as traditional US cars were not expensive to build. Just as in Europe, though, there was an upper wedge-shaped section with Cadillacs and Lincolns sold at a premium over other GM or Ford brands. Again, they were not fundamentally different products but carried more features, had a stronger brand image and earned a price premium.

This segmentation pattern was a simple one, reflecting demand. People would generally start with small cars and, as they became wealthier, they would trade up to bigger ones. A car manufacturer would offer a product ladder for consumers to climb, to meet their aspirations – this was the idea first developed for GM by Alfred Sloan in the 1920s. Consumers would be able to progress up the ladder of brands from a Chevrolet to a Cadillac during their lifetimes. It was similar in Europe. In the 1970s and 1980s, a person's first new car after they started work might have been a Ford Fiesta, a small car. As they progressed in their careers they might have moved on to the Ford Escort. When a family came along they might have traded up again to the Sierra or Mondeo. If they made it into the fat-cat league they bought a Granada. If they made it really big, they would buy a Mercedes or a BMW. The wealthiest people tended to have large fancy cars and the poor tended to have small utilitarian ones.

This pattern became fairly homogeneous throughout the developed world, albeit with the US market still buying somewhat larger and heavier cars than Europe or Japan. From the mid-1970s, however, after the oil shocks and as the economies of Europe, Japan and the US matured, a fundamental change in the nature of market demand set in, which upset the traditional segmentation pattern. As demand changed, some segments were flipped 90 degrees, others fragmented into

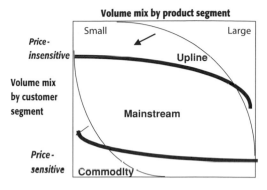

Source: *auto*POLIS

Fig. 1.22 The European segmentation upheaval

subsegments. In Europe, this shift is symbolically portrayed in figure 1.22. It was the result of changes, and *perceived* changes, in consumer attitudes in a maturing developed market. Demand shifted away from product size towards consumer groupings, with buyers affiliated as a function of common attitudes and expectations. With the growth of real disposable incomes and personal wealth, the entry-level or value segment got squeezed, although not totally out of existence.

The result was a product segmentation pattern based more on the common horizontal relationships between different groups of consumers and their expectations than on vertical product class structures. It changed the way vehicles were offered and how they were priced. The number of vehicles developed from a given platform (the basic underlying structure of a car) increased enormously, as did the range of prices across it, to the point at which the price difference between the lowest and the highest specification version of the same basic model exceeded that between the average for adjacent models in the product range. A top-of-the-range Ford Focus, for example, cost 10 per cent more than the entry-level Mondeo, while a basic Toyota Corolla cost 15 per cent less than the highest specification but much smaller Yaris.

This used to be known as the GTi phenomenon in Europe, after the VW Golf GTi and the Peugeot 205 GTi, which pioneered the

trend. The point was to load the car with a more powerful engine and other goodies and sell it at a price considerably inflated above that justified by its real additional content. It encapsulated in a named and branded product what dealers have always tried to do at the point of sale, namely to get the customer to specify high-cost options, which raise the overall margin earned on the car. Vehicle manufacturers strove by every means to shift their sales mix within a model to the more expensive versions.

The change in demand meant that the idea that the rich had big cars and the poor had small ones started to blur. A wealthy individual in the sixteenth *arrondissement* of Paris wanted a luxuriously equipped car but not necessarily a large one, given the difficulties with parking in the street. Conversely, large families with limited incomes wanted bigger, simply featured vehicles, such as an entry-level station-wagon or estate car.

These trends had a nasty consequence, however. There was suddenly a tremendous enthusiasm in the industry for offering as many variants and options as possible. 'Ford in the US offers millions of possible combinations. So should we', said a car company executive to one of us in the late 1970s. This led to a massive proliferation in the number of products on offer. In purely economic terms it resulted in considerable duplication and waste across the industry, as competing firms developed more and more products that were essentially the same as each other. Vehicle manufacturers were trying to deal with their growth problems not by cutting their costs but by raising their average prices, through pushing more products at the market. To a point, of course, the strategy made sense. But they pushed it too far in the end, with predictable and dire consequences for their long-term profitability.

In the early 1980s Ford of Europe had four basic models – the Fiesta supermini, the Escort small saloon, the mid-sized Sierra and the large Granada. Twenty years later it had seven basic models that included SUVs and MPVs. Through acquisitions, it also had four Jaguar models, five basic Volvo designs and four Land Rover options. Within the Ford-badged brand alone, though, the seven models were offered in 110 different configurations of engines and numbers of doors. There were forty-one basic options just for the Focus model. This was before the buyer selected the colour of the car, trim or accessories. Instead of the four basic models it once supplied with a limited range of variations, it now had twenty with more than 200 engine and door configurations. Ford's range had exploded and yet its sales volume and market share had fallen.

Rover, a near-defunct British carmaker, had an average of 25,000 feature variations per model between 1960 and 1990, but saw this increase to an average of more than 2 million during the 1990s, according to a study carried out by Matthias Holweg at the University of Cardiff.

Another factor that changed was the speed with which models were replaced. Holweg says that product lifecycles decreased steadily after the early 1970s from an average of seven and a half years to five by 2001. He thinks that if the trend continues they will fall to little more than three years by 2005 – with the life of a volume model ranging from 'two to no more than five years' by that time.

The continuing multiplicity of vehicle brands caused a continuing proliferation in the range of engines and transmissions on offer too. Most car manufacturers have two or three basic engine blocks, from which engine families are derived. Together with the transmission, what is called the powertrain is the dynamic heart of the car and the most complex and costliest part to develop. According to CAR, the Center for Automotive Research in Ann Arbor, Michigan, the powertrain makes up almost 30 per cent of a car's value. But each brand insisted on having its own proprietary powertrain, because this was considered an inherent part of its distinctiveness. There was some marginal sharing of engines, notably between PSA, Renault and Volvo in Europe, and of automatic transmissions. But the proliferation trend was a feature here too,

so much so that in 1999 we counted eighty-three different engine families (there are far more individual engine models) in production for light vehicles in Europe.

Each additional model that was designed needed a vast array of new components, even if it shared an existing platform. To try to reduce the costs of proliferation, additional models and their variants in the 1990s were often built off a shared architecture – the VW Beetle, Skoda Octavia, Audi A3 and SEAT Ibiza among others use a Golf platform, for example, while the Jaguar X-type used the Ford Mondeo platform as its basic building block. But there were still thousands of other parts that needed to be designed specifically for each new vehicle. In an industry with such high fixed costs, this had a predictable impact on returns.

In a stagnant market so many new products meant that the industry's economies of scale declined. The effects were even more acute in the aftermarket because the number of parts that had to be manufactured and stocked to repair and service all these new vehicles ballooned more and more. The impact of this will affect component makers, parts distributors and repairers for many years to come, as the myriad of vehicles on the roads continue to run around.

The proliferation meant that each car manufacturer was forced to invest heavily for smaller and smaller returns. With competition more intense and each new subsegment smaller than the last, fewer companies were able to make a decent return. (We will look at profitability in detail in chapter 7.) The increase in the range of cars and components they had to provide became a source of financial difficulty, not a solution to their growth problems. It is a trend that will have to be reversed before the industry can become financially healthy again.

Behind the proliferation trend is another wider question. Was the development of so many different models and sub-models a response to the market demand or was it mostly something pushed by the carmakers?

Did they too actively encourage the trend in an effort to build sales? Did they create much of the problem they now have?

Without question, the era of initial mass motorisation had long since passed. There was no longer a market for ubiquitous, functional cars like the Beetle, Renault 4 or 2CV in the developed markets. There was little demand for vehicles that moved the masses cheaply, and were made in very high volumes for years at a time. Consumers expected more choice and were willing to pay for it. The shift in demand patterns in the late 1980s and early 1990s was real and automakers had to respond to it. But it is the extent to which the trend was pushed further by the carmakers that is our concern. Did they themselves contribute to the trend to such an extent that it actually caused them to waste many scarce economic resources? Did they not understand that in such a high-fixed-cost industry any decline in their economies of scale would inevitably lead to financial hardship?

The extent of over-production of different vehicles and components would certainly suggest that they understood the economics of their own business poorly. The bulk of the market's needs was actually still being satisfied by a small number of platforms and engines. As we will show later, as much as 60 per cent of vehicle demand was still being satisfied with 20 per cent of the platforms. Similarly 20 per cent of the engines were able to meet two-thirds of the market's needs. Yet in 2000 there were more than 200 global vehicle platforms, when the industry could have done almost as well with fifty. The rest provided ever diminishing returns.

For the vehicle manufacturers there was a ratchet effect in all of this too – a one-way street. As car buyers, market analysts and competitors became used to an ever wider range of new vehicles, updated ever more frequently and with a host of additional features at lower real prices, they came to expect them. Costs were rising and revenues could not in reality follow them upwards, as this was not reflected in prices. The market was not being charged enough for the plethora of new products. Every manufacturer thought they could get more volume and more of a premium for each product than they really did.

In passing, it may also be that the changing segmentation pattern was encouraged by the biggest carmakers for an almost paradoxical reason. It was a form of risk aversion, even if it was one that added cost. The main models produced by the top manufacturers – the VW Golf, the Peugeot 307, the Ford Taurus or Mondeo, for example – had become ever more important to their fate. If VW got a replacement of the Golf wrong, it would have to live with the decision for four or more years and in the process lose share and revenue in its biggest market sector. As Mark Landler of the *New York Times* said to us, 'Every time it replaced the Golf, Volkswagen effectively bet the company as well as the economy of Wolfsburg', where the car is built. The new model's success became so critical that it would affect the company's ability to invest in any subsequent replacement for the car. Failure would affect its income and its ability to raise finance through its credit rating. The implications of getting it wrong were grave.

To counter the problem of this overdependence on one model there was even more of an incentive to try to identify other, and hopefully more profitable, niches. Yet this also raised costs and reduced efficiency. With such intense competition, few of these niches really were profitable, or at least they were not profitable for long – as everyone leapt off the same cliff in lemming-like behaviour.

For the upline manufacturers, the changing segmentation had another impact. The historical distinction between volume and luxury cars began to blur too, forcing manufacturers to spend ever more on marketing to retain brand exclusivity. The difficulties for the upline manufacturers were reinforced by the fact that more and more of the added features relied on electronics, typically not the technology of the vehicle manufacturers themselves. Traditionally, upline marques had protected the distinctiveness of their brand

and their premium prices by offering superior design, performance, features and finish. They occupied worldwide market niches, mostly building their vehicles in one location. At one time, the fact that Mercedes-Benz or BMW cars were made in Germany was an inherent part of their image and brand appeal.

As the technology and feature content of volume cars continued to increase, this barrier against the entry of the volume producers into upline markets weakened. This is why so many of the traditionally upline manufacturers tried to push further up the prestige ladder into Bentleys, Rolls Royces and Maybachs. The blurring of the traditional segmentation pattern also moved in the other direction too, and pushed down the range into smaller cars. For these firms also, the traditional segmentation of the business was turned on its side – luxury cars spanned all the size sectors, as they were once defined, as did the more utilitarian vehicles produced by their middle-market rivals. A danger for the upline makers in this push into smaller vehicles, of course, was that their brand attractiveness would start to decline. Despite the brave slogan of Marks and Spencer, a large UK clothes and food retailer, 'Exclusively for Everyone', it is hard to make customers feel the brand of product they own is exclusive if everyone has one. As Gilbert and Sullivan said, 'When everyone is somebody then no-one's anybody.'

In the US, the Big Three partially avoided the car model proliferation trap by side-stepping the Japanese attack in that segment through a retreat into light trucks. But this also left them dangerously isolated and vulnerable, as we will see later. It also meant that they still had to maintain a broader model range in cars, with smaller volumes per platform.

The Japanese played a different proliferation game in their home market, based on rapidly introducing many product variants: vehicles that often looked bizarre to Western eyes. This rapid obsolescence policy appears to have matched the peculiar characteristics of the Japanese car market and the near absence of a second-hand market, caused by the forced early retirement of vehicles through draconian safety inspections.

With the financial penalties inherent in the strategy, the option of adding more value and of perpetually increasing the numbers of models on offer as a solution to the problem of lack of growth was not a very sensible one. It worked for a while but got out of control. This is one of the main reasons why the industry as a whole has made rotten returns for almost a decade despite booming, if static, global sales volumes. We explore this further in chapter 7.

A solution to the problems caused by the excessive proliferation of models and components in the 1990s will be forced on the industry, whether it likes it or not. In the short term, as profitability declines further, some car manufacturers may have to increase the prices of all these speciality and niche vehicles to reflect their true cost. As they are well aware, that will be hard in a market where there is intense competition and stable demand. Putting up prices may also blow the 'bubble of perception' about the value of some of these cars – carmakers might find that consumers may not really want them if they have to pay a higher price. The bubble is particularly vulnerable to being pricked by professional buyers in the fleet market, which is steadily becoming the preponderant sector for new cars in Europe, which is still the largest market for them. They have a very accurate perception of what a car's residual value is likely to be when it has to be re-marketed months or years later – and once the gilt of newness has worn off the gingerbread of yet another unnecessary additional model.

In the longer term, then, the industry will have to reverse the product proliferation trend or find a new manufacturing approach. It will have to learn to make fewer variations and perhaps even fewer models, and to focus on mainstream vehicles again. Alternatively, it will have to find new ways to put vehicles together that allow the car manufacturers the ability to offer choice without higher cost.

Without radical change the strategy will lead the industry into further financial trouble. There is another way forward, however, and it is something we will look at in chapter 9.

Illusion and reality – a growing disconnection from consumers

As we now know, vehicle demand in the traditional developed regions of the automotive industry started to slow in the mid-1970s and reached a plateau in the late 1990s which will last for a long time. We know that this is already causing financial strains. Vehicle manufacturers cannot avoid the implications of this slowing-down through building sales in the emerging markets, as these are still small and are unlikely to be easy to access when they do become large. We shall come back to this issue in chapter 4. We also know that the option of cutting costs by developing more standardised global products in response to this growth problem is not open to the industry either. The demands of the different markets vary too much. Besides, the strategy of the carmakers for the last thirty years has been to go the other way and to increase the range of products it offers. This is one of the central pillars of their strategy to counter the slowing of demand. But we also know that trying to grow by 'adding value', by building an ever wider range of more lavishly equipped vehicles, has now run into the spending-power limits on the side of consumers and into the cost-of-proliferation limits on the side of the vehicle manufacturers. So that option has run its course too. Indeed, it has already been taken too far.

There is another potential problem with trying to have too much of a good thing. There is an additional risk within the mature markets which could make life even harder for the big global firms facing a decade of flat demand. It is excessive fixation on branding and the belief that it can solve some of the profitability problems. There is a growing schism between the way the industry likes its products to be portrayed and the reality of how they are used. Sales have become over-dependent on marketing invention and less and less related to the real properties and benefits of products – what we call Hype. There is a growing danger that this could backfire, with painful consequences.

Consumers are increasingly well informed about what they buy. The number of advertising messages to which the average US resident is exposed daily rose from 1,500 in 1960 to 3,000 in 1990 and 5,000 in 2000.[1] Every advanced market is deluged with newspaper articles, TV programmes and specialised periodicals about cars. Few other products are so extensively examined, reviewed and critiqued. New and resale prices, the costs of running cars day to day, comparisons on insurance and repairs – all are easily available for public scrutiny, even more so thanks to the web. The car remains the most functionally complex product that most of us are likely to own. But it has lost a good deal of its technological mystique – not least because it has become so much more reliable and hassle-free. Additionally, we are spending ever more time in our cars, perhaps more than most of us would like. In the UK, for example, the average driver spends $1\frac{1}{2}$ hours a day in their car, more than 9 per cent of his or her waking time. Based on average miles driven, the average speed achieved during this time is just 18 mph.

There is obviously more to the car in the eyes of consumers than a mere means of locomotion. The car has been made into an icon, a symbol, a means of personal identification and differentiation. The package that sells a car today is very different from what sold the utilitarian Model T at the beginning of the industry's history or the semi-utilitarian first-generation Beetle in the 1960s or 2CV in the 1970s. These cars, with their product standardisation and steadily falling real prices, were based on increasing production scale and experience. For the consumer, they were about mobility. Today, cars are sold as much on

[1] 'Better Branding', *McKinsey Quarterly* (2003), p. 30.

image as they are on engineering. They are not only a convenient, cost-effective form of personal transportation; they are also a means of self-expression.

Success in the industry clearly does not only rest on what we call 'passive quality', i.e. that the products work properly and reliably. If it did, the upline brands would not be objectively able to sustain their price premiums, now that the quality of run-of-the-mill volume cars has improved so much – incidentally one of the industry's great triumphs. Passive quality is not difficult to measure, using breakdowns statistics and the consumer satisfaction surveys. Dropping below acceptable standards is quickly punished by the marketplace. But very high levels of passive quality are now a sine qua non of being in the game at all: a qualifier for being a player. They are no longer in themselves a differentiator. 'Active quality' is that differentiator: the factor that gives the owner and driver of a car satisfaction with the product and which creates desire in the non-owner. But it is elusive and much, much more difficult to measure, because it is rooted both in the characteristics of the product and in the complexity of our personal characters and motivations.

Brand strength – of the marque or of individual products – now matters enormously to vehicle manufacturers and is boosted through constantly increasing advertising and promotional expenditures. As Rolf Eckrodt told us when he was the president of Mitsubishi Motors, 'brand and brand identity are number one'. Branding tries to accomplish something subtle and difficult. The basic theory is simple: to encapsulate a good experience of a product or service in some kind of easily identifiable expression – a brand name, a slogan, or both. The purpose is to remind consumers of that satisfaction – their own or that of others – so that they become favourably disposed towards purchasing or re-purchasing the product, while de-emphasising the competitive pricing aspect. It has to achieve consistency between the real attributes of the offering and the emotional attributes of the would-be buyer, and maintain it over time.

Otherwise, no brand value is created. The danger comes when too much reliance is placed on this link as a source of premium pricing and profitability, at the expense of addressing cost problems; when the link is too tenuous, either because the psyche of consumers has been misread, or because the brand proposition is based on nothing of substance; or in trying to transpose a successful branding link from one cultural environment to another; or, finally, in staying with a historically successful theme for too long.

There appear, however, to be very few truly global brands, even looking across all consumer products. Coca Cola and Nescafé seem to qualify, but not many others. It is the same in cars. Mercedes-Benz and BMW seem to have pretty much the same appeal everywhere. And their brand promise is strongly linked to identifiable physical characteristics of their products – 'The best engineered car in the world', 'The ultimate driving machine': plausible claims that appeal strongly to identifiable groups of consumers everywhere and which, for these manufacturers at least, ensure strong branding, sustainable price premiums and superior financial returns.

This condition does not seem to hold in the same way in the volume car market. Perceptions of cars and badges matter considerably for these vehicles – but so do market share and the size and quality of a company's distribution presence. In some cases, there is a curiously negative price elasticity for volume vehicles within a given class in a given market – that is, the greater the volume, the *higher* the price realisation. The VW Golf is the best example of this in Europe. People will happily pay *more* for the car precisely because it is so common. The fact that there are so many around is, paradoxically, what allows the vehicles to command a premium. It is about feeling part of a wide group, about understatement, about a reassurance of belonging, as opposed to a feeling of exclusivity.

Nor do volume brands mean the same thing in the three main automotive regions. Ford, for example, is mainly in the mind of American consumers through its light trucks – its

F-series pick-up is the largest volume vehicle in North America. There is an obvious association between the ruggedness of the vehicles and the American attachment to robust individualism. The whole story of Henry Ford and what he achieved is part of this image, even if the culture of the organisation at the time is now outdated. In Europe, in sharp contrast, the Ford brand simply does not have the same meaning. There is nothing wrong with the products – the Mondeo is seen technically as a leader in its class. But the brand is perceived as a blue-collar one, for which no-one will pay a premium. It is perhaps no coincidence that Ford's strongest individual product in Europe is the Transit light commercial van. In Japan, Ford carries the stigma of the unacceptability of American cars.

As we discussed in the first section, volume-market car buyers in the three main automotive regions expect different things from their cars, because of different conditions and amounts of driving. North Americans (and Australians) are mainly interested in value – a decent-sized car for the money and one which functions decently. Europeans are much more interested in that indefinable quality, 'character' – which includes both performance, particularly road-holding and handling, and styling – and pedigree. We found a good illustration of European expectations in the offices of Christer Ekberg, the managing director of Porsche in Asia. In his conference room in Singapore, along one wall, stretching for perhaps five metres, was a photograph. It was a little like the illustration so often used to illustrate Charles Darwin's theory of evolution: the one that shows a large chimpanzee gradually standing, becoming less hairy and being transformed, in stages, into a man. Only this was not of a chimp but of a car, the Porsche 911. Like the evolutionary picture, it showed the car in the 1960s, 1970s and so on, until it 'evolved' into the car it is today. 'Europeans want something that has heritage, something that has recognisable characteristics which are carried over from one model to the next. They want something that is evolutionary, not something that changes all

the time', Christer told us. This evolutionary tradition is very clearly maintained also by Mercedes-Benz, BMW and the other European upline manufacturers. Peugeot and Volkswagen, with the Golf, also practise it successfully in the volume-car sector.

There are still some quite strong national affinities too, with many consumers – in the car-building countries at least – still persuaded that their national products are better, or at least worth defending. These prejudices clearly apply in Asia, where most Japanese consumers still have a strong preference for Japanese cars, with the same effect in Korea, reinforced by tariff and other barriers. Even in the United States, imported cars achieve their greatest penetration on the west and east coasts and do much less well in Middle America. It is the same in Germany, France and Italy.

These brand attributes are also reflected in the lifecycle of cars. In Europe, a car model's 'life' usually lasts four to five years. When it is launched, sales typically rise rapidly, peaking after about eighteen months. By that time, a rival has usually introduced the 'next big thing' and sales begin to drop back. To prevent this decline from happening too fast, most European manufacturers give their cars a 'facelift' when they are two and a half to three years old. This is much cheaper than designing an entirely new model and typically involves changing the colour of the bumpers and the designs of the lighting clusters. The car is given a 'refresh', so that it looks a little different. This boosts sales again, at least a little, reduces the amount of discount the dealer has to offer, and allows the car to remain in the market for another couple of years until it is finally replaced. In Japan, it is not like that at all. There sales rise quickly, just as they do in Europe, reaching a peak after eighteen months too. But thereafter they just keep dropping. This is because Japanese buyers want something completely new each time they buy a car. No amount of facelifting can convince Japanese consumers that this is anything other than what it is – yesterday's model. In the US, product lifecycles are relatively long and there is less proliferation of products – the count of models on offer is about two-thirds that in Europe.

The impact of all this Hype, of the power of brands and their varying significance between world regions, is almost perfectly illustrated by the case of the Japanese manufacturers. They *do* actually make better cars, by and large, in terms of passive quality. In almost all quality surveys done in the industry Japanese brands like Toyota and Honda come at the top. And yet these and the other Japanese firms have mostly minor shares of the European market and weak brand images there, in complete contrast to what they have achieved in the United States. In the United States, Japanese carmakers have performed spectacularly. In 2003 they controlled more than a third of the car market – and their share continues to climb, while they make less use of cash incentives than the US Big Three in their home market

In the US, the success of the Japanese firms is down to 'value'. Value is more important than the badge, at least up to a point. American consumers can see that a better-built car, which holds its value for longer and which is cheaper to run, is a more sensible buy. The brand matters, but value matters more. The Japanese manufacturers have concentrated on that. They offer very simple product lines, without anything like the kind of variety and rapidity of change they practise in Japan. The Toyota Camry and the Honda Accord are almost part of the furniture in the US and have been so for many years. Even in the upline segment Lexus and Acura were able to knock Mercedes, Cadillac, Lincoln and BMW from their entrenched positions in the US within just a few years because their combination of features and price was so much better. The *value* they offered was higher. American consumers were more rational as buyers. Yet beyond a $50,000 price ceiling even Lexus found it hard. When buyers became less price-sensitive, even in the US, image mattered more.

In Europe the story is completely different. Although Japanese car companies con-

trolled 11.3 per cent of regional sales in 1992, their share a decade later was little different: 11.8 per cent. Even that hid the true picture. Within this total, only Toyota had prospered, raising its share from 2.5 per cent in 1992 to 4.5 per cent in 2002. Honda had 1.2 per cent of the market in 2002, exactly the same share it had a decade before (compared to more than 8 per cent in the US), Nissan's share had fallen from 3.2 per cent to 2.5 per cent over the decade, despite being the first to build an assembly plant in the region, while the shares of almost every other Japanese company had declined too. Why did the Japanese find it so hard?

Part of their decline in the mid-1990s could be explained by the strength of the yen at the time, but, with growing regional production and many years having passed since then, clearly not all. We talked extensively to several Japanese companies, in both Europe and Japan, and found that many of them are perplexed by this. Being rational, they looked at their products. They would say to us: 'Our cars are better equipped, well designed, more reliable, cheaper to run and hold their value better. Why is our market share in Europe stagnant or falling?'

What the Japanese (and the South Koreans and the Malaysians) failed to understand was that Europeans are not (yet) rational buyers to the same extent that Americans are. In Europe that price ceiling barely existed at all. There, buyers were willing to pay more for a less reliable, more expensive-to-run car because it was more fashionable to be seen on the streets of Barcelona, Milan or Paris in a ritzy European-badged model than a functional and often dull Japanese one. They want more variety than US consumers expect in a model line but also products that last longer than in Japan, based on more fundamental innovation. Only recently has Toyota begun to understand this, when it launched its cheekily designed Yaris/Vitz small car. Even then, we are not sure the company has understood the market entirely. It has not followed up on the Yaris with a range of other cars, and its luxury Lexus brand has failed to make a breakthrough at the upper end of the market in Europe. Lexus controlled 1.4 per cent of the US car market in 2003 but just 0.1 per cent of the market in Europe.

These differences in consumer expectations, breadth of product line and frequency of renewal have a huge impact on the economics of the industry, which work significantly differently from one region to another. Simple, value-based products – whether cars or light trucks – with less product proliferation contribute, we believe, to the normally higher profitability achieved in the North American market. The constant churning-out of products in Japan probably accounts for much of the fact that even the most powerful Japanese manufacturers make little profit in their home market. But it does inflate new vehicle volumes there, providing them with a secure base for achieving production scale. Europeans volume manufacturers have arguably become too reliant on brand image and product proliferation to support premium pricing in a saturated and potentially even declining market.

The temptation has always been there to over-exploit the non-product aspects of branding and to play on irrational motivations in consumers. We believe that there is now an increasing risk that this over-exploitation is close, especially in Europe.

Fast, attractive and powerful cars have long been marketed as analogues of the way we see ourselves or what attracts us. Cars are still shown to be shapely symbols of power, influence and fertility. The advertising often evokes images of speed, exhilaration and wealth.

Yet it can be argued that the sexual associations, as well as the emphasis on speed and performance, are increasingly out of step with the market, with reality, with society. There is a sense that much of the marketing is becoming not just sexually but also environmentally and practically outdated too. With the growth in environmentalism and the pressure for recyclable, emission-free, city cars especially in parts of the US, in Japan and in Europe, the continued emphasis on high performance seems increasingly inappropriate. The image

of the car, like that of tobacco, alcohol and fatty foods, could start to change.

For car producers this thought should be worrying. Image, and an image that is often about sexual stereotyping or speed, is still an essential element in the sales 'package' for many cars. Price differences between products cannot often be explained by an analysis of their inherent performance or features. Correcting for objective physical differences such as interior volume, engine power and various features and options still leaves large unexplained residuals – up to plus or minus 20 per cent. This premium is the result of brand strength. The industry's profit margins have become increasingly – and dangerously – dependent on marketing Hype, especially in Europe.

This creates a terrible risk of downfall, if the Hype starts to fall apart. Of course, the car is something special: it is the only means – short of piloting an aeroplane or a helicopter – through which human beings can extend and multiply their physical capabilities to such a degree. But it also just a form of transport, a way to move from one place to another, as is a bicycle or a bus. The danger is that consumers might begin to see through the Hype at some point and that they will see the car for what it really is: not just a safe little cocoon, our own little personal gravity-challenged space-ship with a sound system, but a ubiquitous commodity which simply gets us around, and in the process pollutes the environment, uses up scarce resources in vastly inefficient ways and kills or maims hundreds of thousands of us each year.

The dynamic pleasure of driving which existed during its heyday – when you could throw a sports car around deserted country or mountain roads – is an increasingly rare pleasure. Yet there is a danger that the styling and image components of selling cars have been boosted well beyond rational levels of utility, and that they no longer reflect the needs of the market. What is the good of a 150 mph car with nowhere to drive it? How long will consumers go on paying substantial price premiums for all that hardware they cannot use, for brand image? How long will buyers of 4 × 4s, sports utility vehicles and recreational vehicles pay for lots of engineering and metal that they hardly ever need? The influence of product brands has diminished in many other consumer businesses, like computers, televisions and fast food, in favour of retailer brands:[2] what will happen to the motor industry if this spreads to cars?

Of course, there will always be the car-lover segments in the market – people who want to pay more for a high-performance or luxury vehicle – whether 'objectively' justified or not. The industry has systematically targeted and developed these segments in the last few decades, showering them with new product offerings. But could satisfying the demand of the car lovers end up being counterproductive, a zero-sum game? Could the push to sell cars to these people actually alienate substantial numbers of other buyers?

Do not misunderstand our stance on branding. It is a legitimate marketing instrument – when correctly used. As we said earlier, a brand is a means whereby consumers can identify with a past satisfactory experience with a product or service, so that they feel comfortable in purchasing it again. Then the physically real experience and the emotional value of the brand reinforce each other. The danger comes when the expression of the brand and the reality of the experience start to drift apart.

As we have already explained, we have serious reservations about the economic cost to the industry of excessive proliferation of products. More and more branding cannot produce enough price premium for everyone to defy the laws of cost economics.

While most people in the developed world will always want to have a car for the mobility, freedom and convenience it offers, our concern is that the age of the car as a cult object may be drawing to an end: not in all markets or all segments for sure, but perhaps for some parts of the market and in some countries. As cars have ceased to be rare goods to be striven for and become simply part of the furniture of everyday life, their glamour has faded. The car provided vastly expanded physical mobility for the majority of the population. It is now seen almost as a right. Yet the individual aspirations of today's and tomorrow's teenagers and children may move on different tracks. Witness the vast growth of the video and video games industries. They have developed at a prodigious speed – far faster than the motor industry – and will continue to do so. This is because there is so much more 'stretch' in their underlying technologies. Cars can only become incrementally better means of personal transportation because physical transport cannot be micro-miniaturised.

The potential for developing co-ordination skills, intellectual capabilities and emotional sensitivities through electronic technologies remains far from fully exploited. Telecommunications, too, offers a much wider range of possibilities for us to communicate, reducing the need for travel. These technologies will surely be much more thoroughly exploited, to both desirable and less desirable ends, creating their own sets of personal and social problems and challenges.

In the end, kids will probably end up hanging out as much as ever. They will probably still want access to individual transportation and clamour to borrow the family car. But if environmental concerns rise or brand image declines it will become more of a means and less of an end. The spending priorities will shift, the branding and images will attach to other things, and the premiums will be spent elsewhere. The shift may be gradual but it could quickly accelerate with generational change. It is something the vehicle industry would be wise to think about.

---

[2] See, for example, Judith and Marcel Corstjens, *Store Wars, The Battle for Mindspace and Shelfspace*, Chichester: Wiley, 1995.

2

The problems that can be fixed – dealing with noxious emissions, traffic accidents and congestion

Diseases of underdevelopment (1) – noxious emissions

The car has always had its enemies. In the early years, Anti-Automobile Associations were common, particularly among farmers in America. Many pioneering drivers suffered verbal abuse, vandalism and ridicule, particularly if their cars broke down. Indeed, it was not uncommon for early drivers to give up their machines after a few years, such was the harassment.

Of course, cars have their drawbacks. They are polluting and noisy. Cars and their drivers have been responsible for millions of premature deaths and injuries in the last hundred years. Roads now penetrate some of our most beautiful landscapes, our cities have been reorganised into one-way systems and our gardens and basements changed into parking places. Our city centres are choked with vehicles every day and our lives are blighted by traffic jams. These are probably the most obvious drawbacks. Other negative effects of vehicles include damage to building foundations, emissions from paint shops, leakage from abandoned batteries and air-bag propellants, as well as the dumping of used motor oil. More than 500 million tyres are discarded annually worldwide, as are more than 600 million gallons of engine oil.

This section looks at the socio-economic costs of motoring and the role of governments. In the first part we look at emissions and then road deaths before covering congestion. Finally we look at the role of governments in addressing these problems.

The prospects for noxious emissions can appear exceedingly gloomy to the casual observer. Cars are one of the most visible sources of air pollution, simply because there are so many of them. With places like China and India motorising, even at their current rates, there are also rising concerns about how much these emission levels will increase. In 1950, there were 50 million cars in the world; now there are almost twelve times as many. How many more will there be in twenty years' time? A billion?

The World Health Organisation (WHO) estimates that motor vehicles account for more air pollution than any other single human activity. In a report on the problem it says that 'more than half of the global emissions of carbon monoxide, hydrocarbons and nitrogen oxides from fossil fuel combustion derive from automobiles, both gasoline- and diesel-powered, and the proportions may be significantly higher in city centres'. According to the US Environmental Protection Agency (EPA), driving a car is 'the single most polluting thing that most of us do'.

Transport-associated emissions affect the environment by increasing air pollution levels, particularly carbon monoxide, volatile organic compounds, hydrocarbons, nitrogen oxides, ozone and lead, as well as dust and particles. Diseases and ill-health associated with these emissions include chronic respiratory illness, asthma, reduced lung function, cancer and heart disease, which 'might be caused or exacerbated by air pollution', according to WHO. Benzene and polyaromatic hydrocarbons from car exhausts are recognised carcinogens.

Some hydrocarbons can cause unpleasant side-effects including drowsiness, eye irritation and coughing. Hydrocarbons are important because they react with nitrogen oxides to form ozone at ground level. Ozone, while necessary as a shield against solar ultraviolet radiation in the upper atmosphere, is an aggressive oxidant, which attacks the lungs. It is one of the principal causes of urban smogs. Hydrocarbon (HC) compounds, or volatile organic compounds, are released from exhaust pipes, fuel systems and filling stations.

Cars are the main source of carbon monoxide (CO) in most developed nations too. Nearly 100 per cent of the CO emissions in urban areas are caused by road traffic. CO reduces the efficiency of the bloodstream in carrying oxygen around the body. Exposure to CO can result in impaired vision, co-ordination and judgement, and drowsiness. It also affects the central nervous and cardiovascular systems.

Another major pollutant resulting from the combustion of gasoline is nitrogen oxides (NOx). This covers both nitrogen dioxide and nitric oxide. Nitrogen dioxide reduces the productivity of some crops and can irritate the lungs and respiratory tract, increasing the frequency of lung and bronchial infections. Nitrogen oxides are also precursors to ground-level ozone and contribute to a large proportion of acid rainfall – some claim as much as half.

Diesel fuel with a significant sulphur content is a major source of toxic emissions. Sulphur dioxide (SO_2) irritates the lungs. Suspended small particulate matter (SPM) less than 10 mm diameter (PM10) passes through the filter of the larynx and accumulates in the lungs. According to the European Commission, 50 per cent of particulates in the atmosphere in Europe come from motor vehicles. These have been blamed for aggravating respiratory diseases. There has also been a debate for many years on the possible carcinogenic effects of particulates, although this remains unproven. The International Agency for Research on Cancer stated in 1989,

however, that diesel exhaust particulates were 'a probable carcinogen'. NOx emissions from diesel engines tend to be high, because of high operating pressures and temperatures, which force nitrogen and oxygen to combine. Managing the engine so as to reduce NOx emissions tends to increase particulate emissions, and vice versa. Recommended WHO air quality guidelines for these three pollutants are 'low', as prolonged exposure to even small amounts can be harmful.

A study carried out by the European Centre for Environment and Health of the World Health Organisation in 1999 looked at the impact of PM10 on eight Italian cities on behalf of the Italian Ministry of Health. It found that the mean concentration of PM10 in the cities ranged from 44 $\mu g/m^3$ in Palermo to 54 $\mu g/m^3$ in Turin. The target level in the European Union is 20 $\mu g/m^3$. The study estimated that if PM10 was above 30 $\mu g/m^3$ it would result in another 4,000 deaths a year, out of a population under analysis of 400,000. It would also result in between 4,000 and 7,000 additional hospital admissions as well as tens of thousands of cases of exacerbated childhood bronchitis and asthma a year resulting in millions of days of restricted activity. 'The societal burden of urban air pollution', said the study, 'in terms of mortality, morbidity, hospitalisation and consequent economic costs is very high.' Another WHO study carried out the year before in Austria, France and Switzerland estimated that the impact of PM10 would cause an extra 40,000 deaths a year in these three countries. As both studies noted, the main source of PM10 is 'motor vehicles, including diesels and two-stroke motorcycles'. They both called for intervention to curb motor vehicle traffic.

It all sounds awful – and of course it is.

In one way it is very easy to see that this is all very negative. It is the sort of stuff environmentalists and doom-mongers feed on, and with which they excite the fears of the public – and of electorates. Yet there is also a more positive side, which is often overlooked. The clouds of noxious emissions do have a

Level of noxious emissions from motor vehicles

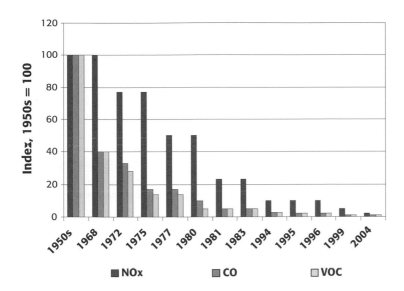

Source: Environmental Protection Agency, Washington, DC.

Fig. 2.1 Breathing more easily in the US

silver lining. In no way would we claim to be apologists for the industry or the damage vehicle emissions have caused and are still causing. Yet the emissions problems, at least in terms of new vehicles, have mostly been addressed. Most studies on motor vehicle pollution, including some of those above, make the classic environmentalist's error (so convincingly documented by Lomborg in his excellent book, *The Skeptical Environmentalist*[1]) of extrapolating from the past. The truth is that technology has given us the means of reversing the trend of rising air pollution from motor vehicles and that success in doing so is already very widely demonstrated – in the developed world at least. We still have a problem. But the means to address much of it exists too.

Over the last twenty-five years, a great deal has been done to solve these problems and with plans already in the pipeline a great deal more will be achieved in the years ahead. Emissions control measures have drastically reduced emissions per vehicle in the last few decades, more than compensating for the increase in the vehicle parc (the number of cars in use) and in kilometres driven – at least where they have been rigorously applied. Thus there has been considerable progress in reducing the problem.

The situation with respect to noxious emissions (nitrogen oxides, carbon monoxide and unburned hydrocarbons) has improved dramatically. The US, led by California and its Air Resources Board, pioneered the improvements, which are summarised in figure 2.1. Exactly the same curve, although reaching back to 1970, can be found for the UK.[2] It shows NOx emissions rising to a peak in 1992 and declining sharply thereafter, with the interesting additional detail of breaking down the sources between petrol- and diesel-powered cars, heavy goods vehicles, buses, light goods vehicles and motorcycles.

The same technologies were applied in Europe, with the same results – shown for

[1] Bjørn Lomborg, *The Skeptical Environmentalist*, Cambridge: Cambridge University Press, 2001.
[2] In RAC Foundation for Motoring, *Motoring towards 2050*, London: RAC, 2002, p. 41.

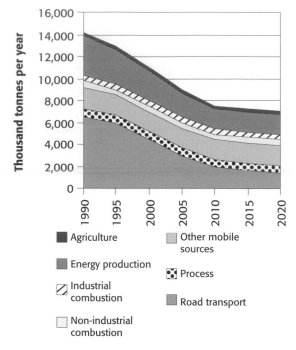

Agriculture

Energy production

Industrial combustion

Non-industrial combustion

Other mobile sources

Process

Road transport

Source: European Commission DGXVII – Energy

Fig. 2.2 Breathing more easily in Europe: nitrogen oxide emissions

nitrogen oxide emissions in figure 2.2. As a result, road transport, despite its enormous growth, is moving from being the greatest culprit to a small contributor.

Noxious emissions were first targeted in California starting in the 1960s because of their contribution to the generation of photochemical smog in the Los Angeles basin. They have been largely dealt with through the use of three-way catalysts, which remove them from exhaust gases, and better management of engine fuelling and ignition. Carburettors and distributors have been completely replaced by fuel injection and highly sophisticated engine management systems, at least in the developed world. This has been a clear example of the successful application of new technologies on a massive scale. Yet this very success simply shifts the focus of our preoccupations back onto the greenhouse effect, global warming and the role of carbon dioxide emissions – and therefore onto fuel effi-

ciency. The steps taken have not yet addressed this problem – but they will. This can be seen in figure 2.3. Despite growth in the parc, carbon dioxide emissions are eventually expected to level off and then gradually start to fall. The carbon dioxide issue is addressed in chapter 3.

Similar technology is now being introduced into the diesel sector. This has already reduced its emissions volumes through higher-pressure fuel injection and more efficient engine design, with a further option of using particle filters in the exhaust system. The situation with respect to nitrogen oxides, carbon monoxide and unburned hydrocarbons has improved enormously in many of the developed markets. The sulphur content of fuels is being dramatically reduced in many parts of the world too, and could be eliminated through the synthesis of gasoline and diesel fuel from natural gas.

From the 1920s, the organo-metallic compound tetra-ethyl lead was added to gasoline in order to inhibit pre-ignition during the compression stroke and to help cool valve seats. Premium-grade gasoline often used to be referred to as 'ethyl' in the United States. Consequently, large quantities of lead oxides and other compounds were emitted in vehicle exhausts. Lead is an insidious and slow-acting poison that is easily absorbed and remains in the body. The serious health impacts of lead have been extensively researched and documented and are well understood. It is particularly dangerous to children.

When people breathe in airborne lead from emissions, it accumulates in the body tissues and leads to anaemia, hypertension and permanent loss of brain function, particularly in infants and children. Exposure to lead has been shown to reduce intelligence quotients in children by 2–3 points for every additional 100 micrograms/litre of lead in children's blood. Children are at the greatest risk, especially very young children, because their digestive systems absorb lead much more readily. It also accumulates in the soil on which they play, getting on their clothes and toys.

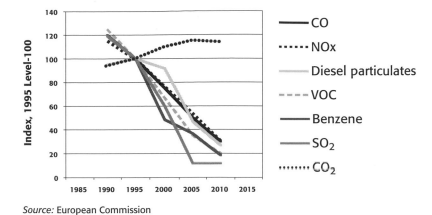

Source: European Commission

Fig. 2.3 Winning the emissions battle

The result is not only illness but permanently stunted mental capacity. Poor children are most at risk because malnutrition intensifies lead absorption. Among adults, lead causes elevated blood pressure, cardiovascular conditions and neurological and kidney-related diseases. Adults lose productivity and die earlier because of airborne lead. World Health Organisation air quality guidelines for lead content in the air are 'low', as exposure to even small amounts can be harmful.

Medical campaigners led a long fight against leaded gasoline. It finally began to be phased out when catalytic converters were fitted into exhaust systems to ensure the full oxidation of unburnt hydrocarbons, carbon monoxide and nitrogen oxides in the US in the 1970s. It could be argued, however, that unleaded gasoline was forced on the automotive industry by technical rather than by ethical considerations, given its initial opposition to the research findings on the harm done by lead compounds.

Today, leaded gasoline has nearly disappeared from developed-country fuelling stations. A 2001 study by the World Bank found that about 85 per cent of all gasoline sold in the world is unleaded. However, this leaves 15 per cent which is still leaded fuel, sold and used mainly in Africa, parts of Asia and Eastern Europe. Africa and the Middle East are among the last regions where motor vehicles

continue to use leaded gasoline almost exclusively. These regions now account for more than a third of annual lead emissions globally. In many of these countries, the report says, there is still a poor understanding of the risks of lead exposure and confusion about the technical difficulty of eliminating leaded gasoline.

Today, much of the lead problem exists because it is hard to sell vehicles with sophisticated fuel injection systems and catalytic converters in these places. This is partly because of added cost but also because the maintenance and repair networks in these countries are not able to look after them. People in the developing markets still want vehicles with carburettors, which can be easily maintained at low cost. As with other noxious emissions, the remaining problems with leaded fuel are really problems of economic underdevelopment. As these countries progress further, and as the numbers of cars rise, it will be possible to introduce newer engine technologies and so unleaded fuel. There are no technical obstacles.

Indeed the automotive industry has, after some initial hesitations and after needing a bit of a shove, made magnificent progress in dealing with the challenge of noxious emissions. The challenge today is really to public institutions to apply what is already available everywhere in the world and to encourage the removal of the older, more polluting vehicles from our roads.

Diseases of underdevelopment (2) – road deaths

Road accidents injure and kill. As cars steadily come off the assembly line, they make an impressive sight: an awesome demonstration of industrial scale, organisation and power. But there is a more depressing aspect. 'Just think', said one car company manager to one of us as we stood by the line, 'about how more than a third of these new cars will end up with blood on them.'

In Europe, one in three people will be hospitalised as a result of a car accident during their lives. Every day, more than 3,200 people are killed across the world. In 2001, 1.2 million people died as a result of motor vehicle accidents. That is the equivalent of Scotland, Israel or Denmark being wiped from the face of the earth every four or five years. It is equal to six jumbo jets crashing, killing everyone aboard, every *day*. The number of accidents where people are injured is roughly twenty times higher. Worse still, the numbers of both are growing.

One in forty-five of us will die as a result of a car accident globally; in the Americas as a whole, one in thirty of us. But that includes Central and South America where the roads are much more dangerous than in the US and Canada. There, the probability is roughly the same as in Europe. But in the US car accidents are the leading cause of death among people under thirty-three years old, according to the National Safety Council.

The World Health Organisation ranks the causes of death in absolute terms and also in DALYs – a disability adjusted life figure. Developed in 1993, this attempts to take account of the number of healthy years lost, either through dying early or through living many years suffering ill-health. In terms of DALYs, motor vehicle accidents are the fourth-largest cause of lost productive years in the Americas.

They are the fifth-ranking cause of all deaths after heart disease, strokes, respiratory infections and lung, tracheal or bronchus cancer. More than 3.5 million people have died in the United States in the last hundred years directly as a result of passenger cars, according to the National Safety Council. More than 200 million have been injured. In 1993 an article in *Automotive News*, the American automotive industry journal, stated that more Americans had died on the roads in the previous fifteen years than in all of the nation's wars since the Revolution. The largest proportion of the dead and injured are young – under thirty-five. Roads deaths in the US cause more loss of life expectancy than cancer or cardiovascular disease.

Road crashes are also a leading cause of head injuries and acquired disability. And even although products like airbags and safety cages have allowed the number of fatalities in the developed world to stay constant in the last five years, in the face of rising traffic volumes, the numbers of hip and leg injuries have grown. Whereas, in the past, someone might have been killed in a particularly severe impact, now the airbag saves them, but often at terrible cost to their lower body.

The sudden and unnatural death or disability of a loved one leaves families traumatised. There is also the impact of the fear of road crashes. Walking and cycling, the healthiest and most non-threatening of transport modes, are made more dangerous by motor traffic and people are put off by the fear of injury. Children are often not allowed to play in the streets as they once did in Europe because parents rightly fear the dangers. This is a further hidden and unquantifiable social cost.

More young adults (aged between fifteen and forty-four years) in Africa were killed by road crashes than by malaria in 1998, according to WHO. Throughout the world road deaths are a phenomenon which hits the younger disproportionately. Just under 70 per cent of all road deaths affect those under

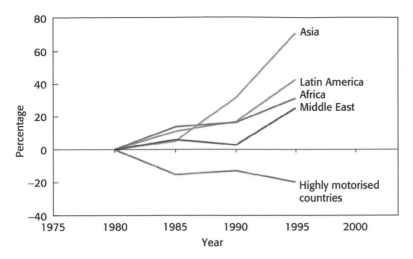

Source: Transport Research Laboratory, Crowthorne, UK.

Fig. 2.4 Percentage changes in road casualties by region, 1980–95

forty-five years of age, with only one in ten occurring to people who are retired and nearing the end of their natural life span. In the EU, road fatalities die on average forty years too early. Extrapolating from the current rate of growth of road deaths, the World Health Organisation predicts that by 2020 road accidents will be the second most common cause of premature death in the world. The growth rates by region are shown in figure 2.4.

It all seems like some horrifying, inevitable, and monstrously growing catastrophe: some sort of divine punishment for mankind's automotive temerity. The number of people killed in road crashes in the developing world continues to increase. Between 1987 and 1995 road deaths in Asia–Pacific rose by 40 per cent, in Africa by 26 per cent (excluding South Africa), in the Middle East/North Africa by 36 per cent (Saudi Arabia rose by 58 per cent), and in parts of Latin America by almost 100 per cent. During the same period road deaths fell by about 10 per cent on average in the most industrialised countries – although since then they have remained almost flat.

Of course rising road fatalities are not inevitable. In fact, the clue is within the figure itself. The percentage change, year on year, has been consistently negative in the highly motorised countries. Once again, this is a disease of underdevelopment. Just look at where the deaths occur (figure 2.5). Ninety per cent of them are in the developing world – the newly emerging automotive markets. Only one in every ten road deaths occurs in the highly motorised industrialised countries, although even there it happens so frequently that our senses to it have been dulled. Two people die every hour on America's roads, the same number that expire on Western Europe's. If a bomb or a natural disaster killed fifty people in New York or London in one day it would be headline news. Yet that number die from car accidents in the US and Europe every day and it barely makes the local paper.

The burden is even more disproportionate when vehicle ownership is considered. Although the car is still very much the preserve of the rich, the road carnage is mostly reserved for the poor. Four in every five cars and light trucks are used in North America, Japan and Europe. Developing and transitional countries own a mere 20 per cent of the world's motor vehicles, but account for 91

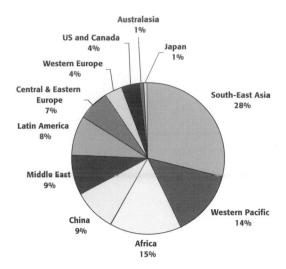

Source: WHO, National Highway Traffic Safety Administration (Washington), Eurostat, OECD International Road Traffic and Accident Database

Fig. 2.5 Regional breakdown of world road deaths, 2001 (1.2 million total)

per cent of the road fatalities. China may have a tenth of the number of vehicles in the US today, yet it has more than two and a half times the number of road deaths each year – more than 110,000 fatalities compared to just over 40,000. Ten years ago China had a fraction of that number.

Road accidents cost between 1 per cent and 3 per cent of a country's gross national product (GNP) and act as a drag on economic development. The estimates made by individual countries vary, from lows of 0.3 per cent in Vietnam to highs of over 4 per cent in New Zealand and the USA – see figure 2.6. In general, the figure is about 1 per cent of GNP in developing countries and 2 per cent in industrialised countries.

According to the Global Road Safety Partnership (GRSP), an affiliate of the IFRC (the International Federation of Red Cross and Red Crescent societies) set up to provide a knowledge base on road safety primarily related to developing and transitional countries, the total global economic cost of road accidents is about $550 billion per year worldwide. This is just over 1.5 per cent of global GDP, which makes the estimate consistent with the figures above. It means that the costs of the deaths to the world are equal to more than a third of the value of the new vehicle industry itself each year.

Moreover, the million people killed each year in developing and transitional countries, together with the 20 million or so injured, are mostly the economically active members of society between the ages of twenty-five and forty. As GRSP says, 'these casualties impose large costs on the economy as a whole and represent a significant drain on the scarce (trained) work force in these countries'. In most developing countries the health sector focuses on communicable diseases and malnutrition. Road accident victims in these places are therefore a particularly unwelcome drain on resources, especially as the casualties tend to stay longer than average in hospital. The cost of accidents today is $60 billion a year in developing and transition countries – more than the entire annual flow of official development assistance to these countries. In many developing countries the net value of the auto industry is negative (we will explain this in

Country	Study Year	Percentage GNP	Value US$mil (1997)
Latin America Brazil	1997	2.0	15,681
Asia Vietnam	1998	0.3	72
Bangladesh	1998	0.5	220
Thailand	1997	2.3	3,810
Korea	1996	2.6	12,561
Nepal	1996	0.5	24
Kerala, India	1993	0.8	
Indonesia	1995		691–958
Africa KwaZulu Natal	199?	4.5	
Tanzania	1996	1.3	86
Zambia	1990	2.3	189
Malawi	1995	<5.0	106
Middle East Egypt	1993	0.8	577
Highly motorised UK	1998	2.1	28,856
Sweden	1995	2.7	6,261
Norway	1995	2.3	3,656
Iceland	1995	3–4	7,175
Germany	1994	1.3	30,173
Denmark	1992	1.1	2,028
New Zealand	1991	4.1	2,441

Source: G. J. Jacobs, A. Aeron-Thomas and A. Astrop, *Estimating Global Road Fatalities,* Report 445, Transport Research Laboratory,

Fig. 2.6 The cost of road accidents

more detail in a later section). But is this a reason to deprive them of the ultimate benefits of motorisation? We think not, as the problems of road accidents are, if not completely soluble, at least very considerably controllable.

Driver error is the sole or partial cause of more than 90 per cent of road accidents (see figure 2.7. The road environment does contribute significantly – it is involved in some 25 per cent of accidents. But road user error alone is responsible to the extent of 70 per cent. We all know about it. Collisions on city streets happen most often at intersections because of lane changing and running or jumping lights, while collisions on freeways are mainly caused by tailgating or carelessness in changing lanes. Excess speed causes two road deaths out of five in France. Dangerous overtaking on two-lane highways can have catastrophic consequences. It is an obvious truism that safer driving would save many lives and injuries, which means much of the solution lies in changing driver behaviour.

With motor vehicle accidents the leading cause of death among the under-thirties, clearly youthfulness has a part to play too. New drivers are proportionately responsible for many more accidents than those who are experienced. In France, for example, drivers with a licence less than a year old are three times more likely to be killed in a road accident than experienced drivers. Again, the roads are the prime cause of death among eighteen-to twenty-four-year olds in France.

Any insurance company will tell you that the number of accidents among the under thirty-fives is so high because they are simply more reckless statistically. A study in the *Journal of Safety Research* in 2002 found that the main causes were inexperience, a lack of seatbelt wearing, fatigue, and the fact that drivers were easily distracted, especially when other teenagers were in the car. It suggested a graduated form of vehicle licensing as a solution.

But a great many drivers involved in fatal accidents, particularly in this age group, have also been found to be under the influence of alcohol or drugs. These play a significant part in European accidents and fatalities. A third of pedestrians killed are under the influence of alcohol. The number of drivers killed in road accidents whose blood alcohol level exceeds the legal limit varies between 15 per cent and 45 per cent in different EU member states. Similarly, of the 42,000 who died on America's roads in 2001, 18,000 were under the influence of alcohol, according to the National Safety Council. A further 500,000 were injured

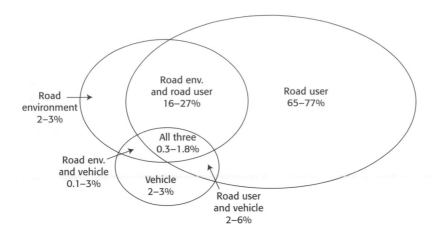

Source: Global Road Safety Partnership

Fig. 2.7 Causes of road vehicle accidents

in drug- or alcohol-related motor accidents. Moreover, the Drivers' Safety Council in the US says that the number of drink-related deaths on the roads is rising. It says that, statistically, 30 per cent of all Americans will be involved in an alcohol-related traffic accident during their lives.

Speeding is a major factor too, and here the industry has at least some responsibility for the way it promotes vehicles as it does for building cars that can so easily exceed legal limits. Cars are much faster than they used to be. In France, for example, only 10 per cent of cars sold thirty years ago could exceed 100 mph and nearly a third had a maximum speed of less than 70 mph. Today nearly all new cars sold can reach 100 mph, while many can reach 125 mph. As the average speed rises by 10 per cent, the likelihood of fatalities rises by 50 per cent, and so this growth in vehicle performance has been matched by a huge rise in the seriousness of injuries. Other French evidence also shows that, while some drivers reduce their speed at night, many actually increase it – which accounts for the disproportionate gravity of night-time accidents there.

Speeding is a contributing factor in 30 per cent of all fatal crashes in the US and Europe. Aggressive driving and 'road rage' play a part

too, with a 1998 *USA Today* article reporting that 'aggressive driving has killed an average of 1,500 people each year and injured 800,000'. Aggressive driving was defined as 'at least one of these four driving offences: running a red light or stop sign, failure to yield the right-of-way and reckless driving'.

The encouraging thing is that the battle for greater road safety is being partly won, at least in the developed countries. Figures 2.8 and 2.9 show how death rates have changed over thirty years in the US and the UK respectively. Clearly, the diminished rate is in part counterbalanced by the increasing number of kilometres driven. But it shows what can be achieved by determined action on road safety. The long-term historical trend in the UK is made clear by the published statistics.[3] From 1950 to 2000, road traffic multiplied sevenfold. Total deaths increased from 5,700 in 1950 to close to 9,000 per year in 1966 and 1967 but declined steadily thereafter, falling below 4,000 in 2000. All categories declined, except that the number of motorcyclists killed increased again slightly in the late 1990s. Traffic engineering is part of that. So is improved vehicle safety and the introduction of seat belts and airbags. The dominant factors,

[3] Ibid., p. 20.

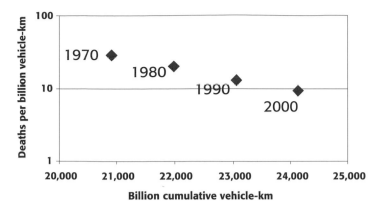

Source: WHO, road transport statistics, *auto*POLIS estimates

Fig. 2.8 Road deaths relative to kilometres driven, US, 1970–2000

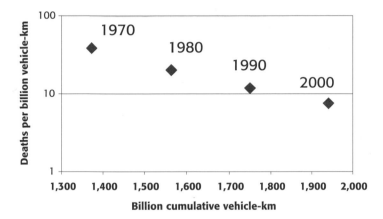

Source: As figure 2.8.

Fig. 2.9 Road deaths relative to kilometres driven, UK, 1970–2000

however, are driver education and enforcement. Figure 2.10 demonstrates that the benefits are not limited to the US and UK. They are achievable everywhere. In this illustration, we can see how Turkey starts at an appalling level but very rapidly makes good progress.

Furthermore, the problem of children and young drivers is being successfully addressed. As figure 2.11 shows, the sharpest reductions in accident rates have been achieved for these two groups. The particular success for children aged up to fourteen years is clearly attributable to the spread of child safety seats,

bans on small children riding in the front of automobiles and the enforcement of rear seat belt laws. Why the rate has got so much worse for elderly people in Japan and the US is another matter.

There is one other important factor, which is perhaps a curious one. It is sex. All that testosterone and perhaps a little (or a lot) of that image and branding by the carmakers (as well as the excessive technical capabilities of modern cars) mean that 70 per cent of all those killed in road accidents are male. These figures are from the Insurance Institute for

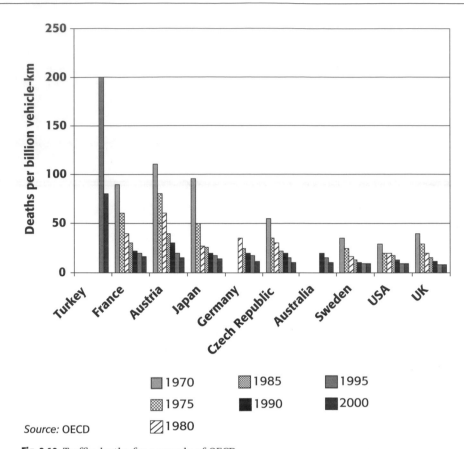

Source: OECD

Fig. 2.10 Traffic deaths for a sample of OECD countries

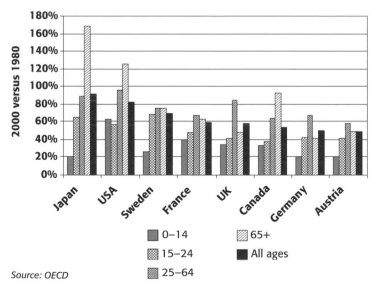

Source: OECD

Fig. 2.11 Road death rates in 2000 by age group, compared to 1980

Driver deaths per million registered passenger vehicles, 1–3 years old

	1981	1991	2001
All cars	177	108	83
All pick-ups	216	169	130
All SUVs	237	109	73
Cargo and large passenger vans	114	60	69
All passenger vehicles	182	117	89
Passenger versions of vans often referred to as minivans are classified as cars			

Occupant deaths per million registered passenger vehicles, 1–3 years old

	1981	1991	2001
All cars	259	169	124
All pick-ups	296	229	170
All SUVs	389	175	115
Cargo and large passenger vans	182	117	143
All passenger vehicles	265	178	131
Passenger versions of vans often referred to as minivans are classified as cars			

Source: Insurance Institute for Highway Safety, 2001

Fig. 2.12 Driver deaths per million registered passenger vehicles, 1–3 years old, and occupant deaths per million registered passenger vehicles, 1–3 years old, in the United States

Highway Safety (IIHS) and are consistent with those from the WHO. Car crashes account for 1.3 per cent of the female deaths worldwide but an astonishing 3 per cent of male deaths. We were not able to find a cumulative figure, but the multiple risk facing young men, with their friends, driving too fast at night, in small cars, after drinking or taking drugs, is huge. No wonder it is the number one cause of death for this social group.

According to the IIHS in the US, the likelihood of crash death varies markedly between vehicle types, according to size. Small and light vehicles have less structure and size to absorb crash energy, so more injurious forces can reach their occupants. People in lighter vehicles are at a disadvantage in collisions with heavier vehicles. Pick-ups and SUVs are proportionally more likely than cars to be in fatal single-vehicle crashes, especially rollovers. However, pick-ups and SUVs generally are heavier than cars, so occupant deaths are less likely to occur in multiple-vehicle crashes. Pick-ups are, however, an exception.

In 2001, according to NHTSA, the death rate for pick-ups was 57 per cent higher than for cars.

Even so, progress has been made in the safety of all classes of light vehicles (see figure 2.12), although significant differences remain between their safety characteristics. Ironically, the trend towards SUVs in the US has been driven partly by the belief that these vehicles are safer. But they are not always safer, mainly because they have a much greater propensity to roll over. SUVs have a rollover rate of 98 fatalities per million registered vehicles, compared to 44 fatalities per million for other light vehicle types, according to NHTSA. That said, they have become safer in the last decade.

What has happened, right across the board, is an enormous improvement in the safety of vehicles themselves, from better braking (particularly through ABS systems) to more protective bodyshells. The automotive industry, after some initial hesitations (the reaction to Ralph Nader in the US, attempts to discredit

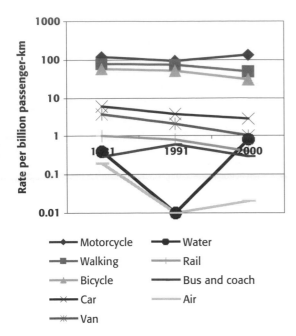

Source: RAC, *Motoring towards 2050*, p. 89.

Fig. 2.13 Passenger deaths by mode of transport – Great Britain

independent crash tests and ratings in Europe), has responded with a huge investment in safety, prodded by governments, insurers and consumer bodies. The results are clear.

Progress in the developed world has been considerable, then, although we should certainly not be complacent about the continuing cost of road accidents.

New technologies can help further. Devices are being developed that will detect 'driver failure', which can identify when a driver violates a traffic regulation, such as speeding or driving through a stop light. They also register the driver's state of alertness and whether or not he is suffering from fatigue or the effects of alcohol or drugs. Other programmes are working on collision avoidance using radar, improved night vision and intelligent navigation systems.

In the US, road deaths should remain relatively constant as the increasing numbers of vehicles on the roads dilute the benefits

of improved safety measures. In the EU and Japan, they are likely to fall as safety measures improve and demographics mean that the number of drivers begins to decline, albeit gradually. Everywhere, too, there is the irony that congestion may actually reduce deaths and the seriousness of injuries, along with the number of accidents, because it simply reduces average speeds. However, preserving safety by reducing mobility is not exactly an attractive policy. We need to maintain our mobility at an acceptable cost.

To give the story a last twist, look at the UK trends for passenger deaths by mode of transport, in figure 2.13. Cars and vans are moderately safe – and improving – as means of transport. Two-wheeling and two-footing are very much more risky.

In the less-developed world, the prospects for road deaths are much less bright. The number of car drivers is still rising rapidly in these countries and the necessary legislative controls have often not been developed to cope with this growth in traffic. The cars bought in these countries also tend to be lower-cost, smaller vehicles that are more likely to result in serious injuries or fatalities when involved in an accident.

There is still an unresolved issue in most developing countries over how these problems should be tackled. If nothing changes, the outlook in terms of the total numbers of deaths is not good. With this goes major damage to the development prospects of these countries. The contrast is perfectly made between long-motorised Western Europe and Eastern Europe and the Baltic states, whose motorisation accelerated with the end of communist rule. In the former region, traffic fatalities dropped 40 per cent from 1970 to 2000, in a fairly steady trend. In the latter, they shot up by 70 per cent from 1988 to 1991. They then went back onto a declining trend but were still up 30 per cent in 2000.[4]

---

[4] European Conference of Ministers of Transport, *Trends in the Transport Sector (1970–2001)*, Paris: OECD, 2003.

Most critically, we think, the issue of road accidents should be accorded much greater importance by society if they are to be reduced – notably by governments. In the past, many governments saw road deaths as the unavoidable cost of the increase in mobility and arguably this still holds true in some of the developing nations, unfortunately. However, as some legislative bodies in developed countries have shown that they *can* reduce the numbers of deaths and accidents, those not following similar policies have little reason not to act. There *are* actually many ways these problems can be addressed and legislators have responsibility for many of the accident-determining factors. These include:

- the road network and how it is used;
- the standards for vehicle manufacturing;
- the laws governing vehicle use;
- influencing the opinions and behaviour of road users through education, training, information, regulation, enforcement and penalties.

Measures that governments can implement include tighter speed restrictions, particularly in built-up areas, to protect pedestrians, or for certain types of vehicles. They can also apply laws more stringently, notably those on drink-driving. Stamping out the overloading of both passenger and freight vehicles is important too.

The motor industry can contribute to the solution as well. Airbags, anti-lock brakes, the compulsory use of safety belts and better brakes on trucks are known to reduce injuries substantially, for example. They can and should be made compulsory.

There are also particular social issues to address in many developing countries, often those that are the result of an undertone of religious faith. When the citizens of some developing countries experience the mobility that the car can offer for the first time, a kind of madness seems to ensue. There is also, unfortunately, often a belief in fate, in karma, in a time to come, which only increases the level of recklessness further. Just

try taking a taxi ride outside any of the major cities in Thailand, India or much of the rest of the developing world to have your own 'faith' tested. Again, these are issues needing improved education and awareness.

Partly, as we indicated, the problem of road deaths in many developing countries is a consequence of economic development. That may seem harsh. But as the economies of Europe, the US and Japan developed they too saw a surge in road deaths when car use began to take off. Drivers were unfamiliar with their machines, road conditions were not ideal, governments had other issues to worry about and there was the thrill of it all. Eventually, though, as countries matured, the priorities of governments changed. They cared a little less about pursuing rapid economic growth and building an infrastructure and a little more about the quality of life of their citizens. They began to think about safety and were more willing to invest in it.

There *are* lessons developing countries can apply, at little cost, to reduce the death toll. It is governments (and to a lesser extent the media) which need to act. The greatest responsibility for reducing the number of accidents, everywhere, lies with the legislative authorities and with those who promote social values. Only they can take actions that will have a lasting impact on the vehicle-driving community. Only they can promote campaigns that will significantly influence driving behaviour. The belief that it is the responsibility of the individual to look after their own welfare is too often used as an excuse for inaction. This is a collective, public responsibility.

The use of motor vehicles can be made considerably safer through government intervention. The automotive industry also has a role to play in helping governments deploy the best safety technologies. Developing countries need mobility in order to develop. They can achieve it at an acceptable social cost if they are prepared to learn the necessary lessons from those who have travelled this route before them, and to make the necessary investments. The potential pay-off for their economies is huge. But action is needed.

Diseases of development – traffic congestion

The third disease of motorisation is one of development. Traffic congestion is a major and growing problem which is important for many reasons. It is an inconvenience for those of us affected, it has an economic cost and it is wasteful of energy and resources. More than that, though, it erodes one of the main benefits of the road vehicle – mobility. If the problems of congestion continue to grow, the balance sheet for the industry, currently so positive in developed economies, as we shall see in the next chapter, will become much less so. In the developing world the net balance or costs of motorisation will become even more negative than they already are.

In economic terms, congestion wastes time and reduces potential economic wealth. According to national US studies carried out by the Texas Transportation Institute (TTI), the cost of congestion to Los Angeles alone was $12.6 billion in 2000, which includes $2.1 billion for wasted fuel. That worked out at an annual cost of $1,155 per person. Of course, LA is the worst affected city in the US, but the costs throughout the country are substantial. In 2003, more than seventeen cities in the US incurred congestion costs exceeding $1 billion. We are probably looking at a national bill of over $100 billion per year. In the EU, road congestion costs $45 billion a year, a figure which is due to double by 2010, according to the European Commission. Heavy goods vehicle traffic in Europe is expected to go up by 50 per cent by then, with the number of cars clogging up the roads increasing at a rate of 3 million a year.

But congestion is not limited to the developed world. It is a global phenomenon, affecting the cities of Mexico, Thailand, India and China just as much as, if not more than, those in the US, Europe and Japan. The largest and fastest-growing cities are now in the developing world. This will increasingly be so in the future because of the disparity in the rates of population growth.

Congestion occurs when traffic demand approaches or exceeds the available capacity of the road system. As we all know, the phenomenon is not constant. Traffic demands vary significantly depending on the season of the year, the day of the week, and the time of day. Studies carried out by TTI and Oak Ridge National Laboratories concluded that roughly half the road blockages in the US are down to recurring congestion – which exists almost every day. The TTI study also estimated that 32 per cent of daily urban travel in the US occurs in congested conditions. It says that the average length of time a 'congested period' lasts has risen from 2–3 hours in 1982 to 5–6 hours in 1999. The average length of congested daily travel in 'small urban areas' tripled during that time. So the problem is getting worse (see figure 2.14. According to the Federal Highways Administration (FHWA), congestion is not just a problem of recurring 'rush-hour' delay in major cities. The other half of all congestion is non-recurring – caused by crashes, broken-down vehicles, adverse weather conditions, special events and other temporary disruptions to the road system.

Congestion can be measured in a number of ways – levels of speed, service and travel time are commonly used measures. Predictability is important. Users in large US metropolitan areas may accept that a 20-mile freeway trip takes 40 minutes during the peak period, so long as this predicted travel time is reliable and not 25 minutes one day and 2 hours the next. Asked about what they wanted displayed on variable message signs on the Boulevard Périphérique, the Paris inner ring road, motorists voted heavily in favour of knowing how long it would take them to reach different exit points. This focus on predictability is particularly prevalent in the freight community where the value of time under certain 'just-in-time' delivery circumstances can exceed $5 a minute.

Congestion in the US is growing. All of the 75 urban areas studied showed more severe congestion, lasting for longer and affecting more of the transportation network in 2000 than in 1982. The average annual delay per peak road traveller climbed from 16 hours in 1982 to 62 hours in 2000. Delays more than quadrupled in districts with less than 1 million people.

Many more trips were accommodated on the transportation system. Passenger-miles of travel increased over 85 percent on the freeways and major streets and about 25 percent on the transit systems between 1982 and 2000.

Congestion costs are increasing. The total congestion 'Bill' for the 75 areas studied in 2000 came to $67.5 billion, equal to 3.6 billion hours of delay and 5.7 billion gallons of excess fuel consumed. To keep congestion from growing between 1999 and 2000 would have required 1,780 new lane-miles of freeway and 2,590 new lane-miles of streets – or – an average of 6.2 million additional new trips per day taken by either carpool or transit, or perhaps satisfied by some electronic means – or – operational improvements that allowed 3 percent more travel to be handled on the existing systems – or – some combination of these actions. These events did not happen and so congestion increased.

Source: TTI

Fig. 2.14 Conclusions and highlights from the Texas Transport Institute Urban Mobility Study 2002

In a speech at the Harvard Conference on Global Cities in 2002, Anthony Downs, a Senior Fellow at the Brookings Institution in Washington, talked about some of the more intractable problems to do with congestion, concluding that it is something we have to learn to live with.

Dr Downs explained that a large part of the problem is down to the strong worldwide desire on the part of people to own their own private means of mobility. But, because selling private vehicles is a profit-oriented business, the automotive industry pursues its ends without regard to the availability of roads. 'As a result, vehicle ownership and use is growing much faster than road capacity throughout the world, even in the U.S.'

The trouble is, as he explained, that roads and transit systems in most of the world are built by governments, which in most nations have incomes that lag behind aggregate private incomes. Furthermore, most governments use some of the revenues generated by gasoline taxes for purposes other than transportation – in the UK, for example, revenue from road and fuel taxes is more than seven times larger than public expenditure

on roads. So the total supply of road capacity to accommodate vehicles is rising much more slowly than the total inventory of vehicles. Add to that the geometric effect that more vehicles have and the problem continues to worsen. One effect of all this has been the increasing pressure to finance new roads privately, to use tolls to raise capital and to charge consumers for road use, as has recently been introduced in central London.

As Dr Downs pointed out, the impact of rising numbers of cars set against inadequate numbers of new roads has been greatly increasing traffic congestion throughout the world, especially in developing countries, where the 'gap' between rising vehicle ownership and new road production is greatest. Another consequence is that congestion tends to put up the prices of housing in city centres because those who live there are willing to pay a premium to travel less. This makes these districts the preserve of the wealthy – which explains one of the other knock-on economic effects stemming from the desire for personal mobility. Lower-income households have to live in the suburbs, or 'on vacant land where they can build their own shacks', as Dr Downs rather poetically put it.

He points out that congestion is not the basic problem, but a symptom of the real underlying difficulty – too many people trying to use the limited supply of road space during the same hours each day. 'Congestion is a balancing mechanism we use to enable us to pursue other goals', he says. Dr Downs's solution to the problem is to 'learn to enjoy congestion'.

But are there any other alternatives? This is a problem that is getting worse and which needs something more than a quick fix. But what should be done? The ever rising tide of clogged roads is actually diminishing the benefits of personal mobility.

In effect, the use of congestion to discourage more people from crowding onto the roads is an inadequate feedback loop. It allows temporary overshoots, which take too long to clear. We know the psychological reason for this. As individuals we value the freedom to start our journey when we wish. We are overoptimistic about how smoothly it will run. We know the roads will be crowded. We still get the car out of the garage. The fundamental defect of this delegated means of management is that it does not address the root cause: excessive demand for motorised mobility in specific places at specific times.

Could we reduce our reliance on the car? It is certainly not easy because of the social ratchet cars have created – something we described in our previous book.[5] There is a one-way street which makes it difficult to limit the desires and aspirations of people for individual mobility.

Put simply, the car has changed the way we live. Patterns of working and living today are built around the car and the truck – which are the result of fifty years or more of social and urban development. This means that limiting future growth in car use and our dependence on cars will be very hard indeed. It will take a long time. Arguably, though, this is why we should start thinking about how it can be done now. Here is an illustration: when the car was initially introduced in the 1890s, the most common source of individual mobility was the horse. Yet it took forty years for the number of horses in use to fall by even half.

If our dependence on motor vehicles is to be managed there are two broad options:

- we can try to limit the number of journeys people take or reduce the distance they have to travel;
- and/or we can try to encourage the use of alternative forms of transport.

As we shall see, neither is terribly practical in the short or even the medium term as a blanket solution, i.e. we cannot expect a large reduction in mobility without catastrophic economic consequences, or a major modal shift away from road transport, as sufficient alternative means of communicating and travelling do not yet exist.

An analysis of the purpose of individuals' journeys shows that most are regarded as essential and that few can be eliminated. In Europe, 85 per cent of personal journeys are by car, 94 per cent are by road. Four trips in five have to do with basic aspects of life – trips to and from work or school, on personal business or for shopping. Only 20 per cent of our journeys are made out of 'choice': that is, for purely social, recreational or pleasure purposes. The remainder are essential to the individual and/or the economy. The Dutch government came to this conclusion when it sought to reduce car use in the Netherlands, with its very high population densities. Not even two car trips in ten were susceptible to being substituted by alternatives, whatever the incentives or means of coercion. Figure 2.15 shows how passenger cars now totally dominate passenger transport in Europe.

The average distance travelled to work has also increased by nearly 60 per cent in the last twenty years, making the need for some sort of personal transportation greater than ever before. In Europe, around 70 per cent of these journeys to work are by car today. The

---

[5] Harlow: Addison Wesley Longman, 1994. Graeme Maxton and John Wormald, *Driving Over a Cliff? Business Lessons from the World's Car Industry*.

percentage is even higher in North America. Similarly, nearly two-thirds of business trips are by car in Europe. Even in households without a car, four times as many journeys are made in other people's cars as are made by train. Banning cars or limiting their use would have a devastating effect on our lifestyles and the economy.

Similarly, the overwhelming bulk of freight is carried by road in Europe (see figure 2.16). Trucks distribute most of the goods we use on a day-to-day basis, such as food, drink and clothing. Just as we cannot change the places where we live and work quickly, nor can we find some other way for goods to get from the factories to the stores. It is this practical dependence on cars and trucks, and the structure of our employment patterns that make blanket solutions to the problems caused by mass mobility almost impossible for the time being.

One solution, at least for some of us, that is often put forward is telecommuting. But the once much-vaunted future world of virtual reality and video conferencing has not achieved what many hoped, and is unlikely to do so for some time. Even if it does, it is only likely to be a real alternative for a very small minority of the working population. You cannot have nurses or shop assistants or people who unload ocean tankers doing their work from home.

What telecommuting does possibly offer is an opportunity to reduce the congestion problems at the margin. If home-working were to become practical even for 10 per cent of the working population in the developed world, this could ease the traffic volumes disproportionately – according to queuing theory. This is clearly an opportunity, although even this will need much more technological development and significant changes in social and working patterns before it can become a reality.

What of the second option? Could we encourage the use of alternative forms of transport in an effort to cut some of the costs of the rise in mobility that result from the car? Unfortunately, that is not easy either. An individual selects a particular form of transport

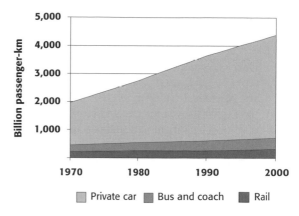

Source: European Conference of Ministers of Transport

Fig. 2.15 Model share of passenger transport in Europe

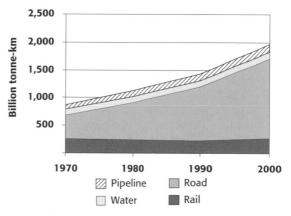

Source: As figure 2.16

Fig. 2.16 Model share of freight in Europe

depending on a number of criteria, whether consciously or otherwise. Although the decision is not entirely rational, he or she will choose the mode of transport that best meets his or her needs primarily on the basis of cost, flexibility, safety, environmental impact, speed and comfort. Each journey and each mode of transport offers a different blend of these on each occasion.

A train, for example, offers a good blend of safety, speed and cost. It is 125 times safer than car travel, does much less damage to the environment per passenger-mile and has a comparatively low cost. For every passenger-mile, trains produce much less atmospheric pollution than any other form of transport.

That means fewer health problems and less damage to the environment. Trains also use up much less fuel and land than road travel. They offer greater flexibility in terms of the type of fuel used too, particularly if they are powered by electricity. It is for these reasons that many countries and cities have been investing heavily in national and light rail systems over the last decade. It is easy to disregard the rail industry as an alternative form of transport, particularly in the US and parts of Europe, such as the UK. But high-speed trains in France, Germany, Spain and Italy, together with the development of an integrated international European high-speed rail network, have led to a resurgence in rail use there.

The US still has a huge track network from the nineteenth-century railroad construction fever. The US rail industry is very large in terms of its economic role. While the trucking industry proudly proclaims that 'America's Needs Move By Truck', in fact rail hauls slightly more tonne-kilometres than road. But that is mostly bulk freight, plus containers (which can be stacked two high, thanks to the generous loading gauge) and trucks on flat cars, moved over enormous distances. It is a very efficient industry too – because it has all but given up on the passenger. Just 0.5 per cent of US passenger-kilometres are by rail, compared to 10 to 20 per cent in European countries and 40 per cent in Japan. Rail's share of freight tonne-kilometres in these regions is almost exactly the reverse of that in the US, simply because of the very different distances – rail is at its best on long hauls.

The European rail industry remains heavily passenger-based. It is also a financial black hole of gigantic proportions. European railways collectively devour some $35 billion of taxpayers' money every year, once the government subsidies paid to them are added to their losses. They are also in many cases stubborn opponents of reform. France, for example, continues a rearguard action against European Union requirements that other freight operators should be allowed access to its tracks. French train drivers retire on a full pension at fifty, appropriate in the age of the steam locomotive, which was brutally hard to drive and stoke, but hardly in that of push-button, air conditioned cabs.

Yet the overall impact of the rail industry will always be limited. The train scores poorly in terms of flexibility, unless the start and end point of the journey are close to stations that have a direct service between them. Although trains offer more comfort and safety, as well as less stress, than a car journey, they force passengers to travel together. While this may seem trivial to many of us, a large number of commuters choose their cars exactly because they allow the individual to be alone. They retain that sense of individuality.

An aeroplane journey scores well in terms of speed, safety and cost, especially since the budget airlines appeared. But it is not terribly flexible, can still be very uncomfortable and is polluting in terms of noise, emissions and land use. Given the air congestion and the time taken to travel to and from airports it is also arguable how fast air travel really is today, at least over shorter distances. This is where high-speed rail has been gaining market share in Europe, at least on the high-density city-to-city axes, albeit at the cost of enormous investment.

A car journey scores well in terms of speed and some aspects of comfort. It is less safe and more expensive (when fully costed – most car owners only consider the marginal price of the fuel used) than rail, air or bus transport and is much more environmentally damaging per passenger-kilometer. The greatest benefit the car offers is flexibility. For most journeys, this is simply not tradeable against the other benefits. Travellers are willing to pay a great deal for the freedom of the car even if congestion means that this is not nearly as great as it once was. In fact, it is sometimes only a *perceived* flexibility. The volume of traffic is now so great that in many cases buses, trains, bicycles or even walking offer faster journey times at far less cost. Even so, the cocoon of the car ranks higher than the rationality of the alternatives.

In Europe, most car journeys are very short. Three-quarters are less than 5 miles; just over

6 per cent are under 1 mile. Yet few drivers are willing to give up their cars, even for short distances. A study done by General Motors, as part of its research into electric cars in the early 1990s, confirmed that most trips in the US were short too. Given the limited range of electric vehicles (EVs), this seemed to indicate that the EV had a market. Unfortunately, the study also found that the great majority of car buyers still wanted the flexibility to take their family and their possessions on a long journey whenever they chose. Even though most journeys were short and people rarely made any long journey without them being planned well in advance, the study found that this was irrelevant. It was the *perceived* flexibility that was critical.

Most journeys may be short and other modes of transport may make more sense, then, but the market is not rational. Car owners are hitched to their perceived flexibility. All in all, the idea of moving large numbers of passengers off the roads and into trains, trams or buses is simply not practical. The personal motor car is here to stay.

Some argue that we could solve some of the problems by moving freight off the roads. Certainly, this would reduce congestion – but not much. Heavy trucks are one-thirtieth as numerous as light vehicles. Even though they drive much greater annual distances, they generally contribute less than one-third of all vehicle-kilometres driven – for the UK, which has the worst road congestion problems in Europe, the proportion is one-sixth. Reducing the number of trucks would also cut the number of deaths and the damage they do to roads. Heavy trucks are more responsible, proportionately, for road damage and serious road accidents than cars or buses. Trucks, being professionally driven, are involved in fewer accidents, per vehicle-kilometre, but because of their momentum the results tend to be much more grisly. Fewer trucks would mean less government expenditure on road maintenance and medical care. Fewer road deaths would also bring economic savings. On balance, though, we would lose more economically than we gain.

However, it is difficult to reduce our dependence on heavy commercial vehicles because of the inherent flexibility of road transport. It is rarely economically viable to move freight by rail unless the goods are transported more than 300 miles. Rail transport brings a loss of flexibility, particularly for part loads or where several drops are required too. The freight also needs to get to the railway station from its point of origin and then to its final destination. These journeys still require road transport. This is why the goods that are most carried on the railways are typically bulk commodities such as coal, concrete and chemicals. Intermodal freight, i.e. putting containers, road trailers or complete trucks onto trains, has been touted as the solution. The problem is, you need to shift a complete train. To do that you need to assemble the train – which means waiting time. It works on high-density, long-distance axes (as in the US), and can be encouraged where road transits have a particularly high environmental impact, as on the trans-Alpine routes in Europe. But at less than two or three trains per day each way on a given axis, the delays are unacceptable in an age of just-in-time delivery. In any case, many rail routes in Europe are saturated already. The costs and lead times involved in increasing capacity are huge. Which is not to say it is not worth doing in some instances. Just that it cannot have anything more than a minor impact on the constantly growing volumes of road freight.

There are other means of transporting freight: pipelines, ships, air and inland waterways. However, all have drawbacks and limitations compared to road transportation. Pipelines can only carry particular goods. Waterways are slow and often indirect. That does not matter with undifferentiated bulk freight, such as coal or oil or iron ore, where a fairly steady flow is delivered. Coastal shipping plays a large role in Japan and a surprisingly large one in Europe, including the shipping of finished cars – partly because of the slowness and unreliability of European rail freight. Most of Europe is surprisingly close to the sea (as the Vikings demonstrated long ago, to the dismay of those whom they visited), or to a major river or canal system which connects with it.

But all this means that any massive reduction in the demand for road transport is unlikely in the short term. Attempting to reduce the need to travel by car and ship by truck, or persuading people to adopt some other form of transport is mostly futile, unless there are major structural changes made to the way we live, which will be hard and very slow to achieve.

There are other reasons why reducing our dependence on the car will be difficult. There are the vested interests of governments, fuel and vehicle suppliers and others in the industry who benefit from the status quo. Not only do the industry and motor vehicles themselves bring substantial revenues to governments, they also brings vast economic activity and employment. The investment in the road infrastructure is also enormous and has taken many years to develop. It makes no sense to see that investment wasted or underutilised: quite the contrary. Governments and politicians want to see a payback; they want to be seen to have spent from the national purse wisely. So there is even a built-in resistance to change among those who are responsible for transport policy.

Simply building masses of new roads is not much help in solving the congestion problem either. According to the Texas Transport Institute's 2002 mobility study, in areas where the rate of roadway additions was approximately equal to the travel growth, journey time still grew at about one-fourth to one-third as fast as it did in areas where traffic volume grew faster than roads were added. This is because the impact of additional cars is geometric not arithmetic. It is a well-documented fact that new roads simply attract new traffic, as people's living and working patterns adjust to take advantage of them.

Besides, as the TTI pointed out, the need for new roads exceeds the funding capacity of state governments and their ability to gain environmental and public approval. Its answer to the question 'Can more roads solve the problem?' was simple. No. It said that in 'many of the nation's most congested corridors there [is not] the space, money [or] public approval to add enough roadway to create acceptable conditions'. Only about half of the new roads needed to address congestion with an 'all roads' approach were added between 1982 and 2000, it pointed out.

There is no easy answer, then, but the growth in congestion over the past twenty years suggests that more needs to be done. In fact the options as to how to resolve the problem vary from area to area. More roads are part of the equation, but they are not the sole answer. More effective use of the existing infrastructure is another solution – improved access management, better signal timing, the introduction of road entrance ramp signals, reducing the effect of vehicle crashes and breakdowns and communicating travel information, for example. All can increase the rate of traffic flow. Information technology and intelligent transportation systems help with this also. In the end, though, it is all tinkering at the margin, dealing with the symptoms and not the causes.

There is an alternative view. As Professor David Begg, the chairman of the UK Integrated Transport Commission, puts it, 'road space is still one of the few economic goods which is allocated along Stalinist lines, by queuing'. His remedy is to use a pricing mechanism, which is what reconciles supply and demand in every market sector of the economy. We believe this is more than just making a point. It is an inevitable conclusion. We know that market mechanisms, properly tempered by regulation where appropriate, are the most efficient means of allocating resources. There is a growing call for those who cause accidents to bear a greater share of their cost. The principle that polluters pay is increasingly well established. So why do congesters not cough up too? A 90:10 rule applies in congestion: it is the last 10 per cent of additional demand put on the infrastructure system that causes it to seize up (or at least slow down very markedly), and that penalises 100 per cent of users.

To the surprise of many, the RAC (Royal Automobile Club) Foundation for Motoring report, *Motoring towards 2050*, came out in favour of road charging as the most effective and equitable means of managing demand for mobility. At the heart of the argument was the discovery[6] that tax revenues in the UK almost covered the high-end estimates of the fully allocated costs of road use and twice the low-end estimates – which exclude the costs of congestion. As the report says, 'the widespread saloon bar view that "we pay enough in road taxes already" can be supported by figures based on average or fully allocated costs. But the marginal cost figures, which are relevant to charging, are much higher and the gap will grow as congestion increases.' These short-run marginal costs are those imposed by an additional road user on other road users. At major urban peak times, they can reach ten times the level of the high-end fully allocated costs.

The automotive industry's major partner in ensuring mobility is government, which provides much of the infrastructure and many of the traffic management systems. The traditional governmental approach has to some extent been one of laissez-faire: let congestion find its own level, such that it discourages extra travel.

Yet we have to grasp the nettle of managing demand. This might mean extending the 'rush hour' by enforced staggering of working hours; changing the timing of the school run in Europe, or even enforcing that admirable American institution, the yellow school bus; or through the much wider use of road tolls. The new road toll in central London has been extremely successful, for example, in cutting traffic volumes and increasing average speeds.

The technology exists. GPS-based navigation systems are now widely available. Less than a tenth of car buyers take up the option, however. The reason is simple: nine-tenths of us drive our cars on regular routes to work, to schools, to shops. The odd vacation trip does not justify the investment in the system. It really works for salespeople, service engineers and delivery drivers, who must constantly find their way to unknown new places, and for

taxis and limousines. The real potential value is not in telling the individual driver where he or she is and where to go next. It is in knowing where any vehicle is at any moment. It is the enabler of universal tolling, which will charge people for the use of the infrastructure, according to cost and as a function of time and route. We already accept the principle of tolling for major highway routes and for specific bridges and tunnels. We are just beginning to accept it for entry into major congested urban areas. It simply needs to be widely generalised, using the available technology.

In the end, it is the only fair means of charging for the use of road space. Unlike blanket charges, such as fuel tax or vehicle licence fees, it does not discriminate against rural users or those who do not need to drive in the rush hour. Provision can easily be made to reduce prices for disadvantaged groups, such as the disabled, or for those whose mobility is a social priority, such as medical staff. The extra revenue raised does not necessarily all have to be handed back to motorists by reducing their other taxes. It can be reinvested in removing critical bottlenecks in the road system – or in public transport.

As the TTI points out, however, this approach needs a wider societal level of co-ordination – more government intervention. 'The key [is] to provide better conditions for travel to shopping, school, health care and a variety of other activities'. Only governments can do this. They will need to conduct many public information and education campaigns to get the new measures accepted. The revolt against increased vehicle taxes in California and fuel tax increases in Europe show how sensitive public opinion is to anything that smacks of 'soak the motorist'. There is, however, a counter-argument that road travel is in fact underpriced, with owners of vehicles not paying the full cost of motorisation. Again, it is a very difficult one to put

[6] Made in Tom Samson, Chris Nash, Peter Mackie and Paul Watkiss, *Surface Transport Costs and Charges*, Institute for Transport Studies, University of Leeds, 2001.

across persuasively. An interesting additional point is made, however, in the RAC Foundation's report, that the visibility of road charges might encourage more telecommuting. Thus we would start to have a positive feedback loop, based on realistic information, rather than the traditional approach of setting out in the car and seeing what happens.

Longer term, it should be possible to change social development patterns – to change the way developments occur. This might mean arranging land use patterns to reduce the use of private vehicles and sustain or improve the 'quality of life' in urban areas, to make walking and bicycling easier for some trips – and this is also a conclusion from studies in Texas, not Europe, where the argument for higher-density living is much more obvious. It is obvious also that Los Angeles-style motorisation is simply not a realistic option for the crowded mega-cities of the developing world.

TTI also says, rightly, that a vision of the future is important – a change in fundamental thinking. That to solve the congestion problem there needs to be consensus about how urban areas should be arranged for jobs, schools, homes, shops, parks and other land uses.

Congestion does not have to be an all-day occurrence and it does not have to be ignored. We can find a better balance. As with road fatalities, therefore, the solutions to the problem lie not with the industry or individuals but with governments and society as a whole.

What then is the nature of the relationship between the industry and legislators? Is it a healthy one? Will it encourage some of the changes needed? We address this in the next section.

Social limits to growth – the role of government in managing constraints on the industry

As we saw in the previous chapters, noxious emissions and traffic accidents are substantial problems, which are having an increas-

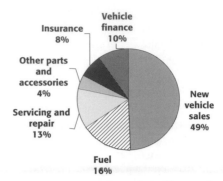

Source: CAR, *autoPOLIS,* Economist Intelligence Unit

Note: Total industry value of $2.6 trillion represents 8 per cent of global GNP and 10.5 per cent of that in the Economic Triad

Fig. 2.17 World automotive industry value added, 2002, in trillion US$

ing impact on society, to the point when they threaten some of the benefits motorisation has brought us. They are, however, local problems by nature, mainly concentrated in the developing and motorising world. The technology and the know-how exist for mitigating their impact very considerably. They are to a large degree problems of underdevelopment, which can be solved. The issues are more those of will than of means. Traffic congestion is a growing nuisance in virtually all large urban areas of the world. Unless it is tackled, it will further reduce the greatest benefit that motorisation has brought us – mobility. It also inhibits economic development. Again, the technology exists for us to manage it actively, rather than be paralysed by the tyranny of individual marginal decisions.

To demonstrate how critical all of this is, we have tried to document the net value of the automotive industry and of motorisation to society, and the potential impact of doing nothing about the problems.

The economic value of the industry itself is the easiest to quantify. Figure 2.17 presents a breakdown of its global value added, which is enormous. At an average cost of $22,000 a vehicle, the value of the global new car and truck sector of industry is almost $1.3 trillion a year, roughly equivalent to the economies of France, the UK or Italy. The sector alone

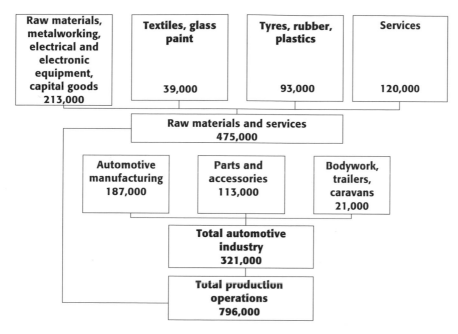

Source: Comité des Constructeurs Français d'Automobiles, 2001 report

Fig. 2.18 Jobs in France related directly or indirectly to the automotive industry in 2000

is twice the size of the Spanish or Brazilian economies, three times the size of those of South Korea or Mexico and nearly six times that of Russia. Even then, this only accounts for the original equipment or new vehicle market – the part of the business directly served by the vehicle manufacturers themselves. It ignores the used car business, which in throughput terms is more than three times the size of the new vehicle market each year – excluded because these are the original vehicles simply being resold to new owners. A further $0.4 trillion is spent on fuelling the vehicle fleet, $0.3 trillion on servicing and repairing it, $0.1 trillion on parts and accessories not included under the previous heading, $0.2 trillion on motor insurance and $0.25 trillion on financing (including value added in the used vehicle market on resale).

When all of these and other sectors are included, the motor business becomes one of the largest and most important industrial seg-

ments in the developed world. Fully loaded, the industry is worth almost $2.6 trillion a year. Like an engine itself, the industry is directly responsible for turning the wheels of many other businesses, making it one of the world's largest generators of wealth and employment. According to David Andrea at the Center for Automotive Research (CAR) in Ann Arbor, Michigan, the industry accounts for more than 10 per cent of the economies of the Economic Triad (North America, Western Europe and Japan). It is responsible for one job in nine, directly or indirectly. In France, a mature industrial European country, the automobile industry provides work for more than 2.6 million people, representing nearly 11 per cent of the economically active population. The industry and its suppliers in France directly employ some 320,000 people, representing almost 10 per cent of all employment in the manufacturing industries. The structure of this employment is shown in figure 2.18.

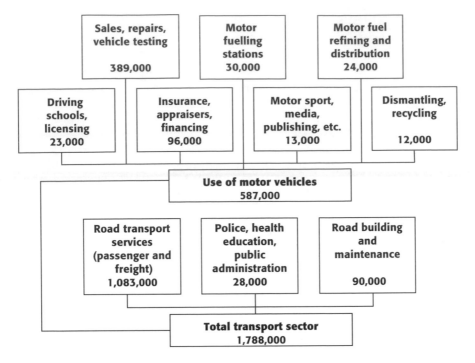

Source: As in figure 2.18

Fig. 2.19 Jobs indirectly related to the automobile, France, 2000

Employment in Europe in the components sector alone is put at 680,000.[7]

Little wonder then that so many emerging countries are keen to develop an auto sector or that there is such a political pressure to protect it in the developed countries. The jobs indirectly created by the automotive industry are even more numerous, as figure 2.19 shows, again for France. The total from the two figures makes up the more than 2.6 million jobs cited above.

In developed countries with a significant automotive industry the sector almost always contributes around 10.5 per cent of GDP. All the numbers add up roughly to this estimate, whether one measures value added within the industry or employment. Globally, the industry weighs in at about 8–9 per cent of world GNP. As 80 per cent of world GNP is generated in the Triad but 85–90 per cent of the industry's value added is produced there, its current relative industrial value to the developing world is probably in the 4 to 5 per cent range.

Using a very direct measure, then, the industry is hugely valuable – although still principally to the developed world. As we saw in chapter 1, the car remains mainly a rich man's possession. It is worth noting in passing, however, that the proportions reverse where heavy commercial vehicles (trucks and particularly buses) are concerned.

What all this does not measure, however, is the social value of the additional mobility that the industry brings: the value of our being able to commute over longer distances easily, travel to visit relatives in far-off places, work in different parts of the country, live in

[7] SESSI, Centre d'Enquêtes Statistiques de Caen, *L'industrie de l'équipement automobile en chiffres*, Paris: Ministry of Economics, Finance and Industry, 2003.

the suburbs. The freedom and flexibility the car has brought us, the mobility it gives to us and to society, is hugely beneficial and is not reflected in these figures. This 'mobility benefit' applies across the globe. Buses are the main alternative for moving people in most of the developing world. Trucks dominate freight transport almost everywhere.

Before the car, people typically lived near their places of work, their friends and facilities such as shops. In the 1930s the car allowed people to move to the suburbs or out of town; it allowed them much greater flexibility in where they chose to live and work. Over the last fifty years this flexibility has increased further, so that what at the beginning was a privilege of the better-off is now a common aspect of the lives of most people in the developed world. Most shopping malls only exist because we can travel to them by car. The very structure of our lives has changed – we cannot conceive of this new freedom being taken away. There is an in-built structural need to travel by car, which is extremely difficult to change.

Moreover, the attachment of individuals and society to cars has become profoundly rooted – not only in the practical necessities of life but also emotionally. There is a deep psychic connection between freedom and movement which the car has fuelled. As an economic phenomenon, the industry, the car, the emotional value of motoring and the mobility it has brought now form a central pillar of modern life in the developed world. Cars and commercial vehicles, and the industry that developed them, have brought great progress.

As a very broad estimate, we think that the all-pervasiveness of motorised road transport in modern life probably makes it worth 20 to 30 per cent of GNP in developed countries, i.e. a total of two to three times the industrial value of the sector. This, is of course, just an estimate and it is a very crude one. The only way to properly measure it would be to try and quantify the indispensability and dependence

that motor vehicles bring; in other words to try to imagine life without the motor car and the truck – a near-impossible task. Making the same estimate for the developing world is even more hazardous. But let us suppose about the same multiplier effect applied to the industry's 4 to 5 per cent industrial value there, giving perhaps 10 to 15 per cent of GNP in all, with, of course, a wide dispersion between different regions and countries.

These are the benefits of the automotive sector. But what are the costs? They are not trivial. All this progress has come at a price. Some sections of society have always seen the automobile as a major evil, a symbol of all that is wrong with modern life:

These are the same people
only further from home
on freeways fifty lanes wide
on a concrete continent
spaced with bland billboards
illustrating imbecile illusions of happiness
The scene shows fewer tumbrils
but more maimed citizens
in painted cars
and they have strange license plates
and engines
that devour America.[8]

One of the most visible examples of the car being seen as evil is the growing anti-car movement in much of Europe and the introduction of car-free days there, either because emissions levels in particular cities have become dangerous, because citizens demand them or because it is a government initiative.

On European Day, in late September each year, 760 cities from twenty-six countries now hold a car-free day. Each year, the campaign aims to be more far-reaching than the last and to push for the implementation of permanent measures to cut car use in the participating cities. Local authorities are encouraged to increase the size of their restricted area each year, to extend the duration of the

---

[8] From Lawrence Ferlinghetti, *A Coney Island of the Mind*, Norfolk, VA: New Directions, 1958.

campaign, and to announce at least one permanent measure for sustainable mobility each year. Together with legislative moves to cut emissions, reduce road deaths and promote other forms of transport, the pressure against the car is growing, albeit slowly.

There are many less obvious aspects of our lives that have been changed by the automobile. Pedestrians have almost disappeared in many towns, especially in the United States. Those that remain are more exposed to street crime – because of the rarity of other pedestrians. Children have lost much of their freedom to play outside, are shepherded to and from school, and spend much more of their youth indoors watching television or playing computer games. These changes have been found to result in less fit and less healthy children, obesity and poorer social skills.

Cars have contributed to the decline of village economies and latterly of city centres as consumers go to out-of-town shopping centres. The village store in most of Europe has become almost obsolete. Without the car, the white upper-middle-class suburb would never have been feasible. According to Stephen Sears' *The Automobile in America*,[9] suburban communities grew dramatically during the 1920s and 1930s, principally because of the increasing use of cars. A study commissioned by the Hoover administration in the 1930s, *Recent Social Trends in the United States*, showed that the city centres of New York, Chicago and Cleveland lost 24 per cent of their populations.

As the number of people with cars has grown, demand for public transport has fallen, particularly in rural areas. It is no longer economic to run bus and train services to remote villages in many parts of Europe. This leaves governments with a difficult choice. They can either subsidise local transport to ensure that those unable, for whatever reason, to run their own car are still able to travel, or allow free market economics to resolve the problem. In this case, it means that the poor and elderly often cannot afford to stay in rural areas. Without a car they can find themselves isolated from facilities such as post offices, shops, schools or medical treatment.

If the poor and elderly cannot afford to remain in rural areas these regions either face decline or become the exclusive preserve of the young and wealthy. This, in turn, changes the demographic structure of the region, creating a distorted social group. The impact of this varies enormously, but it is a little like interfering with the food chain – changing one part often has unpredictable and unexpected consequences on the remainder.

Some of these effects are very visible. Blockley, for example, a village of around 8,000 people in England's Cotswolds region, had twenty-two shops as recently as 1970. It had four public houses, two butchers, a wool shop and a store for photographic equipment. Twenty years later it had just two shops and two public houses, all of which were struggling. Although the nearest large town was 20 miles away, those who lived in the village preferred to travel there rather than shop closer to home.

The car has also made us lazier, lonelier and more unhealthy. The Hoover study in the US concluded that 'car ownership has created an automobile psychology; the automobile has become a dominant influence in the life of the individual, and he in a real sense has become dependent on it'. Gordon Whitnall of the Los Angeles Planning Commission wrote that 'it might almost be said that Southern Californians have had wheels added to their anatomy'. That was in 1927.

There are other costs to our reliance on the car, which are also difficult to resolve. Uncontrolled disposal of cars at the end of their lives is a substantial burden on society. Noise from road vehicles has become extremely intrusive over wide areas. Cars also raise massive and unfulfillable hopes in those who cannot afford them – which remains most of the world. As we have highlighted already, and

---

[9] New York: Scribner, 1977.

	GDP $ trillion	Value %	Value $ trillion	Cost $ trillion	Net value $ trillion	% of GDP
Developing world	24.9	20%	5.0	1.4	3.6	14%
Developing world	6.4	10%	0.6	1.4	-0.7	−11%
Total world	31.3	18%	5.6	2.8	2.9	9%

*Source: auto*POLIS

Fig. 2.20 The global socio-economic balance sheet

will look at in more detail later, the industry is also extremely wasteful in its product development policy. The number of model variations, the number of brands and the frequency with which models are replaced is far from economically efficient. This wastes vast quantities of energy and other resources as a result.

How, then, do we measure the social and environmental impact of motorisation, in order to draw up the balance sheet and to seek a healthier equilibrium between its benefits and its costs? The key, once again, is to distinguish between the already developed, motorised regions and countries and those that are still striving for that status. Our approach is very crude and simplistic – but surely directionally correct.

On p. 38 we saw that the worldwide cost of road accidents is estimated at about US$550 billion per year. We saw that 90 per cent of road deaths occur in the developing world, only 10 per cent in the developed countries. If we 'cost' the economic impact of these deaths in rough proportion to per capita GDP, based on the lost life expectancy of mainly younger productive people, then the burden falls about equally on the developed and developing worlds – some US$275 billion for each. We saw on p. 46 that road congestion costs at least $150 billion per year in both the US and Western Europe. We also have all the other social costs of motorisation, such as visual intrusion and noise.

Let us then apply a generous multiplier of 5× to the costs of accidents, in order to reflect all the other social and environmental costs of motorisation, and approximate its total cost, just as we used a factor of two to three to

estimate the global value of the industry to society. We are therefore looking at $1.4 trillion per year for both the developed and the developing worlds. The results are displayed in figure 2.20.

The simplistic inference is that the further spread of motorisation is having the most ghastly consequences for mankind, but this is only half true. Even with the benefits (including the value added by the automotive industry itself) valued at the lower rate of 20 per cent of GNP and the total costs valued at five times those of road deaths, the balance in the developed world is still handsomely positive. It brings a substantial share of economic activity. It also brings tax revenues and employment, in the manufacturing of vehicles as well as in servicing and repairing them. Millions of people are also employed in providing insurance, financial services and fuel to run them. Most critically, the sector has also brought us personal mobility and freedom in ways that were almost unimaginable a century ago, thereby creating value through a huge economic multiplier effect. As we have explained, this has come at a price. There have been high costs in terms of damaging emissions. There have also been millions of premature deaths and injuries. And there is the congestion, a growing problem affecting almost all of us in the world in some ways. There have also been other social costs. But, on balance, the automotive industry and mass motorisation have been and remain a huge net asset to developed economies.

But the balance is apparently grievously negative in the developing world. Must this remain so? We think not, although we also profoundly believe that each and every region and country will have to make its own deal with motorisation – and seek to control its development, rather than letting itself be overwhelmed by it.

Can we do better in the future? Can we cut the cost side of the equation or stop the costs rising so quickly? Could we even reduce our dependence on the car in some way and respond to the growing concerns about motorisation? What does all this imply for the automotive industry itself? Although there are profound reasons that make it difficult for us to radically change our dependence on the car, the pressures for us to think about the problems cars bring are growing.

War is too important to be left to the generals (Georges Clémenceau).

The duty of government is to govern (Duke of Wellington).

Governments will need to continue to act to address the problems of noxious emissions and road accidents, because they are the ones best placed to reduce some of the most serious costs of mobility. And they will have to act because the costs are continuing to rise – in the developing world and in the developed world, where enforcement is ineffectual.

Governments have long intervened in the motor industry. They mostly do this by imposing requirements and constraints on car manufacturers and drivers. Initially, this was by introducing speed limits and by forcing owners to register their vehicles and fit licence plates. Later it was through taxation, of the vehicles themselves and of the fuels they used. Governments have also established rules for how cars should be built and used, and imposed checks on the safety and environmental conformity of vehicles on the road.

Vehicle safety has become a major issue for governments in recent decades, although this is where the relationship with the industry has often been strained. The automotive industry, like any other business, obeys the laws of industrial economics. A vehicle manufacturer will typically only add a feature to his car if it makes financial sense – that is, if the revenue generated exceeds the cost of adding the feature.

In the 1960s, Ford tried to sell a car on the basis of its safety features, with little success. GM and Chrysler also investigated safety at the time, coming to the same conclusions. GM even offered airbags as a low-cost option, but found very little consumer interest. For many years, therefore, car producers did not place much emphasis on safety. Only Volvo managed to make a virtue out of the necessity. The same problems arose if the vehicles wasted fuel or were dangerous or polluting. Free market economics fails to address these sorts of issues unaided, forcing governments, even the most laissez-faire, to intervene.

A number of key events prompted a change of attitude by governments, however. In 1965, at the Rubicoff hearings, the US Attorney General forced the then president of GM, James Roche, to admit that the company spent almost nothing on vehicle safety. In his book *Unsafe at Any Speed*, Ralph Nader created an outcry when he highlighted the dangers of the Chevrolet Corvair. Nader also highlighted the problem of air pollution when he claimed that the car industry knew about the causes of the Southern California smog as far back as the 1920s.

Unfortunately there is something of a pattern here. The auto industry's leaders have often tried to resist beneficial legislative changes, even those which are clearly improvements in terms of health or safety. This, we believe, is a manifestation of a culture which still pervades much of the industry: a 'Detroit knows best' mentality which is ultimately corrosive. As we will see later, too often it does not. There is a behaviour pattern in the industry, which we will come back to many times in this book.

The industry has fought hard against many pieces of legislation. During the 1960s, in the

US, it was discovered that brakes often failed because the hydraulic fluid boiled, vaporised and was then unable to activate the system. Yet the car giants and the Department of Commerce argued that the government was acting without any mandate in bringing actions against them to address the problem. They argued that the government had no right to legislate on the matter. The car companies also fought legislation on seat-belt anchor points, padded dashboards and safety latches on doors on the grounds that they would 'create stagnation among automotive engineers and designers', which would damage the economy. Some even tried to block the fitting of airbags, on the grounds that 'safety did not sell cars'.

Ironically, and despite this resistance, it has been the US, with one of the freest market economies in the world, that has often led the way in terms of vehicle and safety legislation. The Clean Air Act of 1963 set exhaust emission standards; subsequent laws required the use of seat-belts, catalytic converters and safety glass. Ultimately, governments had to intervene much more extensively in the standards for the design of vehicles. More recent examples include the corporate average fuel economy (CAFE) standards as well as the fitting of airbags and anti-lock brakes. California's legislators, who have been at the forefront of these legislative changes for decades, remain global champions in forcing the development of ultra-low- and zero-emission vehicles (ULEVs and ZEVs), as part of their very ambitious environmental improvement campaign.

Still the carmakers have often resisted. The Big Three, Ford, GM and Chrysler, claimed for many years that catalysts, needed to cut exhaust emissions, would not work. They also resisted legislation that would increase the padding inside vehicles to protect against head injuries on the grounds that it would reduce visibility. The added cost of up to $80 a car was not cited as the principal reason. They also claimed that the development of

cost-effective ZEVs and ULEVs to meet Californian legislation in 1998 was impossible, and had the deadline pushed back. Other companies managed to develop such vehicles, however.

As we discussed earlier, the lead emitted from exhausts caused widespread problems – which were known to the medical profession for generations. When some epidemiologists expressed concerns about lead pollution from motor fuels, they were roundly attacked by the combined automotive and oil industries, and even accused of falsifying their research data. Ultimately, lead began to be driven out of motor fuel in the developed world, not because it might be poisoning people, but because it poisoned the catalysts used to oxidise unburnt hydrocarbons and nitrogen oxides in car exhausts. Throughout the process, the vehicle industry presented a sorry spectacle of resistance to change and, in the case of Europe, internal disagreement about the extent to which exhaust catalysts should be made mandatory.

The irony is that safety and environmental features are now an essential part of new vehicle marketing – but largely because of government intervention. It is not the resistance to outside pressure which we want to highlight here so much as the attitude. The thinking of many of those in the industry has been less than holistic about the wider implications of what they are doing. This is true in terms of the economics of the business too, as we discussed in chapter 1. Again, this is an issue we will come back to. But the attitude was exactly the same with the way the industry reacted to proposals for changes in the way cars were sold and distributed in Europe a few years ago. (We will look at this in chapter 6.) In that case, because most carmakers in the region had got themselves in a financial pickle, and because they were unwilling to accept the idea that an outsider should have the right to force them to change, they got completely tied up in their traditional rhetoric. Some also used their political clout to have their country's presidents and prime ministers pressurise the EU's Competition Commission to drop its proposals. Yet the Commission found that the carmakers were operating a near cartel: that they were fixing prices and that they were preventing consumers from shopping across borders. Although many were fined heavily – Volkswagen was given what was then the largest corporate fine in EU history – they continued to resist and still do. We think this approach is not only counterproductive but short-sighted.

This mindset, and the fact that too many senior auto industry executives have never known what it is like to work in any other industrial sector, has other drawbacks when it comes to introducing reform. If the resistance to outside interference has manifested itself in terms of health and safety legislation in the past, where else might it have appeared? As we will see, in too many places. This sort of thinking has become one of the industry's biggest weaknesses.

Without question, governments will continue to intervene in the industry – indeed, we think there is an overwhelming need for them to do more. Future issues for governments will include the wider adoption of road pricing, restrictions of vehicle use within cities and still tougher laws on safety and emissions. Many in the industry will doubtless continue to resist, certainly in the US and Europe. They will rightly fear the damage such legislation will do to their brand images. If cars become even more functional and more heavily taxed and more restrictions are placed on where they can go, the top managers will have a problem. What value all that Hype, that advertising spend? As we saw in chapter 1, the industry is already in a vulnerable position there. The gap between the reality of using a car and the way it is designed and marketed has grown. This sort of legislation would increase the gap further still.

Which raises the following question. Why does the industry continue to swim against the tide, a little like the tobacco manufactur-

ers once did? It would seem far more sensible to change direction, to take the initiative and to assist in the development of new legislation.

We are approaching a time when there is a need for a change of attitude within the industry, when more legislation will be needed to curb the growing costs of mobility. Yet the industry is too frequently defensive about itself. Information is often manipulated to generate a more favourable image of the industry and of the motor vehicles themselves. The vehicle manufacturers have a great deal of difficulty in working with governments early enough to help them explore the most productive legislative and regulatory options. This parallels the often bitter and dictatorial relations they have had with their component suppliers, distributors and dealers.

There is a clear need for governments to take an ever more active role in the automotive sector. This is a pressure which will test the business in several ways. As we will see in chapter 8, the industry faces a very difficult future if it does not reform and does not approach the business in a different way. How it could do that better is the subject of chapter 9. While most of the changes needed are economic, they are structural in nature, and they cannot be made without a change in attitude and in the way the industry sees itself. We believe that one of the indicators of how successfully the industry can reform will be how it responds to increasing government influence.

What comes out of this discussion for the automotive industry? One thing is certain: it will no longer be 'business as usual'. The benefits of mobility will be maintained in the developed countries and pursued in the developing ones, but under severe constraints. Unconstrained growth of motorisation is over. The design and use of cars will be much more tightly regulated. Selling greater power and speed, and pandering to individuals' fantasies of potency, are out. We have entered a different era in the history of the industry. The use of cars will not continue to grow to any major degree for years to come. It may even regress in some developed regions. We face the choice between having this regression forced on us in a chaotic fashion by uncontrolled congestion and other negative by-products of motorisation, or taking charge by managing the demand for and the delivery of transport in a co-ordinated way. This theme of the choice between the two courses echoes throughout the rest of our story.

3

The global resource challenges – energy and global warming

When the wells run dry – the coming fuel and environmental crunch

Mankind seems to have an insatiable appetite for transport and mobility, which increases inexorably with rising wealth. As we get richer, we travel more. We live further from our places of work to find better housing. We visit our friends more, who live further away. We go further afield on holidays. We travel more on business. The ever rising trend is shown in figure 3.1 for different world regions.

Whereas a hundred years ago the typical distance someone would travel in Europe was 13 miles a year, today it is 13 miles a *day*. Figure 3.2 summarises the differences between different regions of the world. The white bars show income per head in 1985 US dollars. The black bars are passenger-kilometres per person per year. Each pair of bars represents a major grouping of economic power.

There is even a strangely universal law about how much we travel and how much we spend on it. Everyone in the world seems to spend about the same amount of time per year moving around – and the same proportion of income, as shown in figure 3.3. The difference is the means of locomotion employed, the resulting average speed and therefore the annual distance travelled. African villagers walk, Chinese workers cycle, the Japanese mostly use public transport, Europeans and Americans mainly drive. Some of the super-rich even commute by personal aeroplane.

As we get richer, the mix shifts decisively towards individual motorisation: the car. This is illustrated in figure 3.4. For the same geographical groupings as before, the bars represent the consumption of passenger-kilometres a year. They are broken down by mode – high-speed (which is both air and high-speed rail), conventional rail, buses and cars. As we get richer, our preferred mode of passenger transport is more and more the individual motor car, with the advantages it brings in flexibility, comfort, privacy and security. It depends on topography and population density, of course, which is why Japan keeps such a high share of passenger rail transport. But the overall trend is clear. As we will see, there are implications to all this in terms of fuel use and emissions generation. This, in turn, will have implications on the types of engines and fuels we use in the future.

Today, of course, the primary fuel used is oil-derived. Yet in the early years of the automotive industry, at the beginning of the twentieth century, battery electric, and steam-powered vehicles were initially seen as credible alternatives to those powered by internal combustion engines (figure 3.5). Indeed, the first vehicle to achieve 100 kilometres an hour was a battery electric, and Stanley Steamers were quite popular in the United States for a while. But the range limitations of the battery electrics, the inconvenience of long start-up times with steamers and the falling price of oil eventually caused them to be abandoned. The automotive industry's choice of technology for its prime movers narrowed quite rapidly to the internal combustion engine, which has proved increasingly reliable, easy to use and repair, and cheap to mass-produce. The production and distribution of petroleum to fuel these engines was

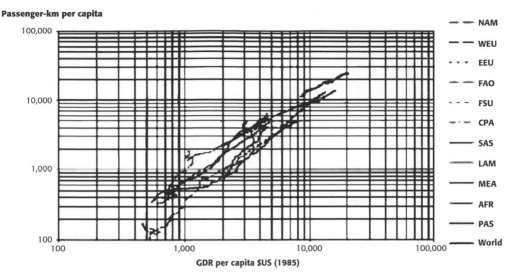

Passenger-km per capita

GDR per capita $US (1985)

WBCSD, *Mobility 2001*

Note: NAM – US and Canada; WEU – EU+CH+N+TR; EEU – Eastern Europe; FAO – Australia, Japan, New Zealand; FSU – former Soviet Union; CPA – China and other centrally planned Asia; SAS – Bangladesh, India, Pakistan; LAM – Latin America; MEA – Middle East and North Africa; AFR – Kenya, Nigeria, South Africa, Zimbabwe, other sub-Saharan Africa; PAS – Pacific Asia

Fig. 3.1 Consumption of passenger transport with rising wealth

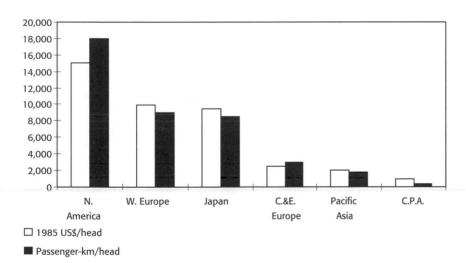

☐ 1985 US$/head

■ Passenger-km/head

Source: Adapted from Andreas Schafer and David Victor, 'The Past and Future of Global Mobility', *Scientific American,* October 1997, autoPOLIS

Fig. 3.2 The well-off travel most

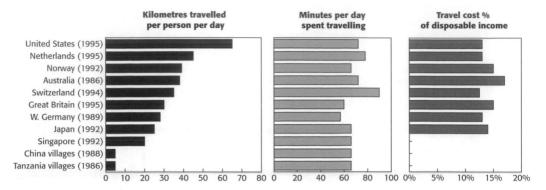

Source: Adapted from WBCSD, *Mobility 2001*

Fig. 3.3 Daily distance, time and cost of travel across the world

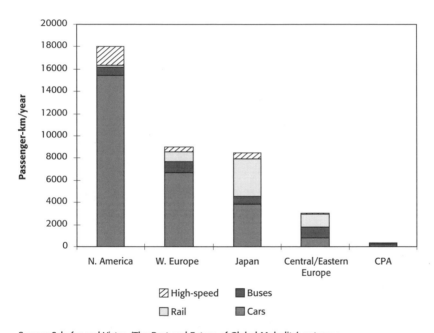

Source: Schafer and Victor, 'The Past and Future of Global Mobility', auto<small>POLIS</small>

Fig. 3.4 Modal mix of passenger travel

one of the major industrial developments of the twentieth century. Today we depend for our mobility on a huge oil industry with its exploration, refining and massive distribution infrastructure.

Will the petrol and diesel engine continue to prevail? Today the whole set of solutions and compromises which were involved in the adoption of the internal combustion engine are being challenged all over again, as the environmental pressures on the industry begin to bite, newer technologies emerge and concerns about oil availability grow. The portfolio of technologies and potential solutions is being broadened out again. We have the opportunity to look at alternative prime

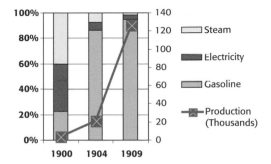

Source: US Census of Manufactures,1910

Fig. 3.5 Where's my Stanley steamer?

movers, different types of fuel and energy sources, other kinds of transmissions, and different structures and materials.

But how real are these concerns over resource depletion and emissions? Is oil about to run out? Will the growth in emissions, especially carbon dioxide emissions, drive a rapid change in the sorts of engines and propulsion systems we use in cars? The answers are remarkably clear.

Certainly, we can be sure that this relentless growth in the world vehicle parc and in vehicle-kilometres driven will lead to a parallel growth in fuel consumption and carbon dioxide emissions. As we explained in the previous section, many of the other emissions problems have been addressed, certainly for new cars in the developed markets. But the carbon dioxide emissions problem has not been solved and diesel particulates remain an issue. Fuel consumption and emissions tend to grow disproportionately fast in the emerging markets, as shown in figure 3.6. This is because people there cannot afford the latest technology and the sorts of vehicles to which the developed world has become accustomed. Nor is the quality of their fuel as high and nor are their vehicles as well maintained. You only need visit one of the developing world's megacities to appreciate the size of the pollution problem they face, largely created by the automobile and the internal combustion engine. Visit New Delhi, São Paulo or Lima-Callao and

see – or choke – for yourself. So to allow an unfettered growth in the parc would mean that the world's fuel reserves would shrink faster and its air quality would deteriorate more quickly – at least for a while.

Transport is a fast-growing emitter of carbon dioxide. Figure 3.7 shows figures for Western Europe. Overall emissions have not increased much but those for transport are sharply up. Although air transport is the fastest growing contributor, its total share remains unsubstantial. Ninety per cent of transport emissions come from road vehicles, predominantly cars. For every litre of gasoline consumed by a motor vehicle, about 2.4 kilos of carbon dioxide (with diesel fuel it is 2.7 kilos) go directly into the atmosphere. In US terms, for every 15 gallon fill-up at the service station, about 300 pounds of carbon dioxide are pumped into the atmosphere. Carbon dioxide is claimed to be a major cause of what scientists believe may be a gradual warming of the planet, the so-called greenhouse effect. Each year the average car puts more than four times its body weight of carbon dioxide into the air. The operation of motor vehicles was responsible for 26 per cent of carbon dioxide emissions in the US in 2002.

Transport is also the fastest-growing user of oil worldwide (see figure 3.8). And oil is a finite resource. As many of the developing markets mature, and as car sales there grow, the demands on the world's oil reserves will rise to a point where they cannot be met.

There has been a curiously persistent myth about the future availability of oil. The conventional wisdom is that, although consumption continues to grow, new discoveries are adding reserves at a more than sufficient rate. This theory is aided and abetted by classical economic theories, which teach us that, as shortages of a commodity develop and prices rise, new suppliers enter the market with increased capacity, until supply and demand come into balance and prices stabilise and fall again. The simplest exposition of this view is the 'pig cycle', which charmingly explains

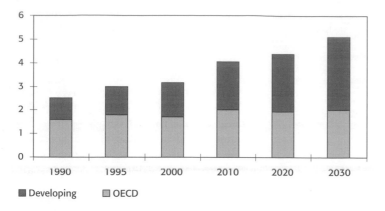

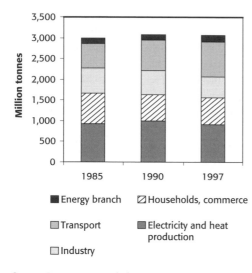

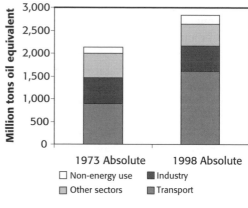

Source: Karl-Heinz Norikat, presentation to Commercialising Fuel Cell Vehicles 97 Conference, Frankfurt-am-Main, 22 October 1997

Fig. 3.6 Time for Kyoto: traffic-related CO_2 emissions by region

Source: European Commission

Fig. 3.7 European carbon dioxide emissions by sector

Source: International Energy Agency statistics

Fig. 3.8 Transport's thirst for oil

that, as pig prices rise because of unsatisfied demand, farmers invest in pig production, only to get out of pigs again when supply exceeds demand. The supposition underlying all these approaches is that supply can adjust to demand – upwards or downwards – in infinitesimal increments and completely reversibly. The real world, of course, does not always function like that.

Giving the keynote speech at the Environment '98 Forum in Ypsilanti, Michigan, Tom Gross of the US Department of Energy asked his audience whether they had read an article which he viewed as essential reading for everyone. This was 'The End of Cheap Oil', by Colin J. Campbell and Jean H. Laherrère, published in *Scientific American* in March 1998. The authors applied well-tried methodologies for evaluating the remaining capacity of individual oil wells, fields and countries, which had been used in the past to give a remarkably accurate prediction of when US domestic oil

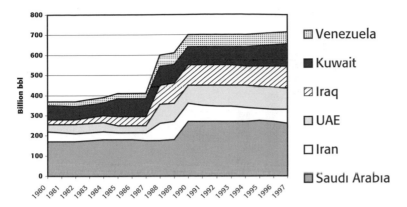

Source: Colin J. Campbell and Jean H. Laherrère, 'The End of Cheap Oil', *Scientific American*, October 1998, p. 65

Fig. 3.9 A false security? OPEC reserves, 1980 to 1997

production would peak. The conclusion of this analysis, applied to world oil reserves and production prospects, was startling. Half of the readily accessible oil has already been used. Production will peak some time in the first twenty years of the twenty-first century.

The authors also identified a factor which has grossly distorted forward projections of the availability of oil. This is the massive upward revaluation of reserves carried out by OPEC members in the late 1980s, without any physical justification, the results of which are shown in figure 3.9. The reason this happened was that OPEC's production quotas were allocated on the basis of reserves, with the result that each country sought to exaggerate the level of its reserves. Interestingly, this revaluation of OPEC reserves is missed by Bjørn Lomborg in his compelling book, mentioned previously, *The Skeptical Environmentalist*. He produces the conventional argument that oil reserves continue to grow faster than production to support the view that there is no immediate problem with supplies of conventionally produced oil. It is ironic that so conscientious a campaigner for the correct interpretation of statistics may have been deceived by some bad data.

The results of a similar forecasting exercise are summed up in figure 3.10. From 2010

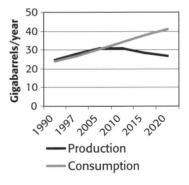

Source: R. C. Duncan, *Heuristic Oil Forecasting Method*, International Energy Outlook 2000 (eia/US DoE)

Fig. 3.10 Trouble in store: world oil production and consumption

to 2020 the inexorably rising trend of consumption diverges alarmingly from the falling curve of production. We periodically lose sight of this prospect, as temporary oil gluts and recessions depress the oil price and have OPEC scurrying to get its members to reduce production. There are strong indications that economic booms are partly fuelled by low oil prices and that recessions are brought on partly by high oil prices. So figure 3.10 indicates decidedly uncomfortable long-term economic prospects throughout the world. Oil is a finite resource and exhausting it will cost

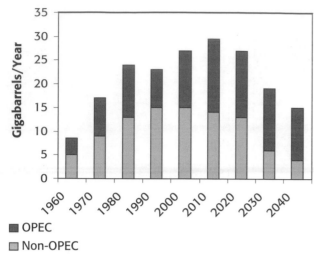

■ OPEC

▨ Non-OPEC

Source: As figure 3.10

Fig. 3.11 Increasing political pressures: world oil production, 1960–2040

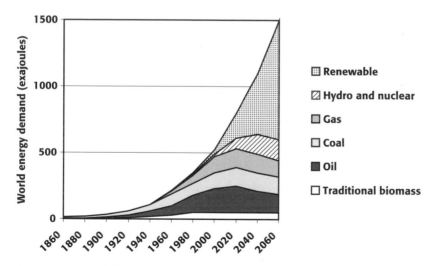

Source: Leo Petrus, Shell, 'Biomass-based Blending Components for Transport Fuels', Global Alternative Fuels Forum, Munich, 19–20 February 2003

Fig. 3.12 Diversifying resources

us dear – not only in economic terms but also politically.

Figure 3.11 forecasts where the declining future supply will come from – increasingly from OPEC countries. The geo-political implications are even more disturbing. Dependency on OPEC sources will increase, as the non-OPEC resources run down first. The more we try to switch away from OPEC in the short term, the worse our long-term dependency will become.

Both Lomborg and Campbell and Laherrère mention the existence of vast reserves of non-conventional oil as a 'back-up' – 1,200 billion

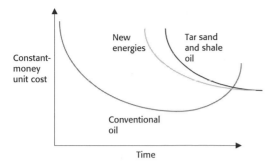

*Source: auto*POLIS

Fig. 3.13 No easy solutions

barrels in the Orinoco heavy oil belt of Venezuela and 300 billion barrels in tar sands and shale deposits in Canada and the former Soviet Union, for example, compared to roughly 1,000 billion barrels of actual and undiscovered reserves of conventional oil. Both also mention the cost of extraction. Orinoco oil is heavily contaminated with heavy metals and sulphur; extracting shale and tar sand oil will have a significant direct cost, also with a heavy environmental impact. Lomborg predicts a rapid decline in the cost of renewable energies – wind, solar thermal and solar electric in particular.

Shell as a major oil company has been the great pioneer and proponent of scenario planning. One of their long-range energy scenarios is shown in figure 3.12, which assumes steady growth of energy consumption at 2 per cent a year. One can, of course, always dispute the details. Will coal and gas use fall off in the middle and later years of the twenty-first century? Will nuclear and hydroelectric power increase so much? It is unlikely that hydroelectric power will, as most large sites have already been exploited, although many smaller ones could be. Nuclear power produces no carbon dioxide emissions but is politically contentious because of the problems of disposing of highly radioactive and long-lived waste. The overall message, though, is clear: either we curb the growth of energy demand, or we need to introduce many more renewable resources.

The problem is that we are looking at complex interactions and possible substitutions, as indicated in figure 3.13. The only real solution, self-evidently, is to reduce the specific consumption and emissions of traditional road vehicles if we want to preserve mobility and allow for growth at acceptable economic, environmental and political costs. The conclusion is clear. We need to limit the use of oil or change fuels or both. The options as to how we might do this are explored in more detail in the next chapters.

Looking for solutions – fixes for the existing technology

Which priority targets should we pursue in order to cut future oil consumption and emissions then? The answer, alas, is that there is neither a single priority target nor a single weapon to throw at the problems. Even so, there are some priorities. As the main users and some of the main polluters, both light and heavy vehicles are good targets, principally in the developed countries. Figure 3.14 represents a segmentation of world road vehicle fuel consumption by region and type of vehicle.

First, by region. From left to right we first have the large, advanced, temperate countries, which really means the US, Canada and Australia, which are the most heavily motorised with the most intensive drivers, precisely because of their size and their dispersed patterns of living. You can see how they dominate the consumption pattern. Next, to the right, are the medium-sized advanced temperate countries, which means Europe. Then came the high-density developed countries notably Japan and Korea; then the high-density developing ones – Latin America and the poor countries of the world. In both practical and moral terms, the responsibility to act and the greatest opportunity to fix the problems lie squarely with the developed countries. The first priority is to address consumption levels in the US, difficult though

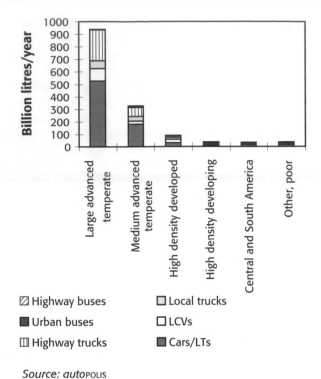

Highway buses   Local trucks

Urban buses   LCVs

Highway trucks   Cars/LTs

*Source: auto*POLIS

Fig. 3.14 The heaviest drinkers: road vehicle fuel consumption

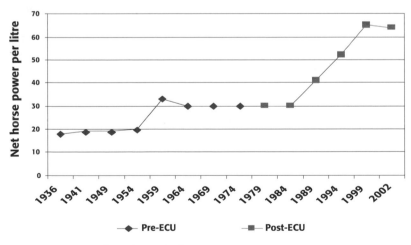

Note: ECU = electronic control unit

Source: Engine development specialist

Fig. 3.15 Getting more out of the old nag: specific output of gasoline internal combustion engines

that may be politically. It may be a hard message to bear, but American-style gas guzzling is an affront to the whole world.

Secondly, cars and light trucks are the biggest consumers – that is the dark grey portion of each vertical bar. But local and, above all, highway trucks – the vertically striped portions – also contribute a substantial share. Individually we cannot live without our cars. But our economies could not live without our trucks. We need solutions in both sectors. That fact, plus the geographical dispersion of the need, plus the diversity of primary energy resource structures between regions and countries, is why there is no single magic solution.

We can target the use of vehicles. We can look at ways of limiting their use, cutting their fuel consumption and reducing their emissions, especially in the developed world. We can improve the existing engine and fuelling technologies further. With a hundred years of progressive development, the technology of the internal combustion engine is not yet played out. The extent of that development in past years is shown for the specific power output of US internal combustion engines in figure 3.15. Average horsepower per litre more than doubled from 1980 to 2002, after a long plateau during the 1960s and 1980s, emissions dropped sharply, and the cost of engines as a proportion of the total vehicle also fell by half. The breakthroughs were in fuel injection, engine management systems and three-way catalysts – all, it must be said, triggered by the requirements of the Clean Air Act and its amendments and of the CAFE standards. Projections are for a continued improvement of 1.5 per cent per year – remarkable for a basic technology as mature as that of the internal combustion engine.

There have been further major advances in recent years, notably with high-pressure direct-injection diesel engines and variable valve timing in petrol engines, both of which greatly improve control over combustion and so fuel economy and emissions. But there are also limits to the possible gains. For example, it is becoming increasingly difficult to reduce consumption – and thus carbon dioxide emissions – in diesel engines, while also limiting emissions of nitrogen oxides and microscopic soot particles to levels desirable for public health. As we shall see later, this is leading to major controversy about which new technologies to adopt, with a split opening up between Europe and Japan.

Had they lived earlier, William Heath Robinson in the UK or Rube Goldberg in the US might have invented such an improbable engine as the internal combustion engine today. 'You mean to say that the fuel *explodes* in the cylinders and that those pistons and rods thrash up and down thousands of times per minute, Mr Benz?' Yet the two fundamental forms of reciprocating piston internal combustion engine, the Otto and the diesel, are still with us over a hundred years later. The cumulative output of them exceeds 1 billion units.

Most of the features of today's internal combustion engines have changed little since they were adopted between 1900 and the start of the First World War in 1914: multiple cylinders, V-banks, electric spark ignition, electric starting, carburettors – these last starting to be replaced by gasoline injection in high-powered aircraft engines in the 1930s. A four valve per cylinder design helped Mercedes win the French Grand Prix – in 1914. You can see the car in their fine museum in Stuttgart. Figure 3.16 shows a photograph and an engineering drawing of the Peugeot 'L3' 16V 3 litre In-Line 4 of 1913. Four valves per cylinder are used in almost all modern engine designs today, with the same objective as then – to ease the intake and exhaust of gases into and out of the cylinder.[1]

Similarly, diesel engines have remained much as they were first designed. Diesel engines are almost universally applied in

[1] For those with a more detailed interest, an excellent and richly illustrated account of the history of the internal combustion engine has recently been produced: Jeff Daniels *Driving Force, the Evolution of the Car Engine*, London: Haynes Publishing, 2002.

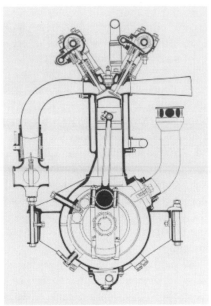

Source: David Taitt, Engineering Director,
Lotus Cars, 'Creating the Future Engine', Federation of Automotive Parts Manufacturers Convention, Queensland, July 2002

Fig. 3.16 There is nothing new under the sun

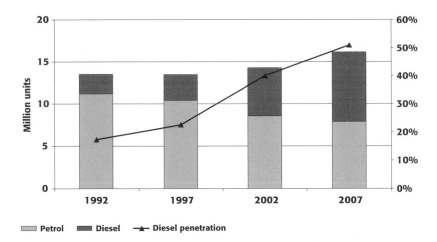

Petrol   **Diesel**   —▲— **Diesel penetration**

Source: JD Power-LMC, from *Vehicle News,* 266 (April 2003), p. 76

Fig. 3.17 The inexorable rise of the diesel engine in
Europe

heavy trucks, as they are in marine propulsion (apart from outboard motors), because of their exceptional energy conversion efficiency and durability. They have long been popular in light commercial vehicles in Europe, despite their initial lack of refinement, for the same reasons. They have also penetrated the European passenger car market in a major way, with every expectation that the trend will continue, as figure 3.17 shows. Indeed, diesel is the European industry's chosen technology today although it has never achieved such a degree of acceptance elsewhere. Diesel engines have even made major headway in upline European cars. VW-Audi and Daimler-Chrysler sold more diesel than gasoline cars in Europe in 2002.

Diesel has never been as popular in the US. Following the second oil shock in the late 1970s, diesel car penetration reached just 6 per cent in the US, compared to 10 per cent in Europe at the time. It then collapsed, partly because of the very unattractive nature of the diesel-powered vehicles put out by Detroit then, partly because having to buy fuel in unattractive truck areas at filling stations was a disincentive to consumers. Resistance in the United States and Japan has also been largely motivated by fears about the potentially carcinogenic properties of microscopic soot particles in diesel exhaust gases and by their high noise levels and comparatively poor acceleration – although recent innovations have largely addressed both these issues.

Controlling diesel engine emissions is a delicate balancing act between the level of nitrogen oxide and the particulates produced. PSA (Peugeot-Citroën), one of the major pioneers of light vehicle diesel engines, has opted for particulate filters. At present these have to be cleaned part-way through the life of the vehicle, but future versions will not need this. They are, however, relatively bulky and slightly reduce engine performance. The hope of German manufacturers was to do without them, if possible, through further improvements in combustion, which requires both higher pressures and precision in the fuel-injection system and essentially sulphur-free diesel fuel. There are now signs that they, too, are turning to particulate filters, in the face of the very stiff requirements of the forthcoming Euro 5 emissions standards. Europe has set itself a target of an average of 140 grams of carbon dioxide per vehicle-kilometre. Figure 3.18 shows the rate of progress towards achieving this. As can be seen from the figure, diesel plays a major role.

Indeed, now that modern diesel cars are every bit as attractive to drive as gasoline-powered cars, governments are starting to

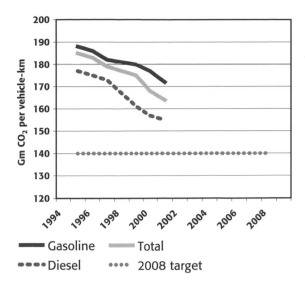

Source: Richard Dobson, Exxon Mobil, 'The Future of Vehicles and Fuel', Global Alternative Fuels Forum, Munich, 19–20 February 2003

Fig. 3.18 A challenging objective: progress towards the carbon dioxide target

implement consumption-related incentives which will increasingly favour them. There are even signs of a revival of interest in the US, as diesel engines have become far more powerful, refined and quiet. They offer a particularly attractive solution for reducing fuel consumption and carbon dioxide emissions in larger light vehicles – notably US-style light trucks and SUVs – in which their strong low-speed torque is a significant advantage. There are even signs that the California Air Resources Board (CARB) may relent on its historical aversion to diesel emissions, as its attention shifts towards carbon dioxide targets. J. D. Power-LMC forecasts an increase in diesel penetration in the US from 4.5 per cent in 2002 to 16 per cent in 2014. Siemens-VDO (a European supplier of diesel injection systems) is even more bullish, expecting US light vehicle diesel sales to increase from 750,000 units in 2003 to 2.6 million in 2007, driven by the use of these engines in light trucks and SUVs. Delphi suggests a penetration range of 6 per cent to 15 per cent by 2010, depending on technological progress and regulatory decisions.

However, US 2007 emissions standards would seem to require the use of an expensive nitrogen oxide catalyst. The US and Japan are much tougher on nitrogen oxide than Europe or China. They are also more concerned than Europe with noise levels. Passions rage: Jean-Martin Folz, the chairman and CEO of PSA, believes that carbon dioxide is an infinitely more important issue than nitrogen oxide and has called for greater transparency in emissions standards. The oil industry has expressed concerns about unbalancing the refinery mix and pointed out that refining diesel fuel produces far more carbon dioxide than refining gasoline. One should also remember that diesel fuel is denser, so that each litre has a higher energy content than a litre of gasoline, which biases the litre-per-hundred-kilometres or miles-per-gallon figures in its favour.

As energy prices rise in future decades, it will also become increasingly attractive to synthesise completely clean fuels, both gasoline and diesel, from natural gas. The technology has long existed, based on the Fischer-Tropsch process, originally developed in Germany in the 1920s and 1930s to make oil from coal, and further perfected by Sasol in South Africa – in response to both political isolation and the pursuit of autarchy. Any synthetic process has a considerable disadvantage in capital investment requirements over oil extraction and refining, however, until oil prices rise substantially. This recourse will nonetheless further extend the life of the internal combustion engine.

The other obvious way to save on fuel consumption and reduce emissions is to reduce the mass of the vehicle. Today, most cars are made from pressed and welded sheet steel. Steel bodies are complex to design and build. It is a specialised activity, resting on massive investments in design and simulation systems, manufacturing hardware and people's know-how. But they are unbeatably cheap in volume production and offer attractive energy-absorbing properties in case of an accident. Corrosion problems have been almost totally solved, through modern protection systems. The steel industry has also counter-attacked against the threat of aluminium as a weight

saver through the co-operative ULSAB (ultra-light steel auto body) programme.

There has been a notable increase in the use of aluminium cylinder blocks for engines, and the proportion of aluminium in the total weight of cars has increased significantly in recent years. Relatively less progress has been made in the use of aluminium chassis and body structures. The BMW 5-Series uses an aluminium rear subframe, but this is still a rarity. Only a few vehicles have entered series production with full aluminium bodies, including the Audi A8 and the Audi A2, now abandoned. Nonetheless, we can expect more gradual progress with aluminium bodies but no breakthrough is likely at current fuel prices, as the fuel savings achieved through weight reduction do not justify the additional cost of the bodywork, at present fuel prices at least. Even the proponents of aluminium are not projecting a major breakthrough in its use – see figure 3.19. The fast growth in body applications mainly represents individual opening units – hoods and some tailgates.

Despite these improvements with the engine technology, with the potential to synthesise fuels and alternatives to change the designs and materials used in the manufacture of vehicles, we are almost certainly entering a period in which there will be more alternative solutions to the fuelling, propulsion and emissions challenges, even within the general family of internal combustion engines. As we will see, we are entering a period of some technological uncertainty, as the vice of consumption and emissions standards continues to tighten. We will explore the more radical options in the next section.

Really new technologies – the radical alternatives

The key to a step change in environmental performance and a way to reduce our dependence on oil is to move away from conventional mechanical engines. In 1992 the State of California initiated a major attempt to

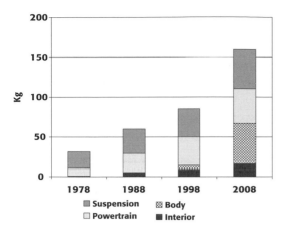

Source: European Aluminium Association, reproduced in *Vehicle News,* 271 (October 2003)

Fig. 3.19 Past and projected use of aluminium in different parts of the vehicle

revive battery electric vehicles by requiring 10 per cent of all new vehicles sold in the state to have zero emissions. The two show-stopping features of battery electrics, however, are limited range and recharging time. One might have hoped that Californian families, many of whom own more than one vehicle, would accept the concept of a specialised commuter or urban vehicle. In reality, product planning studies everywhere generally show that consumers want all their vehicles to be fully capable, meaning more than the 100 mile or so range for a battery electric. Of course that might not be such a handicap if the batteries could be recharged quickly. The standard to which consumers are accustomed, that of refilling a fuel tank in 5 to 10 minutes, including paying, is simply not achievable for battery recharges. None of this is an obstacle for fleets operating from a central point and which can recharge overnight, or in a planned shift pattern. Shuttles to move disabled and elderly passengers around airports, golf carts, indoor forklift trucks and specialised delivery vehicles are all valid and long-standing examples of applications where battery power is suitable.

Also, electric vehicles do not necessarily reduce overall emissions. It is possible that they simply displace the sources away from city centres. A substantial proportion of California's electricity is generated by out-of-state coal-fired power stations. To be comparative, one must consider the oil-well-to-wheels or coalfield-to-wheels energy conversion efficiency ratio in evaluating the overall impact of alternatives to the internal combustion engine. Using this method, an experiment with an all-electric vehicle fleet on the island of Rügen off Germany's Baltic coast showed that the overall energy and carbon dioxide balance was actually somewhat worse than for a fleet of conventionally powered vehicles of equivalent performance.

In short, battery electrics are not the way forward, using current battery technologies, essentially lead-acid. A large amount of research has gone into alternative systems but with no sign of a breakthrough. Their much greater cost is not sufficiently compensated for by gains in power density, battery life or speed of recharging. A miracle is unlikely. The fundamental barrier is that mass and energy transfers are relatively slow in what have to be systems capable of repeated charging and discharging.

There are two main alternatives – hybrids and fuel cell vehicles, with internal-combustion-engine-based hybrids the essential first step. American vehicle manufacturers have shown considerable interest in hybrids through the Program for a New Generation of Vehicles and in trying to develop an 80 mpg family sedan.

A hybrid powertrain consists of an engine, a bi-directional energy storage device and a means of storing and recovering energy to and from that storage device. A hybrid electric vehicle (HEV) system seeks to operate a conventional engine at maximum efficiency or turn it off. It then provides propulsion through an alternative source. This is more efficient in terms of fuel use and less polluting in terms of emissions. Even so, hybridisation generally provides the greatest gains in stop–go city driving and far less (it can even be less efficient because of the extra weight) at highway speeds.

In HEVs the electric storage device is normally a battery, but it can also be an ultra-capacitor. Flywheels can also be used as storage devices – the city of Yverdon in Switzerland had a brief flirtation fifty years ago with flywheel-powered buses, called gyrobuses, the flywheel being revved up electrically at each bus stop. Even compressed air has been proposed; it was originally used as a power source for locomotives in building railway tunnels through the Alps, which filled up from the supply for the rock drills.

Illustrating the options, Dr Tamor of the Ford Motor Company amusingly presented what he called the HEV Smorgasbord Menu at the Hybrid Vehicles 2000 Conference in Windsor, Ontario:

- Choose a configuration between
  - series (trans-axle or wheel motors, motor types, etc.)
  - parallel (motor before or after transmission, type, etc.)
- Chemical energy converters:
  - piston engine
  - turbo-generator
  - Stirling engine
  - fuel cell

- Energy storage:
  - electrochemical battery (lead-acid, lithium ion, etc.)
  - ultra-capacitor
  - mechanical 'battery' (flywheel, compressed air, etc.)

But he sounded a wise note of caution in his 'HEV Smorgasbord Disclaimers':

the management is not responsible for the unexpectedly high price, unexpectedly poor performance or interminable delays in delivery of any item. The management is not responsible for inappropriate technology combinations or poor operating strategies that result in poor performance, unacceptable vehicle behaviour, or much lower than anticipated fuel efficiency.

So a 'hybrid' covers a multitude of possible propulsion architectures and there are trade-offs in terms of costs and performance. Figure 3.20 explores the span of possibilities, which run from a pure battery electric with a small internal combustion engine (ICE)-powered generator on board to extend its range, to a pure ICE driveline with a bit of additional power and regenerative braking capacity via a special starter-alternator.

The former appears as EV ER (electric vehicle, extended range) on the right-hand side of the figure. Work at the University of California has shown that such vehicles can achieve very low levels of fuel consumption, although their performance characteristics are unlikely to endear them to the average driver. They can also achieve very low emissions.

The latter come under electric boost on the left-hand side. Characteristic examples are the Honda Insight and the Ricardo-Valeo concept vehicle, with Ricardo providing the direct-injection diesel engine and Valeo, one of the leading European producers of starters and alternators, the combined starter–alternator machine. In passing, it is perhaps noteworthy that it has taken an independent engineering consultancy and a component supplier to produce this in Europe, rather than a vehicle manufacturer. But then it was Valeo that virtually created the mass market for vehicle air

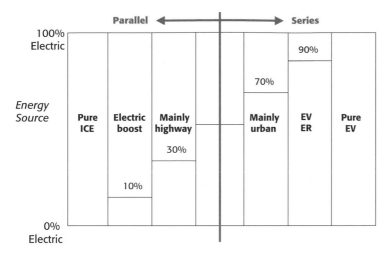

Source: *auto*POLIS

Fig. 3.20 Range of hybrid types

conditioning systems in Europe too, overcoming the scepticism and inertia of the vehicle manufacturers.

The Toyota Prius sits to the left, in the mainly highway category, with around 30 per cent electric power capacity. The Prius has probably been the most successful hybrid so far, and was the first such vehicle to be put into series production. Its sales history is shown in figure 3.21. The overall numbers remain relatively modest but are nevertheless impressive for a vehicle with such a novel driveline. They are comparable to those for the all-aluminium-body Audi A2, another daring innovation. Note the particular interest in North America, with its continuing nitrogen oxide emissions problems – which the Prius is particularly designed to tackle – and the weak interest in Europe, where there is more concern about carbon dioxide.

Hideshi Itazaki's book, *The Prius that Shook the World*, describing how Toyota developed the world's first mass-production hybrid vehicle, is worth reading. It is a testimony to Toyota's engineering and project management skills. It underlines the challenge that Toyota set itself by deciding to develop a small car requiring very tight packaging, rather than a more 'open' large vehicle. This was not some lash-up job done with off-the-shelf components. Because of the very challenging performance objectives, almost everything had to be specially developed.

The battery required a considerable development effort, working with Matsushita. The Japanese electrical engineering industry has vast experience of electric traction motors, from light rail systems to the Shinkansen Bullet Trains. Yet these were too big, too heavy, too costly and not reliable enough for automotive applications and mass production.

The Prius project was clearly not without its pains and anxieties, as the book honestly relates. What seems clear, however, was that it was successful in large degree because of Toyota's ability to manage relationships – between functional departments, across engineering disciplines, within itself and with outside partners. In our view, the lessons learned put Toyota years ahead of its rivals in its ability to develop such a complex and refined system.

Driving the Prius was, and is, a revelation. It glides away from the curb under silent electric power and makes an almost imperceptible transition to conventional engine power, with the engine starting up automatically at a set threshold speed. It is a seamless piece of

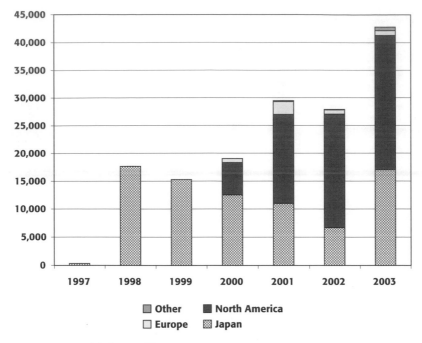

Source: Le Journal de l'Automobile, 16 May 2003

Fig. 3.21 Sales of the Toyota Prius

engineering. The only disconcerting feature is a powerflow display on the instrument panel that is so fascinating to watch that it risks distracting the driver's attention from the road ahead. The Prius has now been in series production for some years, with a second version recently launched. Toyota is now extending hybrid drivelines to the Lexus 300 and other models.

So what of that Great White Hope of at least some in the industry and outside it – the fuel cell? Perhaps surprisingly, it is no revolutionary idea: Groves discovered the fuel cell principle in 1839. It has taken a long time – and it is likely to take a longer time yet – to come to fruition as a major source of tractive power for road vehicles, however.

A fuel cell is an electrochemical cell which can continuously convert the chemical energy of a fuel such as hydrogen into electrical energy, using oxygen from the air. Unlike well-known electrochemical batteries, the chemical energy is stored outside the fuel cell where the electrochemical reaction takes place. As long as the fuel cell is supplied with fuel and oxidant, electrical power can be generated. The power of the system and capacity depend on two self-contained units: the fuel cell stack and the capacity of the fuel storage. The principles of operation of internal combustion engines and fuel cells are contrasted in figure 3.22. All ICEs are heat engines, limited in their thermal efficiency by the Carnot cycle; fuel cells are not subject to this limitation. There are five basic types of fuel cell, distinguished by their different electrolytes:

- In the alkaline fuel cell (AFC), the electrolyte is potassium hydroxide (KOH) in a water solution. The AFC is being used for the Space Shuttle Orbiter, and was used in the earlier manned *Apollo* space flights. It is expensive, and requires pure oxygen.
- Proton exchange membrane fuel cells (PEMFCs) – also known as solid polymer membrane fuel cells (SPMFCs) – are expected to be the best technology for vehicle applications,

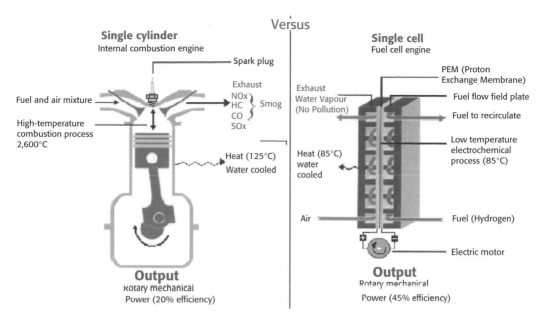

Source: Ballard Power Systems, Inc., reproduced in A.M. Branco, and G.M. Branco, 'Hydrogen Fuel Cell Buses as an Alternative for the São Paulo Metropolitan Area', March 1999

Fig. 3.22 Working principles of ICE and fuel cells

because of their high power density, smaller size and faster start-up. They use hydrogen as fuel obtained from methanol, ethanol, natural gas or another source. Key development problems remain, principally in membrane and catalyst technology, in which Du Pont, Ballard, Johnson-Matthey, Degussa and other companies are investing.

- Direct methanol fuel cells (DMFCs) use methanol directly as a fuel. Only limited progress has been made in developing these.

- Phosphoric acid fuel cells (PAFCs) are now in use for electric power generation, in the range of 57 to 375 kW, and are also being developed for transportation applications. H Power Corporation uses the fuel cells together with batteries (as hybrid systems). PAFC-powered buses, using methanol with on-board reformers, were built in 1993, but polymer electrolyte membranes (PEMs) have shown better results since then.

- Substantial efforts have been made to commercialise molten carbonate fuel cells (MCFCs). Stacks have been tested and small demonstration plants are expected within a couple of years.

- Solid oxide fuel cells (SOFCs) are the fifth option. These operate at high temperatures, have high fuel efficiency, high-power density and low cost. SOFCs can be of tubular or planar construction. For tubular SOFCs, Westinghouse has completed hours of operation, and is in the process of scaling up the size of the units. Ceramatics is a leader in planar SOFCs, which are expected to have low cost, high performance and high reliability.

Proton exchange membrane fuel cells (PEMFCs) are the most promising candidates for automotive propulsion today, although advances in solid oxide fuel cells may also make this technology suitable for automotive applications.

When the fuel is hydrogen, a fuel-cell/electric (FCE) propulsion system does not generate any pollutants. The only emissions are unused oxygen, nitrogen and water, which

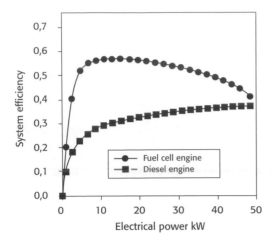

Source: W. Schnurnberger, 'Hydrogen Supply, Storage and Refuelling Techniques', February 1999

Fig. 3.23 Part-load characteristics of hydrogen–air fuel cell module and diesel engines

may be present in either liquid or vapour form. As an energy conversion device, the FCE system is superior to the best diesel engine across the whole of the power range, and especially under part load, as shown in figure 3.23.

There is, however, a big catch in all this: getting the fuel to the system. A conventional engine simply needs a tank of gasoline or diesel fuel. A fuel cell engine needs a supply of very pure gaseous hydrogen. Impurities inactivate the cell. And pure gaseous hydrogen is not available at every street corner. Fuelling infrastructure, cost, reliability and durability are the critical hurdles that fuel cell drives have to overcome before they can achieve mass deployment.

For us, there is another major issue too. It is very significant that the great majority of the subsystems and components being developed for fuel cells are based on technologies that are almost wholly alien to the conventional vehicle industry. This will create substantial challenges and the need for carmakers to build up new supplier bases. We also think it will create some sources of conflict. Either the new suppliers will have to adapt to the styles of relationship and to the working practices of the industry, or the auto industry

will have to change the ways it works with suppliers. Certainly, the idea that so much of the heart of the vehicle should be technologically under the control of outsiders will not sit easily with most vehicle manufacturers. The fact that the company that has done the most to develop proton exchange fuel cells based on road vehicle propulsion systems, Ballard, is owned by DaimlerChrysler and Ford is an additional challenge to their competitors.

Set against these developments, or potential developments, conventional vehicles continue to develop too, as we have seen. Whether the conventional engine remains the prime mover of choice, or whether hybrids will make a breakthrough into real mass production or whether fuel cells become an important source of propulsion is the subject of the next section.

The cavalry to the rescue – how and how soon will new engine technologies arrive?

A new source of power . . . called gasoline has been produced by a Boston engineer. Instead of burning the fuel under a boiler, it is exploded inside the cylinder of an engine . . .

The dangers are obvious. Stores of gasoline in the hands of people interested primarily in profit would constitute a fire and explosive hazard of the first rank. Horseless carriages propelled by gasoline might attain speeds of 15, or even 20 miles per hour. The menace to our people of this type hurtling through our streets and along our roads and poisoning the atmosphere would call for prompt legislative action even if the military and economic implications were not so overwhelming . . . the cost of producing [gasoline] is far beyond the financial capacity of private industry . . . In addition the development of this new power may displace the use of horses, which would wreck our agriculture (*US Congressional Record*, 1875).

Is it fear of the dangers of hydrogen as a fuel that inhibits the rapid deployment of fuel-cell-powered vehicles? Many remember the disaster that befell the German airship *Hindenburg* at Lakeside, NJ, in the 1930s. Its gas bags were filled with hydrogen, the US government having refused to supply helium to National Socialist Germany.

Hydrogen certainly has some problems, notably that of burning with an invisible flame. It can explode when mixed with air in the right proportions. But then so will any gaseous or liquid fuel. On the other hand, its lightness means that it disperses upwards if there is a leak, provided this does not take place in a confined space. That may be a problem in winter climates, as fuel cells will freeze. Chicago Transit had to install elaborate hydrogen detection and venting mechanisms in the bus garage which housed its experimental fleet of three fuel-cell buses. There is also a sense of unease because hydrogen is stored in vehicle tanks under very high pressure, in order to pack in a sufficient amount to get adequate range, and has to be loaded into the tanks at that pressure. But this is really no more alien, particularly to a growing number of transit operators or taxi drivers, than the use of compressed natural gas (CNG).

In practice it is not fears of the dangers, it is the economics that are the real barrier, plus the problems of refuelling. The environmental benefits are also not necessarily what they seem to be. There are space penalties within the vehicle to be overcome too. Let us cover these in reverse order.

Liquid hydrocarbon fuels – like gasoline – have some immense advantages. They are, by definition, liquid at room temperature and pressure, so they can simply be poured and pumped into and out of thin-walled tanks. Vehicle tanks used to be made of coated steel but are now increasingly in blow-moulded plastic, which is lighter and can be shaped to fit the available space within the body structure. These fuels also have a high energy density, and can readily be shipped by road or rail tanker, by barge and by ship. They are ideal transportation fuels. They normally come from petroleum but can also, at a pinch, be synthesised, starting with other carbon-containing feedstocks, from methane (natural gas) to coal.

Hydrogen, in contrast, does not liquefy under slight pressure, which the liquid petroleum gases (LPG), propane and butane, do. To get any useful weight of it into a tank, and a reasonable operating range for the vehicle, it must be highly compressed. High-pressure tanks of this kind are already widely used in CNG vehicles. Even so, no reasonable amount of compressed hydrogen will both fit into a car without eating an unreasonable amount of luggage and/or passenger space, or giving it a wholly unacceptable range, comparable to that of the pure battery electric vehicles.

So what to do? How can hydrogen be fed to the fuel cell but carried in a dense enough form? The production technology has long existed in the chemical and fertiliser industries. Hydrogen is produced in millions of tonnes a year by these industries by the steam reforming process, which reacts water vapour with natural gas to yield carbon dioxide, which is mostly discarded, and hydrogen. The hydrogen is then forcibly combined with nitrogen from the air to form ammonia, which is a fertiliser in its own right but also the starting material for all the other nitrogenous artificial fertilisers, and for explosives.

But then there is the distribution problem. There are very few hydrogen pipeline systems and those that do exist are typically within oil refineries and chemical plants. But we have natural gas distribution systems, at least in the great majority of the OECD countries. So it is perfectly possible and would be cost-effective to carry out the steam reforming of natural gas on a local basis. This could feed a fuel cell installation which will conveniently generate both electricity and low-grade (60 to 70 degrees Centigrade) heat – perfect for powering and heating an apartment complex, a hospital or an office block – or a hydrogen filling station for vehicles. We can also generate hydrogen locally for a filling station by electrolysis of water – reversing the reaction in the fuel cell, which combines hydrogen and oxygen to generate electricity. That can be an attractive option where there is plenty of cheap electricity available.

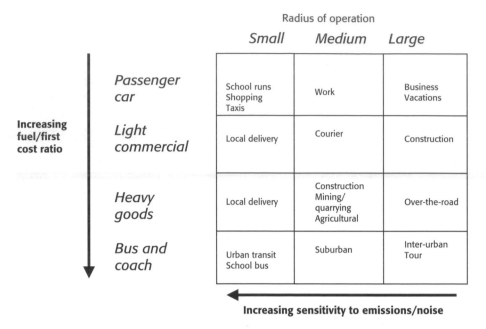

Source: autoPOLIS

Fig. 3.24 Segmentation of vehicle applications

These are exactly the routes which have enabled the development of the first practical fuel cell vehicles – urban buses. Figure 3.24 explains the logic of why this should be so. The whole set of road vehicles and the uses to which they are put have been arrayed following both an economic and an environmental logic.

The rows in the matrix represent vehicle families, ordered by the amount of fuel they use, relative to their initial cost. Passenger cars, in the top row, are mainly not used very intensively – at European fuel prices, they will on average consume fuel during their life costing about as much as the vehicle cost to buy. Light commercials are more intensively used by professional operators and consume more, relative to their purchase cost; heavy trucks, buses and coaches even more so. So this segmentation into rows relates to the sensitivity of their operators to fuel consumption. Heavy consumers of fuel are more likely to buy more expensive vehicles, which use novel technologies to cut their consumption. Fuel consump-

tion also determines the amount of noxious and carbon dioxide emissions.

The columns group the ways in which vehicles are used. The right-hand column covers uses involving a large radius of operation from base – in the extreme case, driving across a country or continent. The middle column represents medium-radius operations, e.g. within a city and its suburbs. The left-hand column represents small-radius operations, much of which will be within inner cities. This has two effects. First, inner-city environments are more sensitive to the effects of automotive emissions, the noxious ones at least. Second, if the new technology (notably fuel cells or rechargeable electric vehicles) needs a new fuel distribution and retailing infrastructure, that will be a big problem for the passenger car fleet, which is very widely dispersed. But an urban transit bus or a taxi, operating within a limited radius from a fixed base, does not suffer from this constraint. A fuel-cell-powered urban bus can refuel at its base overnight, whereas a similarly powered car

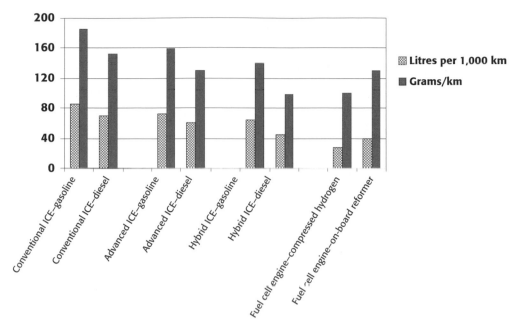

Source: *auto*POLIS; industry sources

Note: Compressed hydrogen from fossil fuel sources, consumption in liquid-fuel equivalent

Fig. 3.25 How clean are they really?

either needs an incredibly expensive new network of hydrogen filling stations, or must resort to carrying liquid fuels and extracting hydrogen from them by means of an on-board processing plant (called a reformer).

On this logic, then, the obvious first candidate for fuel cell power is the urban bus, in the bottom-left box of the matrix. By definition, urban buses operate in urban environments. Many of the passenger-kilometres they provide are run in rush-hour conditions, with the bus starting and stopping even more than it normally does at bus stops. The fuel cell engine is most advantaged at part-load – which is ideal for an urban bus. At part-load, the fuel cell engine is at its most efficient and up to twice as efficient as the diesel engine. At full load, the two efficiency curves converge again – which is why diesel engines are likely to maintain their position in long-distance buses and trucks for a long time. Taxis are another possible candidate, to the extent that they are designed as specialised vehicles, as

in London, not simply ordinary passenger cars painted yellow, as in New York.

Both categories of vehicle need only a limited operating range – single-deck buses can carry enough hydrogen tankage on the roof for 350–400 km, which is plenty for an urban bus route. Both categories of vehicle can refuel from the central depot from which they operate. The buses can refuel overnight, so that hydrogen can be pumped into their tanks as it is generated, from steam reforming or electrolysis. There is no need for extensive (and expensive) static storage: it is just-in-time.

It all looks terrifically good for fuel cells, if you can fuel the vehicle with hydrogen (see figure 3.25) achieving the equivalent of 94 miles per US gallon of liquid fuel, compared to 56 mpg for the best advanced conventional diesel engine, in the left-hand part of the figure. But note how that figure collapses as soon as one puts in an on-board reformer, so as to be able to carry denser liquid fuels.

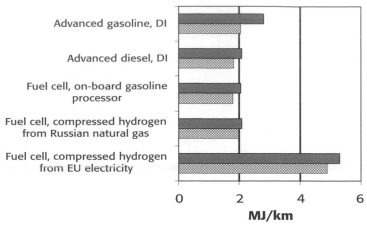

Source: Dobson, 'The Future of Vehicles and Fuel'
data from GM European well-to-wheels assessment

Fig. 3.26 Selected 'well-to-wheels' efficiencies

And look at the overall carbon dioxide emissions, in the right-hand part of the chart. The hydrogen-fuelled fuel cell vehicle only just edges out a good diesel-engined one – and is a lot less good than a hybrid.

The method of generating the hydrogen to be used is extremely important in assessing the overall energy efficiency of the system, however. Figure 3.26 gives some selected examples of this. There is a certain amount of controversy over the figures and their interpretation. But it is clear from this limited set that the conventional engine is by no means played out. Advanced direct injection gasoline and diesel engines will give a fuel cell with an on-board gasoline reformer a good run for its money. The additional conversion losses in the reformer cancel out the conversion efficiency gain of the fuel cell engine over the internal combustion engine. A methanol-fuelled reformer hybrid (not shown) is not all that different – the reformer is more efficient than a gasoline reformer but additional losses are incurred in making the methanol. All these four can be refuelled from a conventional pump, although methanol will need its

own, perhaps taken over from lead-containing gasoline. The fourth, using hydrogen locally steam-reformed from Russian natural gas (a principal source of energy within the European Union) also looks all right, assuming, of course, that one has installed that network of reforming/refuelling stations. Using the other decentralised means of generating hydrogen, electrolysis, looks awful, if we use EU sources of electricity. It has the same problem of building a new network of filling stations as the previous case.

In some ways, then, the future has arrived. Or it would have done, given that we still need a special fuel, that the overall 'well-to-wheels' efficiency is no better than for a good direct-injection diesel driveline, and that the fleet demonstrators run on compressed hydrogen, for which there is only a very limited and purpose-built refuelling infrastructure, with the kind of range limitation which killed the battery electrics.

The cost of a full hydrogen distribution network for the US, reaching down to the corner gas station, has been estimated at $100 billion. Furthermore, it would have to operate in

New vehicle fuel economy

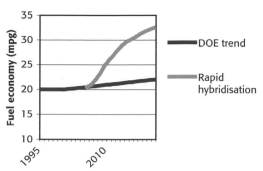

Light vehicle carbon emissions

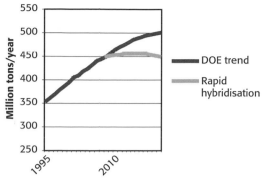

Source: Dobson, 'The Future of Vehicles and Fuel'

Fig. 3.27 Projected benefits of rapid hybridisation in the US

parallel with the conventional fuel distribution network, as it would take decades for the huge parc of vehicles to switch over completely. All this does not make the widespread deployment of fuel cells a wildly attractive proposition, either financially or environmentally speaking – unless and until the world's whole energy balance and pricing structures change. That does not mean that we should not continue research and pilot projects to prepare for the future. Just do not look for massive change within the next twenty years. Despite optimistic pronouncements from some industry sources, large-scale deployment of fuel cell light vehicles is not for tomorrow, and perhaps not even for the day after tomorrow, meaning more than a decade from now.

So what is our prognostication? Our reasoning is summed up in figure 3.28. Passenger cars – and light trucks used as substitutes for them – could become hybrids-based, but still use conventional engines, as they are extensively used in urban areas and stop–go traffic. But it will take some pretty strong incentives and straight diesel engines will remain a strong competitor, at least in Europe and possibly elsewhere. Light commercials and local delivery trucks do a high proportion of low-speed, stop-and-start work and would benefit considerably from hybrid drives. Urban taxis

	Urban Use Proportion	Preferred Driveline Technology
Cars and light trucks	50%	Hybrid
Taxis	100%	FC
Light commercials	80%	Hybrid
Local delivery trucks	80%	Hybrid
Over-the-road trucks	10–20%	ICE
Urban transit buses	100%	FC
Long-distance buses	10–20%	ICE

*Source: auto*POLIS

Fig. 3.28 Potential applications of new driveline technologies

and transit buses are the only immediate obvious 'natural' application for fuel cell engines. Long-distance trucks and long-distance buses will continue to use diesel engines, whose 'well-to-wheel' efficiency is hard to beat for most of their operating pattern.

How soon will this happen? Figure 3.29 is our attempt at a forecast. It may well be too optimistic – or pessimistic in terms of the energy and emissions controls environment. And that comes down to highly political issues. If we do not make some changes, though, we expose ourselves to facing possible future storms without an ark. The forecast

	2000	2010	2020	2030	2040
Hybrid cars/LTs	–	–	2,700	22,500	50,500
FC taxis	–	35	200	450	550
Hybrid LCVs	–	350	2,500	8,000	14,500
Hybrid local trucks	–	30	350	1,300	2,500
FC urban buses	–	1	35	100	150

Source: autoPOLIS

Fig. 3.29 Projected growth of new driveline technologies (thousand new vehicles per year)

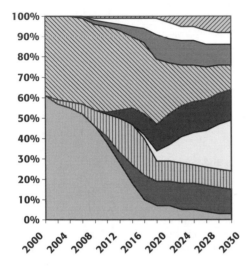

Source: Dobson, 'The Future of Vehicles and Fuel'

Fig. 3.30 Share of engine technologies in new light vehicles, 2000 to 2030

is one that Japanese and US manufacturers might side with but definitely not Europeans, who have shown very little interest in hybrids. Their position appears to be based on the cost and weight penalty that a hybrid, or at least a full hybrid of the Prius variety, imposes on the vehicle. They are confident that they can reach the target of 140 gm of carbon dioxide per kilometre without hybridisation, using advanced diesel and other internal combustion engines. But they also admit that they will have great difficulty in getting below this level of emissions with these essentially conventional technologies.

Figure 3.30 shows one future view of the engine mix in European light vehicles (under 5 tonnes gross vehicle weight). In this view, over 85 per cent of drivetrains will still be internal combustion piston engine based in 2030, with hybrids (which would themselves still require an internal combustion engine) making only a weak showing and fuel cell engines only arriving in quantity after 2020. What is noteworthy is the projected continuing growth of diesel-based engines and the ultimate emergence of the homogeneous charge compression ignition engine, sitting between gasoline and diesel engines.

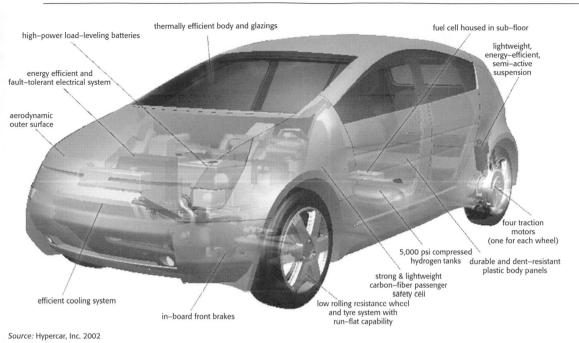

high–power load–leveling batteries

thermally efficient body and glazings

fuel cell housed in sub–floor

lightweight,
energy–efficient,
semi–active
suspension

energy efficient and
fault–tolerant electrical system

aerodynamic
outer surface

four traction
motors
(one for each wheel)

5,000 psi compressed
hydrogen tanks

durable and dent–resistant
plastic body panels

strong & lightweight
carbon–fiber passenger
safety cell

low rolling resistance wheel
and tyre system with
run–flat capability

efficient cooling system

in–board front brakes

Source: Hypercar, Inc. 2002

Fig. 3.31 The Hypercar

It is clear, then, that we shall not see radical improvements or changes for many years. This is partly because we would need to break free from the conventional design constraints that the industry continues to impose on itself. It is a sad fact that we are really still tinkering at the margins of what the vehicle could become with these ideas, altering only one parameter at a time and only to an extent that does not upset the traditional paradigm of what an automobile is. We stick to the steel unitised bodyshell, except for very marginal exceptions. That shuts us into an assumption that a vehicle of a certain size inevitably has to have a certain bodyweight – it is one of the ratchet effects in the industry. That, in turn, virtually condemns us to continuing to use the internal combustion engine, running on liquid fuels, as they alone can provide the power density required to haul that bodyshell over the required range with the required speed and acceleration. Note, however, that those two requirements are themselves ratchets which we impose on the vehicle by the way we have built it into our patterns of living

and working, with low-density housing and long distances to work. If we can mentally break out of these constraints, then immense changes would become possible.

Figure 3.31 shows an example of more radical thinking. It is the Hypercar developed by Amory Lovins at the Rocky Mountain Institute in Colorado. Their brochure includes a marvellous quote from Henry Ford: 'We build our vehicles as though dead-weight increased speed . . . I cannot imagine where the delusion that weight means strength comes from.' Their slogan is: 'Hypercar . . . breaking the rule of iron in the auto industry', the rule of iron being that customers always want more features and performance, that one must use iron and steel to fulfil these expectations, and that this inevitably means adding further weight to the automatically assumed large base weight, which sets the powertrain expectations, and so on.

In a nutshell, the Hypercar concept aims to halve the total weight of the vehicle and reduce its power requirements by two-thirds, while at least maintaining existing standards of safety, performance and comfort and also achieving full manufacturability with no increase in cost. Because the power requirement is so much reduced, the vehicle can house a tank needed to carry 3.4 kg of compressed gaseous hydrogen to fuel its fuel cell powertrain. If really achievable it is indeed a true breakthrough.

Arguably, we need to stop trying to put the wine of the new technologies into the worn-out old bottles of conventional design thinking if we are to make the improvements that could be achieved. Yet to change would require the industry to let the wolf into the fold: to allow radical outside views and actors onto the stage, which is a difficult task, especially for an industry which too often has tried to crush creativity by imposing its traditional ideas and stifling relationships on newcomers. It certainly seems to us that the conventional engines and their derivatives will be with us for many decades yet.

4

A global industry and the changing international order

The structure of world vehicle markets – which countries will make it and which will not

In chapters 1 and 2, we showed that the automobile industry is large and important. It has a significant role to play in economies, accounting for 10 per cent of a developed nation's GDP. We know too that the global market is mature and that the growth in places like China and India is unlikely to make up for the stagnation and decline elsewhere. These conclusions raise several questions. First, we look at the countries that are trying to develop an auto industry, that see the importance it has and the kudos it brings, and ask which ones will actually make it. Many are trying to become large, scale-intensive manufacturers of cars and trucks. Which will succeed? Conversely, which countries with a major role to play in the industry today will see their influence wane? Second, how much of a role do trade agreements have to play? If markets are completely open and there is plenty of capacity in the industry already (and there is), then demand in many emerging markets can be satisfied with imports. So how open will they be?

The automotive industries in different countries are not equal. Some are massive and scale-intensive, others are emerging and protected, and some are little more than jobbing shops, making cars from kits using substandard local parts and pretending to their governments that they are serious scale-driven competitors in this tough global business. The situation is not static, however. At first, it was just Europe and the US that made cars. Then Japan joined them. During the first hundred years of the industry, in different proportions, those three places have accounted for four in every five vehicles built.

But is that it? Is that the end of history? Most assuredly not. Other countries have tried to join this triad and still more are trying. In the 1970s South Korea started to develop an auto sector. A decade later so did Malaysia. The Russians have an auto industry and so do the Brazilians and the Romanians. Most recently of all, the Chinese and the Indians have started to build in volume, as have the Iranians. So the world's auto industry is changing.

Is it possible that we might see car and truck output steadily decline in the big countries, like Japan and Germany, as these newer countries ramp up production? Will Americans, Europeans and even Japanese customers be buying Shanghai-Auto cars in ten years' time or even Iranian ones? Of all these entrant-upstarts, who will make it and who will not? To answer these questions we need to look first at the world's auto markets, to find out where the demand will be. For a country to build a robust industry it needs the base of a substantial local market. That is why so few countries have made it into the club so far and some have been ejected.

We already know that most cars are used and bought in the Triad today – North America, Europe and Japan. We know too that production today is still largely based in these places. Figure 4.1 shows a global sales map with vehicle volumes represented in a very simplified form, with the size of countries

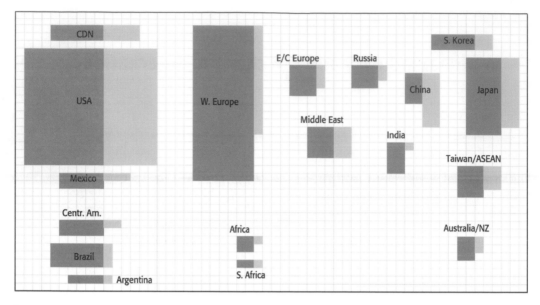

*Source: auto*POLIS
Note: One square represents 100,000 vehicles sold per year

Fig. 4.1 The world market today

and regions proportionate to sales. The dark grey is the passenger car market, the light grey, trucks. As of today, the world automotive market is still largely dominated by the OECD countries, mostly the Big Three.

The next question, to help us map where sales and production will focus tomorrow, is, where is the market potential? As we discussed in chapter 1, those OECD markets are mature and largely saturated. So any growth will come in the emerging markets, by definition. Even so, by 2010 these will still be very far from catching up, as you can see in figure 4.2. The market areas on this map are the same in size as in the last one. You can see that, even although we expect massive growth in places like China and India, the overall map is not very different. Even a decade from now, the bulk of car and truck sales – and that means two out of three – will be in North America, Europe and Japan.

In fact it will take until nearer 2020 before the sales volumes in the emerging markets begin to rival those in the developed world today. Figure 4.3 summarises what we expect

to happen to world demand by region by then.

By 2020, the balance will have shifted decisively, with Asia becoming the largest automotive region in the world. Note that Asia is more of an archipelago than a continent, with China and India as its largest 'islands'. Much of the rest literally consists of islands. So it is not now and probably never will become a single, integrated market. We count Russia as European in automotive terms, as its capital is in Europe, even though much of its land-mass is in Asia.

So there will be growth – but not where it used to be, and not soon enough to solve the industry's current problems. At best, there will still be at least another decade with very little global growth, after many years of virtually none at all. Then there is the issue of market access. Will these emerging markets be open to imports from other countries? Or will they try and put up trade barriers to stop the scale-intensive producers from the US, Europe and Japan crushing their emergent industries? Could they even attempt to build

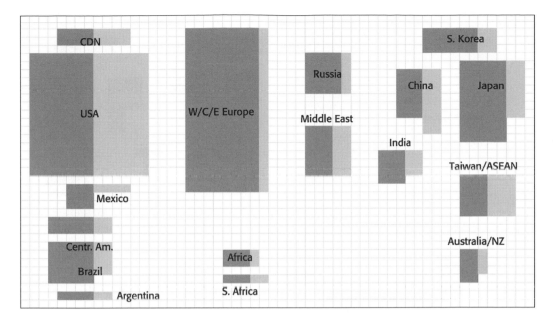

Source: *auto*POLIS

Fig. 4.2 The world market in 2010

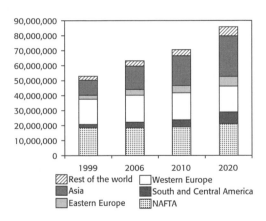

Source: *auto*POLIS

Fig. 4.3 World vehicle sales to 2020

their own exports, upsetting the balance in the developed markets? After all, Japan and South Korea both developed their auto industries by developing exports quickly.

Curiously, perhaps, we think that the impact of trade agreements on the industry can be largely (but not entirely) ignored. More open markets do not always lead to more open trade, certainly in the auto industry.

South Korea and Japan have had very open markets for years (in terms of tariffs), yet foreign vehicle sales in both places are negligible or small. Trade agreements focus on tariffs and openness and on the mechanisms of importing and exporting. In the auto sector, as in some other businesses, there is more to it than that. Because of the importance of the auto sector, because it is a pillar industry, politics and national interests often get in the way. Developed country governments do not want their primary industries hollowed out by lower labour cost countries. Similarly, developing country governments do not want their emerging auto sectors wiped out in their infancy or taken over by the big global majors. They want to protect them until they are big enough to compete on their own.

Figure 4.4 looks at the degree of openness to importing complete vehicles in the world today. You can see that the degree of openness has little to do with tariff levels or trade agreements. This is partly because there are a great many non-tariff barriers which affect

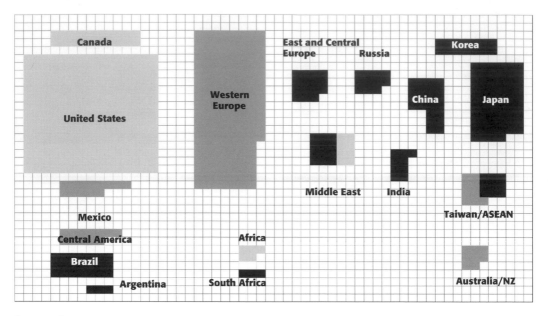

Source: *auto*POLIS
Note: One square represents 100,000 vehicles sold per year

Fig. 4.4 Accessibility of automotive markets today

the industry – which are permitted under WTO. This is also partly because trade barriers are often invisible in any normal sense. They are often cultural or customary barriers, not material ones.

The US and some others are almost wholly open markets. That is the light colour. There are no major tariff/non-tariff barriers, nor what we might call 'customary barriers', although there is the UAW pact with American manufacturers which requires them not to 'export' jobs. Other customary, non-tariff barriers, for example, might be difficulties in securing adequate dealer networks – a real problem in Japan and to a significant degree in Europe. This can take the form of the government threatening car buyers with a tax audit if they order a foreign car, as was once the case in South Korea, or general prejudices against foreign products. The French, for example, still have much less experience of Japanese cars, as they were subject to a

3 per cent market-share ceiling for decades. So Japanese cars and brands are still often seen as quirky and 'not for me', even although most French consumers can claim to be open-minded. These are customary barriers and they are perfectly legal under WTO.

In fact, large parts of the world automotive market, the medium grey areas, are still subject to this kind of discrimination. Equally large areas are also, quite frankly, protectionist – the dark colour. Note that some regions have been aggregated together in the figure for simplicity, such as the ASEAN markets and Taiwan. These comprise a set of national markets, each with their own characteristics and national policies.

So how open will world automotive markets be in 2010? We believe the picture will change, but not much. Figure 4.5 is our estimate of how it might look. The world automotive market is significantly more open than it was but by no means uniformly so. The

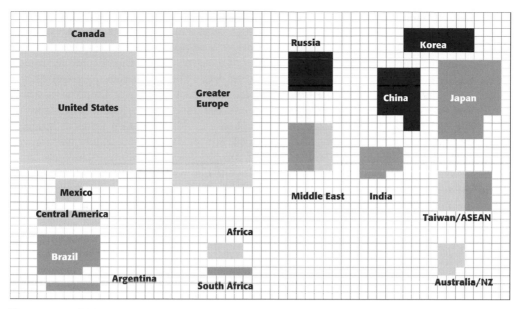

Fig. 4.5 Accessibility of automotive markets in 2010

biggest shift is expected in Europe. In 2002, the European Commission published the New Block Exemption Regulation and this is likely to have a progressively widespread impact. The regulation sets the framework for the sales and servicing of light vehicles in Europe, and for how carmakers can exercise control, or not, over their dealers and car repair shops. The aim of the new law is to make the market substantially more open and competitive than it was under the previous regulation, which gave the vehicle manufacturers pretty much a free hand to control distribution channels as they saw fit. The changes this legislation will bring are not likely to happen overnight, but they are the harbinger of a major shift in the balance of power in the whole downstream sector of the industry within the region – and perhaps further afield. That story is described in detail on pages 185–97.

But even by 2010 much of the world will remain closed or partly closed. Latin America, South Korea and Japan will still not be open markets by then. Russia and large parts

of Asia will remain mostly closed too, as governments continue to protect their domestic vehicle industries while they grow.

Ownership and control in the auto sector are very important political, economic and social issues, and in practice the choice as to whether or not to develop an indigenous industry only affects a few countries. Only a very few have the potential to develop auto sectors that will one day be internationally 'core' – independent, open and global. It is very important not to confuse the fact that a country builds large volumes of vehicles with the idea that it has a domestic automotive industry under its own control. Because the industry brings such wealth, and because it accounts for 10 per cent of the GDP of developed economies, there is a very powerful incentive for almost every emerging economy to focus on the sector. That is not to say they will succeed, even if it might look as though they are doing for a time. The difficulties facing a developing country that wants to develop an auto sector are curiously complex. They are also, too often, misunder-stood.

The ideas that lead countries to try and develop an auto industry are simple enough. As countries grow, their citizens become wealthier. As they become wealthier, they demand more of the goods that make life easier. They want television sets and radios and refrigerators and music systems. Of course, as the penetration of television sets and the internet grows – two of the first steps up this acquisitive ladder today – the citizens of emerging economies also become more aware of the lifestyles of those in the developed world which they then seek to emulate.

As they move up the mobility ladder, the first stages are bicycles and then motorcycles. The motorcycle market in China is already by far the biggest in the world – with more than 10 million new machines now sold annually – while the Indian market is not far behind. Hero Honda in India is the world's largest producer of powered two-wheelers.

At this stage, there is not much of a problem. The technology used in bicycles and emerging-market motorcycles is pretty rudimentary, their value is comparatively low and the economies of scale needed to manufacture them are not very onerous. This is obviously not true of advanced-country motorcycles, such as BMW, Harley-Davidson or Honda. So countries wanting to motorise at this level can quickly establish local manufacturing facilities, perhaps using designs licensed from established global players, and begin making them locally. Even when demand was comparatively low, motorcycle manufacturers were well established in India and China. They also had high levels of localisation – that is, most of the components needed to make the motorbikes were made locally too.

This is important, because the last thing a developing nation needs is to become a net importer. What it needs to develop are jobs, higher levels of economic output and then exports to fuel the foreign exchange coffers through trade. This approach encourages inward investment and a further healthy inward flow of foreign funds.

In the car and, to a lesser extent, in the truck sector, the economics do not work like this. As a rule of thumb, developing countries begin to see a surge in the demand for motorcycles when the GDP reaches around $750 a head: around the level in China as a whole today. For the car sector, the average is much higher, more than thirteen times as much in 2003. But, of course, that is only the average. In most developing countries, income levels and income distribution vary hugely. While most of the people in Thailand, India, China and Indonesia are still extremely poor, for example, a growing proportion are not. So, even although these countries as a whole are not yet ready for mass motorisation, a large number of people in these places are able to afford cars.

This is where the difficulties begin. To provide these people with cars, they have to be imported, in small numbers at first, and that is not a problem. But because the average value of a car is so much higher than a motorcycle, say, and because the rich in these places are often very rich, they tend not to skimp. So the gradual inflow of cars often starts with high-value Mercedes, Lexuses and BMWs to transport the country's elite.

Again, in small numbers, this is not a problem. But demand then tends to rise as the middle classes begin to grow in number. Then, many countries start to import second-hand vehicles or middle-market vehicles in more substantial numbers. Within a remarkably short time this becomes a real problem. Take a country like Indonesia, which had vehicles sales of just 317,000 units in 2002, which was equal to just a week's sales in the US that year. If it imported all these vehicles, Indonesia would have a net outflow of funds of almost $8 billion, equivalent to 6 per cent of the country's GDP. It would increase the value of the country's imports by a quarter.

With a population of 220 million people – not much less than in the US – sales would not have to grow very much before the entire Indonesian economy would be crippled. If vehicles sales reached just 950,000 units a year, and these all had to be imported, then the cost would wipe out the country's entire trade surplus. Instead of being a net exporter (thanks mostly to oil and gas reserves), Indonesia would become a net importer. This would have a catastrophic effect on growth, the exchange rate and the country's foreign exchange reserves.

The way to try and stop this happening, of course, is to impose hefty tariff barriers on imported vehicles. But these are always politically sensitive and, in any case, have been made more difficult by free trade agreements like AFTA and WTO. The other option is to start local manufacturing and assembly. The trouble here, however, is that this is much more easily said than done. It also explains why national vehicle programmes, like Malaysia's Proton and Indonesia's Timor initiative (now abandoned) run into such difficulty so quickly. But the scale requirements in the auto industry are immense. To make a car in any sort of economic quantities using current production technology needs an output volume of at least 250,000 units a year per model and preferably 400,000 units a year. Above that, the advantages diminish. It is for this reason that the creation of a local car business in these countries is often called a development economist's nightmare.

So, think again of Indonesia. It barely has the demand for *one* world-class competitive car plant today, and yet the market is already being served by around ten different companies, each providing many different models. So even if such a car plant were built today, it would mean that the citizens of Indonesia would suddenly lose all the choice they have had. It would be impractical in other ways too. The 317,000 vehicles sold in Indonesia in 2002 were not just cars, but trucks, pick-ups and buses too. It is simply not realistic to force the market to adopt one model in the interests of scale economies and the national foreign exchange balance.

Besides, there are other problems with this idea. First, while it may only need 250,000 units a year of output to make a car efficiently, the skills to design and engineer one are also needed. Few sustainable car companies exist in the world that make less than 1 million units a year unless they are protected by governments or tariffs. Second, the scale requirements for many of the components are even higher than they are for cars. A starter or alternator factory is only really efficient when it churns out 1.2 million units a year, almost four times the demand that exists in Indonesia today. Indonesia simply cannot develop a local car industry with a sustainable parts sector with the demand volumes it has today.

So the next best option for these governments is to encourage local assembly; and to do this, they have to impose high tariffs on fully built imported vehicles. This allows those that are assembled locally to be competitive, under a price umbrella. Only then will the world's carmakers see that if they want to sell cars in that country they have no alternative but to assemble them locally.

The way assembly starts is with carmakers importing kits, known in the industry as CKDs or SKDs – complete or semi-knocked-down kits. These are then put together, giving the importing country some of the added value. However, there is often controversy about even this. In some cases, the vehicle manufacturers, reluctant to have the hassle and happier to use up some of their expensive manufacturing plant elsewhere, import cars that they claim to be partially built up but that are, in reality, almost entirely finished. There was a scandal in the EU a few years ago, for example, when Daewoo cars were being imported to Poland as part of a trade pact with the EU. Daewoo had claimed that the cars were being assembled in its factory outside Warsaw, when they actually arrived at the country's ports complete in every way other than needing their door mirrors attached. The local added value was almost nil. Or parts that are difficult to procure locally are simply smuggled in, concealed in the CKD crates.

To get around such abuses, developing countries typically bring in more legislation, forcing the assemblers to buy some of their components locally too. Carmakers are forced to buy batteries, tyres and glass in the country, for example, or to cast the engine blocks there (although only if they absolutely must, as this is a complex and very scale-intensive process). Even here, though, there are abuses, or at least there is a reluctance on the part of the big global carmakers to do it, often for good reason. One Japanese carmaker we found in Thailand would, for example, buy all the car radios for its vehicles locally, as it was required to do by law. But because it found that the quality of the locally sourced devices was so poor and because such things matter to owners, it ended up putting all of them in the bin and importing superior units from Japan.

Developing country governments are therefore faced with considerable problems in their efforts to develop an auto industry. Another difficulty exists over how to measure local content: the amount of value added put into the vehicle in the country in which it is being produced. Some governments in developing countries try to force carmakers to increase the local value added by specifying the products they have to buy in the country of assembly. Others say carmakers must achieve a local content level which is a proportion of the final weight of the completed vehicle. Still others say that it must be a proportion of the value. Whatever the definition, as soon as local integration goes beyond the simplest commodities, sourcing them locally at acceptable levels of price and quality becomes a nightmare. Governments want more local content, to save imports, and will typically also expect parts of vehicles to be exported, to earn foreign currency to pay for the the imports. Car manufacturers reluctantly invest in local production and try to drag their home suppliers in to join them. They seek to minimise local content, as (paradoxically, for developing country governments) imported components are cheaper and better. The twain have great difficulty in meeting.

Yet all the methods used by governments to force carmakers to increase their local content are flawed and open to abuse. We cite the example of a country where we were called in to help the government develop its national industry policy for the auto sector. How, the government there wondered, did it have such a huge trade imbalance in the auto sector when the local manufacturers were making vehicles with a 70 per cent local content? Why was its trade balance so out of kilter in the automotive sector when the cars being made within its borders had such a seemingly high locally added value?

We went out to nose around. In one factory we found the answer. It made air conditioning systems, which the government stipulated had to be locally produced. Sure enough, we discovered, tens of thousands of systems were being made in the factory every year and often in very labour-intensive ways, to take advantage of the low costs of hiring people in the country. And, as promised, all the systems left the factory and were fitted and used by cars for the local market. All – 100 per cent – were locally supplied to carmakers, as the government decreed.

Only there was a catch. The compressor, the most expensive part of the system, was being taken from a box at the side of the assembly line which was labelled 'Made in Brazil'. It was removed from its packaging, a rubber tube was attached to a nozzle coming out of it and a sticker saying 'Made in xxxx' (the country in question) was stuck on the side. The last stage of the manufacturing process unquestionably took place in the country we were investigating, but very little of the value added was really created there. It was the same with the raw materials for the system: the metals, tubes and rubber nozzles. They were all imported too. In fact, around 90 per cent of the value of this air conditioning system was actually imported, even though it was 'made' locally.

In the end, this country's legislators were horrified to find that the real added value of the cars being produced locally was not 70 per cent, as they had decreed and as they thought, but just 18 per cent. This explained the massive trade imbalance.

This sort of phenomenon is not just a developing country problem either. One of us also visited a factory in Europe making parts for the steering systems fitted to Japanese cars made in the UK. Sure enough, the parts were assembled in Europe, but all the metal, the designs, the machining – the real added value – came from Japan. Again, 90 per cent of the added value was imported, even if the end product was classified by the authorities, or at least by the carmaker, as European. We saw exactly the same going on with Japanese-made heater units imported into a Central European country. Simply sticking on a label that read 'Made in Transylvania', for example, meant the unit was deemed to be national. The relabelling helped the manufacturer achieve sufficient 'European' content to gain free access to the markets of the European Union.

There is, unfortunately, no easy solution to this problem and it is where developing country governments have very substantial difficulties, made worse, we suspect, by their misunderstanding of the way the industry functions. The fact is that carmakers and their suppliers often have to import very basic commodities like steel and rubber trim into a country because the volumes needed to make these products in the grades suitable for car manufacturing are immense. Making automotive-grade steel requires a huge investment. This is part of the chicken-and-egg problem facing so many developing countries in both industries. They need to have an auto industry to build a steel industry, but it makes very little sense to set up a cold-rolled steel mill to make automotive-grade steel without substantial local demand from a domestic car industry. But, in the meantime, until either has the scale needed to compete, to make this investment sensible, what do you do? You have to import.

As we will see later, there *are* countries that are getting around this today, and that are successfully developing their own auto industries. But there are only a few, and fewer will ultimately succeed. Most places, sadly, will never have sustainable indigenous auto industries. Others will only create one successfully if it is protected and where there is substantial domestic demand.

This is a critical issue and it is one few developing country governments really grasp. Most governments look to the sector, correctly, as a pillar for future industrial development. They see that it is almost impossible for them to develop many other industrial sectors without an auto business to act as a demand catalyst. But few really understand the economics of what they are taking on.

So what are the likely future roles of different countries in the global automotive economy of tomorrow? This is no exact science, if only because of the significance of the industry within national economies, the continued attachment of many countries to protecting it, and the consequently highly political and local nature of the game. We have, however, tried to loosely group automotive manufacturing countries into four groups to see who might make it. These are what we have called core, peripheral, autarchic and networked-in countries.

The groupings are shown in figure 4.6. Production volumes per country have been added to the figure to illustrate the point that volumes have little to do with strategic position, and that merely having assembly plants does not make a domestic automotive industry.

The first group, the core countries, consists of the United States, Japan, Germany and France. These are the only countries in the world today that have been able to sustain an automotive industry complete in all its functions, that have scale, and that have ownership and leadership in different aspects of its technology. These are the core countries of the world automotive industry. Their national players have enough scale to survive in the global league.

We may be stretching the point a little including France in this group, as it has two major domestic vehicle manufacturing groups but only part of a complete components industry. Also, France's PSA (Peugeot-Citroën) has chosen a regional European strategy, not a global one. It has flanked this by alliances in specific product areas, such as a joint venture plant with Toyota to build small cars

Core
- ❖ US – 16.7 m
- ❖ Japan – 10.2 m
- ❖ Germany – 5.5 m
- ❖ France – 3.7 m

Peripheral
- ❖ Spain – 2.8 m
- ❖ Belgium – 1.1 m
- ❖ Poland – 0.3 m
- ❖ Czech Republic – 0.5 m
- ❖ Hungary – 0.1 m
- ❖ Turkey – 0.3 m
- ❖ Romania – 0.1 m
- ❖ Canada – 2.6 m
- ❖ Brazil – 1.7 m
- ❖ Mexico – 1.8 m
- ❖ Argentina – 0.3 m

Autarchy
- ❖ China – 2.9 m
- ❖ India – 0.9 m
- ❖ Russia – 1.3 m
- ❖ Iran – 0.3 m
- ❖ Malaysia – 0.4 m
- ❖ South Korea – 2.6 m

Networked in
- ❖ UK – 1.8 m
- ❖ Italy – 1.4 m
- ❖ Sweden – 0.5 m
- ❖ Thailand – 0.5 m
- ❖ Australia - 0.4 m
- ❖ South Africa – 0.4 m

Source: autoPOLIS

Fig. 4.6 Countries grouped by role in the world automotive industry, 2002

in the Czech Republic. But PSA aims to be a global leader in specific technologies, such as diesel engines, for which Ford and Toyota have turned to it for help. Note, too, that we have not included Italy, which is in the process of dropping out of this group, because of Fiat's decline, or the UK, which dropped out twenty years ago and has only other people's satellite plants.

Around these core countries are clustered what we have called the peripheral countries – Spain, Belgium, Poland, the Czech Republic, Hungary, Turkey, Romania, Canada, Mexico, Brazil and Argentina. Their national automotive strategy – consciously or otherwise – has been to integrate themselves into the major regional poles. Briefly, their history or position in the world is as follows:

• In the 1970s Spain was autarchic, as it attempted to develop its own industry, protected from the outside world. The government imposed high tariffs on vehicle imports. There was a 90 per cent plus local content requirement in national production which was backed by investment and export

incentives. SEAT, the then national manufacturer, dominated the market. Today Spain builds a good number of cars but there is no longer an independent Spanish automotive industry and SEAT is part of the VW group.

• Belgium builds the better part of a million cars and light commercials a year. VW has an assembly plant in Brussels, GM in Antwerp, Ford in Genk. Renault used to have one in Vilvoorde. But these are purely satellite operations. Belgium has no vehicle design or development capability and only a very limited components industry.

• Poland, with a population similar to Spain's, is going the same way, after selling part of the previous national industry to Daewoo (which then collapsed). Assembly and components manufacturing plants in Poland are now extensions of Western European industrial networks.

• The VW group is the largest foreign investor in the Czech Republic. It has saved and transformed Škoda, a once national champion, turning it from producing communist-era joke products into a serious global contender. Again, though, the price has been a complete integration into VW's engineering and manufacturing network.

- Apart from Rába, which was formerly the Soviet bloc's specialised supplier of heavy truck axles, and so a considerable enterprise, the Hungarian automotive industry now consists entirely of satellite plants of European, US and Japanese groups.
- Turkey is largely in the same position with its automotive industry increasingly integrated into that of Europe.
- The Romanian automotive industry only survives because Renault has chosen to acquire its former licensee, Dacia, and use it as a base for producing entry-level vehicles for emerging markets.
- Canada has long been a manufacturing satellite of the US.
- Mexico has moved to this status, abandoning its past independent stance in favour of its Maquiladora strategy.
- Brazil is the dream that keeps fading. With 180 million inhabitants, it should be a good base for a national and thence a global automotive business. But it lurches from one economic crisis to another and lacks the technological capability and determination. This is why the attempts to pursue an export-led growth strategy from a protected national base have mostly failed. Brazil is largely a satellite of European players, led by VW, and likely to remain so.
- Argentina attempted such a strategy through Mercosur. This strategy fell apart because of currency and economic misalignment between Argentina and Brazil, however, and also because Brazil is not a substantial enough automotive economy to be a core country.

Other countries have tried or are trying to be core, in that they are attempting to develop their own auto industries. These 'autarchic' countries are China, India, Brazil, Russia, Iran and Malaysia. The problem for these places, however, is that they will need enormous actual or potential markets plus a good measure of ruthlessness to pull their plans off:

- China probably has the best chance of success although it will take time for a substantial enough domestic market and industry to emerge. But they will come. So far, China has been very careful to keep control of the industry's destiny and pretty clever at making use of its foreign partners. It is increasingly possible that China will emerge as a major exporter of bottom-of-the-line cars to Europe and the US using its own technology within a decade. We shall look at China in detail later.
- India has the population to become a core automotive country too but it does not have China's economic dynamism or national unity of purpose. It continues to hesitate between open competition and state-controlled development. In our view, it may become a major exporter, and one company, Tata Engineering, may emerge as a global industry power, but India is unlikely to provide a useful national model unless it radically changes its approach.
- Russia is still in something of a mess but has managed to keep control of its auto industry through the ups and downs. It is an untapped large-area country, with considerable hydrocarbon resources as well, and with a huge automotive market potential to become core – just so long as its politics and economics come right.
- Iran is trying to build its own automotive pole, partly focused on the Muslim and Arab world by political necessity, and to free itself from the control of its present largely French providers of technology. Whether the Middle East and a motley collection of ex-Soviet Central Asian republics can provide a sufficient base is a tough question.
- Malaysia's automotive industry is a wholly artificial construct, based on imported technology, a protected national market and opaque finance. It will not survive.
- South Korea's has perhaps been the most heroic attempt to become a core industry provider, based on massive capacity investment, technology replication and exports. It has failed, however, as economic reality

overtook the hastily constructed adventure. All of the Korean manufacturers are now under total or partial foreign control, except Hyundai. What was once a national automotive industry risks moving from autarchy to the networked model. South Korea may even find that, in time, it faces the same fate as Italy or the UK and that it moves to being 'networked-in'. With China planning to take the market for low-cost vehicles and Japan retaining the high end, South Korea risks being squeezed out of the business – and indeed many other businesses.

Finally, there is the last group, which we have called the networked-in countries, into which we have put the UK, Italy, Sweden, Thailand, Australia and South Africa:

- In reality, the UK ceased to have an independent domestic automotive industry twenty years ago, as the domestic assemblers collapsed or declined and dragged much of the components industry down with them. Yet there is a good deal of the industry left, based on the principle of supplying multiple automotive businesses rather than a single national one. Each level of the industry in the UK has had to find its own markets, define its scope and scale – or die. A few components firms such as GKN have made it to be global players; most have not.
- With the progressive deliquescence of Fiat, Italy is on the same track as the UK. Again, there are some very fine specialists there – one only needs to think of Ferrari and the design houses – and some good technology within Magneti Marelli. The overall prospects for Italy's auto sector are not good, however, especially in an industry with 25 per cent too much global capacity already.
- For many decades Sweden managed to maintain an independent car industry with two players, Volvo and Saab. That eventually broke down, with GM acquiring Saab and Ford taking over Volvo, after the latter tried to ally itself with Renault. While the brands retain their distinctive Scandinavian characters, their cars increasingly share platforms

and components with their parents. Sweden still owns some strong independent suppliers, such as Autoliv in safety systems and the world's largest bearing company, SKF, but it cannot sustain a widespread components industry any longer.

- Thailand is perhaps a bit of an odd example of a networked-in country. We actually worked for the Thai government on its national automotive strategy a few years ago and we found it hard to identify any automotive sector in which Thailand had a genuine comparative advantage. Yet with the help of tax-based distortion of its internal market and the benefits of being the only sensible place to invest in the ASEAN region, it has become the global pick-up king and a supply base for these products for global groups. Whether or not its position can be maintained after 2010 if the ASEAN countries form a free-trade link with China is questionable, however.
- Australia has followed a version of the networked-in model since the Button Plan[1] took it away from autarchy. The market has opened up to imports and yet, thanks to tariff protection, the assembly of a limited number of models continues. Vehicle exports are even on the increase, thanks mostly to a drop in value of the Australian dollar during the 1990s and the manufacture of products that find niche markets abroad. There is a fairly complete components industry, although much of it is under foreign control. Longer term though, it is likely to become a satellite manufacturing

[1] Until the 1970s, Australia used to be a totally protected market, with a large number of local assemblers and manufacturers operating inefficiently behind the tariff and non-tariff walls. A process of dismantling the barriers was started in the 1970s. In the early 1980s, Senator Button was asked to review the situation. The Button Plan was announced in 1984, with the aim of further reducing Australia's automotive isolation and of reducing the number of vehicle manufacturers from five to three and the number of models produced from thirteen to six by 1992. See Richard Johns, *Australian Automotive Intelligence Yearbook*, 2002: www.aaintelligence.com.au.

location for only one or two carmakers, each building one model for regional sales.

- South Africa is virtually the counterexample, at least in part. It was long a protected mature market, at least for the benefit of the white population under apartheid. Today, while it has developed exports thanks to the drop in the value of the rand, there are still far too many vehicles being assembled and the components industry is too weak to sustain anything substantial. If one excludes catalytic converters, which need platinum, and leather seat trim, both based on local natural resources, there is little that is internationally defensible. The government has been pressuring vehicle manufacturers to export more, with the incentive of earning credits to bring in built-up vehicles and components, and VW, BMW and Mercedes-Benz have responded to this by making South Africa the source of right-hand-drive versions of the Golf, 3-Series and C-Class, respectively. As the economy stagnates, however, there is a real risk that South Africa could slip back onto the protectionist track – a road to nowhere. The Australian option would be the most economically rational one for the country's automotive industry, but is very unlikely to be affordable for South Africa for the time being.

In conclusion, there is a need to be very cautious when attempting to think of the automotive industry as some open global marketplace, or believing that it will become one any time soon. There are simply too many complicating factors, based on national economic development and, sometimes, sheer pride. This is not something that will change quickly, even over the next fifteen to twenty years.

That, then, is the way that vehicle sales and assembly looks geographically today and how it will look over the next decade. Yet that is only half the story – or one way to look at the world. In the next two sections we will look at it another way – competitively. We will look at how the industry shapes up not in terms of

countries but in terms of the big global companies – the carmakers themselves. In the next section we will look at the cultural and competitive history of the business. In the following section we will look at who is best positioned to exploit the growth that is available.

Different inheritances – the cultural basis of competition

We now have a much better idea about which countries will make it in the auto industry of the future and which will not. What about the other side of the equation? Which carmakers will make it and which will not? Which are best positioned to take advantage of the growth that there is? Which suit the nationalistic dynamics of the industry in the future, in the long term?

These questions are complex. To answer them, we need first to understand the long-term competitive balance of the industry. Then we can look at the competitive positions of firms today and which are likely to gain most from these national plans. Looking at it this way throws up another dimension. If there are certain competitive characteristics that have determined success in this industry in the past, how might they change in the future? How might the winners in the current model become the losers and vice versa?

The competitive dynamics of the industry, its style of management and the way it collectively thinks are all very much part of our story. They are immensely influential. They also change from time to time. There have already been three fundamental revolutions in the style of the business in the hundred years since the industry was born. As with all revolutions, elements of pre-revolutionary thinking and behaviour still linger in places, long after the major change has taken place. These are important too. The alternative futures that we see for the industry, which we have mapped out in chapters 8 and 9, are highly dependent on these elements and on the style of doing business adopted by the industry. If the style remains as it is now, then a Graceless Degradation, which we discuss in chapter 8, is the future. If the industry can be made to change, then a much brighter future becomes a real possibility. But this would require a Fourth Revolution, which we have defined in chapter 9.

The First Revolution was the introduction of mass-production. This was important in itself, as it had a profound impact on the manufacturing of many other products. It is still important today for the thinking and management approach that lay behind it and for the style of doing business it brought to the industry. This is something that has had a legacy which can still be seen throughout the business today. It is at the root of many of the industry's problems and is still a major issue going forward.

The Second Revolution was instigated by Alfred P. Sloan. He effectively created the corporation as we recognise it today, in the form of General Motors. Again, though, what is important to our story is the thinking behind Sloan's ideas and the approach to business that he introduced. As well as refining the ideas of mass-production, he introduced new ideas as to how to approach the market. Again, these have had a lasting impact and are at the root of some of the other woes confronting the industry today. The ideas of 'planned obsolescence' and of making cars emotional objects – reflections of our ambitions and achievements – brought major benefits to his company. But they also sowed the seeds of the brand-driven industry we discussed in chapter 1, where vehicles are replaced and renewed at such a frequency as to have created what we call the 'economics of the madhouse'. As so often happens in history, the latter-day disciples do not really understand the prophet's true teachings and end up applying an exaggerated and perverted form of them.

The Third Revolution was lean production. Although not invented by the car industry it was perfected by it – by Toyota this time. Again, our story is not about lean production per se but about its implications. It has created a competitive fracture down the centre of the industry which has been taking a long time to heal and which has had enormous consequences.

The car as we know it does not have one single inventor. Both Leonardo da Vinci and Isaac Newton conceived of a variety of motorised vehicle. The first steam-driven vehicle was built as early as 1769 by Nicolas Joseph Cugnot and used by the French military. The car, as we know it today, finally came into existence about a hundred years later, thanks to a number of inventions. In 1876, Nicolaus Otto built the first effective gasoline motor engine in Germany, the 'Otto Cycle Engine', which was initially used in a motorbike. Nine years later, Gottlieb Daimler (who had worked with Otto on the motorbike) and Wilhelm Maybach designed, developed and patented the first prototype of the modern gasoline engine. This Maybach engine was small, efficient and light enough to allow it to be fitted to a coach chassis. Later versions of the vehicle included gears and could travel at up to 10 mph.

The first car of the sort that we might recognise was designed by another German engineer, Karl Benz, using the Otto engine in 1885. In 1893, the Benz Velo became the world's first affordable car produced in any volume. There are many other people who played important roles in the industry's early days. John Lambert built the first American gasoline-powered car in 1891; the Duryea brothers founded the first American company to manufacture and sell cars.

For the first decade of its history, the automotive industry was mainly a European affair. Its customers were the wealthy and adventurous – eccentrics, many of them. Their cars were individually built for them, on the English craft principle. A running chassis would be built, whose parts were individually hand-fitted together, so that each vehicle was mechanically distinct. Often the customer would have a coachbuilder build an individualised body on top of the chassis.

In the First Revolution Henry Ford turned the industry upside down. He introduced mass-production which transformed it and allowed it to blossom into something infinitely more than a producer of elaborate toys for the rich. The importance of Ford and of his development of mass-production is difficult to overstate. Mass-production completely changed the automobile business and a great many other industries as a consequence. It introduced working methods and a management style that have remained a feature of much of the industry to this day.

In terms of the production process, Ford's approach was revolutionary. There are two critical elements to it, although Ford actually invented neither. The first was the idea of interchangeable standard parts, which was the basis of the 'American' approach to manufacturing, pioneered for weapons production by Samuel Colt during the American Civil War. It contrasted sharply with the 'English' approach, which was based on the craft-fitting of individually produced parts. With interchangeability, the parts could be fitted to any of the vehicles being made. Spare parts for service or repair would also fit any vehicle requiring them.

The second element was the use of a continuously moving assembly line, where the vehicles were brought to the components. The line workers could then carry out the different stages of the manufacturing process one step at a time. Until then, cars had been assembled while stationary, with the workers bringing the parts to them.

By combining interchangeability and the moving assembly line, Ford made it possible to mass-produce highly complex, multifunctional objects economically. The process was first fully adopted at Ford's Highland Park facility in 1913 with the Model T. The power of the approach was undeniable. As the system was perfected, output increased from just over seven cars an hour to 146 – something that terrified competitors. It allowed Ford to increase volumes and cut costs simultaneously. This meant that prices plummeted too. The Model T cost $825 in 1908. By 1926 it cost just $290. The competitive effect was not long in coming:

by 1919 the Model T held 42 per cent of the US market. Driven by Ford, the US automotive industry leapt ahead of Europe. The huge productivity gains also made it possible for Ford to increase the hourly rate for line workers to the now famous $5 a day. This made life even more difficult for his rivals, who had to match the wage rates without the benefit of large volumes.

The key to mass-production and the element that distinguished it so fundamentally was repetitiveness. Ford changed the car from an objet d'art to an industrial product. It meant that complex products could be broken down into their components which could then be repetitively produced and repetitively assembled – *because* the parts were interchangeable. Careful adjustments, made to the component as it was fitted, became a thing of the past, taking most margins of error out of operations.

To achieve this also required a fundamental change in management style and a major change for those working on the production line. Parts production could be automated and assembly tasks subdivided, just as Adam Smith had once famously described in relation to his pin factory. This is the opening story in *The Wealth of Nations* and illustrates the value of what was termed a 'division of labour'. In Smith's factory, instead of every worker performing all the steps needed to produce a pin, each was assigned a separate task. Worker A would cut the wire, worker B would sharpen the ends, worker C would stamp the heads and worker D would solder the heads. By organising the work in this way, the factory could vastly increase its production of pins.

Ford made it possible to apply Smith's ideas to a much more complex product, to dramatic effect. But it was not just the technology that Ford changed; it was the process and the style of working. Ford's application of mass-production was as much a social transformation as an economic one. It gave rise to what was called Fordism, or Americanism. It is also sometimes referred to as the second Industrial Revolution.

Ford's approach meant that it was not only the parts that became interchangeable; the labour did too, because the skills required for each task were much less complex than before. Instead of specialised craftsmen, the factories could be filled with more simply trained fitters. The exhaust (muffler) shops were to repeat this fifty years later in the repair sector. Fordist production needed careful co-ordination to achieve a steady flow of output. Tasks had to be specified in great detail by managers. While craft-based workers exercised considerable control over their work, mass-production workers did not. According to *The Machine that Changed the World*, a book on the application of lean production in the industry, the mass-production system adopted by Ford was the ultimate application of the division of labour:

[T]he assembler . . . had only one task – to put two nuts on two bolts or perhaps to attach one wheel to each car. He didn't order parts, procure his tools, repair his equipment, inspect for quality, or even understand what workers on either side of him were doing . . . Special repairmen repaired tools. Housekeepers periodically cleaned the work area. Special inspectors checked quality, and defective work, once discovered, was rectified in a rework area after the end of the line . . . The role of the assembly worker had the lowest status in the factory. In some . . . plants, management actually told assembly workers that they were needed only because automation could not replace them yet.[2]

In the mid-1920s, one production worker described the relentless pace and intense effort that his job required, and the consequences of failing to meet that standard on a daily basis:

You've got to work like hell in Ford's. From the time you become a number in the morning until the bell rings for quitting time you have to keep at it. You can't let up. You've got to get out the production . . . and if you can't get it out, *you* get out.[3]

Ford's assembly line work was boring and repetitive. Yet it required high levels of concentration and was often physically demanding. This meant job turnover was high –

another reason to pay higher wages that were double the normal daily rate.

It meant that rivals had to emulate both Ford's pay and his methods. Automobile firms were offering a premium for putting up with what Antonio Gramsci, a Marxist thinker, described as mass-production's 'monotonous, degrading, and life draining work process'. The corollary, of course, was that the pay rates and processes adopted meant that standards of living for line workers in the US rose quickly.

Another core element in Ford's approach was the need for different power relationships in the workplace. The promise of massive increases in productivity led to the widespread imitation and adaptation of Ford's basic model of production through the industrial heart of the US economy and in other industrial capitalist countries. But it also brought about an economic, social and workplace transformation, the implications of which are still very visible today.

The model for Ford's management system was actually first perfected by the Prussian army during the nineteenth century. It included innovations such as centralised planning, control by rules, standardised operating procedures, the merit principle, functional administrative design and sequential processing. Once Ford had developed it further, another army subsequently used it a few years later. The planning and control system used by the German military under Ludendorff to mobilise the country's resources during World War I, the *Kriegwirtschaftsplan*, was almost identical to Ford's system. It was so rigid that when the Kaiser got cold feet about going to war in August 1914, the military told him that the mobilisation was irreversible. The centralised planning system, Gosplan, used in the Soviet Union was, in turn, an

---

[2] James P. Womack, Daniel T. Jones, Daniel Roos and D. Carpenter, *The Machine that Changed the World: The Story of Lean Production*, New York: HarperCollins, 1991.

[3] Mark Rupert, *Producing Hegemony: The Politics of Mass Production and American Global Power*, Cambridge: Cambridge University Press, 1995.

adaptation of the *Kriegwirtschaftsplan*. Lenin explicitly joined the two elements of Ford's system in his definition of socialism: 'socialism = Soviets + electrification' and 'socialist production combines Prussian railway administration and American industrial organization'.[4]

Ford's methods have often been described as paternalistic. Authoritarian might be a better term. An important element of Ford's approach was that there would be no unionisation, no counter-power – an idea that still seems to be deeply anchored in the hearts of many vehicle manufacturers today, despite the presence of unions. During the 1930s, however, the labour movement was gaining in power in the US and it had other ideas. At the time, Detroit remained firmly non-unionised, but the battles to make it share power have become legendary.

Inspired by European sit-down strike movements, the Reuther brothers of the United Autoworkers Union (the UAW, now the International Auto, Aerospace and Agricultural Implement Workers of America) sought to persuade the big automobile makers to allow unions into their factories.

In January 1937 they organised a sit-down strike at the GM Fisher No. 2 plant in Flint. This subsequently became known as the Battle of the Running Bulls because it deteriorated into a three-hour pitched battle with police in which the strikers were gassed and shot at and fought back with water hoses and makeshift slingshots. It led to the start of a concerted effort by the UAW to break the approach of the auto majors to labour control.

The following month the UAW staged an attack on the Flint Chevy Plant No. 4. This eventually forced GM to sign a contract with the UAW. In March that year almost 200,000 workers staged sit-down strikes before Chrysler signed, then Studebaker and Cadillac. They won an hourly minimum wage, abolition of piecework pay and, most importantly, a voice. With other businesses willing to come out in sympathy and the UAW gaining in respectability, it then decided to go after the

most difficult company of all to crack, Ford Motor Company.

Henry Ford possessed tremendous political and economic clout. His cousin was the mayor of Detroit and the chief of police was a former Ford security officer. According to Curtis Hansen at Wayne State University, 'Ford tried to nurture an image of himself as a benevolent father figure. He claimed that no union was needed at the Ford Motor Company to take care of the needs of his workers; his personal control and management of the company would best serve his employees.'[5] Union sympathy or activity meant instant dismissal.

In truth, Ford wanted complete control over his company and his workers. According to Fred Thomson at the Willamette School of Management, Ford believed that 'men work for only two reasons: one is for wages, and one is for fear of losing their jobs'. As the *Detroit News* put it,

he ruled by fear: Harry Bennett, his right hand man, hired spies and thugs (many were ex-convicts), 2,000 of them, to man his 'Service Department.' Bennett had served in the navy and was a talented boxer. He was also confrontational, ready to assert himself physically. He ran the Rouge Plant like a Central European police state. Anti-union groups were encouraged, workers were urged to spy on each other and they feared losing their jobs if they participated in any union discussions.[6]

As part of its campaign, the UAW put up posters saying 'Fordism is Fascism' and 'Unionism is Americanism'. Walter Reuther then scheduled a massive leaflet campaign at the Rouge plant for May 1937 and invited reporters, photographers and government officials to join the organisers. As soon as they

---

[4] Thomas Parke Hughes, *American Genesis: A Century of Invention and Technological Enthusiasm, 1970–1970*, New York: Viking, 1989, cited in G. Frederick Thompson, *Fordism and Postfordism*, Atkinson Graduate School of Management, Willamette University 26 August 1998, availble at: www.willamette.edu/~fthompso/MgmtCon/Fordism_%26_Postformism.html.

[5] Curtis Hansen, 'The Battle of the Overpass', Reuther Library, Wayne State University, Detroit, n.d.

[6] See www.detnews.com/history/overpass/overpass.htm.

arrived, however, the newsmen were harassed and threatened by members of the 'service department'. Reuther and others climbed two flights of iron stairs to an overpass but Ford's men punched and kicked them back down the stairs. One man was thrown 30 feet over a bridge. A union man walking two blocks away was so badly beaten that he spent months in the hospital with a broken back.

Reuther described some of the treatment he himself received:

Seven times they raised me off the concrete and slammed me down on it. They pinned my arms . . . I was punched and kicked and dragged by my feet to the stairway, thrown down the first flight of steps, picked up, slammed down on the platform and kicked down the second flight. On the ground they beat and kicked me some more.[7]

Bennett's men also attacked the reporters and photographers that had remained, ripping out notebook pages and destroying photographs. What became known as the Battle of the Overpass is one of the most famous events in American labour history. It was a turning point. Although Ford won the fight it lost the battle for public opinion, and three years later Ford eventually signed a contract with the UAW.

Curiously, and despite the frequent and very close link between Ford's methods and Frederick Taylor's Scientific Management, Taylor actually criticised the automaker. He said that Ford's approach in reducing the skills needed was flawed, and likened Ford's workers to 'trained gorillas'. Nonetheless, the similarities between Fordism and Taylor's ideas are clear. Scientific Management was also based on an extreme division of labour and on rigorous control. Taylor recommended using time-and-motion studies to monitor workers, standardised tools and implements, the use of 'slide-rules and similar time-saving devices', as well as instruction cards for workmen which detailed exactly what they should do, just like Henry Ford. Taylor called these 'the elements or details of the mechanisms of management'. He also recommended 'task alloca-

tion', i.e. breaking a task into smaller and smaller subtasks to create the optimum solution to the job needing to be done. 'Work can be done more economically by [the] subdivision of labour', he said.[8]

So mass-production and Fordism introduced an approach to management and a style of business that was revolutionary. With Ford the largest company in the industry and his methods so successful, economically at least, other companies were forced to mimic his style. Components suppliers and competitors also adopted a system of rigorous top-down management and strict labour control. Ford's practices became the roots of subsequent management development in the industry. And, a little like the thinking that became so pervasive in the Soviet Union during seventy years of communist control, they have proved difficult to shake off. This is partly because they were so effective on many levels. But it is mainly because they have become part of the culture: part of the heart (or heartlessness) that is at the centre of much of the industry's personality. The command-economy mentality is still recognisable in much of the behaviour of the industry.

A final aspect of Ford's approach was his strong urge to develop a vertically integrated business, including building the Rouge steel mill and having his own iron mines to feed it, plus glass production and many other items. Again, this is reminiscent of the integrated industrial Kombinat that characterised the communist economic system.

The Second Revolution in the history of the industry, which is equally important to our story, was the result of another legend in the business, Alfred P. Sloan. Sloan discovered that the combination of suppliers and several vehicle manufacturers into a conglomerate, General Motors, brought economies of scale of a different kind. The creation of GM produced

---

[7] Ibid.

[8] Frederick W. Taylor, *The Principles of Scientific Management*, New York: Harper Bros., 1911.

an integrated supplier network that could maximise revenues, as well as a car manufacturer that could further control the sequence of operations and the companies that supplied it.

GM's innovations in marketing and organisation allowed each major operating division to serve a distinct product market. When Sloan took over GM in the early 1920s, it was little more than a loose confederation of car and car-parts companies. Sloan reorganised the car companies to create a five-model product range from Chevrolet to Cadillac. He also established a radically decentralised administrative control structure, although with many of the elements developed by Ford.

General Motors had been struggling to overcome the stranglehold Ford had on the market. Instead of engaging in an outright price war, which GM would lose, Sloan designed a different approach to mass-production and consumption. He persuaded GM to offer cars that were more individually distinctive and that lacked the stigmatising signs of mass-production. GM's cars were not just a means of physical transportation; they became symbols of social status, personal prestige, sexual power or financial clout. They were the beginnings of auto industry 'brands', each with their own personality. The company also created a hierarchy of different makes to encourage consumers to upgrade as they progressed through their car-owning lives: utilitarian cars for the poor, luxury cars for the rich. GM's cars had 'planned obsolescence' too, in that older models would decline in value with the introduction of newer ones. Moreover, Sloan was successfully able to mass-produce cars but still make them look custom-built.

As well as creating five car divisions, GM had component divisions such as Delco-Remy. Each division used Ford's organisation model and a small corporate headquarters managed the entire business, using the Du Pont system of financial controls, developed by Sloan's predecessor, Pierre du Pont. Each division kept its own books, with its managers given specific return-on-assets targets. If they failed to meet those targets, the managers were changed, while those that met the targets were promoted. Again, the system rested on the presumption that activities should be simplified and controlled from above, with engineering and administrative functions delegated to staff specialists. Only those at the top were able to exercise any real judgement.

GM's revolutionary ability to reconcile diversity and effective scale made Ford's standardised product largely obsolete. It also undermined Ford's policy of vertical integration through a more effective division of responsibilities between specialist enterprises. Again the results were not long in coming: in less than two years, Ford's share of the market had dwindled from close to 50 per cent to just 15 per cent.

But Sloan's approach was much less dirigiste than Ford's. He advocated shared knowledge and flexible planning. Importantly, he tried to balance overall corporate control with divisional autonomy. Yet he was anti-union too, and was eventually forced to step down as a result of battles with the UAW.

The Third Revolution in the history of the motor industry that is important to our story was the introduction of lean production. This stands in stark contrast to the style and approach needed for mass-production and has played a major part in the direction of the industry ever since. Unlike the previous two developments that were the result of American innovation, this was the result of pioneering work by a Japanese firm, Toyota.

It was actually IBM that first introduced the ideas of lean manufacturing, just-in-time delivery and 'total quality management' twenty years before Eiji Toyoda and Taiichi Ohno implemented the Toyota production system. But it was Toyota that used it to best advantage and routed its Western competitors in the process. (It could perhaps be argued that Henry J. Kaiser initiated lean manufacturing, in his shipyards that could build a Liberty Ship in three weeks. There were also elements of it in the massive acceleration of armaments production in all the major combatant countries in World War II – including Japan.)

In conventional mass-production, each stage in the process – and there are many stages in producing an automobile – functions at its own best pace. As cycle times differ considerably, for example between producing some parts on highly automated machinery and assembling them into subassemblies by hand, the faster processes are run in 'campaigns', piling up inventories of finished products, which the next stage draws on as needed. This minimises production costs at each stage. But it has serious negative consequences too. Flexibility is inhibited: if the downstream stage is required to do something different – perhaps because of a change in market demand, or an unexpected shortage of another component – the upstream inventory of parts is now wrong. Similarly, if a defect occurs, it may not be picked up until a great pile of parts has been made. Assembly-line workers force-fitting mismatched parts with a hammer is part of the legend of traditional automobile production. Moreover, when the overall costs of the total production system are added up, they do not look good. Unfortunately, standard costing systems, which are estimates based on normal, i.e. semi-idealised, operating conditions, typically do not show this.

In contrast, one key aspect at the heart of the lean production system, and one of the elements that distinguish it so fundamentally from mass production, is the precept that each stage of the manufacturing and assembly process *pulls* intermediate products from the previous stage. If the previous stage has a faster cycle time and/or requires time to switch from one product specification to another, the effort is put into loosening that constraint. A classic example was the press shop, which uses lines of mighty hydraulic presses equipped with massive pairs of steel dies to shape steel body panels, which are then welded together to form the unpainted structure of the car. Traditionally, it could take up to 36 hours to change dies on a

press line and get them adjusted so that they produced the complex shapes without errors or tears. Visitors from Western manufacturers were amazed to find Japanese press shops changing dies in 15 minutes, with operators guided by whistleblasts from the foremen, almost like a military assault team, operating in perfect synchronisation. Returning home, one group discovered that a key blocking factor in a major Western press shop was that a forklift truck was needed to lift the dies, that the shop did not have its own and that it had to be reserved for borrowing from the maintenance department 36 hours in advance. For want of a forklift truck . . . but the fundamental answer was, do not be awed by the constraints; overcome them.

The elimination of intermediate inventories initally developed by Toyota, whether within a plant or (and this is equally crucial) between plants, for example from supplier to manufacturer, through the just-in-time or *kanban* system, led to the elimination of waste or *muda*, i.e. activities which do not add real value to the overall process.

The other important element is that of personal responsibility. In mass-production, the process operator was made to operate equipment or perform assembly tasks, with his movements reduced to minute sub-units of the whole process. Most importantly, the operator needed to have no deeper knowledge of what was going on. He or she could have almost no influence upon it. Productivity was prescribed by the machine cycle, the industrial engineer or the time-and-motion analyst. The phrase 'wage slave' was apposite. Lean production turns that on its head. It does not seek to gain a competitive edge by treating workers like machines. Instead, it works on the principle that it is actually the operator who adds the value, who is best positioned to improve the process and who can ensure it is done perfectly. Lean production requires a very different approach and a different way of thinking – a different way of behaving even. It requires more numerate and literate workers, capable of a higher degree of self-direction. The Japanese words *kaizen,* meaning 'continuous improvement', i.e. self-improvement, and *poka yoka,* which means the use of simple control devices that help the operator to keep his or her process within its normal range of operating parameters, have become part of everyday manufacturing vocabulary. All this and the tremendous gaps in productivity and quality that opened up between Japanese and Western vehicle manufacturers as a result are eloquently documented in the best-selling book, *The Machine that Changed the World,* based on extensive academic research, piloted by the Massachusetts Institute of Technology.[9] This book was very influential, although the title is a misnomer, implying a wider discussion of the socio-economic role of the automobile. A more accurate title might have been *The Production Approach that Changed Vehicle Manufacturing.*

Lean production involves a fundamental change in emphasis, then: in the way people work but also in the way they think and act. Shop floor jobs become more challenging but they are also more demanding, requiring more initiative. Lean production often means that product designs need some adaptation for the process to work well. Most fundamentally, though, it requires the whole industry to function on a new structural and operating basis. Fordism worked on unified, central and detailed control of everything. Sloan broke this down into divisional entities, which were still internally complex and multifunctional. Lean production works through the constitution of natural process entities, capable of self-management and linked by harmonious working relationships. A partial political analogy for these three stages might be, first, the unitary Europe attempted by the Roman Empire, Napoleon and Hitler; second, a Europe of nation states; and, third, the desire of a certain number of Europeans today to structure it as a set of regions. We shall return to this concept of networking between internally homogeneous and semi-autonomous entities when we look at the need for a Fourth Revolution in the industry at the end.

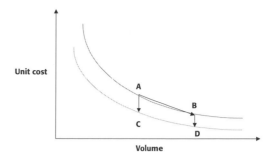

*Source: auto*POLIS

Fig. 4.7 How the Japanese used leanness to defeat a scale disadvantage

The pioneering work by the Japanese in this area brought them considerable competitive advantage. In effect, they were able to leapfrog over the scale advantage of the established Western manufacturers, as shown in figure 4.7. Starting at point A, they could not hope to catch up with larger competitors at point B, on the upper scale curve for conventional manufacturing. Instead, they used the indirect approach and dropped down onto the lower scale curve for lean manufacturing at point C. From there they could accelerate to D before their competitors woke up to what was going on.

The result of this was the third huge competitive upheaval. Its introduction by Toyota led to a bifurcation of the industry which is still reflected in business attitudes today, in approaches to market, responses to legislators, the treatment of retailers and, most critically, in financial success. As a rule of thumb, those firms that have genuinely embraced lean production and a co-operative approach to business have prospered, while those that have done it in a mechanistic way have not. There are exceptions, but as a whole lean production has proved a better model – but only when it has been applied properly. Some observers view it as an incomplete revolution, as we do: 'The essence of lean production has been to seek compliance from the supply base and the

[9] Womack et al., *The Machine that Changed the World.*

vehicle distribution network to the demands of the vehicle manufacturing process – not to optimise the system as a whole.'[10] This certainly seems to have been true in its application by Western manufacturers. Leopards with blue oval spots do not change them that easily.

The trouble comes in making it work. Transferring a very deep know-how, accumulated over a long period of time, was never going to be easy. This is at the root of why its development is so important to our story. Time will tell, perhaps, but it seems possible to us that lean production is not actually the best model for many Western firms to consider. Culturally, when applied properly, it appears to be at odds with so many of the social mores in the US and Europe, where the needs of the individual are often regarded more highly than the needs of a group. Teamwork is fine in many of these countries, but individual destiny often comes first. The counterweight to individualism is forceful central authority.

So while GM, Ford and many others in the industry can claim that they have adopted or adapted the Toyota manufacturing system for their own use – and they can claim this perfectly fairly – they have often not fully grasped the thinking which goes behind it. For Toyota, throughout the value chain, there is a co-operative approach. Doing business with Toyota is always tough, suppliers say, but it is based on maximising mutual interests. If you get into trouble, Toyota will come and help you out.

With American and European firms it is different. They often talk of co-operation with their suppliers, with governments and with their distributors and dealers. Too often, however, the Bennett boxing-glove mentality returns, especially when times get hard or margins are thin. Sometimes it is simply down to organisation. Those running the engineering and product development functions of the Western carmakers are often happy to take a collaborative approach with their suppliers. When the time comes to place the order, however, it is often the purchasing department or the finance function that takes control. 'This collaboration is all very well', they will say, 'but this is a tough market and keeping cost down is critical. Cut your prices by 10 per cent or we go elsewhere.' The collaborative trust is shattered.

Box 4.1

Pay up and then we'll give you some business (Not the mob, the motor industry in 2003)

The following is an article from *Automotive News Europe*.[11]

Visteon (one of the world's largest auto components manufacturers and once part of Ford) is demanding large cash payments from US sub-suppliers who want new contracts.

The 'pay to play' demand is part of Visteon's plan to cut its US supplier roster from 1,800 to 500 within five years. Visteon promises to give more business to the survivors.

In documents circulating among US suppliers, Visteon said it would choose only two or three companies per business segment. Current and future business will go only to the selected companies.

To injection-moulding suppliers, Visteon's demands look like this: The company wants big price cuts for new contracts, at least 6 percent annually for five years. Visteon wants an up-front cheque for the first-year's reduction and portions of future years' reductions. The total prepayment will be a least 10 percent of the first year's contract.

So if an injection moulder agrees to supply $25 million worth of parts annually, Visteon wants a $2.5 million payment [up front]. Similar demands are being made for other parts, suppliers report.

'We are going to consolidate our supply base, and we want to make sure we're all on the same page,' said Visteon spokeswoman Liane Smyth-Bilicki.

Note: Visteon eventually shelved this plan.

---

[10] P. Wells and P. Nieuwenhuis, 'Why Big Business Should Think Small', *Automotive World*, July/August 2000.

[11] '"Pay to Play", Visteon Tells Subsuppliers', *Automotive News Europe*, 10 March 2003.

Thus lean thinking has not been applied evenly throughout the industry, with the result that many of the old control attitudes remain, especially in the US and Europe. Lean manufacturing works best when there is a desire to achieve mutually best results. Unfortunately many of the relationships in these Western countries (indeed Western societies) remain adversarial – they are about one side gaining at the expense of another, about costs being squeezed out of suppliers regardless of the impact on them, or about legislators being opposed, almost on principle.

This mindset has restricted the value of lean manufacturing to the industry and its rate of application. Too often those who have implemented the process have talked of systemic thinking but have actually retained traditional vertical hierarchies and control relationships.

Despite many decades of change, the Fordist emphasis on control remains a strong feature throughout much of the industry. Although vehicle manufacturers contract large proportions of the chain to suppliers and dealers, their determination to control – in detail – remains strong.

Much of the industry is still male-dominated, domineering in its relationships, presuming to know 'what's good for America', oligopolistic and often introverted. As a friend who is the managing director of a large parts maker in North America, told us, 'success in Detroit is determined by how hard you punch someone else' – a brutal macho culture still.

After several discussions, we came to the conclusion that Toyota's real lifeblood is the quality of its relationships. As part of our research into this we met Richard Chitty, a senior vice-president of Toyota, who was based in the Asian regional headquarters in Singapore in 2003. An American and a thirty-one-year Toyota veteran, he was the man who helped put Lexus on the map when it was first launched in the US.

What, we wanted to know, made Toyota different?

Dick explained that there was a 'Toyota way', which is the 'DNA of the company', he said. 'There are two pillars to it', he went on. 'The first is respect for people. The second is *kaizen* or continuous improvement.'

We sat with bated breath, keen to learn more.

But that was it. That was the answer. We probed harder. Surely the secret of Toyota's success had to be down to something more than this – something that sounded suspiciously like 1980s-style socio-babble?

Richard explained further, and with some patience this time. He said that the reason that Toyota's parts suppliers and dealers were so trusted and the relationships with them were so strong was because they, in effect, became part of Toyota when they were selected. They represented Toyota. That meant that there had to be mutual respect. Toyota looks on these relationships in a fundamentally different way from others in the industry – or indeed many other industries. It is not just a commercial relationship and it is certainly not an exploitative one: 'We know these businesses have to make a profit, so we see ourselves as partners to make them successful too.'

Toyota would never, he said, go to a supplier and simply demand a price reduction. *kaizen* does not mean cost reduction; it means improvement. It is about finding a better way to build something, to design something, to use something. If we can save money by doing that, good. But it is not about cost reduction. We might go to a supplier and ask them to think about how to take cost out or try and work with them to do that. But we would never simply demand a cost reduction.

We explored further. Toyota would not change its suppliers readily either. It would not sell a supplier it already owned. It would not announce a decision, to build a plant say, and then change its mind. That would be poor planning. It would not think about outsourcing something (that is not improvement). It would not make a commitment and then break it.

'The strength of the manufacturer is down to the strength of the dealer network', said Richard. And Toyota does not own the dealer network. So it has to be about respect.

We were beginning to understand.

Richard talked about how the company is regarded; about how it was the *application* of these two central pillars of its philosophy that made the difference; that it was the belief in these that was important. That it was about humility even. He said, 'Thinking that way becomes natural.'

All very Asian and foreign then? Not at all. When Toyota launched Lexus in the US one of Richard Chitty's jobs was selecting the dealer network in America. Of those dealers selected, 40 per cent had no previous relationship with Toyota. Yet they were willing to invest between $3.5 and $5 million each in facilities as well as working capital to sell a product they had not even seen a picture of. 'They had faith in Toyota', he says.

Toyota will happily let you or any of its rivals into its factories. You can see the Toyota production system in operation and, if you want to, you can copy it. But as it is subjected to *kaizen*, continuous improvement, what you copy will always be behind what is being used. And it is far more difficult to copy the mentality that goes with it.

This raises the following question: have all those attempts by rivals to copy this lean manufacturing system been in vain? Our conversation reminded us of another tale, this time from Richard Best, managing director of GKN in North America. GKN, a British company which is one of the world's largest manufacturers of driveshafts and constant velocity joints, is a supplier to Toyota. One day, Fujio Cho, now president of Toyota in Japan but then head of Toyota in North America, announced that he wanted to visit the GKN plant in Alamance, North Carolina, as part of his trip to the US. He asked to be shown around the factory. During the visit he stopped at one of the production cells. He asked Mr Best and his colleagues to leave him, if they would not mind, so that he could spend some time understanding what was being done there.

When he returned to the office an hour later, Cho took off his jacket, rolled up his sleeves and picked up a pen. On a whiteboard on the wall he proceeded to explain how he saw the work going on in the production cell and then suggested ways that it would be improved, to the immense delight of Richard Best. This is not something the president of most other car companies would take the time to do, or even be able to do.

As Mr Chitty kept talking, the real value of the Toyota system began to dawn on us. He had been right when we began the discussion. Toyota's secret *was* based, very simply, on those two pillars – respect for others and *kaizen*, continuous improvement. It was exactly what everyone already knew – what they tried to replicate. The difference, though – the thing that made it so powerful – was that unlike almost any other company in the industry, in the world perhaps, Toyota really *believed* in it.

As a global economic phenomenon, the automotive industry made a leap ahead of the times with mass-production. In our view, much of it may still be running behind in terms of lean production – or barking up the wrong tree entirely.

Lean production has opened a schism in the industry. Those companies that have embraced it fully tend to have prospered and become strong. Those that have tried to apply it retrospectively, gluing it over the top of a previously top-down control model, have not. This gives a clue to the future of the industry and it is something we will come back to at the end. Unless there is change, we think, companies have to adopt the lean production model properly to prosper, even to survive. Or they need to find a different model. We will look at both alternatives in the last two sections.

One final point. It may seem at times that we have a bias: that we appear to favour Toyota and some other Japanese firms too readily; that we criticise some of the other Japanese firms as well as many of the Americans and Europeans a little too quickly.

Yet we genuinely think that Toyota and a few other firms are rare companies in this industry – certainly the way it is structured today. Toyota, in particular, is a slow and ponderous company and, outside Japan, it lacks the sort of dynamic leadership, the personality-led style with which we are more familiar. Yet, by almost any measure, Toyota stands head and shoulders above its rivals in this business. It makes more money, it has improved its market share in more markets, it has some of the most efficient plants in the industry and it consistently produces the best-quality vehicles. Moreover, and almost uniquely, its suppliers like working with it, as do its dealers. Ask almost any supplier who once worked for the big American or European firms and who now works for Toyota and they will tell you, 'It's tough, but I wouldn't go back.'

Toyota is not perfect. Its cars are often dull, it has not performed anything like as well as it should have done in Europe, and its top managers lack a broad knowledge of international cultures. Similarly, Ford, GM and others are not entirely staffed by knuckle-heads unable to see any other way to do business than banging their fists on the table. But Toyota really *is* different. It clearly has a different approach to business and a very different culture, even compared with many other Japanese firms.

It does not seem to be a culture that is easy to emulate, however, although many have tried, often encouraged by academics who make it seem easy to replicate the physical aspects of lean thinking, but not the soul. As Richard Chitty says, 'Toyota is a people business.' The difference between Richard and others saying this apparent platitude is clear. In Toyota's case they really mean it.

Corporate cultures do not change quickly or easily in huge and complex organisations. Like national cultures they can take decades to change. They can be a *constraint* on change. Yet, as we have said, there is a need to change in this industry. The growth has gone and there are new pressures which suggest a different approach is needed.

The industry has already gone through three very different and distinct revolutions. Each brought substantial gains to the instigators, wrong-footing their rivals. Each changed the economics of the business. Determining which companies will win in the future is greatly to do with their position today, management attitudes, their hunger for change and their flexibility. It is also, self-evidently, to do with their ability to challenge conventional thinking.

In the next section we will look at the competitive outlook for the industry today and the prospects for the main companies. We will look at which is likely to gain in the global industry model we discussed in the last section, and which is likely to be able to access the growth that there is. The results are not as many would like.

The vehicle manufacturers as global enterprises – a false impression

The world's vehicle industry is currently dominated by little more than a handful of firms, each wielding colossal financial, emotional and political power. They are, or have been, the puppet-masters of the business for more than a decade. They clearly believe that they will continue to play this role in the future. They are obsessed with globalisation, in the belief that salvation lies in global scale. Very few have achieved it. Very few will, as the Eldorado of global scale looks more and more like a mirage.

Moreover, one of the most important trends in the industry over the last hundred years looks like ending. In the early years of the industry there were hundreds of different car-makers around the world. Over time their number has steadily dwindled. There has been a consolidation which has meant that there have been progressively fewer firms pulling the industry's strings.

Going forward, that dynamic looks likely to change. Although the industry is controlled by a handful of big firms today, it looks likely that it will be controlled by ten or more lesser ones a decade from now. Some of the big boys will be smaller big boys tomorrow, we think. Some of the big groups face fragmentation, while some new entrants will emerge. This is important for a number of reasons, although probably not scale intensity. It is important because it reverses a trend that the biggest firms have become used to. They have become used to the power and influence that goes with being a major global firm with a turnover bigger than many countries. This is partly why they often behave as they do. In the future, though, they will not have quite as much power. They will not have the same control. Instead of engines of economic development, controlling the technology, managing the value chain, telling dealers how to sell, they are going to be gradually emasculated. Few will grow as much as the economies in which they operate. Most will have to downsize. All will have their power to manage the downstream end of the business curtailed, especially in Europe. They are going to have their wings clipped, and it will change a lot of the attitudes and bravado of the past into something a little more contrite in the future. Expect a great deal of noise, as well as tantrums and filibuster, during the process of transformation, however.

The first important wave of competitive consolidation in the industry got underway forty years ago as the many tens of competitors remaining (there were once 270) coalesced into a few national champions. Then the Japanese started to invade the US and Europe and there was another round of acquisitions and withdrawals. By the early 1990s most of the companies that dominate the industry today had established powerful positions. Volkswagen came to dominate Germany and eventually Europe; Renault and PSA led France and were among the top six in Europe too; Fiat led Italy; Toyota, Nissan, Honda and Mitsubishi were the clear leaders in Japan; and

GM, Ford and Chrysler accounted for the bulk of sales in the US. Ford and GM had established strong positions in Europe too.

Globally, GM (including Saab) and Ford (including Mazda and Jaguar) were top, with Volkswagen (which included Audi, SEAT and Skoda) and Toyota further behind, followed by a host of middle-sized firms including Fiat, Nissan, PSA, Honda, Renault and Mitsubishi. After these firms came the upline specialists like Mercedes-Benz and BMW, as well as companies like Suzuki, Subaru, Volvo, AvtoVaz (Lada) in Russia and Maruti in India. Smaller still were niche specialists like Ferrari, Porsche and Rolls Royce, making a few thousands or tens of thousands of cars a year.

Towards the end of the 1990s, after rather too many years of people like us predicting it imminently, came another wave of consolidation. This was driven partly by merger mania (M&A was all the rage at the end of the dot.com bubble) and partly by genuine opportunity. It is the implications of this consolidation that are important, however, because they created a stasis from which the industry can only disintegrate.

Within a few years Chrysler had been bought by Daimler which then aligned itself with Mitsubishi. Ford acquired Volvo Car Corporation (Volvo Trucks remained independent) and Land Rover. Nissan was subsumed (but nicely this time) into Renault. Suddenly, six companies accounted for more than 75 per cent of global production and the top ten were responsible for almost 90 per cent of all the cars and trucks produced and sold. One of the world's biggest industrial sectors was, ultimately, in the hands of just a few people. This consolidation is sometimes difficult to visualise because figures are often still reported as they used to be and articles are usually written about the brands or vehicles themselves, not the companies that ultimately control them. Ford is usually talked about separately from Mazda, Volvo and Land Rover, for example, even though they are all under the same umbrella. Similarly, Renault is discussed separately from

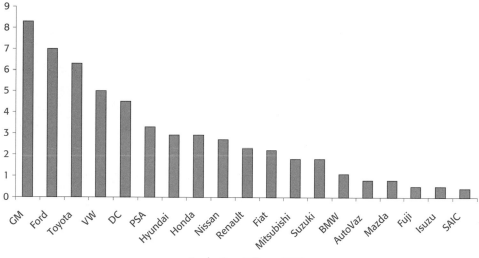

Source: vehicle manufacturers, *Automotive News, Global Market Data Book*

Fig. 4.8 Unconsolidated production by
manufacturer in millions, 2002

Nissan. As Rolf Eckrodt pointed out to us
when he was president of Mitsubishi Motors in
Japan, 'This is because consumers buy brands
not alliances.' The unconsolidated picture is
shown in figure 4.8.

Equity links between the world's light vehicle manufacturers are shown in figure 4.9.
They are numerous and complex. But most
have been built up as part of drives to secure
global presence. This means that the consolidated picture is very different. The top six
groups have extensive holdings:

• GM, whose main brands are Buick, Cadillac, Chevrolet, GMC, GM, Oldsmobile, Pontiac, Saturn, Holden, Hummer, Opel, Vauxhall and Saab, is linked to or owns part
of Suzuki (and through this, its subsidiary
Maruti), Daewoo, Subaru, Isuzu (although it
has reduced its stake) and Fiat (although
it has an option to acquire the business,
it wants to get out of it). Fiat owns Alfa
Romeo, Ferrari, Iveco (heavy trucks), Lancia
and Maserati.
• Ford, whose main brands include Ford,
Lincoln and Mercury, owns a controlling

stake in Mazda, Aston Martin, Volvo, Jaguar
and Land Rover.
• DaimlerChrysler owns Merecedes-Benz (both
cars, light commercials and heavy trucks),
Chrysler, Plymouth, Jeep, Smart, Freight-
liner (heavy trucks), Setra (buses), Sterling,
Thomas Built Buses and Western Star. It
had a minority stake in Mitsubishi, as
well as Hyundai (which owns Kia). Proton
(which owns Lotus – not shown) is partially
technology-dependent on Mitsubishi.
• Toyota owns Daihatsu, Lexus and Hino.
• Renault-Nissan controls Renault, Nissan,
Alpine, Infiniti, Samsung, Dacia and Nissan Diesel, Volvo Trucks having acquired
Renault Véhicules Industriels (heavy trucks
and buses).
• Volkswagen controls VW, Audi, SEAT, Skoda,
Bentley, Bugatti and Lamborghini.

The effect of this consolidation, logically
enough, has been to increase the concentration among vehicle manufacturers. The ranking of the leading groups, based on consolidated production volumes, is shown in

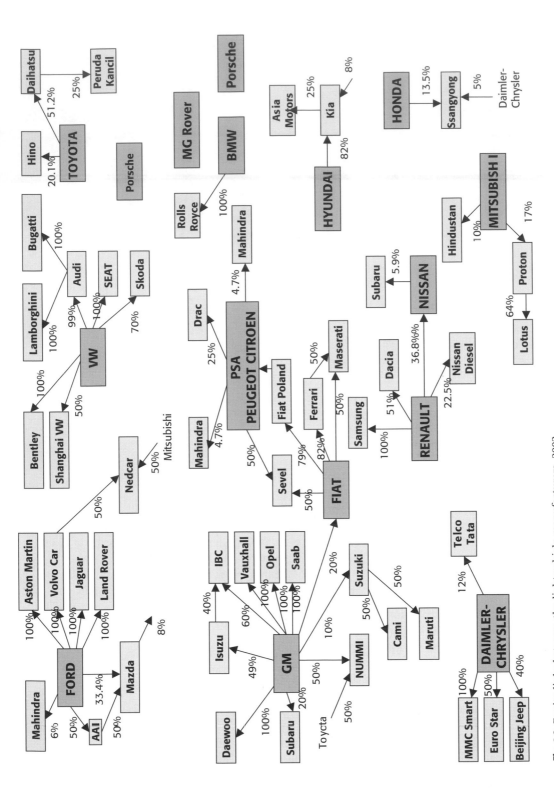

Fig. 4.9 Equity links between the light vehicle manufacturers, 2003

Source: The Automotive Industry, A Guide, Centre for Automotive Industry Research and British Telecom plc, 2001, updated

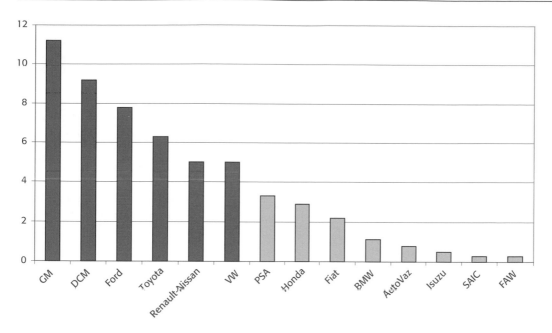

Source: vehicle manufacturers, *Automotive News*
Note: DCM includes Mitsubishi, Hyundai and Proton.
GM includes Suzuki, Maruti, Fuji-Subaru and Daewoo.

Fig. 4.10 Consolidated production by manufacturer
in millions, 2002

figure 4.10. In 2002, the top six groups accounted for 77 per cent of the industry's output. After the top six firms, the next tier is much smaller. Next come PSA (Peugeot-Citroën) and Hyundai (partly owned by Daimler-Chrysler), then Honda and Fiat – which is also partly linked to GM but in something close to terminal decline.

After the top ten comes Mitsubishi, at the time part of DaimlerChrysler too. Then there is Suzuki which is also partly under the wing of GM. Suzuki owns Maruti, the largest carmaker in India. Then comes BMW and Auto-Vaz in Russia, and then Fuji-Subaru, also part of GM, and then bankrupt Isuzu, which was once closely linked to GM but is now, thanks to its financial troubles, much less closely linked. Then there is SAIC, Shanghai Auto Industry Corporation, and First Auto Works (FAW), both in China. These are two of the largest auto companies in China which have the potential to become global majors one

day. Others in the same category include Dong Feng, once known as Second Auto Works, and Tianjin Auto Works, an affiliate of Toyota and a subsidiary of First Auto Works. After FAW in our global league table comes South Korea's Daewoo (now part of GM too) and then Maruti in India, the Suzuki subsidiary. Finally comes Iran Khodro which is based just outside Tehran, the Ukraine's AvtoGaz, Malaysia's Proton, India's Tata Engineering and Britain's MG Rover – all of which are around the same size and in various states of health. Finally, there is a long tail of smaller companies including Dong Feng in China, Ashok Leyland and Mahindra & Mahindra, both in India, Porsche, Scania Trucks and tens of little companies in China.

There is a huge difference between the largest and the smallest vehicle manufacturers. While the largest company, GM, built and sold 8.3 million cars and trucks in 2002, the smallest shipped less than 100.

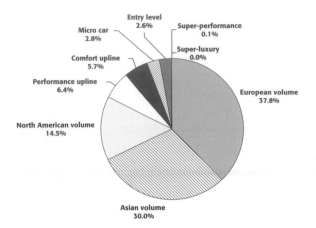

Fig. 4.11 Passenger cars, product segmentation, 34.9 million units

The trouble with this consolidated view, however, is that it is in many ways deceptive. As we argued in chapter 1, there is no global light vehicle market, and there are few global light vehicles outside specialised niches. The rest of this section explores the real positioning of the manufacturers, which requires a more disaggregated view of the global light vehicle industry, broken down into product and market segments. This is the classical stuff of strategic business analysis, all too rarely practised in this industry.

Figure 4.11 segments the 35 million passenger cars sold per year worldwide into broad product segments. We distinguish the following classes, conveniently identified with well-known names, with one segmentation variable being size (North American volume cars, for example, being typically rather larger than European or Asian ones) and the other being price per unit of weight, with mass-produced cars cheaper than smaller-volume, more exotic ones:

- There is a tiny super-luxury segment, in which cars are worth $250,000 or more each. Typical names are Rolls Royce, Bentley and Maybach. They are large comfortable cars, silent, smooth and superbly finished and equipped. They sell to a limited but faithful

following of the very rich, in very limited numbers – less than 10,000 per year in all. The segment is truly global, in that owners range from British aristocrats to American film stars to African tyrants. The segment is very small but survives world recessions surprisingly well, as most of the clientèle are fairly well insulated from economic cycles by massive personal wealth.

- The super-performance segment is significantly different, with some 75,000 cars per year, also sold worldwide in essentially the same specifications, mainly to wealthy enthusiasts. Porsche is far the biggest producer, with Aston Martin, Ferrari, Lamborghini and Bugatti as smaller-volume examples. Prices range from $75,000 upwards. The economics of these first two segments are virtually those of craft production, or at least low-volume production.

- Next, in increasing order of size, comes the entry-car segment, which is utterly different from the preceding two in its economics, with cars priced down to $3–4,000. These are semi-utilitarian products, the successors to the Renault 4 and Citroën 2CV, mostly intended for the motorisation of the developing world but present in Europe and other places too. The low volume so far, 900,000 units, is because not many products are yet on offer. This is a segment with growth prospects, mainly – although not exclusively – in the developing world, where even lower-priced cars are in the pipeline.

- We then have the micro-car segment with 1 million units per year, mainly in Asia, including developed countries, notably Japan, because of urban crowding. The leading brands there are Suzuki and Daihatsu, plus Hyundai and Daewoo in Korea. Micro-cars and entry-level vehicles are largely peculiar to Asia, but there are also European cars of a similar size, such as the Fiat Seicento.

- Next, and substantially up in size at 2 million units, is what we call the comfort upline segment, typified and led by Mercedes-Benz. These are the cars that featured in the European large-car sector of figure 1.13. They are not functionally different from other cars of a similar size or from smaller volume cars. Only the depth and quality of engineering, the overall fit and finish, give them a significantly different 'feel' of comfort and security. Unlike those in the next segment, they are not designed for sporty handling. They have strong brands, based on their engineering quality and reputation, and are able to secure a substantial price premium over run-of-the-mill volume cars. Other well-know brands in this segment are Lexus, Cadillac and Lincoln – although it is a moot point whether Cadillac and Lincoln differ sufficiently in quality from GM and Ford volume cars to justify inclusion. Mercedes-Benz clearly occupies a global market segment, with significant sales in the US and Japan. Apart from the M-Class SUV, built in the United States, Mercedes-Benz cars are still built in Germany and shipped worldwide.

- At 2.2 million units, the performance upline segment sits in parallel to the comfort upline segment on the price per kilo scale. BMW, Audi, Jaguar, Saab and Alfa Romeo are brands that stand out in this segment. It is a worldwide segment, with BMW selling strongly in the US and having a leading position among European brands in Japan.

We then enter the volume car market, 29 million units strong, i.e. almost 85 per cent of the world's car market. As we said on page 17, this is not a 'global market' or business in the sense that there is much standardisation. There remain very distinct product differences between continents:

- The first segment within this is the 8–9 million annual units of North American volume cars, 60 per cent of which are built on distinctive North American platforms belonging to GM, Ford and Chrysler – the Detroit Big Three. Notice, though, that this segment is considerably smaller than the next two. This is because half the light vehicle market in the US has been taken over by light trucks, as we showed on page 15. These man-

ufacturers, in their North American manifestation, are therefore small players on the world scale, with less than 15 per cent of world volume car production. The other 40 per cent of this segment has been captured by foreign cars, mainly Japanese, on world platforms. If one word can characterise what Americans look for in these cars, it is 'comfort', consistent with much driving on mainly uneventful roads.

- Asian volume cars are produced at the rate of 10.5 million per year. They are mainly, although not exclusively, Japanese, led by Toyota, Honda and Nissan, with the growing presence of Hyundai. The key market appeal here tends to be 'features': gizmos and electronics which are valued in a dense urban environment.

- Far the largest segment is European volume cars, at over 13 million per year. The leading brands are VW, Peugeot-Citroën, Renault, GM Europe, Ford Europe and Fiat. One of the distinguishing factors in this segment is 'handling', reflecting European driving styles.

This segmentation, which is not the way the industry normally looks at itself, is important, as it largely determines how competition actually takes place. The market positions and shares of individual manufacturers reflect this heritage and this structure. The world market for cars (not light trucks or light commercial vehicles) is shown in figure 4.12. It is worth dwelling on for a little while, as it says so much about the competitive dynamics of the industry and about how they are constrained.

The North American car market (the left-hand bar in the diagram) is actually relatively small. It is only 60 per cent of the European market and barely bigger, even today, than the Asian market. Within North America, the volume car market is led by fairly distinct North American products (the light grey part of the column), offered by the Big Three domestic manufacturers.

Brand market shares within the North American volume car sector are shown in

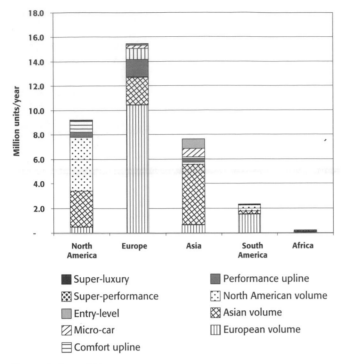

Source: As figure 4.11

Fig. 4.12 World product/market segmentation

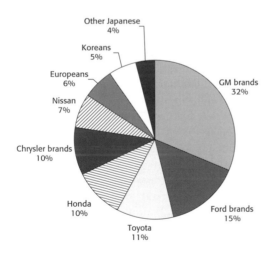

Source: As figure 4.11

Fig. 4.13 Brand shares in the 7.8 million unit North American volume car sector

figure 4.13. The impact of the Japanese is striking. GM still holds a quarter of the market, while Ford and Chrysler were down to 16 per cent and 10 per cent respectively in 2002. While the Big Three have 51 per cent, the Japanese in combination have reached 35 per cent – a share which was still climbing in 2003. This is the direct consequence of the combined impact of the Third Automotive Revolution, pioneered by Japan, the windfall gift to its manufacturers of US car downsizing in the 1980s, and the diversion of US manufacturers' efforts into light trucks. The two Japanese leaders – Toyota and Honda – have overtaken the no. 3 native manufacturer and are pushing close on no. 2. The European manufacturers hold only 9 per cent of the market, with more than half of it in the hands of the VW group. The South Koreans led by Hyundai are almost as significant, mostly satisfying the segment that demands lower-cost smaller cars. This picture is very different from a decade ago and reflects a major change. Apart from GM, the domestic American manufacturers are in the process of being squeezed out by the Japanese.

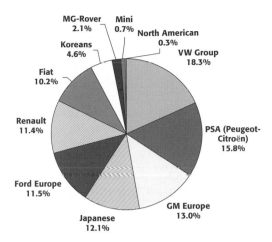

Source: As figure 4.11

Fig. 4.14 Manufacturers' shares in West European volume cars, 11.2 million units

The European volume car market is dominated by European players, as shown in figure 4.14. The VW group, with its three volume brands – Volkswagen, Skoda and SEAT – and its upline brand, Audi, which are built on common platforms, using common engines and gearboxes, is in the lead, followed by PSA, following a similar strategy with its two brands, Peugeot and Citroën. GM Europe is in third place with its lead brand Opel; its Vauxhall sub-brand uses the same vehicles, rebadged for the UK market. The Japanese are collectively at 12 per cent, led by Toyota, which is starting to grow strongly in Europe. They have been limited in their penetration by offering products too often taken off the US shelf, which are seen as too insipid to European tastes.

Ford Europe has got itself into trouble and lost market share, particularly in the critical German market, the largest in Europe. Much of this is attributable to two enormous product planning blunders: the failure to appreciate the growing role of diesel engines in Europe and therefore to provide second-generation high-pressure direct-injection units in time; and a very belated recognition of and entry into the new mini-MPV segment pioneered by Renault with its Scenic. Renault, which has gone through suc-

cessive crises of profitability, including the disaster of its 1970s foray into acquiring American Motors in the US, relies on creativity in its products to hold onto its market share. But a sense of insecurity with that situation drove it to seek a global alliance partner, achieved through taking a minority holding in and operational control of Nissan.

Fiat, which remained overdependent on its Italian home market for far too long, never managed to build a real pan European presence. It was also distracted by its involvements in Russia, Eastern Europe and Brazil. Fiat is virtually at death's door in financial terms. The Koreans provide basic entry-level low-cost transportation, as in the US, having taken over the role historically played by imports from Eastern Europe, sold by the former communist regimes at non-economic prices to earn desperately needed hard currencies. MG Rover, the last remains of an independent UK volume car industry, is effectively a failing operation, unable to finance product line renewal. The Mini is BMW's volume-market entrant, which has been very successful – the last relic of the firm's abortive relationship with Rover, its English patient. Finally, US-designed volume cars are virtually unsaleable in Europe, with only Chrysler making volumes of any significance, with the Neon positioned in the low-cost entry-level segment.

Market shares in the volume car sector in Europe have moved relatively little over the last decade, in contrast to the steady climb of the Japanese in North America. The Japanese have not broken through, despite the menace they seemed to pose in the late 1970s and early 1980s. There are still six major European-based players (we view Ford Europe and Opel/Vauxhall as European, as their businesses are substantially distinct from their North American parents). Fiat refuses to die. No-one ever withdraws. It has been a kind of persistent stalemate, in which no-one has achieved dominance and – as we shall see in chapter 7 – no-one has been able to make a decent financial return. The calm may, however, be disrupted in the future, as the reality of the lack of growth opportunities sinks in,

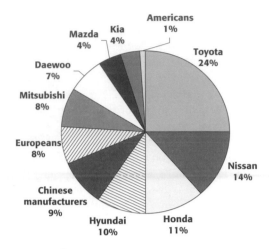

Source: As figure 4.11

Fig. 4.15 Brand shares in the Asian volume car sector, 5.6 million units

as Fiat declines and as Toyota finally begins to power up in the region.

Figure 4.15 shows the situation in Asia. The volume car market is still dominated by the Japanese, who control over 70 per cent of it, with their major volumes in their home market but also having strong penetration in many of the smaller markets. The Koreans make a respectable showing, based on their highly protected home market. But not all of them could succeed in their characteristically Korean export-led strategies. Daewoo has gone back to GM. Kia has been absorbed by Hyundai, which alone remains independent. The fledgling Samsung, built on Nissan technology, now belongs to Renault. Chinese manufacturers – until recently mainly affiliates of European companies – have collectively become significant. The Europeans are weak. Half their volume is Volkswagen in China. They have had great difficulty in penetrating the large Japanese volume car market. Once again, American cars play an absolutely marginal role. US manufacturers have very little market share, which is portentous for them, given that Asia is the region in which almost all future growth will take place. They are being strongly attacked by the Japanese in their US home market and have little effective means of retaliation in Asia, the problem

being, of course, that Japanese cars have been attractive to American consumers for three decades, whereas American cars have little appeal in Asia.

Contrary to some impressions based on now fairly distant history, South America is no longer a US automotive province but largely a European one. Even if Chevrolet is a leading brand in Brazil, the product is in fact a rebadged Opel Corsa. The market is fragmented into individual countries, apart from Brazil – which hugely dominates the region – and Argentina being part of the Mercosur trading area. The Brazilian market and industry are controlled by VW, GM Europe, Fiat and Ford. European cars dominate the volume car market. Other entrants, such as Renault, with its initial bases in Argentina and Colombia, have had a difficult time. The Japanese have been notoriously absent from these protected markets. The rest of the world, other than Central and Eastern Europe which is small, is simply not consequential for the industry.

Figure 4.16 shows the structure of regional markets for light trucks/light commercial vehicles, with their sizes and how they are shared out by manufacturers, grouped by continent of origin. The world market is totally regional. As we saw in chapter 1, there is very little commonality of products across regions. Apart from some Asian incursions into North America and Europe, each region remains dominated by producers from that region. Asia is, of course, itself no unified market, unlike the two other major regions. Again, the Japanese dominate Japan itself and most of the smaller Asian markets, while China and India are mainly held by domestic producers. The large size of the Asian LCV market is understandable, as these vehicles serve as all-purpose carriers of people and goods in emerging markets. The virtually equal size of the North American market is caused by the peculiar American light truck phenomenon, already discussed.

Figure 4.17 segments the world sports utilities vehicle (SUV) market, which is half the volume of light trucks/light commercials but nevertheless substantial. It has a curious

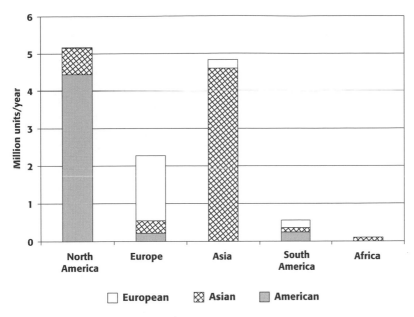

Source: As figure 4.11

Fig. 4.16 World light truck/light commercial
vehicle markets, 14 million units

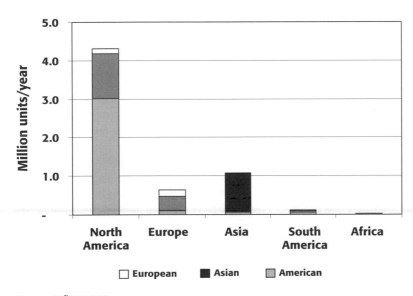

Source: As figure 4.11

Fig. 4.17 World SUV market, 6 million units

structure. Half of it is occupied by the US Big Three, whose products sell overwhelmingly in North America. Once again, they are too crude – and energy-inefficient – to be saleable to any great extent elsewhere. Everywhere else is the realm of the Japanese. The only Europeans of consequence are Land Rover, Mercedes-Benz with its M-Class and BMW with its X-5 and X-3 products. All of these (except for the Land Rover Defender and the Mercedes G-Wagen) are in a distinct upline niche rather than in a true all-terrain segment. Incidentally, we do not count the numerous 4 × 4 derivatives of passenger cars in this product segment.

Apart from the extreme upline niches and the true all-terrain 4 × 4s, therefore, the one true global segment is probably in performance upline cars – and this is dominated by European brands. In cars, therefore, there are only two categories of really global manufacturers: the European upline and the Japanese volume players – and the latter are still not fully into Europe, the largest car market of all. In terms of the competitive positions of the manufacturers, globalisation is still very far from being a widespread reality in this industry. Everyone seems to be striving for it and talking a great deal about it. But is it a realistic prospect, or even a goal worth striving for?

A changing view of scale – the emergence of new competitors

As we have seen, competition between vehicle manufacturers and how it really takes place is a complex subject. It is riddled with emotions and unwarranted assumptions. The automotive industry, although claiming to be a global business, is only partially so. Driving habits differ from one region to another and even between countries. So do product requirements. The idea of a 'world car' has proved mostly elusive, except in some niches. Vehicle manufacturers are variously far from having freed themselves from their national origins.

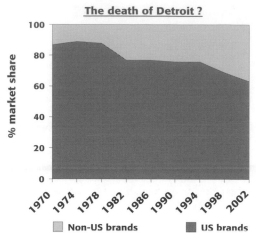

Source: Automotive News, Wards

Fig. 4.18 Detroit loses the US light vehicle market

There are very few truly global brands: most of them are predominantly regional. The competitive basis of the industry is really pluriregional, not global. Although the Japanese come close to having global platforms, this is essentially because of the lack of effective opposition to their passenger car products in the United States. The Detroit Big Three went to the ball in their light trucks, leaving Cinderella passenger car in the kitchen, looking dejected and sad. After all, who could love this shabby midget, the fruit of the forced CAFE union with Uncle Sam, after the glorious era of fins and horsepower races? Who could make money in *that* sector? Until, that is, Cinderella met her Japanese prince(s) – the shocking result for the Big Three can be seen in figure 4.18. The big slide in their share has been entirely caused by Japanese incursion into passenger cars. Moreover, it will continue, as the Japanese – mainly Toyota and Nissan – move on to attack the lucrative light truck market, the last bastion of the Big Three's defence.

In terms of companies, the only effectively three-region volume car and light truck/SUV manufacturer today is Renault-Nissan, which brings together an almost perfect match of complementary skills and geographical positions. It stands in sharp contrast to the absurdly misconceived takeover of Chrysler and Mitsubishi by Daimler, the first of these initially misrepresented as a merger of equals. We return to this subject in chapter 7. Toyota is probably on its way to being a truly global company, but by the slower route of organic growth. It is strong in the US and Japan and is already ahead of its penetration target in Europe, where it is ultimately aiming for 10 per cent of the market. Globally, it overtook Ford to become the world's no. 2 manufacturer in the third quarter of 2003 – a victory of the sober and rational over the showy and aggressive which is worth contemplating.

All the other big car and truck manufacturers are either specialists or regional players, only partially global. Indeed, in our view, the importance of scale, certainly the importance of being global, has been greatly misunderstood in this industry and treated in far too cavalier and aggregated a fashion. Moreover, unlike most industry watchers who talk of further consolidation to come, we actually foresee the emergence of new competitors, fragmenting the future business structure and rotating the traditional thinking even further on its head. This is because the fastest-growing markets will not be easily accessible to the big global names. Newcomers will take most of the additional sales in these places. Similarly, we think that the consequent overextension of some of the big groups and their financial troubles could force them to break up, as did BMW-Rover. Their fate will be determined by their financial situation as much as by their market position. We will look at their financial situation in chapter 7. For almost all these top groups, however, there are uneasy challenges ahead. Many are financially weak and all have the bulk of their sales in the mature slow-growing markets in Europe, the US and Japan. Access to the fast-growing markets will not be as easy as they anticipate.

In terms of market position, we think that the fastest growers of the next decade will be those companies that are mostly on the fringes of the industry today: Chinese firms, such as First Auto Works and Shanghai Auto Industry Corporation, as well as Tata in India,

Iran Khodro in Iran and AvtoVaz in Russia are examples. These are companies with more protected, faster-expanding domestic markets as well as the determination and will to win. In contrast, most of the big carmakers are stuck in lower-growth markets, facing maturity.

Why do we think the newer manufacturers will grow? Essentially because they have markets with significant potential, as well as some sort of protection, or simply the pride and determination to succeed. Because of the shift of power in the industry to the systems and component suppliers (discussed in the next section in more detail) the transfer of technology to entrants is also much easier than it once was. Most of all, though, these companies and their national governments are aware of the importance of the auto industry to their economies. A business that amounts to 10 per cent of GDP is a pillar of growth, an engine of development. It is not something that should be given to foreign companies to control, especially for some of the most populous nations on earth.

Why will they succeed? Let us look at these companies a little and what they are planning. First, the Chinese entrants.

China is key to the growth assumptions of most of the big carmakers. Indeed, almost every business in the world sees China as a massive opportunity. Yet we think that almost all will find it a graveyard eventually too. China is, we think, a lure in which most foreign investors will get snared.

There are reasons to think twice about China, no matter what business you are in. There are good reasons to think that foreigners, in many sectors, will fail in China. There is an already established pattern of industrial development, which can be seen from studying the fate of other businesses. Telecommunications is perhaps the best example. In the late 1980s demand for telephone services in China started to take off. To help fuel and fund the growth, the authorities encouraged foreign telecoms companies to establish Chinese operations. But they insisted that these had to be in joint ventures with then weak local firms.

The government also established a Ministry of Information Industry (MII) with a powerful head to co-ordinate development. Demand for telephones mushroomed, of course, such that by the end of the 1990s China had become the largest fixed-line telecoms market in the world. By 2001, it had become the largest mobile telephone market too.

Yet the role of foreign firms today is not as might be supposed. In land-based telecoms there is now almost no foreign participation, while in mobile phones, apart from a few base stations and a declining share of the handsets market, the Nokias and Motorolas of this world are in the process of being squeezed out by rising local producers. Moreover, China, not content with running the show itself, specified its own third-generation (3G) technology standards in 2002, forcing the already financially stretched foreign phone companies to develop yet another costly system, as well as the ones they had produced for the US and Europe. It was either that or lose out entirely on the world's biggest market. So China has cleverly used foreign know-how, foreign technology and foreign investment. In telecoms it has built an industry of its own over a decade and then squeezed the foreigners out again. It is now intent on leading the industry globally and on setting future technical standards.

Is this a one-off? Not at all. Talk to people in the pharmaceuticals sector, in computing, in white goods, in some logistics businesses, and many other industrial and service businesses and they will all say exactly the same. This is precisely what happened to them.

In the auto sector one of the main issues for China is control. Who will control the destiny of China's auto industry? Will foreign investors like GM, Ford and Toyota – companies with the size, technology and cash – eventually dominate? Or can the country develop indigenous Chinese manufacturers successfully? Our answer is that China will keep control of its own automotive destiny and not allow itself to become a mere province within the multinational vehicle manufactur-ers' global empires. But the battle will be hard.

Certainly, China is immensely attractive to the industry. Given the lack of growth elsewhere, it is also a prize worth fighting for. China has fast (but perhaps not always robust) economic growth, a huge population, surging car sales (they rose tenfold between 1992 and 2002 to almost 1.1 million cars a year and 1.5 million light commercial vehicles a year and grew by another 60 per cent in 2003) and, undeniably, massive long-term potential. Figures put out by the Chinese government predict a market for 5–6 million vehicles in 2010 – 8 per cent of global demand then – and a 250 per cent increase on the volume experienced in 2000. Demand for cars (as opposed to other types of vehicles) is expected to grow by more than 500 per cent during the decade, the government says. Other figures suggest a market for almost 12 million light vehicles a year by 2020, almost as big as that in Europe. Almost everyone agrees that China will become the dominant vehicle market in Asia within fifteen years.

Competitively, China's auto sector was nearly virgin territory throughout the 1990s. Because it was tightly controlled by the government and entry was restricted until 1998, there was only one serious competitor in the car business – Germany's Volkswagen, in partnership with SAIC, a regional state-owned company. It also had a partnership with FAW in the north. Through these ventures, VW held two-thirds of the market.

With the country's WTO membership in 2001, the opportunities that China seemed to offer took on a new impetus for the world's car manufacturers. The market appeared to be becoming more liberalised, import tariffs were falling and many of the rules surrounding the granting of licences for local vehicle assembly were eased. Under the terms of China's membership, the duties on vehicles were to drop to 25 per cent by mid-2006 compared to 70–80 per cent in 2001. Import quotas were increased too, and would continue to grow by 15 per cent a year until

2006. Provincial governments were allowed to approve higher levels of foreign investment – up to $150 million by 2005, a fivefold increase (though this is still a trivial sum for the auto industry, where investment in a car plant can cost ten times as much). Modifications were also made to the laws governing the ownership of vehicle distributors, to allow for greater foreign involvement and even majority control of a joint venture after 2003. The market finally appeared to be opening up.

In response, almost all of the world's top car and truck makers announced plans to set up assembly operations. Almost all claimed that they would have a substantial share of the market within a few years. It was, and remains, in our view, like a rush of corporate lemmings. All dismissed the difficulties, the risks of losing their technology to Chinese firms or the threat of a capacity glut. These were only problems for their rivals, it seemed.

Yet the problems were formidable. First, the entrants would have to take on the might of VW. Second, there was the issue of volumes. While the growth rates were high and a market for 5–6 million vehicles a year by 2010 might have sounded good, prices were falling, two-thirds of the market was still for utilitarian light commercials, competition was becoming ever more intense and the *incremental* volume opportunity – the difference between sales in 2000 and the end of the decade – was comparatively small. Even by the government's estimates there was to be a net increase of around 2.8 million annual new car sales between 2000 and 2010. That is like adding another UK or France to world vehicle demand. It is good, but not that good, given the level of inward investment. Although it was almost impossible to calculate accurately because there were so many unannounced investments by Chinese firms too, the additional investment planned by foreign firms would add another 4–5 million units of capacity by 2005 to a market with 3–4 million units already – and sales of just over 2 million units a year in 2003.

There was also the issue of the Chinese government's own plans: its intention to make the auto sector a 'pillar' economic industry. Most of the entrants seemed to ignore these or dismiss them. Perhaps they believed that the might of the multinationals would be enough to overcome the determination of a country so recently emerging from years of communist thinking. Yet, since 1994, the Chinese had made it clear that they had other ideas. The government had stipulated that its long-term objective was the establishment of a strong, *independent* domestic automotive industry, not one overrun by foreigners. The Tenth Five Year Plan, which runs until 2006, made these intentions clearer still, with detailed objectives for the auto sector. These specified the pace of technology development for the industry, the competitive structure (including the numbers of companies in each product segment) and the types of vehicles that would be needed by when. The auto industry's progress was also specifically linked into the nation's wider plans – its urbanisation plans, the city construction agenda, into future tax revenue assumptions, into environmental controls and, most critically, into carefully managing the country's oil dependence.

Subsequent announcements have made the plans clearer still. In May 2003 a draft automotive industry policy was published that suggested that the government would further curtail the ability of foreign automotive manufacturers and suppliers to protect their proprietary technology and intellectual property. One translation of the document suggested that foreign partners, even those with just 10 per cent of a venture, were to be forced to hand over their products, patents, designs and processes to their Chinese partners as part of their entry requirements. The document even said that the foreigners could not object if their technology was then used against them. It added that, by 2010, half of the market had to be in the hands of firms wholly owned by Chinese investors using their own technology.

Whether or not these ideas become law is irrelevant in many ways, although that has not stopped many in the industry dismissing them as illegal and counter to the documents signed by China for its entry to the WTO. More important, certainly in the view of many industry watchers, is the thinking that goes behind them. Even if such plans never reach the statute books, their airing has given a taste of the way that the bureaucrats are thinking. China will *not* be overrun by the big foreign carmakers in such a critically important industrial sector.

The Chinese have not just been explicit about their intentions for the industry, however. They have also been clever at playing one foreign investor off against another. There have also been problems with counterfeits – complete counterfeit cars.

Foreign companies that have formed relationships with one local firm have subsequently found that it has set up a venture with their arch-rival too. Volkswagen, for example, had long-established partnerships with SAIC in Shanghai and with FAW in Changchun. But after many years of working together, SAIC then formed a partnership with VW's rival GM. Similarly FAW, in the north, established a venture with arch-competitor Toyota. Another large local player, Dong Feng Motors, has relations with PSA Peugeot-Citroën of France, the French–Japanese group, Renault-Nissan, and Honda.

Today, all of the foreign parties in these bigamous relationships fear being played off against each other and worry about technology being leeched to either their partners or, worse perhaps, a global rival. As Berndt Pischetsrieder, the head of Volkswagen, says of China, 'It is difficult, just as it is in real life, to share a good partner with someone else.' It is more difficult still in China, we think, where the invisible hand of central control is at work too.

The development of counterfeits took almost everyone by surprise and has become another headache. In 1996, we spoke about the possibility to the head of VW in China at the time, Martin Posth. 'Could they ever make counterfeits cars in China?', we asked. 'No!' he said, laughing. 'Cars are not like watches or CDs, you know! A car is too complex. The engineering required to design and manufacture one is much too difficult to copy.'

Yet within four years he was proved wrong. The first copy of VW's Jetta car appeared in late 2001, rebadged, slightly altered in appearance and about 20 per cent cheaper. More surprising, the build quality of the car was very high – close to VW's own standards. The reason was simple: the car was actually being made in a VW factory. SEAT, its Spanish subsidiary, had sold a car plant to a Mexican group but they had sold it on to a company in China. Moreover, the company that bought the plant, Anhui Chery, was 20 per cent owned by VW's main joint venture partner in the country, SAIC. Despite protests from VW, Chery's cumulative volumes broke through the 100,000 mark in early 2003, an output nearly half of VW's own for the car. VW was therefore faced with a flood of counterfeits made in one of its own factories by a company partly owned by its 'partner'. The car even used original VW branded components at the start, although this practice has since ended.

In mid-2003 Chery launched another car too, in a bolder move yet. It introduced the QQ, a copy of a car that had not yet even been introduced by its original designers. The car was about to be launched as the Chevrolet Spark by SAIC's other main foreign partner, General Motors (see box 4.2).

Chery is not the only counterfeiter either. Since 2000 another company, Zhejiang Jili Geely, has produced three different models of cars which look remarkably similar to those made by Toyota's Daihatsu subsidiary and which are made under licence by another Chinese firm, Tianjin Auto. The Geely cars cost as little as half as much as the Tianjin car and controlled 14 per cent of the subcompact car market in 2003. There are also reports of copies of Mercedes cars.

So, because it is policy, because of the strategies of the main carmakers today and because

Box 4.2
Copycat cars

GM probes 'copying' of its car by Chinese maker[12]

SHANGHAI – Foreigners have long railed against pirated software and CDs in China. The latest complaint? Copycat cars.

Car-makers in the country's booming vehicle sector, frustrated with what they deem intellectual property theft, suddenly face a new threat: The copying of cars, which take anywhere from US$500 million (S$880 million) to US$2 billion to design from scratch.

America's General Motors (GM) says it is investigating media allegations that Chinese car producer Chery's just-launched QQ minicar bears a striking resemblance to GM's Chevrolet Spark, due to enter the market later this year.

SAIC-Chery Automobile Co Ltd, which sold 50,000 cars last year, denies the allegation.

The Spark is based on the Matiz, made by GM's South Korean unit GM Daewoo Automotive and Technology Co., so experts reckon it cost little to adapt for China.

The Matiz probably cost some US$500 million to develop, according to car consultancy Autopolis.

'As the market matures, you are getting more mature attempts to rip off other people's intellectual property rights,' said Mr Ben Goodger at intellectual property consultancy Rouse & Co. International.

'The big players are going to have to be much more sophisticated in taking action,' he said. 'We're talking about suing people.'

Besides GM, Japan's Toyota Motor Corp. and Honda Motor Co. and Germany's Volkswagen AG have also been ensnared in disputes as they pursue a market where car sales leapt 56 per cent last year to break the million barrier for the first time.

'The Chery case is a little bit unique,' said a senior executive with a rival car-maker. 'All I can say is, it's really worth the effort of all parties to look into this.'

GM executives say they told Chery about a year ago they would 'not appreciate' them copying GM's products, without referring to any specific model, and Chery assured them it would not.

'We're concerned about public and media comment that the two vehicles look very similar,' said Ms Daphne Zheng, GM's China spokesman. 'We need to look at the ramifications.'

The irony is that Chery is 20 per cent owned by Shanghai Automotive Industry Corp – GM's main joint venture partner.

The Chery dispute follows other high-profile disputes over intellectual property theft or violations of copyright in a land where copying – from DVDs to goods on supermarket shelves – is rife.

It is hard to copy a car: The reverse engineering would have to involve the complicity of systems suppliers or a direct exchange of designs between a company and its would-be imitator. Most piracy in the industry now centres on parts such as brakes and windshields and can be hard to detect, legal experts said.

But they do not discount the possibility.

Last year, Volkswagen said parts produced by it had been used illegally in one of Chery's cars.

The Chinese firm said that it used technology bought legally from Volkswagen, which finally agreed with Chery suppliers that they would stop using original Volkswagen components.

Yet another complaint revolves around the Geely Group and Toyota, which is demanding 14 million yuan (S$207,000) from Geely for using a 'mini-globe' logo similar to Toyota's in its Meiri sedan line, a charge Geely denied.

---

[12] Ben Blanchard, Reuters, 27 June 2003.

of the counterfeits, we think that foreign automobile firms will eventually lose out in their attempts to dominate the sector in China. We think that the market will eventually resemble that of Japan or South Korea, where non-national companies have a small and specialist share. In China's case this is because of government decree, because it is the intention of local companies and because it follows the pattern of industrial development the country favours. Although much invaded, China has never been successfully colonised and it is unlikely to be so economically, in the world's largest manufacturing sector and in such a 'pillar industry'. Our view is that the growth in the fastest-expanding auto market in the world is likely to go mostly to Chinese firms and not the big multinationals in the long term. Companies like FAW, SAIC, Dong Feng and others will gradually come to dominate the business. They will develop their own technology and progressively squeeze the foreigners out. This is what the government plans – and very explicitly.

So, of the middle-sized companies we have listed as being the biggest winners in the industry in the next decade, two – SAIC and FAW – are expected to prosper, thanks to some sort of explicit government protection and support. It will probably be much the same in Iran, for Iran Khodro, for now (see box 4.3). If Russia wants to retain its industry, it will need to protect its local firms as the market grows too, in which case AvtoVaz is likely to benefit as well.

In India, the situation is different, with one company growing at the expense of foreign investors without explicit government support. We have classed it as a winner for other reasons. That company is Tata and it offers a lesson in how to overcome the apparent barriers of scale which are seen as so insurmountable in this industry, without using government support. It is a lesson for others in this otherwise difficult-to-enter industry.

Box 4.3

The top twenty carmakers you've never heard of

Here is a puzzle. Think of a carmaker. A carmaker that is in the world's top twenty. A carmaker that exports. That is more than twice the size of Malaysia's Proton or Britain's Rover. That has a very high domestic market share in one of the world's fastest-growing auto markets. A market that in 2001 was two-thirds the size of the fast-growing Chinese car market.

Give in?

You should, because you are very unlikely to guess. It is a company called Iran Khodro and if you have not heard of it now you might soon. Iran Khodro is the largest carmaker in Iran. Well, so what?, you might say. Who wants to do business with Iran?

Actually, a growing number of people, despite all the political problems. It may still be a difficult place to get into, certainly if you carry an American passport. It may still face US sanctions and it may have many other troubles that stem from a religion-based government that is often at odds with US and much global opinion. But, aside from the politics, the country is changing rapidly. If the politics ever catch up, Iran could be one of the world's most exciting new auto markets.

In 2001 around 450,000 new cars were built and sold in Iran, with the order books full for two years ahead. The demand was so high that buyers often sold their vehicles as soon as they received them, such was the premium they could receive.

So what is the hitch? Well, for one thing, the technology. Iran Khodro still makes the Hillman Hunter, a relic from 1970s Britain. It even makes a natty new pick-up version in pretty pastel shades. 'We'll build more than 130,000 Hunters this year', Dr Sakhavi the factory's American-educated quality consultant told us proudly. They will be built on a line transferred from Linwood in Scotland decades ago.

The technology and products are being upgraded though. In the late 1990s the company started making the Peugeot 405 as well, on lines transferred from France. It makes spare parts for its French partner too. It has also developed models of its own, the Persia, which is a modified Peugeot 405, and the RD. This blends the body of the 405 with the drivetrain of the Hillman, an odd marriage, for sure. But what it loses in performance it gains in local content. Almost the entire vehicle is made in Iran. In 2002, the company introduced the latest Peugeot 206 and the X7, an entirely locally designed car. In 2003, a number of Renault vehicles were introduced too.

There is also export potential. The company – and its smaller competitors such as Saipa – already export a limited number of vehicles. As Dr Amir Albadvi, Iran Khodro's strategic planning manager, pointed out, Iran shares fourteen different borders. This gives the country access to places most other firms would not touch. Turkmenistan, Azarbaijan and Tajikistan are hardly on GM or Ford's list of top potential export markets, after all.

That is not to say exporting to these places is easy. Iran Khodro shipped a few hundred cars up to Turkmenistan in 2000 as part of an initial sales contract. When they went to check how the vehicles had performed six months later, they found most of them were wrecked. It was not that the vehicles were no good. It was the fact that they had been driven 450 miles a day, on roads where achieving an average 20 miles an hour is a challenge. They had been used around the clock. And they had never been serviced or even had their oil changed. One of the company's engineers took a measuring device with him for the journey north. He wanted to see how many potholes they would drive through, to calculate what sort of suspension specifications the markets needed. He stopped the machine after two hours because it told him all he needed to know. There had already been more than two and a half thousand.

Luckily these are not the only places with export potential for Iran. There are also the Arab countries, particularly along the North African coast and around the Middle East. The demand for vehicles is stronger there and some of the markets are greatly undersupplied. While Iran is not, like these places, an Arab country, it does at least share a religion and years of isolation from the West. That makes doing business slightly easier.

Another developing role for Iran Khodro is to become a pillar for Iranian industrial development. Mr Esmaeli, vice-chairman of the company, told us that he thought that the country's oil had been 'a curse in some ways'. It brought the country wealth but not prosperity, he said. It has done nothing for long-term development. It has created few jobs. It has built few skills. And it has cemented no new economic foundations. The oil has brought trade but not industry. Mr Turkan, the head of Iran's Industrial Development and Renovation Organisation (IDRO) put it more succinctly. 'Iran needs to reintegrate itself into the global economy and make an intelligent contribution, where there is give and take. We don't just want to play the role of the buyer', he told us.

Many of the most influential people in the country have been thinking carefully about how they can invest for the future – and a key part of that is building an auto sector. Many of the Iranians we spoke to were increasingly aware of the need to re-establish relationships with US and Western companies. Many were thinking about how to rebuild local industries and embark on what may be a twenty-year plan for economic regeneration: to re-create Iran as it once was, as an economic powerhouse in a politically sensitive region.

Convincing some of those in the government and indeed many Iranians that this is the best policy is still difficult, however. Many are still wary after so long being spurned internationally. With so much at stake it is likely to be some time before it becomes clear which direction the country will take. Even so, for the world's auto industry, there may be growing reasons to rebuild some sort of dialogue with the place.

The Indian market is still comparatively small in global terms, with sales in 2003 of around 900,000 vehicles a year – compared to around 16.5 million in the US. It is today dominated by Maruti, a Suzuki subsidiary still partly owned by the Indian government and originally a national project, and by Tata.

Tata is a rare firm in the automotive industry. It is filled with smart, creative and ambitious people. It has already achieved massive growth against the odds and it has plans to become a major global competitor while going it alone.

We first came across Tata Engineering in 1999, shortly after it launched its first car. More than 600 of India's most senior auto industry managers had gathered for a special meeting in Pune, about 100 miles east of Mumbai. Without enough seats, many sat on the stairs or huddled around doorways, squinting to see beyond the TV cameras, photographers and newsmen.

They had come to hear the views of one man, Ratan Tata – head of one of the country's largest conglomerates, a leading light of the protectionist Mumbai Club and the father of the Indica, the first truly Indian small car. To their great unease, however, even those squashed in the corners felt more uncomfortable after he had spoken than they had before.

Despite his achievement in making the first Indian car, he said, 'I have a sense of remorse', which seemed odd when he had just created something that most Indians were proud of. 'Five or six years ago I had a dream to build a small car for India and in a way that dream has been fulfilled', he continued, 'although in another way it has not.'

Mr Tata then explained carefully that he had been disappointed, saddened even, by the lukewarm support that had been given by the rest of India's auto industry to his plans. 'I wanted to get the components industry together with the automobile industry to create something that would make its mark not on India alone, but on Asia. [A car] built for Asia and conceived in Asia.'

'That dream was not fulfilled', he said. More galling still, he added, 'It attracted criticism'.

He explained how Tata Engineering had been forced to undertake the work to develop many of the components itself. 'We did produce a car – and I'm very proud of it – but I still have a sense of remorse.'

When he was finished the room was quiet, heads were down and people shuffled uncomfortably. Here was a man who was a national icon, whom the audience, India's auto components industry, had failed, and no matter how nicely he said it, many felt suitably chastened.

We spoke to some of them afterwards. Of course they felt bad. But, they explained, there were so many carmakers in India, and sales were rising so rapidly that they had to focus their efforts on the biggest and most global firms first, not an unproven newcomer. What else could they do?

We found that Tata's struggle has certainly been a difficult one. It had been hard to develop the manufacturing and product technology and to identify supplier companies with the potential to build millions of components a year who were willing to bet on a newcomer.

What made Tata different? Why had it succeeded? We think Tata managed to break into the industry partly because his conglomerate – which is more than 150 years old – had an established reputation for having long-term ideas, an understanding of the hurdles and a history of achievement. It was as much because of the culture of the business, its determination and the creativity of its approach as the business model. As India's largest truck maker, it was also a company with an established range of vehicles already, its own technology and the potential to create a regional, if not a global, brand.

The company found the going hard though, especially with support from the local parts industry so lukewarm. With intense competition, sales development at the start was also much slower than it would have liked.

Yet the half-hearted support of India's components makers forced Tata to develop much of its technology in-house (see box 4.4). But it was not able to do everything – and this led to problems in some areas. The supply of

Box 4.4
You spent *how* much?

In May 1999, Ratan Tata stood at the end of the line inspecting the latest cars as they came off the track. The car coming off the line was the Indica, the auto industry's latest addition. Designed and developed in just 31 months, it boasted a 99 per cent Indian content – higher local content than any comparable car in the world. It was also one of the cheapest cars to manufacture, yet it would sit happily on the roads of any fashionable city in Europe. Most amazing of all, perhaps, was the thought that all this had been achieved for the cost of a model facelift in the rest of the world – around $400 million.

Unlike all its local competitors, who depend greatly on foreign technology, the Indica has had no such support. The car was designed with the help of an Italian design house, Idea. The engine, which was also new, was developed in-house. The assembly plant was bought from Nissan when it pulled out of Australia.

'We needed something that was very low-priced to compete with Maruti [the dominant Indian car company]. We got this entire plant for $22m', Tata told us. 'After they closed the plant, Nissan had run it every day to keep the hydraulics and pneumatics in good shape. So we got a plant that was terrific. Although of course, we have added a lot since then.'

Tata Engineering boasts engine testing expertise with the capability to meet the latest European emissions standards, crash-testing facilities, a high-speed track and an NVH (noise, vibration and harshness) laboratory. Pulling on India's already world-class software industry, the company had also set up an extensive CAD/CAM design house. There were also in-house tool-making facilities and a depth of engineering skills that would be the envy of many more established carmakers.

'We didn't achieve a milestone nationally', Tata told us with some regret. Yet he achieved a milestone in another way: no-one has ever entered the car industry so successfully for so little.

good-quality plastic parts was difficult to achieve and the quality of the rubber trim in early vehicles was extremely poor, for example.

The Indica was sold for less than $6,000, including tax at 40 per cent. In the first year the company sold more than 70,000 of the stylish little cars and still had waiting lists longer than any of its competitors. Despite this, quality surveys suggested more than teething troubles. The finish of much of the trim, the harshness of the engine and the ride and handling were all comparatively poor, even by Indian standards.

Yet through determination and growing local sales, as well as the launch of another model, the Indigo in 2002, Tata became the third-largest carmaker in India within three years. By mid-2003 it was the second largest. We think it achieved this partly through its

approach but also by introducing models that Indians actually wanted and that suited their needs. Foreign rivals typically sold cars which they made elsewhere but had been decontented to make them cheaper. This is a very important factor. We once heard an Indian marketing expert castigate the industry for not listening to what Indian consumers really want and need.

With some foreign tie-ups and further product development plans, Tata now hopes to become bigger still in the years to come. A tie-up with Britain's MG Rover will allow it to sell cars in Europe and build volumes further. Other tie-ups are in the pipeline. It also has plans to develop a new low-cost car – which will retail for just $2,000 and will be aimed at other developing markets. The company also has big plans to make an assault on the foreign truck business, competing with the big global names by using lower prices and better service.

In conclusion, then, we think that the companies best placed to win from the growth that there will be in car and truck sales in the next decade will be some of the entrants, not just the big global majors. Some of the latter face disintegration. This is something we will come back to later. But it means that the industry will become more fragmented, not more concentrated, and that has substantial implications.

There is an important lesson here. It seems, finally, that it *is* possible to grow in this industry and to make it, despite the apparent enormity of the scale requirements. There are different ways to approach the business to succeed. This idea brings us back to the previous section, to the attitudes of the managers inside the big car companies. By thinking slightly differently, by using the assets of rivals perhaps, it is possible to make a breakthrough in the business and to establish a position against the odds. It is as much about attitude as approach. After decades of consolidation, a number of new entrants have shown that it need not be like this in the future. They have challenged the scale requirements, which were for so long a barrier to entry.

The fundamental reasons for this reversal of the tide of global consolidation among vehicle manufacturers are fivefold:

- First, markets, products and competition between manufacturers are not global but regional, outside a limited number of product segments.

- Second, as we have seen in chapter 3, basic automotive technologies are increasingly mature and slow to evolve, with no immediate prospect of a revolution in the structure of vehicles. Although there is more electronic content, this is not a barrier to entry for more utilitarian vehicles and is, moreover, available to them through suppliers if they wish.

- Third, technological, engineering and manufacturing know-how has steadily been moving out of the hands of the manufacturers, as we shall see in chapter 5. It has therefore become much more easily acquirable by upstarts, provided these get adequate protection during their period of emergence and can control a sufficiently large regional market.

- Fourth, as we shall see in chapter 6, the protection afforded to incumbent players by proprietary distribution channels in the largest single car market in the world, Europe, is starting to be stripped away. This will greatly facilitate market access for emerging new players from outside, who can play into niche segments of a huge regional market.

- Fifth, as we shall see in chapter 7, the hitherto dominant established volume players are mostly in no financial condition to continue to impose their worldview upon the industry.

We are on the threshold of the Fourth Revolution of the world's automotive industry, a subject we shall return to in chapters 8 and 9.

5

The supplier industry – the catalyst for the profound changes to come?

No easy task – the complexities of developing and producing vehicles

Automobiles are complex products. They are complex to design and develop because so many functions are incorporated. They must function together as perfectly and as reliably as possible.

The major subsystems of a car are the body, the chassis, the driveline, the electrical power subsystem, and the command, control and communication subsystem, shown in figure 5.1. Each subsystem divides into a set of functional areas, i.e.:

- The body subsystem divides into: bodyshell (the fixed superstructure of the vehicle), doors and latches, internal trim and climate control.
- The chassis subsystem divides into: platform (the underpinnings of the vehicle) and corners (the vehicle's links to the road).
- The driveline subsystem divides into: engine and transmission (the means whereby the engine's power is delivered to the driving wheels).

Each functional area further subdivides into a set of specific functions, for example:

- The corner function contains the running gear (wheels, tyres, wheel bearings, suspension), braking and steering functions.
- The engine function contains the short block (cylinder block, cylinder head and all the mechanical moving parts), and the fuelling, de-pollution and cooling systems.

Each specific function is assembled from a set of individual components, for example:

- Seating contains frames (which give the seats their strength); foam (which makes them comfortable to sit on for long periods); covers (which make them attractive and practical), and mechanisms (which allow them to be adjusted to the size and shape of particular drivers and reclined or tilted to allow access to the rear of a two-door or three-door car).
- Fuelling contains a tank to store the fuel; a fuel pump (usually in the tank, to move the fuel to the engine); a pump (to generate the pressure needed to inject it into the cylinders in the case of a diesel engine); and injectors (to squirt the fuel into the intake manifold or cylinders); and, the necessary low- and high-pressure tubing.

Vehicles are also changing. The automobile is moving increasingly from being a mainly mechanical engineering system to one based on electronics and electric power. Virtually all subsystems are already under the control of electronic control units (ECUs), consisting of sensors, logic circuits (hardware), control algorithms (software), actuators and man–machine interfaces. These include:

- engine management – control of the fuelling system, ignition, turbo-compressor, variable valve timing, cylinder shut-down;
- management of engine ancillaries – radiator ventilator;
- management of the transmission (automatic, automated manual or continuously variable);

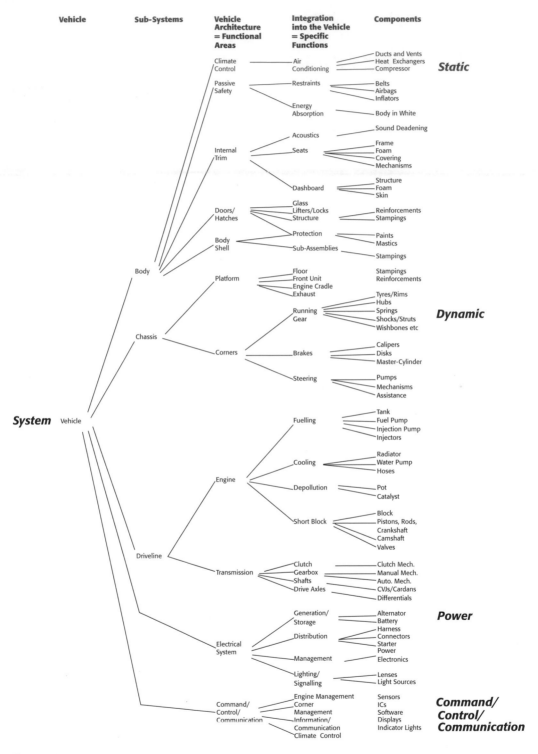

Fig. 5.1 Systems structure of an automobile

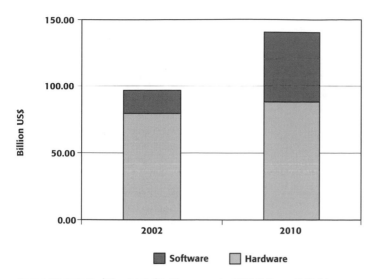

Source: Strategy Analytics, quoted in 'Components: 1000 Units per Vehicle',
Vehicle News 271 (October 2003), p. 61.

Fig. 5.2 The software revolution: value of
electronically controlled systems

- anti-skid braking, emergency brake assist, electronic stability control using yaw sensors, intelligent cruise control and traction control, ultimately brake-by-wire;
- hydraulic or (increasingly) electric power-assisted steering, ultimately steer-by-wire;
- parking assistance;
- adaptive suspension control;
- intelligent lighting systems – automatic lighting up, dipping;
- rain-detecting wash and wipe systems;
- memory seats and rear-view mirrors;
- head-up displays;
- driver condition monitoring;
- airbag controls, internal and external (to protect pedestrians);
- climate control;
- vehicle security and remote locking and entry;
- navigation, communication and entertainment systems;
- automatic toll collection.

The value of electronically controlled systems is also rising rapidly. The popular figure is that 40 per cent of a new car's value in 2010 will consist of electronics, as against 22 per cent in 2000 and 10 per cent in 1990. This in fact refers to the value of the systems that are or will be electronically controlled – the actual electronics are worth much less than that. The numbers are striking nevertheless. As shown in figure 5.2, it is the software element that is increasing the fastest. Today's car can contain up to eighty electronic components or systems. These are only partly interconnected today but will be completely interconnected by data-buses by 2010.

The breakdown of this growth by functional area is shown in figure 5.3. Powertrain electronics is relatively mature; the major growth areas are in safety and body/chassis, i.e. the other core areas of the vehicle. Leisure components are growing but remain relatively unimportant – a matter we shall return to in chapter 6.

Moreover, putting these functions under electronic management enables them to be almost endlessly enriched. Whereas in previous generations of vehicles they were mainly isolated islands, they will be increasingly able to communicate with each other. Fuelling and

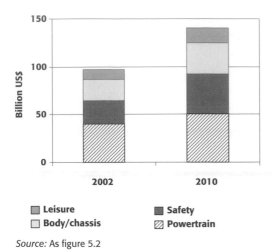

Leisure
Body/chassis
Safety
Powertrain

Source: As figure 5.2

Fig. 5.3 Growth of electronics by area: value breakdown of electronically controlled functions

ignition controls working together were an early example. But engine management can be integrated with the transmission, and the braking, steering and suspension controls can talk to each other and to the cruise control system. All this has some important consequences for the industry, going well past the technologies themselves:

- The characteristics of vehicles are being increasingly determined by their electronic control systems and how they are programmed. That includes the interactions between individual systems, so that overall complexity rises exponentially.
- Control algorithms for individual functions and for vehicle-wide integration and management of them is increasingly software-based, which creates a rich source of potential malfunctions. We return to this subject in chapter 6.
- Multiplexing, which channels command signals and electrical power through separate ring-mains, into which remotely controlled functions connect, is finally breaking through. This allows considerable savings in the bulk and weight of the wiring harness, which has hitherto consisted of an ever growing number of pairs of wires, and is the

single largest and fastest-expanding component in the vehicle. The downside is the vulnerability of these circuits to breakdowns, particularly at interfaces bridged by connectors – which have always been a bugbear.

- The differentiation of, for example, an upline vehicle from a volume car will reside increasingly in its fancy integrated electronics, and relatively less in high-quality mechanical engineering. This may pose a long-term threat to the ability of upline manufacturers to differentiate their vehicles and has the potential to bring structural change to the industry more widely.

Most critically, the ownership of the technologies involved in creating the 'feel' of a vehicle is passing from the vehicle manufacturers to systems and components suppliers. Some of these are new to the automotive industry and may be unwilling to operate to the old order, especially as their influence grows. This has a number of implications which we will come back to.

Vehicles are not just becoming more complicated pieces of machinery, however, and the shifting balance of power from the manufacturer to the supplier is not just in the provision of parts. It is more widespread than that. It begins even further back in the production cycle, with the vehicle's design.

Speaking to those responsible for vehicle design, one gets the sense that the designer is a kind of tightrope artist: pushing for innovation while having to respect the commercial constraints of the marketplace; being avant-garde while not getting too far out of line (look what has happened to Fiat, which has produced some wonderful designs but a bit off-centre for the bulk of European market taste); promoting visual quality while respecting engineering constraints.

Technical constraints weigh heavily: if you want a tight package, with low aerodynamic resistance and dead weight for fuel economy, and good survivability in crashes, the laws of physics and engineering tend to drive everyone towards the same solutions.

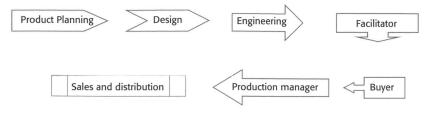

*Source: auto*POLIS

Fig. 5.4 The old approach to product development

In good times and in bad, vehicle design and development is a difficult business – probably more so in the bad times, when readiness to invest and take risks is low and the risks of failure are so high. The creation and introduction of a new vehicle is a mammoth project, involving very big commitments of time and money – it is quite capable of breaking a company if it goes wrong. For the design engineers there is a permanent struggle, to put it negatively, or creative tension, to put it positively, between the need to maintain the integrity of technical functions and the imperative to produce creative new products which reflect or – better still – anticipate the requirements of the market.

Figure 5.4 shows the old approach to product development – how it used to be done in a more leisurely age, fifteen or twenty years ago. In those days, the product design and development process was sequential and task-driven for all vehicle manufacturers. The process would start with product planning, would be handed over to the design department, and gradually follow a course through separate parts of the organisation, until the production department received its instructions. The process was a long one – the introduction of new models could easily take seven years, with frequent revisions caused by the incompatibility of the design with the individual objectives of the departments involved, such as purchasing and production. In addition to being lengthy, it became prohibitively costly because of the constant revisions and reworking, resulting in frequent cost and time overruns. As there was no single person accountable for the whole

process, it was also hard to pin the blame on anyone when things went wrong – or, more importantly, to make the process faster and less haphazard.

One of us spent months helping to reorganise and decongest the product engineering department of a European truck manufacturer. On the office wall was a complicated flowchart that showed the stages of the process, from the marketing department's input and the initial concept through to final detailed design, manufacturing engineering and production launch. It was hard to find anything 'wrong' with it, except that one more intermediate design review might have been beneficial. Yet that wholly missed the glaring flaws: it all took far too long and what emerged at the end of a long pipeline was all too often out of date or inconsistent with what marketing thought it had asked for. Interfacing with subcontractors was poor. In one instance, a complete cab was engineered by a highly reputable exterior design house – and was found not to fit over the engine. Although all the steps and interfaces were there in the official description of the process, the discussions between the different departments were not real and there was far too much of 'throw it over the wall to the next set of actors'.

One solution to all these problems was simply to telescope the process, shorten it and make it more iterative, so that there could be feedback and checking for consistency with the original intentions. But that is not ideal either. The fundamental problem with the approach is that it is too extrapolative, i.e. it works in stages from what is already known. It

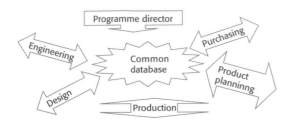

Source: *auto*POLIS

Fig. 5.5 The modern approach to product development

is cumbersome and slow, especially for a fast-moving market.

In response to these difficulties the whole design and development process was turned around and tasks are now run in parallel under the co-ordination of a programme director (see figure 5.5)

When a new project is identified ('develop a sports car with a price of X') it is now handed over to a multidisciplinary team, who have instructions to get the maximum margin in that sector. The project works by contributions from the various disciplines. The glue that holds it together is the constant interaction with a central database from which they all work – no matter where their location. In practice of course, each vehicle manufacturer has its own approach and seeks its own balance between market-facing generalists and technical specialists. The whole process remains an extremely complex and delicate balancing act, unmatched in any other industry we can think of.

This change in approach has had profound implications. It has halved development time, improved accuracy of budgeting, and allowed component suppliers to 'design in' from the earliest stages. Most critically, it has greatly increased the role and power of the systems and component suppliers in the process. In theory, it seems, all the design–engineering–market requirement problems have been solved by this new approach. However, this is far from the case, as we will see.

The sequence of the final manufacturing processes involved in building an automobile is shown in figure 5.6. Their basic nature has not changed for decades. The assembly plant takes in coils of steel, which are cut into blanks – or pre-cut blanks may come from steel producers. From these blanks sheet steel parts of varying sizes and shapes are stamped. They are welded together to form the raw steel bodyshell, known as the body-in-white. The doors, bonnet (hood) lid and boot (trunk) lid are produced in a similar fashion. The whole is dipped in a rust-inhibiting bath and gaps that need sealing are filled with mastic. Special protection is applied to particularly sensitive areas. Undercoats and finishing coats are applied by spraying, until the desired glossy finish has been achieved. In parallel, components are produced and assembled into modules, as far as possible. These range from the headlight clusters to the fuel tank and fuel pump subassembly, from the engine and gearbox to the seats. The mechanical elements – drivetrain and running gear – are fitted to the body on the mechanical assembly line. The seats, dashboard and other pieces of trim are fitted on the trim line. Wheels and tyres are fitted. Tanks are filled with fluids – fuel, engine and gearbox oil, radiator cooling solution, gas for the air conditioning system, a detergent solution in the screenwash. The car is started and driven away.

As with the design and development process, there have been huge improvements in the manufacturing process too. Everyone has learned how to change dies in 10 minutes instead of 36 hours. Welding robots make it possible to run different models down the same line. Paint spraying has been extensively automated. Doors are often removed from the body after painting, so that they may be fitted with their various mechanisms (locks and window lifters) away from the main assembly line.

There has also been a major effort to reduce the number of operations on the assembly lines. Complete engine and gearbox assemblies are mounted on carrying cradles off line

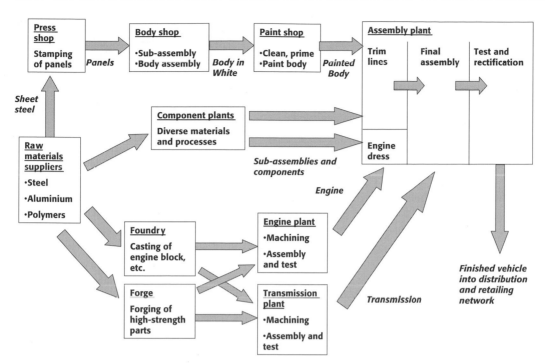

Fig. 5.6 Steps in producing an automobile
Source: As figure 4.9

and offered up for mating with the body in one piece. Fuel tanks, fillers and pumps come as complete assemblies, as do dashboard and instrument panel assemblies. Seats are assembled within the confines of the assembly plant or very close to it, in the exact versions and colours required for each vehicle moving down the final assembly line – with the lead time given to the seat assembler often as little as an hour or two. Wheel hubs, brakes and steering components are integrated into corner units, pre-assembled off line.

Automation is applied wherever possible, although it will never be possible to do away with manual assembly completely. Vehicles are often held in cradles, so that they can be rolled over, in order to avoid tiring overhead working. Flexible automation, including programmable robots, has made it possible to reconcile all this with an increasing variety of products moving through assembly.

Above all, the philosophy of automotive manufacturing has changed hugely. Along with the lean production idea of not producing anything until the next process stage actually requires it, has come a completely new sense of responsibility for quality. Three decades ago, some of VW's US adverts boasted that the company had more quality inspectors than assembly line workers. It helped sell cars, particularly to an American public deeply fed up with Detroit's then awful quality. But it was a very Taylorian approach, implying that assembly line workers (and component suppliers) were feckless incompetents, whose misdeeds had to be rectified all the time.

Today, the responsibility for quality is placed where it should be: on the producer at each step, with prevention insisted on instead of cure. Process operatives are expected to understand their process, to devise means of improvement and to take corrective action whenever needed, to the point of halting the entire assembly line if needed – something which used to be absolute anathema in the industry.

The changes are a very, very great achievement. In human terms, it has meant that there has been a shift from intentionally mindless wage slavery to dignified responsibility. In product performance terms, this has been a continuous and considerable enrichment. Quality and durability have been vastly improved. Time to market is a fraction of what it once was.

Behind these achievements, there remains the awe-inspiring scale of this industry of industries, the amount of investment it requires, and the depth of specialised knowledge in such a multitude of components and disciplines. There is, believe us, enormous complexity involved in the creation and production of such humble products as door handles and oil filters. Think of the entire car and multiply it a thousandfold.

While the vehicle manufacturers have clearly played the leading role in all this growth and change and improvement, they could not have done it without the support of the systems and components industry. Its critical and growing role and the changing power balance in the industry are examined in the next section.

The revolt of the masses – the growing power of suppliers

We tend to think of the automotive industry in terms of its leading players, the vehicle manufacturers. These are the stars, the household names, the brands with which everyone is familiar. These, and the families behind them, were the initiators of the industry – the Daimlers and Benzes, the Fords, the Toyodas (the family behind Toyota) and Hondas, the Renaults and Citroëns, the Rollses, the Royces and the Ferraris. They invented practically everything to do with the automobile at the beginning. But it could not go on that way. As the industry grew, and as its products became ever more complex, they were forced to delegate, sometimes very reluctantly.

The American giants – Ford, GM and Chrysler, in descending order – had such scale that they could keep control of most of the functions and technologies of the vehicle for a long time. This control collapsed more quickly in Europe, in part because its automotive industry was initially fragmented along national lines. It never existed in the same form in Japan, whose industry had to emerge out of the ashes of the Pacific War, practising an extreme economy of style, of which the Toyota production system, or lean manufacturing, is an example.

Henry Ford managed to keep control over almost everything for years, with his own steel works and glass production, and even his own sources of iron ore. GM, on the other hand, established internal components divisions from an early stage, having invented the divisionalised form of corporate organisation. Harrison Radiator, Fisher Guide, Delco-Remy – to name only three – were an early recognition of the need to specialise component development and production, while serving the four car divisions of the corporation: an early example of a matrix organisation. But who among the broader American public, outside the industry, was familiar with these names? They were hardly household brands. Everyone in Germany knows of Bosch in white goods, brown goods and power tools. But how many are aware of the crucial role the company played in the early development of the

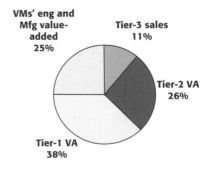

*Source: auto*POLIS

Fig. 5.7 Breakdown of the industry's industrial value added (total $893 billion)

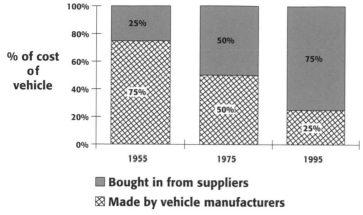

Source: *auto*POLIS

Fig. 5.8 The world turned upside down

German automotive industry? Bosch invented the magneto, the first effective electrical spark ignition system. The shape of the magneto's rotor is the heart of Bosch's corporate logo to this day. Similarly, in Europe air conditioning has become widely available on cars. But who is aware of the crucial role played by Valeo, the largest French systems and components group, in making this happen? They identified the latent unsatisfied market and sold the feature to the vehicle manufacturers.

In many respects the system and component suppliers are the unsung heroes of the automotive industry. Today, the vehicle manufacturers only control 25 per cent of the value of the products coming out of their assembly plants, as figure 5.7 shows. Three-quarters of the cost of those products is in the hands of the companies that supply them with raw materials, individual components and subsystems.

This was not always so. At the dawn of the age of the automobile, the pioneer manufacturers designed and made a very large proportion of their vehicles. Quite simply, they had to, as there was hardly anyone around from whom they could buy what they needed, beyond basic products such as steel and other materials. As the industry grew rapidly – starting in the 1910s in North America, in the 1930s in Europe and in the 1960s in

Japan – vehicle manufacturers could not keep up with the technological, financial and managerial burden of looking after all the functions of the vehicle. Although Henry Ford strove mightily for decades to maintain complete control and a high level of integration, even Ford had to concede that he could not carry on – and ended up with a lower degree of integration than GM, although higher than Chrysler. This was in the good old days, before GM and Ford spun off their component divisions in the form of Delphi and Visteon in the 1990s.

So the deintegration movement goes way back in time and was started because it makes economic sense. It has continued steadily too, as figure 5.8 shows. When Lord Cornwallis and the British army were shown off the premises in Yorktown, Virginia, in 1781, the band played 'The World Turned Upside Down'. It has been much the same in the automotive industry.

Today, the systems and component suppliers are, if not kings, at least very large barons. Figure 5.9 shows just how large some of them are. It ranks automotive groups by sales. We can see what gigantic undertakings groups such as GM, Ford or DaimlerChrysler are. With a turnover of $100 billion per year, some are equivalent in size to a not-too-small country.

The twelve largest companies, in turnover terms, are vehicle manufacturers. After all,

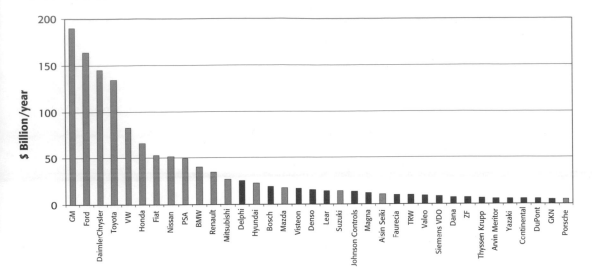

Source: *auto*POLIS, based on data from Automotive News Data Center, 313-446-6000: www.autonews.com

Fig. 5.9 The relative sizes of vehicle manufacturers and component suppliers

they make and sell a high ticket product – the most expensive consumer durable – at the rate of thousands per day. What is fascinating, though, is to see how high some of the component suppliers rank, based purely on their automotive turnover. (Some, such as Bosch, have other large areas of business as well.)

Delphi, the largest supplier group in the world, comes in after Mitsubishi but ahead of Hyundai, the largest Korean vehicle manufacturer. Then there follows a whole string of suppliers, of various national origins and with different areas of technological focus. Delphi groups together most of the former component divisions of GM and covers many areas of vehicle technology. Bosch has always been independent and is today controlled by a foundation, which helps to protect it from some of the short-term and more arbitrary pressures exercised by the capital markets. It is extremely powerful in all areas of engine fuelling and management, having pioneered both diesel and petrol injection since the 1920s. It was also the first to introduce the electronic anti-lock braking system (ABS) and is a major force in the electronic command and control structures of vehicles. Visteon is the ex-Ford equivalent of Delphi, also covering

many aspects of the vehicle. Denso is the Japanese equivalent of Bosch and originally its licensee. Lear and Johnson Controls design and supply seat assemblies and interior trim, as does Faurecia, which is also a large supplier of exhaust systems in Europe. Magna is Canadian, a huge supplier of structural assemblies, such as chassis and subframes, and the creation of an emigrant Austrian toolmaker, Frank Stronach. It also assembles vehicles under contract, raising again the intriguing possibility of a supplier ultimately becoming a manufacturer.

In reality, the sales ranking understates the relative importance of these suppliers. As the manufacturers now control only 25 per cent of the value of the vehicle, that is their real economic value added. Suppliers tend to add more than 25 per cent. Figure 5.10 shows the value-added rankings for the industry. The rankings shift perceptibly, with Delphi now almost as significant as Peugeot and ahead of BMW and Renault (taken here in isolation from its partner Nissan), while Bosch comes just behind the latter.

Figure 5.11 brings the phenomenon a bit more to life, showing who supplies what on an actual new car. The omnipresence of the

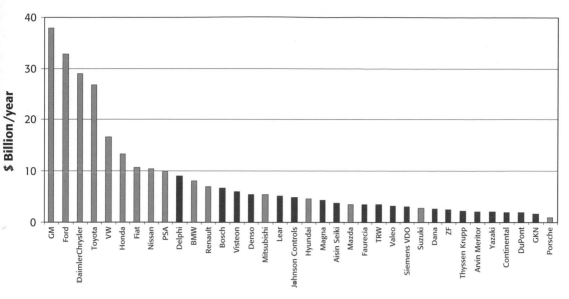

Source: As figure 5.9

Fig. 5.10 How manufacturers and suppliers compare on value added

independent systems and component suppliers is made obvious.

The whole trend is a very long-term one of specialisation in the industry: a greater division of labour, following the precepts put forward by Adam Smith in the eighteenth century. Co-operating in trade so as mutually to exploit each party's comparative advantages is a powerful force for economic growth, enabling as it does the optimal allocations and use of resources. So it is in the automotive industry.

The Japanese led the way. They had to restart their automotive industry literally from the ashes, following World War II. They were desperately short of resources, which forced an economy of style upon them – it was also native in the Japanese tradition of elegant and economical craftsmanship. This led to the lean production revolution, discussed on pp. 109–13, but also to the structural principles of tiering and delegation of responsibility down through the tiers of the supply industry. This is illustrated in figure 5.12. The Japanese vehicle manufacturers simply had to do it, in order to access the necessary engineering and manufacturing resources. They

did it, however, within their own constraints, notably that of the so-called *keiretsu* structures. These were systems whereby a family of suppliers was uniquely affiliated to a given vehicle manufacturer, reinforced by equity cross-holdings. A supplier in the Toyota *keiretsu* would typically not supply to Nissan, for example, and vice versa.

A very few suppliers were large and powerful enough to escape this constraint. Honda tended to be less *keiretsu*-reliant than its two large competitors, Toyota and Nissan, for example.

In some respects the *keiretsu* approach reproduced the features of the great *zaibatsu*, the industrial and financial combines that had powered the industrialisation of Japan following the Meiji Restoration, and which were dissolved under the occupation of 1945. The closeness of the relationships helped the Japanese vehicle manufacturers enormously when they established their first transplant assembly operations in the US and experienced the then inadequacies of the US supply industry, particularly in terms of product quality. Japanese suppliers were persuaded to transplant too, and versions of the automotive

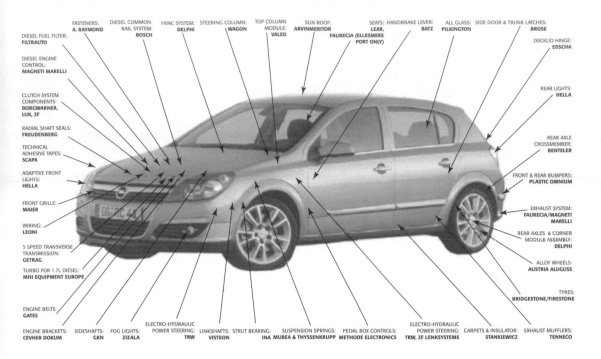

FASTENERS: **A. RAYMOND** · DIESEL COMMON-RAIL SYSTEM: **BOSCH** · HVAC SYSTEM: **DELPHI** · STEERING COLUMN: **WAGON** · TOP COLUMN MODULE: **VALEO** · SUN ROOF: **ARVINMERITOR** · SEATS: **FAURECIA (ELLESMERE PORT ONLY)** · HANDBRAKE LEVER: **LEAR, BATZ** · ALL GLASS: **PILKINGTON** · SIDE DOOR & TRUNK LATCHES: **BROSE**

DIESEL FUEL FILTER: **FILTRAUTO**

DECKLID HINGE: **EDSCHA**

DIESEL ENGINE CONTROL: **MAGNETI MARELLI**

REAR LIGHTS: **HELLA**

CLUTCH SYSTEM COMPONENTS: **BORGWARNER, LUK, ZF**

RADIAL SHAFT SEALS: **FREUDENBERG**

REAR AXLE CROSSMEMBER: **BENTELER**

TECHNICAL ADHESIVE TAPES: **SCAPA**

ADAPTIVE FRONT LIGHTS: **HELLA**

FRONT & REAR BUMPERS: **PLASTIC OMNIUM**

FRONT GRILLE: **MAIER**

EXHAUST SYSTEM: **FAURECIA/MAGNETI MARELLI**

WIRING: **LEONI**

REAR AXLES & CORNER MODULE ASSEMBLY: **DELPHI**

5 SPEED TRANSVERSE TRANSMISSION: **GETRAG**

TURBO FOR 1.7L DIESEL: **MHI EQUIPMENT EUROPE**

ALLOY WHEELS: **AUSTRIA ALUGUSS**

TYRES: **BRIDGESTONE/FIRESTONE**

ENGINE BELTS: **GATES**

ENGINE BRACKETS: **CEVHER DOKUM** · SIDESHAFTS: **GKN** · FOG LIGHTS: **ZIZALA** · ELECTRO-HYDRAULIC POWER STEERING: **TRW** · LINKSHAFTS: **VISTEON** · STRUT BEARING: **INA** · SUSPENSION SPRINGS: **MUBEA & THYSSENKRUPP** · PEDAL BOX CONTROLS: **METHODE ELECTRONICS** · ELECTRO-HYDRAULIC POWER STEERING: **TRW, ZF LENKSYSTEME** · CARPETS & INSULATOR: **STANKIEWICZ** · EXHAUST MUFFLERS: **TENNECO**

Source: Automotive News Europe; by permission

Fig. 5.11 Suppliers to the new Vauxhall Astra, 2003

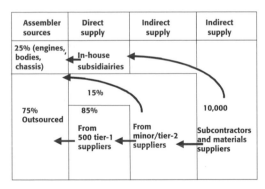

Fig. 5.12 Japanese tiered supply structure
Source: Richard Lamming, *Beyond Partnership –
Strategies for Innovation and Lean Supply*, Hemel
Hempstead: Prentice Hall, 1993

keiretsus were established on the other side
of the Pacific. This could be done gradually,
however, as the US imposed no local content
conditions.

It proved more difficult in Europe, where
the British government imposed an early 80

per cent European-content objective on the
Japanese transplant operations in the UK. The
Japanese vehicle manufacturers there were
forced to work with local suppliers, an effort
pioneered by Nissan, the first transplant. Nissan chose mainly to work with local UK
suppliers, rather than the established Europeans, as they would conform more readily with Japanese manufacturing and quality approaches. In some cases, the local UK
suppliers were selected only to carry out the
final assembly stage, however, with most of
the product design, raw materials and added
value still coming from Japan, to maintain
quality. This conveniently met the regulations
and also allowed Nissan to control the end
product.

The difference in manufacturer–supplier
relationships between the transplants and the
established European firms is summarised in
figure 5.13. The Japanese initially preferred
to get their local suppliers up to speed on

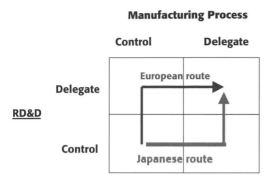

Manufacturing Process

Source: Supplier Innovation, UK Department of Trade and Industry, 1992

Fig. 5.13 European and Japanese supplier relations priorities

the manufacturing process, Japanese-style, in order to replicate the cost and quality lead they had established through the *keiretsu* structures and lean production in Japan. Suppliers were not asked to innovate in terms of research, design and development, as the product design was simply transferred to Europe largely as it was, apart from the need to conform to local regulatory requirements. European manufacturers relied far more on their suppliers for technical and design innovation.

This was ultimately to have profound consequences. The cost of the semi-corporatist Japanese approach placed a constraint on the participation of their suppliers in the globalisation of the supplier industry.

For all the investment made in supplier development by the transplants in the UK, notably by Nissan's supplier development teams, the effort essentially dead-ended, as the suppliers invested in were too small and parochial to break out of the confines of the UK. Even the most successful found it extremely hard to break into other European markets against established competitors. As a consequence, the transplant manufacturers were privately concerned about the lack of engineering resource and management dynamism in the UK supplier base.

The established European suppliers eventually learned the Japanese manufacturing techniques – leanness, continuous improvement, self-control of processes by production teams, etc. With the introduction of the euro, removal of local content requirements, failure of many of these chosen firms to develop, and other pressures, Nissan later reduced the percentage of UK value added in its British-built cars by a substantial degree.

European vehicle manufacturers each had their local origins and therefore their primarily national supplier infrastructures. A European manufacturer of thirty years ago would work directly with thousands of local suppliers, large and small, largely on a build-to-print basis. In other words, they faithfully executed the manufacturer's designs and competed with other suppliers within the same manufacturing technology, primarily on price. But that changed with the advent of the European single market. Just as vehicle manufacturers increasingly interpenetrated each other's national markets, so did the components industry. As in Japan, a tiered structure emerged. Figure 5.14 shows an early example of that: BMW's planned sourcing model from the early 1990s.

European supply structures made a ninety-degree flip, in effect, from multiple national suppliers supporting their national vehicle manufacturers to international specialists supplying all manufacturers. Nor did it stop there. The openness of Western equity markets encouraged transatlantic rationalisation, from which the Japanese had largely excluded themselves. National champions mostly disappeared, although there are still some vestiges of protectionism: for example, the unwillingness of the French government to see Valeo come under foreign control. Those who failed to follow the trend suffered. Some of those who anticipated it did well.

The fates of Lucas and GKN in the UK make a poignant contrast. Both were left exposed by the progressive collapse of the UK's domestic vehicle industry in the 1970s and 1980s. Lucas was a multiline supplier, far the largest in the

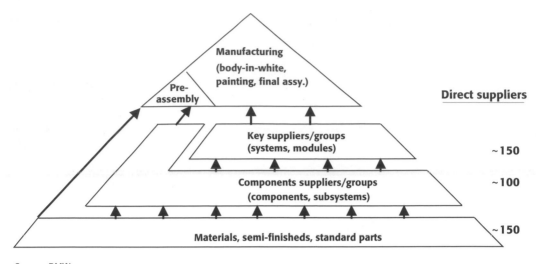

Source: BMW

Fig. 5.14 BMW planned sourcing structure

UK, the equivalent of Bosch in Germany, Valeo in France or Magneti Marelli in Italy. While it managed to internationalise some of its activities, notably in braking, it spread its assets too thinly and made some major errors of technological judgement. It has now been dismembered, with its diesel injection business (once a serious rival to Bosch in light vehicles in Europe) owned by Delphi, its lighting business long since disposed of to Magneti Marelli and most of the rest owned by the US group TRW.

GKN, in contrast, made a crucial early acquisition in Germany, buying UniCardan, the national supplier of constant velocity joints, the essential component for transmitting power to the driving wheels of front-wheel-drive vehicles. This established its dominance in Europe in this specialised sector, the major hold-out being Citroën, which had pioneered front-wheel-drive cars in the 1930s. When downsizing and, by implication, front-wheel drive were forced on the US industry, Ford bought GKN's drives, while GM was supplied by its own Saginaw Division. This, plus the European business, plus its Japanese affiliates afforded GKN a 40 per cent global

market share – and made it arguably the earliest global component supplier. The constant velocity joint business remains the GKN group's almost unassailable cash cow to this day. (Note that in response to criticism from the capital markets for this over-dependence on one product and one industry, GKN spent much of the 1990s building a number of other successful businesses with considerable success. Unfortunately, as a result of subsequent pressures from the financial markets and a change of leadership, these businesses were then spun off, leaving the group back where it started. It remains, in our view, however, one of the brightest stars of the industry in terms of its technical and managerial competence.)

The major US manufacturers also recognised the need to open up systems and component supply to more competition. Under pressure from the capital markets, GM and Ford made the major strategic move of divesting themselves of their component divisions, Delphi and Visteon respectively. These two groups still have a major share of their sales with their former parents but are moving as quickly as possible to diversify their customer

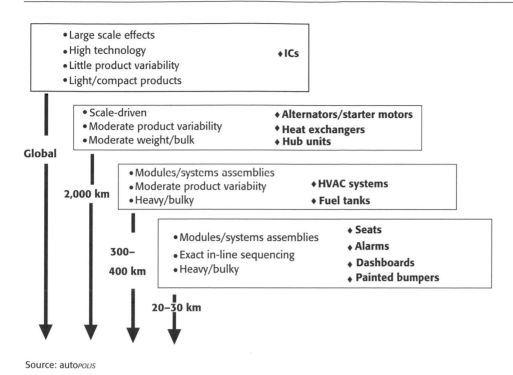

Source: auto*POLIS*

Fig. 5.15 Global sourcing – the theory

base. Delphi, in particular, has been active in making international acquisitions.

The Japanese suppliers, having been the first to go through the tiering process but having also remained isolated, are exposed to this globalisation trend. Not the least of the shocks to the Japanese system experienced when Renault took over the controls at Nissan was the opening up of its supply structures. This is a process which still has a good way to go. A similar one is underway in Korea, whose supplier industry still contains many small players and which is still very largely a technological satellite of Japan.

The changes mean that there is an increasingly rational global supply industry, illustrated in figure 5.15. Sourcing is increasingly dictated by product performance, supplier competitiveness and logistics. Some components can be supplied globally, others need to be produced near the vehicle assembly plant.

• Products such as integrated circuits (ICs), which are subject to large-scale effects in development and manufacturing, favour large centralised plants. They are high-technology, high-value products. There is relatively little product variability – that is put into the applications software – and therefore a long supply pipeline does not matter too much. They are small and light. It is cost-effective to ship them over considerable distances.

• Heavier, more bulky, but still scale-driven components, such as alternators, starter motors, heat exchangers (radiators) and wheel hub units, with little product variability from one vehicle to another, will stand shipping over a continent, such as North America or Europe. The effective supply radius is some 2,000 kilometres.

• Larger assemblies that are more dedicated to the vehicle model into which they are built, such as heating ventilation and air

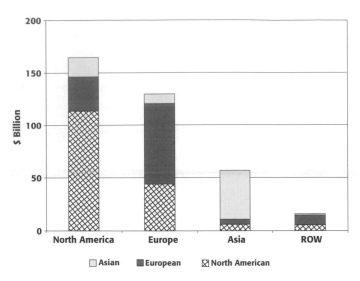

Source: As figure 5.9

Fig. 5.16 Shares of regional markets, 2002, top 100 suppliers by regional origin

conditioning (HVAC) systems, or fuel-tank filler-pump assemblies have to come from closer at hand, or the shipping costs and delays become prohibitive.

• Finally, bulky items, which must exactly match the specific vehicle being assembled and be provided in sequence, such as seating systems, alarms and immobilisers, dashboards and painted bumpers, must be produced very close at hand, to very short lead times.

As vehicle manufacturers have gone global, so have their suppliers. This has happened to a large degree for the tier 1 systems suppliers, although not so completely for the more specialised tier 2s.[1] Figure 5.16 shows that regional automotive supply markets are still mainly dominated by suppliers originating from, and having their ownership within, the region. The North American market is still mainly held by North Americans, although Europeans have made some inroads – more than the Japanese. Europe has been quite extensively penetrated by North Americans, mainly through acquisitions. Asia – dominated by Japan and to a lesser extent Korea –

is still largely separate. The rest of the world – mainly South America (itself mainly Brazil) and Australia – is shared between North Americans and Europeans. Figure 5.17 shows where the top hundred suppliers in the world automotive industry achieve their sales. North American groups are in the lead and have achieved the greatest globalisation of their sales footprints, with Europeans second. Asian groups are well behind.

---

[1] Vehicle manufacturers typically work with their components suppliers in 'tiers'. Tier 1 companies are those in the top tier, immediately below the vehicle makers. They supply the most technically complex parts, as well as what are called systems or modules, such as a complete air conditioning unit or a bumper or fender with the lights and trim already installed. A tier 2 manufacturer typically supplies the tier 1s (although it might also supply the VMs directly). It might make smaller components like the dials for the speedometer, the door locks or the lights. Tier 3 manufacturers make castings (although not complex castings like engine blocks), seat cloth, simple plastic parts or components like fastenings and screws. Below them come the raw materials suppliers. Those in the top tiers are afforded more access to the carmaker, have more influence on the performance of the final product, and have greater legal liability if things go wrong.

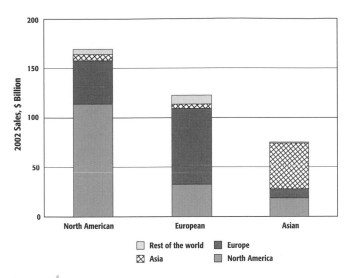

Source: As figure 5.9

Fig. 5.17 Regional footprints of top 100 suppliers,
by region of origin

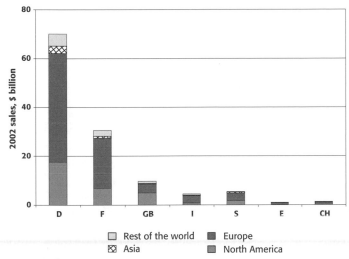

Source: As figure 5.9

Fig. 5.18 Sales footprints for the top thirty-four
European supplier groups

Figure 5.18 performs the same breakdown
for the thirty-four European groups within the
top hundred. The dominance of German suppliers and their lead in globalisation is clear,
although they have not yet penetrated Asia
very much. The French come second, with all
the others a long way behind. The remaining UK groups are well established in North
America – they had to globalise or die, given
the demise of their national vehicle industry. The small and overwhelmingly European
presence of the Italians graphically portrays

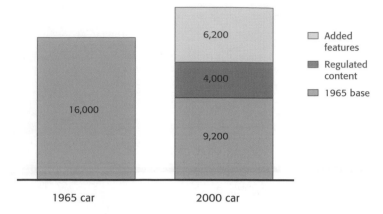

Source: Glenn Mercer, 'The Global Automotive OEM and Automotive Supplier Industry', McKinsey & Company, 26 September 2002
Note: Values are in year 2000 constant dollars, for an average-sized US car

Fig. 5.19 Content enhancement trend

the hollowing out of the once strong Italian automotive industry. Even the Swedes (led by SKF and Autoliv) and the Swiss do proportionately better. But that is the sorry price of national corporatism – of Fiat is Italy and Italy is Fiat.

The components industry is supposed to be on its way towards an automotive brave new world, in which every layer is rationally organised, everyone concentrates on their specialised area of competence, comparative advantage works, and everyone can make a decent living. There is, however, a problem. It is the subject of the next section.

More for less – the problem of growing complexity

The first hundred years of the automotive industry have been marked by the gradually growing technological complexity and sophistication of motor vehicles. While they perform the same overall roles as they always have done, their functionality has been enriched and enhanced almost out of all recognition. Half a century ago, turn signals were not universal. There were cars on sale in the UK for which a heater was an optional extra. We have come a long way since then. Figure 5.19 shows

the amount of value which has been added to a standard car for two main reasons: comfort and convenience, and regulatory requirements for safety and emissions.

It has been an extraordinary performance. Yet it has not made cars more expensive. At constant definition, new cars have become much cheaper in the last fifty years. Even with added features – demanded by the market or pushed on it by manufacturers – they are still cheaper in deflated money. Only the additional content imposed by government safety and emissions control regulations has pushed their real price higher. Moreover, as figure 5.20 shows, once a feature is introduced by one manufacturer, it spreads like wildfire, as every other manufacturer wants to be able to offer it.

The technical complexity of automobiles will continue to grow during the next years and decades, as more and more new technology is installed in them, from propulsion systems to navigation, communication and safety devices. Technology is not the only trend driving increased complexity in the business of engineering and producing vehicles, however. There are visibly more and more products out there in the marketplace too, as we discussed in chapter 1 and is illustrated in figure 5.21.

Pace of market penetration in US

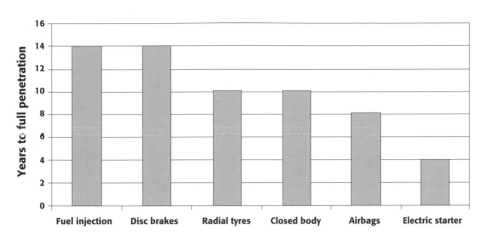

Source. autoPolis

Fig. 5.20 Spreading like wildfire

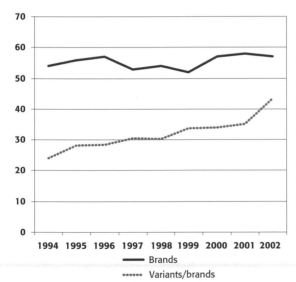

Source: Centre for Auto Industry Research, Cardiff University, from *Autocar* data

Fig. 5.21 Growing proliferation of product in the
UK market

The top trend line shows the number of brands. Contrary to some popular impressions, these have not greatly increased. This is because very few new firms have entered the industry since the South Koreans – indeed, for the last twenty years or so, there has been a brand stasis. The real change is in the bottom trend line, the average number of variants sold by each brand. This has increased by almost 80 per cent. At the most visible level of its product offerings, the industry has almost doubled its burden of maintaining and renewing its product lines. This trend also has enormous implications in terms of cost and complexity for suppliers.

Having to provide new and replacement parts for such a vast and growing array of vehicles greatly increases design and development costs as well as stocks. It also creates the need for short runs to manufacture the parts in ever smaller and less efficient volumes. And all this raises the costs of motoring for the consumer, or it cuts margins in the industry, or both.

Any market will welcome more rather than less variety – assuming, that is, that there is an acceptable additional cost to the proliferation of products. A key issue for any producer of any kind of goods or services is to find the right balance between the incremental volume, revenues and profits earned by adding more products, and the incremental costs of adding them. In the auto industry, the real cost implications of all this proliferation have not been thought through – or at least not properly. Moreover, because they have been forced on the rest of the industry by the vehicle makers, who do not bear many of the additional costs created, there is little awareness of the extent of the problem among those creating it. This is one of the reasons why it has been allowed to continue to an extent that has become unhealthy – no-one is taking a holistic, rational economic perspective, even though many firms suffer from the consequences.

The vehicle industry thought that the faster introduction of more products aimed at more market niches or micro-segments was the route to salvation. We believe this to be a tragic misinterpretation and abuse of what the Japanese pioneered in rapid product development, extensively documented at the time by Professor Kim Clarke at Harvard.[2]

Certainly, product development times had been cut in half. But they did not disappear. Yes, it used to be commonplace that a new model needed five years to be developed and brought to market. Now the general expectation is more like two to two and a half years.

The number of engineering hours required for this has been cut in half. But it still takes time and much effort. If you double your output of new products and cut the time to develop them by half, the total time and money spent stay the same.

Because the Japanese desperately needed to find economical means of production in a time of desperate post-war shortage, they accelerated their product development pace sharply, in order to have the products they needed to conquer foreign markets in the 1970s and 1980s. But this was a means to an end, not an end in itself. Part of the industry's continuing tragedy is precisely its frequent inability to distinguish such means from ends.

There is a striking analogy here with some of the abusive interpretations of the benefits of lean production. There seems to be a belief in the industry that the industrial cost of product proliferation is nil or at least negligible. Part of this is based on an observation made during MIT's International Motor Vehicle Program, related in *The Machine that Changed the World*, that increasing the number of products had no measurable detrimental effect on the productivity of a lean assembly plant. This is undoubtedly true in a pure assembly operation. But it glosses over the extra costs that are induced further back upstream and downstream in the supplier industry and the aftermarket.

The other misleading generalisation, made to us in direct response to our challenging product proliferation at an industry–government meeting at 10 Downing Street in London, is that the variable cost penalty of additional variety is nil in a flexible manufacturing environment. Again, this is true in the strict sense. If your production machinery is designed to accommodate different product designs, then one design will not be penalised against another in terms of machine times or

[2] K. Clark and T. Fujimoto, *Product Development Performance: Strategy, Organization, and Management in the World Auto Industry*, Cambridge, MA: Harvard University Press, 1991.

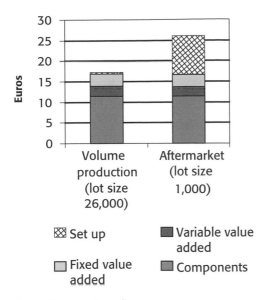

Source: Component supplier

Fig. 5.22 Production cost comparison, Drivetrain component

direct labour hours. Yet the argument ignores the indirect costs of having extra product references, design and development costs, and the costs of producing at lower volumes and of manufacturing set-ups and multiple inventories.

Figure 5.22 shows a real recent example of the costs of product proliferation. It shows the cost build-up for the same physical product, a driveline component, first under the conditions of high-volume production, feeding both the assembly line and the spare parts aftermarket, and second once assembly of that particular vehicle ceases but the aftermarket must still be supplied, at much reduced volumes. The data comes from a respected component supplier, a world leader in its sector, which is highly specialised and requires huge capital investments in its manufacturing. The product needs high-speed machinery and very high levels of precision, which simply cannot be made to function in exact sequence with the requirements of the final assembly line, on which the product is built into the vehicle. The same is true of the aftermarket. One

simply cannot make the product one by one, as orders come in from distant garages. So there has to be production to stock, with different economic lot sizes in the product's two lifetimes – for the vehicle maker and for the aftermarket.

The cost of producing it, in its first life – its original equipment (OE) life – is shown on the left. In its second, aftermarket-only life shown on the right, it is produced on more flexible machinery to account for the lower production runs. Variable and fixed value added are therefore contained and there is no explosion of costs. What goes through the roof, however, are the set-up costs, which are unavoidable. Total cost leaps by 40 per cent. That is, the same product, produced at one-fortieth of the volume for the aftermarket, costs 40 per cent more to make.

Yet this example is probably grotesquely optimistic, in that the bought-in components that go into the assembled final product have been left at the same cost. In reality, they are likely to cost much more too, for the same reasons.

We think the real cost of manufacturing the small-volume item is more likely to be three or four times that of the high-volume one. Repeat that across all the parts and systems that go into a car, and ask yourself what is the real cost to the industry and the consumer of that extra model, version or variant. It is substantial.

In response to our arguments against proliferation, an industry executive once accused us of wanting to make everyone drive around in Trabants, the much derided, low-cost utilitarian car made in former East Germany with body panels of papier mâché and little expectation of reliability. That is not the case at all. We would never advocate a return to a time of a handful of national models as if the result of some government-imposed austerity measure. Nor do we wish to throw away the enormous gains achieved by the industry over the last fifty years. We simply believe that the industry is not operating in the optimum part of its price/cost trade-off map any longer. It is down to economics. Too many people seem to believe that more new product will bring incremental sales volumes at better prices, by unlocking the hidden and hitherto unsatisfied desires and longings of consumers. We think this is simply wrong-headed beyond a certain point. We are advocating balance – a more rational, economically viable approach, not proliferation for its own sake, which is what seems to exist today.

This short-sighted, unbalanced approach to products and the ever increasing fitment of added features has brought the components industry considerable difficulties. Moreover, it has created an unhealthy relationship between the vehicle makers and their suppliers which cannot continue. Vehicle makers are forever demanding more variability and lower prices – as we illustrated in chapter 4. Yet suppliers cannot keep cutting prices forever, especially when they are being given added costs. Putting endless pressure on them to do so will simply drive them out of business. The whole approach is flawed. Do you sit down at the start of each year and work out how to cut your costs of living? Do you think about how you can move to a *smaller* house, buy *cheaper* clothes, eat *less* well? Of course you do not. You might not want to spend more, but you will probably want to live better. And so it is with the auto sector and this whole global, accountancy-led mentality of cost cutting. Everything is being driven to be forever cheaper and to last for a shorter time. It is hopelessly wasteful of resources and counterproductive in the long term. The mindset that never seeks to improve, only to cheapen, is not a road to anywhere in the end.

Figure 5.23 shows an instance of the complaints coming from the supplier industry which appeared in *Automotive News* in 2003. Some of the comments made are alarming. One supplier said, for example, that 'pressure for cost reductions with GM has broken down many processes and created a total breakdown in supplier partnerships and trust'. Others were as blunt. We are not out to

> **Suppliers' complaints about GM**
> - **Aggressive price-cut demands**
> - **Unrealistic quality standards**
> - **Too optimistic volume forecasts**
> - **Higher product recall paybacks**
> - **Lower profits on GM work**

Source: Automotive News Europe, 1 December 2003, based on a survey of suppliers by Supplierbusiness.com

Fig. 5.23 An example of pressure on suppliers

castigate GM. We want to highlight a behaviour pattern which is, unfortunately, all too common across the industry. There are differences, notably with some of the Japanese. But the wider problem remains.

There is a need for the relationship between carmakers and their suppliers to change because the balance of power is changing. As more of the value has shifted, the suppliers have more power than they once had. With their precarious margins and ever greater reliance on image, vehicle makers risk having less.

At some point, like a warring couple, there will come a fissure between the carmakers and their suppliers. It may break open through the introduction of new technology, by new entrants into the industry in a variety of sectors or by economics. But it will come. This is something we will explore further in the last two sections.

In the meantime, there is a positive side to this whole sorry tale, perhaps. The growing power of suppliers, should they decide to wield it, also creates an opportunity for change. This is the subject of the next section.

The growing strains – overloading the beasts of burden

As we have seen in the preceding sections, developing and producing vehicles is more and more about the art of managing relationships, although there is still a lack of

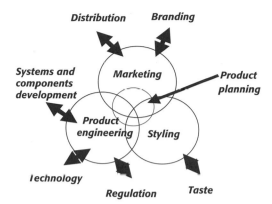

Source: *auto*POLIS

Fig. 5.24 Managing the relationships

awareness of this importance in many quarters. Yet, as soon as the genius founder entrepreneur gave way to the structured corporation, the development process involved the conscious and active management of relationships across internal specialised functions. As the manufacturer's market footprint widens beyond its original home market, more distant entities have to be dealt with.

As soon as suppliers' capabilities have to be brought into play, relationships need to be managed across different enterprises, without the benefit of authority that springs from ownership. Government, the capital market and downstream relationships have to be managed too. The automotive industry is obviously not unique in this respect. But it is an unusually complex industry, whose internal and external relationships are correspondingly complicated and have become more difficult.

Figure 5.24 summarises the interlocking set of relationships that come into play during product development alone. The engineering function must ensure that the right technologies are available and brought into application effectively. It must also ensure compliance with and, ideally, a suitable influencing role upon regulations imposed by national governments and international institutions. It must also ensure that the right combinations of systems and component suppliers

are used during product development. Styling must read, anticipate and interpret market tastes and needs, in conjunction with engineering. Marketing must ensure compatibility with distribution partners and with available means of communication. Product planning holds the whole together – and interfaces with the equally complex realms of production and finance, each with their interlocking set of relationships. General management has to balance the whole, internally and externally.

It is all getting more and more complex. Society expects more and more of road vehicles in terms of performance, attractiveness, safety and environmental compatibility. More and more advanced technologies are being brought into play to ensure this. Reaching further into global markets adds further twists along all dimensions. The industry makes life more complicated for itself by constantly intensifying the product race.

By the late 1990s product proliferation had become a very real problem in the industry, particularly in Europe. The world had far, far more platforms than it needed, as figure 5.25 shows. Europe had a staggering diversity of engine families too, half of which were produced at less than 30,000 units per year (see figure 5.26).

All this suggests that the vehicle industry only has a partial understanding of relationships and its own economics. Arguably, the vehicle makers have chosen not to develop such an understanding, for the problems could always be unloaded onto someone else – the supplier in many cases. At the same time, cost-down expectations have become universal. Only this all too often means price-down, regardless of what the supplier can realistically hope to achieve. It is a long way from the Japanese approach of working on cost reduction and quality improvement opportunities together. In the US and Europe, it has degenerated into one-sided bullying of the worst sort.

Some years ago a supplier in the US related how his team, having painfully learned how to work with the Japanese, no longer wanted to work with Detroit. A European supplier friend

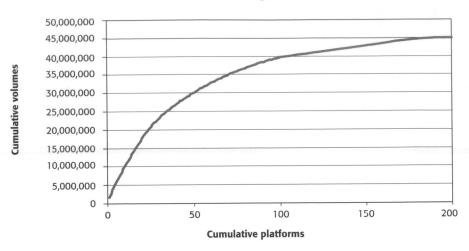

abc curve, light vehicles, 2000

*Source: auto*POLIS

Fig. 5.25 World platform proliferation

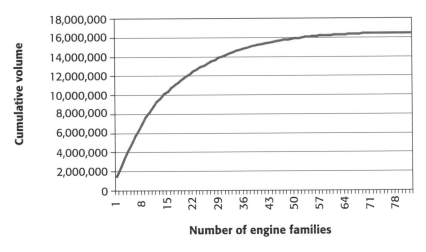

*Source: auto*POLIS

Fig. 5.26 European light vehicle engine production,
1998

related to us how a Japanese manufacturer had stepped in to help with a problem he had had in his plant, whereas a leading European manufacturer had found no better solution than to excoriate him. Another told how a manufacturer had demanded a retroactive 30 per cent price cut on a particular supply contract, threatening to cancel all contracts if it was not honoured.

There are beginning to be timid signs of protest from the suppliers, however (notably from the tyre industry), though precious few actual revolts, against these price pressures and constant demands to develop new components for marginal vehicles which then do not meet their volume objectives.

The hurt is certainly real. The Center for Automotive Research of the Altarum Institute made a thorough and compelling analysis and part of the introduction reads: 'this value chain, which constitutes over 10 per cent of the US economy, and much more of the private sector of the economy, appears to generate surprisingly little in the way of consistent net earnings for many of the companies involved'.[3] Very significantly, the study finds that the split of the assembled value of vehicles was 28 per cent in favour of OE (i.e. vehicle manufacturer) value in 1990 but that this actually grew to 33 per cent in 2000 – which the authors describe as a 'counter-intuitive result'. We do not think it is counter-intuitive at all but the logical consequence of enormous pressure on prices exercised by a monopsony. The numbers are displayed in figure 5.27.

In the words of the study report, 'To put it bluntly, the Big Three were not profitable in 1990 but they certainly were in 1997 and 2000'; and – most damningly:

the enormous fixed costs of capital depreciation and R&D expense place a severe pressure on vehicle producers' margins. However, the typical reaction of vehicle firms to [exert] downward pressure on vehicle prices has been to demand further material cost cuts from their independent suppliers. In other words, supplier fixed costs have been treated by their customers as variable, while vehicle firm fixed costs, which produce less and less, have been treated as almost permanent. Vehicle firms have sought to increase their margins at the expense of suppliers while failing to increase OE asset turnover performance in good or in bad sales years in the 1990s.

The conclusion is particularly interesting: 'A strong movement towards the transfer of vehicle firm R&D and capital expenses to the supplier sector and to operating OE earnings would both improve the vehicle companies' operating performance and the supplier sector's bottom line.'

So there we have it. Much of the supposed delegation of responsibility is fake and the

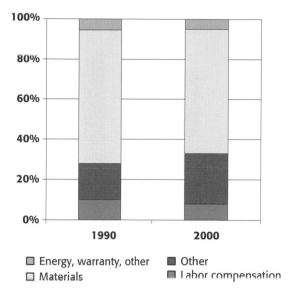

Source: CAR, 'Estimating the New Automotive Value Chain'

Fig. 5.27 Breakdown of 1990 and 2000 US auto manufacturing value chains

'partnerships' between carmakers and their suppliers one-sided power plays. Much the same is surely going on in Europe. It certainly is on the other side, the downstream sector, in which European vehicle manufacturers in particular have resolutely refused delegation and continue to micro-manage their enslaved distribution partners, at enormous cost to all concerned, as we shall see in chapter 6.

The supplier industry continues to consolidate, shown for Europe in figure 5.28. The pressures, challenges and risks are rapidly getting transmitted to the other end of the pecking order. In a report[4] for the French Ministry of Economics, Finance and Industry, the consulting firm Algoé identifies the pressures on the tier 2 automotive suppliers in France. The upper levels of the tiered structure having

---

[3] CAR, 'Estimating the New Automotive Value Chain', Center for Automotive Research, Altarum Institute, University of Michigan, November 2002.

[4] Algoé, 'Adaptation structurelle des équipementiers de second rang et des PME de la filière automobile', Paris: Ministry of Economics, Finance and Industry, 2002.

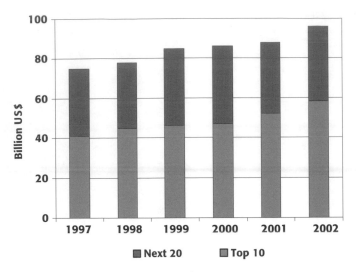

Source: Automotive News Europe, 20 October, 2003

Fig. 5.28 Sales to OEMs by European suppliers

	Weak	Strong
Weak	Production capabilities	Function integrator
Strong	Production capacity	Module supplier

Source: Algoé, 'Adaptation structurelle'

Fig. 5.29 Potential roles for tier 2 suppliers

largely consolidated, they now face considerable challenges in terms of investment in technical capabilities, geographical market reach and ability to relate to their tier 1 customers. This forces them to choose a clear role, as summarised in figure 5.29:

- as a local provider of production capacity – largely price/cost driven and with little protection against customers re-sourcing, e.g. to lower-cost countries;
- based on production capability, allowing them to add value beyond simply provid-

ing capacity. These, too, are also subject to price/cost pressures, although perhaps less vulnerable to re-sourcing than the first category;

- as a module supplier: this means adding extra capabilities and value, which implies major investments as the role expands. It can also force internationalisation on them as a condition of survival;
- as a function integrator: this is in effect a move from tier 2 to tier 1, with all the capabilities that that implies. There are few successful examples.

The upshot of all this is clear. The vehicle manufacturers continue to micro-manage their suppliers, to exert almost intolerable pressures upon them, and to duplicate what they should be doing. They risk killing those geese which lay the golden eggs for them.

Beyond this lies a wider issue. It is an issue which we introduced in the previous section, about the requirements for scale and the potential emergence of a virtual manufacturer. What should be the future role of a vehicle manufacturer? How should they define their core businesses? It was clear enough in the past: they were superior mechanical engineers, who ensured the integration of the mechanical-engineering-based subsystems and functions of the vehicle into a satisfactory whole. They were the absolute masters of the supply and manufacturing chain. But now what? They have created a model which is increasingly unsustainable. What does the future hold?

The basis of product performance and differentiation is moving away from its old foundations, electrical actuators increasingly replacing mechanical and hydraulic systems, electronic control modules taking over from the driver's neurones. At the same time, new partners are emerging, who have sources of business other than the automotive industry and may not take so willingly to being bullied and price-pressured as the industry's traditional supplier base.

We think the bully-boy game is up for the vehicle manufacturers, or at least some of them. The old way of all doing the same things, offering up pretty much the same products, staying cosily within the same core business is going. How could they redefine their future core? How might they relate to their partners in a more healthy way? We will look at the prospects if things do not change and at the potential for more positive change at the end.

6

The downstream sales and service sector

A command economy – the franchised dealer sector

What happens after a car leaves the factory is the 'downstream' end of the business – it is the process of buying a car, having it serviced and reselling it. Although we tend to think of the purchase of the car itself as the biggest cost item, the downstream sector is a major part of the cost of motoring. It is also the profit engine of the industry. Figure 6.1 shows how significant the downstream sector is for the global automotive industry. It is where the money is made. Everything downstream excluding fuel, the government and the wider social arena, contributes over half of all profits. No wonder it is fought over so strenuously.

Figure 6.2 shows a breakdown of the cost of motoring in Europe, expressed as the lifecycle costs of a vehicle. The owner, or succession of owners, carry the depreciation of the vehicle, of which 70 to 75 per cent is its ex-factory cost and 25 to 30 per cent the costs of marketing and distributing it. Within the 25 to 30 per cent, 10 to 12 per cent is the discount or gross margin given to the dealer who retails the car. Excluding only the financing cost (the cost of the capital tied up in the vehicle during its life), insurance, and taxes and tolls, the downstream sector costs about 60 per cent of the whole. Even without fuel (here at European prices), it is still about 40 per cent, with that split about 50:25:25 between the vehicle manufacturer's internal marketing and selling costs, the cost of dealers' new car retailing, and service and repairs. That is from a consumer perspective.

The financial numbers involved are gigantic. Dealer new car sales are worth some $1.3 trillion per year, with used car sales – not all carried out through dealers – probably worth about the same amount. Dealers typically earn fairly limited amounts on new car sales – we discuss how this is controlled by the vehicle manufacturers later. Even so, their value added in this subsector amounts to some $150 billion per year. The common factor, in developed countries at least, is that dealers are the sole route to retail sales for new cars. As we will see, this is important – and also rare for a consumer product.

Vehicle manufacturers have traditionally enjoyed a protected and controlled franchised dealer channel for retailing new cars. Indeed, this right of manufacturers to choose and control their channels is one of the most important and distinctive features of the industry. It is also one of most contentious ones.

The industry is at odds with most retailing sectors, where multiple channels usually compete, targeting different consumer sectors. Think of the different types of outlets in which we can buy PCs, household appliances or food. They range from the upmarket speciality store to the no-frills 'stack-'em-high-and-sell-'em-cheap' deep discounter. Not so for new cars. It is the dealer of the vehicle brand or nowhere when a consumer wants to buy a new car. There are websites of course. You can browse them to get information about products and prices and so on. But you are almost always driven back to a franchised dealer. In Europe you may buy with the help of an intermediary, arbitraging price differences between countries. But he buys from a dealer in another country, in your name. He cannot buy new cars speculatively as a reseller.

This protection of the vehicle manufacturers' dealer channel and networks is enshrined in law. In the United States this is in state dealer laws, which protect the dealers, notably making them the exclusive route to market. In Europe, it is a piece of legislation called Block Exemption that exempts the franchised dealer system from the provisions of the Treaty of Rome. This, the founding constitutional instrument of the European Union, forbids restrictive vertical trade agreements, of which dealer franchises are a clear example. The 'exemption' is just that. Both have been the products of enormous lobbying by the automotive industry – by the dealers in the US, and by the manufacturers in Europe. In defending its franchised dealer system, the industry in Europe has occasionally claimed that it should not be modified, as it is the same throughout the world and notably in the highly competitive United States. The vehicle industry claims that the US approach to automotive sales and service is similar to that used in Europe. The only difference is supposed to be that the US is a single market, with little government interference, while Europe is a fragmented set of national markets with interference. 'A system that works perfectly well in the US is controversial in the EU. The reason is not the system but the context in which it works: the EU.'[1] As we shall see on pp. 185–97, this cosy protective environment has taken a bad knock recently in Europe, with enormous implications for the future – and not just in the region.

The US franchised dealership system is held in place by tough dealership laws. The system is fairly watertight, in that these laws generally prohibit manufacturers from selling direct, i.e. by-passing dealers, particularly when selling large volumes of vehicles into the fleet market. The laws have been separately negotiated in each state of the Union and vary from one state to another. Attachment to states' rights is strong in the US. This makes these laws extremely difficult to attack

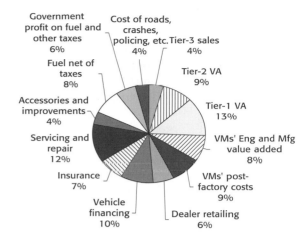

*Source: auto*POLIS

Fig. 6.1 The significance of the aftermarket: breakdown of industry value added ($2,600 billion)

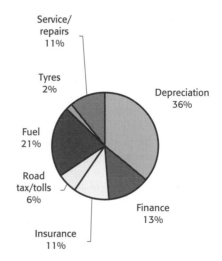

*Source: auto*POLIS **estimates**

Fig. 6.2 The cost of motoring in Europe

in aggregate. They were originally instituted to protect consumers, but now in effect protect dealers against excessive exercises of power by the manufacturers. Dealers are licensed annually by mixed private/public commissions

---

[1] ACEA-CECRA press release 25 October 2000, following a review of the functioning of distribution of new motor vehicles and automotive after sales services.

in each state. The balance of power swung in favour of dealers in the US in the 1980s, although there has been some partial reversal since.[2] Dealers as a group are far more powerful vis-à-vis both vehicle manufacturers and legislators in the US than in Europe. In general, US dealers are far better protected by law than their European counterparts. They have also consolidated more and are relatively less dependent on service revenues for their profitability.

A major difference compared to Europe is that the dealer population is far more concentrated. There are one-third as many dealerships as in Europe. The top twenty-five dealers sell 1.3 million new cars per year, controlling over 7 per cent of the whole market. AutoNation Inc., the largest dealer group, sells almost half a million vehicles, through 290 outlets, i.e. over 1,600 per outlet. Behind the shelter of the protective laws and commissions, much more concentration has taken place.

As a result of the different balance of power, US dealers are less constrained in their commercial dealings. They aggressively discount models in stock. The majority of vehicle advertising in the US is dealer advertising in the local press, based on product and price. But they also charge considerable premiums over list price for 'hot' models, which is very rare in Europe. They appear to achieve much better profitability on new vehicle sales than their European counterparts, suggesting that a more liberal regime may actually be healthier for dealers than a very controlled one. They even manage to do it on a much lower gross margin on new vehicles – 7 per cent, compared to the 10 per cent or more common in Europe – although they make up profitability on other items, notably finance and insurance (which we shall return to in a later section).

In fact, there is a world of difference between the two environments. Figure 6.3 shows that the US dealer population is incomparably smaller and also rationalising more quickly. As a result, US dealers have a much higher 'productivity' in terms of the number

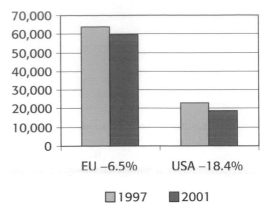

EU −6.5%   USA −18.4%

□1997 ■2001

Source: International Car Distribution Handbook

Fig. 6.3 US and European dealer populations

of new units sold each year (see figure 6.4). As fleet deals in the US are largely controlled by the dealers, their profitability is also better. They also make a great deal of money on financing vehicle sales. It is, however, characteristic of the industry's thinking that productivity is measured in terms of sales, which is the obsession of vehicle manufacturers, whereas the money is in service.

This is still a very fragmented sector. There is nothing in Europe to compare in size with America's NationWide – see figure 6.5 – although this only controls 3.8 per cent of the national new car market and the top ten chains control 10 per cent. The nearest would be Austria's Porsche Holdings, which has sixty-one dealerships in that country, a hundred in France, twenty-five in the Netherlands and others in Germany, Eastern Europe and the US. Belgium has no culture of large dealer groups. Automobilgruppe Nord is the largest in Germany, with 102 outlets. Porsche Holdings is the largest in France. Grupo Quadis has a hundred outlets in Spain. Car World Italia has all of twenty-six outlets in Italy. Kroymans Corporation has sixty-two in the Netherlands with a handful in Germany and Belgium. Grupo Santogal controls 35 per cent

---

[2] 'La distribution automobile aux Etats-Unis', *La Lettre de l'Automobile*, July/August 2000.

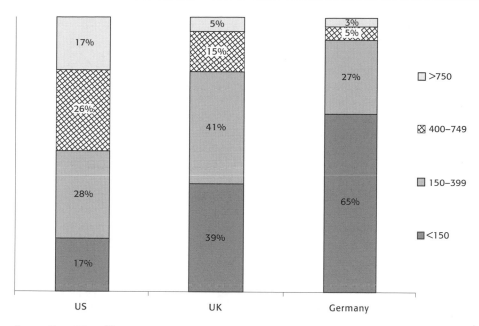

Source: Mercer Consulting

Fig. 6.4 US and European car dealer annual new vehicle sales

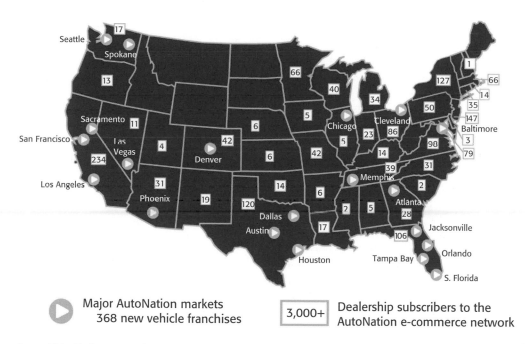

Source: Michael Jackson, AutoNation, presentation to Automotive Fellowship International, 2002

Fig. 6.5 The giant of US automotive retailing

of Portuguese sales through fifty-two outlets. The UK has the largest concentration of dealer groups, led by Pendragon with 132 outlets.

So far, all these operations have been financial holding companies in effect, with the contractual relationship continuing to operate directly between the manufacturer and the individual dealership within the group. (How this system has been challenged in Europe by the public authorities and by economic better sense, and what this may portend for the future are the subjects of the third and fourth sections of this chapter). Manufacturers in the US cannot carry out wholesale restructuring of their networks, their dealers being so strongly protected by the dealer laws. Yet the dealer sector itself has rationalised and operates in a far more competitive market than in Europe, where networks are in effect controlled and managed by the manufacturers – who have only lately begun to rationalise them, such has been their fear of losing distribution presence. In Japan, manufacturers have almost total control over their dealers, even though the great majority are independent businesses.

Another fundamental distinction is in the degree to which dealers are exclusive to one make. In Europe – see figure 6.6 – 70 per cent or more of dealers are exclusively devoted to one brand in the majority of markets. In Norway, Sweden and Finland single-branded networks of dealer outlets would simply be uneconomical because of low population density, but these markets are really the exception. The vehicle manufacturers are profoundly attached to their single-brand networks and regard them as an essential component of their overall brand position and expression. Not so in the US, where the great majority of dealers represent more than one brand. The average number of nameplates per dealer outlet is 2.4 in the US versus 1.2 in Europe.

Having the dealer totally identified with one brand is arguably what customers want in the upline sector of the industry, as it is part of the feeling of exclusivity the customers

Box 6.1

Single brand car dealers prepare for the big squeeze

Step into a car showroom and you enter a rarefied world. It is like no other store: cars of a single marque are arranged proudly, carefully polished and tended. Sales people sit at desks, staring at screens and looking vaguely under-occupied. The receptionist ushers you to a sofa and offers you some coffee, while you flick through some swatches of fabric.

This must be some industry to have such bespoke service! It must be a sector blessed with high margins and elite brands, which can afford to cosset and flatter its rich and devoted customers. Not for this industry the hustle and bustle of supermarkets, where you have to chase assistants around the aisles to find out where the cans of soup are hidden.

Well, actually, no. This is an industry of razor-thin margins, and often huge losses, one in which every sector and sub-sector has been infiltrated by global competitors. It is a market in which each innovation is rapidly copied, and produced more cheaply. In short, it is an industry making commodity returns on what it treats as exclusive brands.[3]

enjoy – and for which they are prepared to pay. But it is fundamentally a nonsense in the volume market, and has been cruelly but accurately lampooned (see box 6.1).

Imagine having to go to a dedicated Whirlpool store for a refrigerator and then another to look at another brand – and you can begin to see how out of kilter with other sectors the car retailing business has become.

The other major structural problem in the dealership system is its reliance on financial cross-subsidies. US dealers make 90 per cent of their sales turnover in vehicles (see figure 6.7). Despite this, they are heavily dependent on parts and workshop labour sales for their profitability (see figure 6.8).

[3] John Gapper, *Financial Times*, September 2003.

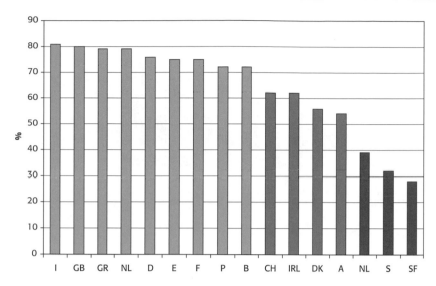

Source: As figure 6.3

Fig. 6.6 Proportion of single-brand dealers in Europe

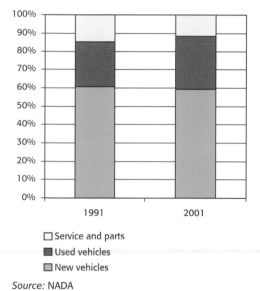

- ☐ Service and parts
- ■ Used vehicles
- ■ New vehicles

Source: NADA

Fig. 6.7 Sources of US dealers' sales

The situation in Europe is even more skewed towards dependence on service. As figure 6.9 shows, European dealers depend on service hours and parts sales for 20 per cent of their turnover, twice the US proportion, and derive 50 per cent of their earnings before interest and tax (EBIT) from this source. The proportions of course vary between European countries. Thus the contribution to profit, reputation and brand image of parts sales, workshop and servicing, bodyshop and the rest greatly outweighs that from vehicle sales, with the proportion having generally increased over recent years. The remaining gross profit contributions in franchise dealers are obtained through sales of new and used cars, finance and insurance packages and extended after-market operations which subsidise vehicle sales (particularly sales of new vehicles), both financially and in building a relationship with customers.

This is generally recognised and indeed promoted by the industry as a positive virtue. For the consumer, there is an evident element of comfort and security in dealing with one organisation, which supplies the new vehicle, offers a complete set of services to support it in operation, and is set up to take the vehicle back in part exchange for a new one, if desired.

The bundling together of sales and service in the one local, mainly single-branded (in Europe) franchised dealership, which forms

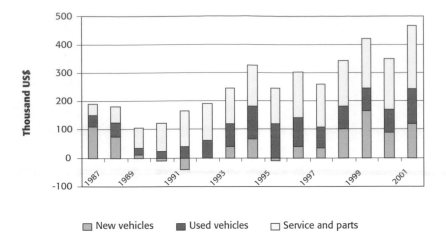

Source: NADA

Fig. 6.8 Sources of profit for US dealers

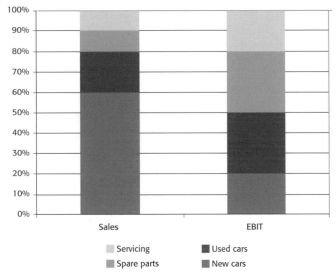

*Source: auto*POLIS and Goldman Sachs Research estimates, from client briefing paper, 2003

Fig. 6.9 Sales and profits breakdown for UK dealers

part of a national network of such dealerships, is a long-established tenet of the vehicle manufacturers' approach to the downstream sector. The sales–service link is a fundamental structural and operating premise of the automotive industry. Its visible manifestation to the consumer is the combination of sales and service outlets within the franchised dealer format. Its invisible basis is the internal cross-subsidy of sales by service that keeps the dealership financially alive. The very limited margins dealers earn on new car sales limit their ability to discount – which gives the manufacturers indirect control over

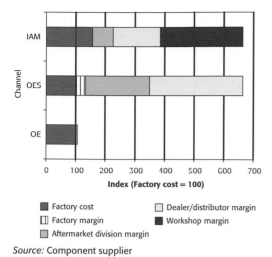

Legend:
- ■ Factory cost
- ▥ Factory margin
- ▦ Aftermarket division margin
- ☐ Dealer/distributor margin
- ■ Workshop margin

Source: Component supplier

Fig. 6.10 Parts margins structures by major market sectors

transaction prices between the dealer and the end customer.

Yet it goes much further and deeper than that. Component suppliers are put under severe price pressure by their vehicle manufacturer customers in the OE business, i.e. the supply of systems and components to the vehicle assembly lines. They often have to make up for these low margins by obtaining higher ones in their aftermarket business. This is illustrated in figure 6.10, which shows margin structures in a component supplier's three routes to market for a given part: OE business, supplying the assembly line; original equipment spares (OES), selling into the vehicle manufacturer's spare parts business; and independent aftermarket (IAM), selling to independent parts distributors. In each case, the factory cost of the part has been set at an index value of 100 – physically the same parts, made on the same equipment. That is the left-hand part of each horizontal bar.

The next part to the right is the margin earned by the supplier's factory. The disproportions – and thus the internal cross-subsidy between businesses – are evident. The third part of the OES bar is the gross margin earned by the vehicle manufacturer's parts and

service division, on selling the part on to its dealers. This is huge, although manufacturers do incur substantial costs to conduct their spare parts operations, as we shall see. The third part of the IAM bar is the equivalent gross margin earned by the service division of the supplier, which performs the same tasks as the vehicle manufacturers' parts operations, although serving a different customer base, the independent distributors. The other part of the bars are the margins given to the distributors and workshops to cover their costs and allow them to earn a profit on parts sales. Suppliers are understandably extremely concerned about the protection of their right to sell their OE parts through all possible channels into the aftermarket. There have been numerous instances of vehicle manufacturers attempting to restrain them from selling into the IAM, claiming that the parts are theirs, by virtue of design or ownership of tooling.

Notice that the downstream part of the OES chain is kept on much tighter margins than its IAM equivalent. Here again we have indirect control by vehicle manufacturers of the prices consumers pay, through limiting downstream gross margins to inhibit discounting. The right-hand ends of the two bars tend to coincide quite closely, as each sector generally aligns its list prices against those of the other. It is this continual alignment, carried on country by country, which has produced large differences in the prices of both new vehicles and spare parts between European countries – a subject we shall revisit in the next section. The fact that the end list price is up to six times the factory cost sounds horrendous, but one must remember that there is a very large cost to making hundreds of thousands of different parts almost instantly available everywhere. The old complaint that a car made from spare parts would cost an unreasonable amount is not wholly fair – yet it does contain an element of truth.

Only 20–25 per cent of spare parts are designed and made by the vehicle manufacturers, while 75–80 per cent are bought in

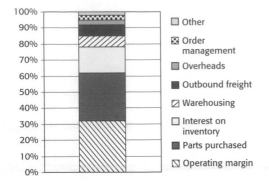

Source: Automotive Advisers & Associates, presentation to Automotive Logistics Conference, Bremen, 2001; *auto*POLIS estimates

Fig. 6.11 Cost and margin structure of a European vehicle manufacturer's spare parts business

from suppliers. As mentioned above, the vehicle manufacturers act as range assemblers and distributors to the dealers. They take a considerable gross margin on the parts, often in the 60–65 per cent range. They have invested heavily in very sophisticated and efficient parts procurement, warehousing, logistics, cataloguing and IT systems for this purpose. Even so, they make enormous operating profits on their parts business, as figure 6.11 demonstrates for a European manufacturer. Almost 40 per cent of sales revenues are absorbed by the cost of running the very complex business of sourcing parts from multiple vendors, assembling and cataloguing the product ranges, centrally stocking them, taking in orders and getting them out to the dealers. Another 30 per cent is the cost of the purchased parts, which still leaves over 30 per cent as the operating margin. This is pretty good in an industry which generally struggles to make 5 per cent.

The spare parts business typically makes a large contribution to the profitability of vehicle manufacturers. As this is generally low (see the McKinsey study),[4] spare parts business frequently subsidises marginal profits or losses on vehicle operations. The same applies to income from vehicle manufacturers' financing subsidiaries, a matter we shall return to in chapter 7.

Another fundamental point to appreciate is that the tied dealership system, although covering 100 per cent of retail new car sales, is in fact a minority phenomenon in terms of overall car sales. As figure 6.12 shows for Europe, the great majority of car sales transactions concern used cars, rather than new cars. This is no surprise in a mature and essentially saturated car market. Averaging across Europe, manufacturer control over new car sales covers only one-third of all transactions.

All this suggests that the sales/service link so beloved by the vehicle manufacturers and claimed as the only way is not a wholly natural one, that it may be forced under some circumstances, and that at least some alternatives exist. Furthermore, the cross-subsidy mechanism within dealerships is coming under increasing strain, as we shall see in the next section.

Further arguments are produced in support of the existing system, which are presumed not to be available in a 'free-for-all' distribution situation. Manufacturers claim that the cross-subsidies ensure network coverage, even in less-populated areas; that all elements of service and repair are available everywhere, even if the more complex repairs are not naturally profitable in all outlets; that the full range of vehicles is made available for sale and supported with full service everywhere; that a close relationship with selected, exclusive dealers is essential to ensuring the range and quality of both sales and service functions; that a strong brand identity is vital to the manufacturer's survival; and that a close relationship with selected, exclusive dealers is essential to preserving it. As we shall see on pp. 185–97, many of these arguments fail to stand up under closer scrutiny – and especially when the true economic motives are revealed.

While it may seem to the petrol-heads like an obscure and uninteresting backwater, the automotive aftermarket plays a key role in the profitability of dealers, vehicle manufacturers

---

4 Glen Mercer, McKinsey and Co., 'Road Work Ahead', *Automotive World Opinion*, June–July 2000.

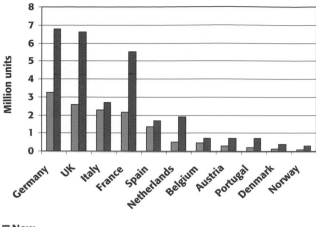

■ **New**
■ **Used**

Source: The used car market, 2002, BCA Europe

Fig. 6.12 Used and new car sales in Europe

and many component suppliers – a matter further explored in the next section. Jac Nasser of Ford correctly perceived this fact and sought to orient Ford to achieve a stronger control of the downstream sector and of the aftermarket in particular. He never had the chance to carry this through.

Where the money is earned – the fight for the aftermarket

If the franchised sector and its suppliers are having to make so much money out of service, in order to cross-subsidise new vehicles, why do other competitors not attack it? Answer: they do. The challenge to each of the locally bundled sub-businesses of the franchised dealer is that they are increasingly exposed to focused, scale-driven competitors:

- new car sales by direct sales from vehicle manufacturers to fleets (in Europe), which later generate flows of six-month to three-year-old used cars back into the marketplace – we shall return to this destabilising factor in a later section;
- used car sales by a growing breed of used car supermarkets, with a much greater ability to

display and maintain a wide range of cars, as well as the traditional local independent traders;
- service and workshop activities by independent garages, at least for routine service and repairs, offering lower labour rates (often 30 per cent lower), and by chained service specialists for the routine tasks such as tyre, exhaust and glass repair, which do not need qualified mechanics and fit well into multi-bay, service-while-you-wait outlet formats;
- body repair by independent bodyshops, as there is no restrictive franchise in this sector;
- other services, notably financial, by a plethora of independent agencies;
- technical repairs by specialists, such as diesel fuel injection workshops.

The fact that all service is not performed by franchised dealers is a matter that vehicle manufacturers and dealers prefer to try to ignore or obscure. But the facts are there: 80 per cent of service aftercare in the US and 50 per cent in Europe is performed by independent workshops of one kind or another. Because it matters so much to everyone's profitability, we need to take a closer look at the aftermarket.

Component suppliers

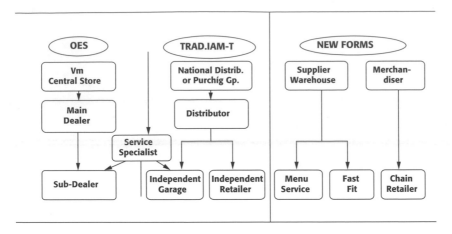

End customers

*Source: auto*POLIS

Fig. 6.13 Generic structures in the European automotive aftermarket

This really is the Cinderella of the industry, whose managers were described as barrow boys by their original equipment colleagues at one major supplier group. It is a neglected and poorly documented sector, which does not help the rest of the industry and other stakeholders achieve an adequate understanding of it. Its generic basic structures are displayed for Europe in figure 6.13, and they can be found, under differing guises and in different proportions, in every aftermarket in the world. But it is also still a national business and even very local in some respects – far from the great pretensions of globalisation that have swept the top levels of the automotive industry. The fact that the same structural elements are present everywhere is in practice about as helpful as saying that all men and women are alike because they all have two arms, two legs and a nose. The subtleties are in the detailed structures and the interrelationships, especially the latter, as the aftermarket is still a very relationship-driven sector.

Across the top of the figure are the component suppliers, who provide spare parts to the aftermarket. Note that 75–80 per cent of this production is conducted by independent suppliers and only 20–25 per cent by vehicle manufacturers – another important fact all too often deliberately obscured by them, as we shall see in the next section. They feed three distribution macro-sectors.

On the left is the OES sector. The entry points are the parts and service departments of the vehicle manufacturers, which operate huge centralised warehouses, in which they accumulate the spare parts ranges needed to support the vehicles of their brand. This involves not only vehicles currently in production but also an obligation to support older vehicles, out of production but still in operation, for up to ten years. This is a hugely complex task, involving multiple sources: the cataloguing of hundreds of thousands of parts references; providing detailed information to the workshops in the dealer network about which parts fit which vehicle and how to fit them; organising the physical distribution of these parts to the dealers, who act as local parts stockists and wholesalers; and ensuring that the right part is kept at the appropriate place for the right balance between maximising local availability and minimising the costs of carrying parts inventories in the distribution chain. The dealers carry the local parts inventories, selling them to their own workshops, to those of service sub-dealers, where these exist, and also to independent service and repair garages, when these cannot obtain the right parts from the independent parts distributors.

The distribution chains in this sector are mainly exclusive to each vehicle group and therefore very duplicative. Conversely, they are the only ones run on a pan-European basis – although this notably does not apply to prices, as we shall see in the next section. They are also very tightly controlled by the manufacturers, in terms of both margin control and the imposition of equipment and training standards on dealer workshops. Margin control is essential to protect the cross-subsidies described in the previous section. The OES sector is an integral and vital part of the command economy, which would not survive without the protection of tight controls and coercion of customers to return to it.

In the middle is the traditional independent aftermarket (or IAM-T for short). Independent service and repair garages have to deal with any make or model of vehicle. They cannot afford to carry inventories of the spare parts they need to service and repair them – the range of parts references required is huge and constantly growing – other than a few current and standardised items, such as engine oil, electric bulbs and wiper blades. All the rest comes from a network of local parts stockists – called jobbers in the US, factors in the UK, *grossistes* in France, *Teilefachhändler* in Germany, *ricambisti* in Italy, and so on. These have to be very local – the expectation from the garages is that most parts will be delivered to them (there is also a proportion of walk-in counter trade at the stockist) within 20 to 60 minutes, which requires regular van delivery rounds several times per day. Thus these local stockists are very numerous: 900 in Germany, where they are fairly well rationalised; 1,400 in France; 2,000 in the UK; 5,000 in Italy; 20,000 in the US.

For each aftermarket component supplier to reach enough local stockists to achieve full coverage of a national territory is a logistical and organisational nightmare. There is no simple solution to this and so different intermediate structures have arisen in different countries. A cocktail of different structures has emerged to fill this role in Europe, none of them wholly satisfactory. Germany used to have an intermediate level of distributors called *Werksvertreter*, literally factory representatives, who were the exclusive franchised regional distributors of the component suppliers, matching the federal political structure of the country. These had multiple franchises for different product lines, although not competing franchises within a given product line. The surviving larger members of this club have transformed themselves into regional distributors, selling directly to the garages in their home urban areas and via local stockists elsewhere, in part imitation of the roles of the US warehouse distributors (WDs) (discussed later). A number of strong regional distributors have emerged in France. Italy has one notable national importer/distributor in the form of Rhiag, a kind of national WD, whose role resembles that of van Heck and other large importers in the Netherlands or of Mekonnomen in Sweden. The UK had two national distributors, owning large chains of local outlets, Partco and Finelist. The latter collapsed shortly after being acquired by one of the large French purchasing groups – a classic example of 'look before you leap', as Finelist's structural weaknesses were clear for most to see. Partco was acquired by the contract distribution group, Unipart. Much of the running in the UK parts distribution scene is now made by major regional distributors. The French scene is dominated by the large purchasing groups, which combine the purchasing power of numerous local stockists to exert pressure on suppliers but do little to resolve the logistical problems of supplying to all these local outlets. Cecauto from Spain and Doyen of Belgium are the only attempts to create European-level structures. Other than that, the IAM-T remains largely a set of national markets. Participants in it largely try to cover all makes and models of vehicles. The different levels are linked by open market interfaces typically only weakly co-ordinated between them, which leads to many inefficiencies, such as duplication of parts inventories down the chains.

The third pillar of the aftermarket are the 'new forms', on the right-hand side of figure 6.13 These encompass fast-fits, which concentrate on simple repair operations that do not need a trained mechanic but can be executed by fitters. The two classic offerings are tyres and exhausts, with the latter pioneered by Midas Muffler in the US. By extension they also cover the tyre merchants, well developed everywhere, and the menu service outlets or auto centres. These have bays for fitting tyres and exhausts and for the simpler service items. They may or may not have associated retail shops, offering parts and accessories to the DIYer and perhaps other items, such as bicycles. The Halfords auto centre chain in the UK is an illustration, now split into AA Service Centres and the retail shops, which are owned by venture capitalist CVC. This was one of the two national chains of cycle stores that emerged before World War II (the other being Currys, now an electrical and electronic goods store chain). The French equivalents are Norauto and Feu Vert, and the German counterpart is ATU, the very successful creation of a local parts distributor, Auto Teile Unger, in the small town of Weiden, near the Czech border in Upper Bavaria, which now has effective national coverage with over 400 branches. French-owned chains have made some penetration in Spain. The new formats have made almost no impact in Italy, which is still dominated by 50,000-odd very small traditional independent garages and by a national aversion to DIY, which is not favoured by the tra-

ditional pattern of high-density urban apartment living.

Channels in the new forms subsector are quite tightly controlled, at least by the larger fast-fit and auto centre operators, some of whom are vertically integrated backwards into parts distribution for the resupply of their workshop centres. There are two very considerable differences, however, with respect to the OES channels. First, there are no proprietary or contractual links to individual vehicle brands. As a result, this subsector also deals with all makes and models of vehicles, within the limits of practicality – you might not find a muffler for a Rolls Royce at every Midas store but they will cover all the common vehicle applications. Second, it does not attempt to offer every kind of service. Quite the contrary, the whole name of the game is focus on a single kind of service, or a very limited range of rationally grouped services. This allows a considerable economic rationalisation, from the ability to offer 'while-you-wait' service to using labour that is trained in those services only and costs far less than fully qualified automotive mechanics.

Above and behind these subsectors lie the technical specialists, in areas such as diesel injection, automotive electrical systems, air conditioning, engine and transmission repair and rebuilding, etc. These are sometimes controlled as networks by systems and components suppliers upon whose technologies they rely. They are almost always all-makes operations. A further category is crash repair. This is a specialised craft sector, which does not readily lend itself to the creation of large-scale networks. Although a proportion of crash repair shops are owned by dealers, they still mainly operate on an all-makes basis – the deep skills required are not significantly brand-specific.

And here the genericity ends. As we have already been indicating, there are big differences between countries within Europe, not so much in the kinds of subsectors and actors present as in their relative market shares. Essentially it has to do with how quickly vehicle owners and operators desert the

Service spend and retention

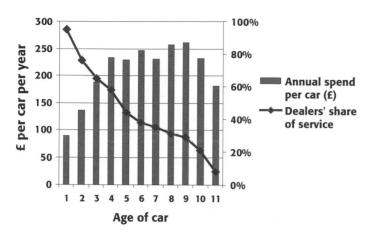

Source: Vehicle manufacturer

Fig. 6.14 Running away from the dealer – the UK pattern

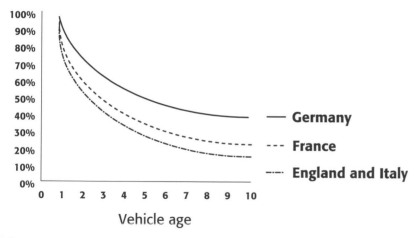

*Source: auto*POLIS

Fig. 6.15 Simplified dealer service retention curves in Europe

over-priced franchise sector. The detailed pattern for the UK is shown in figure 6.14. The collapse of dealer service retention after the first two years is spectacular. The high initial penetration, in the first two years of the vehicle's life, is mainly due to habit (or inertia), notably on the part of fleets (which dominate the UK new car market, as we shall see in a later section), but also to the perceived threat of invalidation of manufacturers' warranties if non-dealer workshops are used. The UK has some of the weakest dealer retention figures in Europe and is the country most akin to the US in this respect.

The different rates at which dealers' retention of service collapses as the vehicle ages

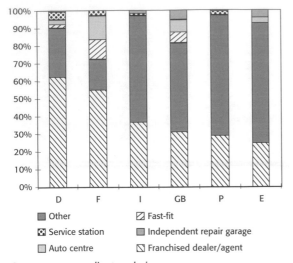

Source: *auto*POLIS client analysis

Fig. 6.16 Where brake pads are fitted

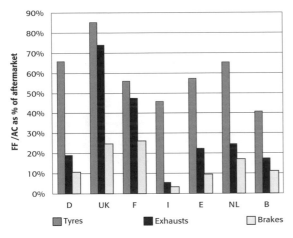

Source: *auto*POLIS

Fig. 6.17 Fast-fit and auto centre penetration in Europe

(and passes from one owner to another) are shown in simplified form for four European countries in figure 6.15. German customers stay faithful the longest and the British and Italians the shortest, with the French in the middle. This shows the differences in national propensities to have recourse to franchised dealers for service in any of the three car market sectors. These are rooted in long-established traditions. Combined with the dif-

ferences in the structures of the new car markets, this results in very large differences in overall retention of service business by dealers for the vehicles of their make in the national parc. At one extreme, dealers in Germany typically achieve 65–70 per cent retention, those in the UK 30–35 per cent. There are of course further variations by brand, with upline and Japanese makes usually achieving higher retention than volume makes.

This is obviously also true at the level of specific jobs, as shown for one of the most common (and safety-related, although simple) service jobs, changing brake pads, in figure 6.16. Again, this demonstrates that the market split is not simply between the OES and IAM subsectors. In their classic service sectors of tyres and exhausts, fast-fits and auto centre chains have achieved a huge penetration (see figure 6.17). Conversely, they have not done nearly so well in the more technical area of brakes. Motorists have long since learned to segment their own demand and to seek out the formats and offerings that best satisfy it, disregarding the voices of the vehicle industry, at least when they can self-diagnose the problem (as with exhausts, tyres and glass) and do not feel they are running any risk.

The upshot of all this is reflected in the national patterns of parts distribution in Europe, shown in figure 6.18. Germany remains OES-dominated, France has an intermediate position, and Italy and the UK among the other larger markets are dominated by the independent sector. France and the UK have the most vigorous new forms sectors, although Germany – a late comer – is now catching up.

Nor are the technical specialist service and repair sectors wholly tied to vehicle sales. The two major diesel service networks have always operated under the Bosch and Lucas (now Delphi) brands, these being the two leading suppliers of diesel injection systems. These are major independent systems and components supply groups, which serve multiple vehicle manufacturer customers. Radiator suppliers, such as Valeo, Behr and Serck-Marston, have long operated all-makes specialist service

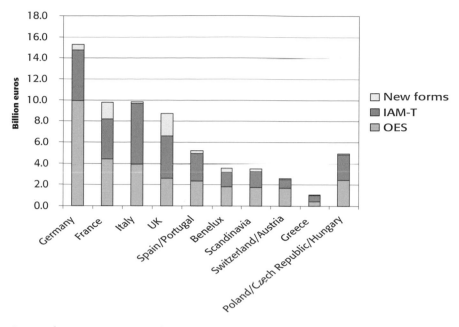

Source: Industry sources, *autopolis* estimates

Fig. 6.18 Macro-segmentation of the spare parts market in Europe

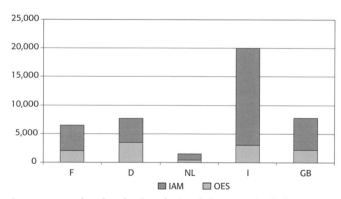

Source: autopolis, based on data from the Association Internationale des Réparateurs en Carrosserie (AIRC)

Fig. 6.19 OES and IAM bodyshops

networks, now extending into the growing market for air conditioning maintenance and repair.

Body repair is a major technical activity, involving substantial investments in equipment and training. Yet the bodyshop profession is numerically dominated by independent shops (see figure 6.19). While some of the larger bodyshops are dealer-controlled, the independents are able to obtain both vehicle manufacturer and insurer approvals. The physical and training investments required for body repair are generally not specific to vehicle makes or models. There are, however, some links where mechanical or electrical/electronic re-assembly is required. One key difference between the bodyshop sector and the rest of the vehicle repair sector is

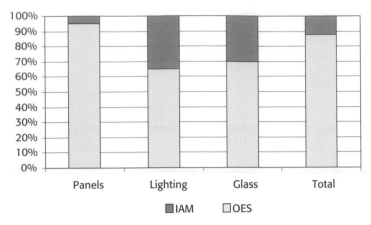

Source: ECAR[2]

Fig. 6.20 Distribution channel shares for body repair parts

the nature of the customer. Insurance companies pay for the majority of body repairs, which makes the insurance company, not the vehicle user, the buyer of services. Insurance companies will usually direct the customer to their own approved, local body repair shop, regardless of whether this is an independent or a franchised outlet. They can exercise considerable purchasing leverage, unlike individual retail customers. Here is some evidence from two national trade associations.[5]

70 per cent of bodywork repairs are conducted by independent bodyshops. 1050 of the total 1500 all-makes bodyshops are independent, 450 belonging to franchised dealers. There are some problems with equipment only being available to the franchised sector. Of the 1 million repair jobs per year, 50 per cent involve manufacturer's warranties.

Although half or more of these are on vehicles that are within the warranty period, 75 per cent are actually performed by independent shops. Nevertheless, the manufacturers, each in their own way, try to get owners to commit to the dealership. They issue repair insurance policies, which require return to the dealership, at non-economic prices. There are threats of warranty invalidation if work is conducted in non-franchised shops. The work of independent body shops is denigrated to customers who have made use of them, although most of our affiliated shops use fully trained personnel and OE parts.

There are some indications of vehicle manufacturers trying to use threats of warranty invalidation to dissuade motorists from having body repairs conducted in independent bodyshops (see quotation above). There also appears to be a distortion of parts supply into the bodyshops, with OES channels dominating, particularly through vehicle manufacturers' hold on the supply of body parts (figure 6.20).

The US shows the same aftermarket macrostructures as Europe, but with a huge growth in the new forms sector (see figure 6.21). The traditional channels have shrunk a good deal – IAM-T is now mainly concentrated in rural areas and small towns. Franchised dealers hold at the most 20 per cent of the service market for domestic brands, maybe 40–45 per cent for imported brands. The traditional role of servicing gas stations has shrunk dramatically too, with 222,000 in the 1970s and less than 40,000 today, mainly doing oil and filter changes, replacing tyres and a few tune-ups. They can be part of oil company care programmes. There are also about 130,000 independent repairers performing the more complex jobs. They are gradually being

5 Evidence submitted in connection with the European Commission's review of the Automotive Block Exemption Regulation, 2001.

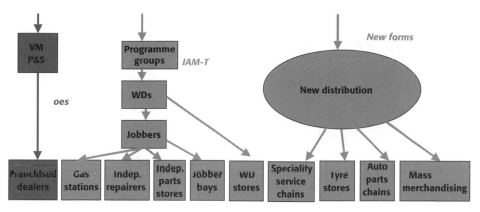

Fig. 6.21 Macro-structure of the US aftermarket

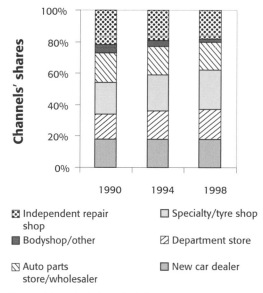

- ☒ Independent repair shop
- ■ Bodyshop/other
- ◩ Auto parts store/wholesaler
- ☐ Specialty/tyre shop
- ▨ Department store
- ▤ New car dealer

Source: Automotive Industry Statistics Report, 1999, MEMA

Fig. 6.22 Low services retention by US franchised dealers

squeezed in regular maintenance, however – shares of the service market for regular maintenance are shown in figure 6.22.

There is the same dropping-off of dealer service retention as the vehicle ages – see figure 6.23 – except that US dealers start off with a much weaker retention on one- and two-year-old vehicles than European dealers. There has been an explosion of new form retailing and servicing in the US, which now dominates urban aftermarkets. There are the speciality

service chains, e.g. 5,000 exhaust shops (Midas, etc.), the lube specialists (Jiffy Lube, etc.), doing mainly lube/oil/filters, with 70 per cent of this in oil changes, 3,500 glass replacement stores, 3,000 front-end alignment specialists, 6,000 automatic transmission repairers; tyre stores, mainly working on domestic cars. There are the huge auto parts chains (Pep Boys, etc.), mass merchandisers, discounters (KMart, Wal-Mart – with narrow parts lines), food and drug chains, home centres and department stores. The traditional distinctions between classes of players are breaking down: jobbers have acquired repair bays; only 60 per cent of WD business is now with their traditional trade customers, 40 per cent being with retail customers.

There is both growth and consolidation, and a merging of retail and servicing. As much as 45 per cent of component suppliers' business is now in the form of direct sales into the large chains. There has been a clear move back from 'do it yourself' to 'do it for me', with more two-income families with less free time from work, together with more complex vehicles and systems. The new forms retail stores sector is highly concentrated (see figure 6.24). The top five chains have over 90 per cent of all stores and sales within this sector – Pep Boys dwarfs all the others, with 662 stores, 6,900 bays and $2.4 billion sales.

The US has an extensive network of WDs acting at the regional level and supplying

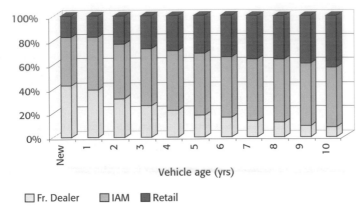

□ Fr. Dealer ▨ IAM ■ Retail

Source: Automotive Industry Statistics Report,1999, MEMA[3]

Fig. 6.23 US – outlet share by vehicle age

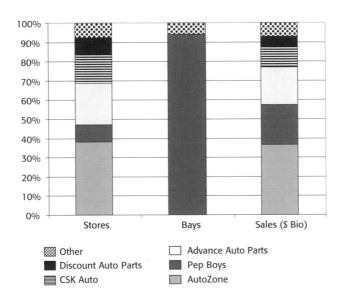

▨ Other   □ Advance Auto Parts
■ Discount Auto Parts   ■ Pep Boys
▤ CSK Auto   ▨ AutoZone

Source: Automotive Marketing

Fig. 6.24 Retail store concentration in the US

the jobbers in their networks. Many WDs are themselves organised into programme distribution groups, which are very large, exercise huge combined purchasing power, and are able to organise (programme) the rational stocking of parts throughout the long distribution chain. The distributor sector shows considerable chaining and concentration. Shares of stores, bays and sales are shown in figure 6.25. The top five programme groups

have 82 per cent of members, 85 per cent of stores and 90 per cent of sales.

Within the US spare parts trade, buying patterns are changing. There is much more HQ purchasing – a very visible change – by both auto parts chains and programmed groups, with very similar buying patterns. Customers throughout the chain have become more demanding. Apart from the obvious pressures for low prices and rapid availability

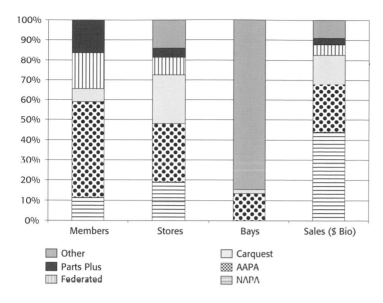

Source: Automotive Marketing

Fig. 6.25 Concentration in the US parts distribution sector

of products, they also want financial support for advertising and marketing (on their own or in co-operation with the supplier), tailor-made packaging and displays, help with in-store merchandising, and training in the use of products. Velocity/variable pricing is becoming the norm, with a trend to 'cost plus' rather than percentage off published list prices.

Competitive intensity in the US aftermarket as a whole keeps on increasing. Lines of demarcation between channels are fading and disappearing. Market segments resemble one another: customers, store design, display, buying practices, packaging. Branded products are present in all outlets, but private label brands are highly prevalent in jobber and jobber/retail outlets, as they are more price competitive. Programmed WD group 'private brands' are becoming national brands, with their own boxes, catalogues and parts numbers. Retail chain 'private brands' are also becoming national brands. Traditional three-step distribution channels are in steady decline, together with a decline in the number of traditional independent jobbers.

There is not a lot to be learned from the remaining regions of the world, not helped by the lack of consistent data. Figure 6.26 shows the split between franchised dealer and independent workshops in the Asia-Pacific region. There is no evident consistent pattern. The total contrast between its two current major automotive producing countries, Japan and South Korea, is notable. The independent aftermarket scarcely exists in Japan, so tightly is the market controlled by the domestic vehicle manufacturers. In South Korea one scarcely saw a dealer until fairly recently.

So the important territories, from the standpoint of the aftermarket, remain the US and Europe. The US is a shining example of free competition in the aftermarket. This has enormous implications for what could happen in the independent aftermarket, particularly in Europe, and to its relationships to the OES sector, on which dealers and manufacturers so depend for their profits. The apparently greater loyalty of customers in Europe to the franchised dealership system is not always

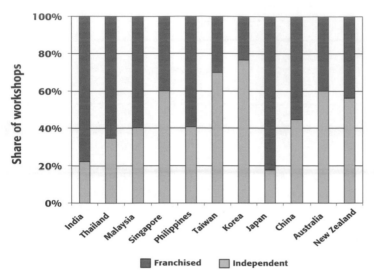

Source: oil company

Fig. 6.26 Structure of national workshop
populations in Asia–Pacific

what it seems. While there is an element
of convenience and reassurance in having all
products and services available from the one
local source, the vehicle industry's interest in
protecting the system is far from altruistic.
It enables the vehicle manufacturers to protect their revenues and those of their dealers
by artificial means, particularly through the
forced bundling together of vehicle sales and
service.

The vehicle manufacturers in Europe have
long tried to convey the impression that the
only serious alternative is theirs with the
sales/service link, with some grudging recognition of the new forms sector. The real picture is significantly different:

- Averaged across countries, half of current
service, repair and parts sales in Europe take
place in the independent aftermarket sector,
including safety-critical work.
- By the manufacturers' reasoning,[6] therefore,
either half the cars on European roads are
unsafe, or their presumption that only franchised dealer workshops are competent is
false.

- By that same logic, either half of car owners
are irresponsible, or half the market has good
reasons for disagreeing with the proposition
that the vehicle manufacturers' system of
the sales/service link is the only valid one.
- There is already an extensive disconnection
between sales and servicing of cars, through
the existence of an IAM that is as large as
OES. An even more pronounced disconnection is evident in the US for both routine
and complex servicing and repair.
- The OES sector has no monopoly of the more
complex, technical repairs. Some of the most
technical service and repair interventions
are referred to specialist workshop networks
that depend not on vehicle manufacturers
but on systems and component suppliers.

The US is hardly likely to move in the direction
of Europe. If Europe moves in the direction of
the US, the results for the franchised sector
and for vehicle manufacturers will be dire. As
we explain in the next section, a giant step
has been taken in just this direction.

[6] ACEA press release, p. 1.

Catastrophe in Europe – David sees off the Goliaths

The last section described the fault lines, forced relationships and strains introduced into the downstream sector of the industry by the franchised dealer system and the way it is run by the manufacturers. When two major systems rub up against each other too hard, the stresses become excessive and have to be relieved. The resulting adaptation is not necessarily gentle or orderly and can lead to systems collapses. We saw this, once the strains induced by its internal contradictions and the constant threat from the more successful order in the West put paid to communism, at least in Europe. Fortunately, the East German leadership gave way semi-gracefully, paving the way for the long-hoped-for reunification of Germany. Mikhail Gorbachev prepared Russia for change so that we were spared the doomsday scenario of a desperate attack by the Warsaw Pact on Western Europe. When tectonic plates in the Earth's crust move too far and too fast relative to each other, however, we get earthquakes, with devastating consequences for those living on or close to the fault lines.

What happened in Europe in the period 2001–3 constitutes an earthquake for the downstream sector of the industry, the aftershocks of which will continue to be felt for many years. To appreciate its nature and importance, we need to go back in time, in order to understand what led up to it. We have been, and continue to be, witnesses to a titanic clash of power and wills between a very large, pervasive and important industry and the political executive power of the European Union. One could hardly ask for a more potent piece of street theatre.

The European automotive industry recovered from the destruction and disruption of World War II with remarkable speed. Mass motorisation, which had begun in the 1930s, two decades after the US, resumed. Europe went through its one-size-fits-all Model T era in the 1950s, with mass-production of the VW Beetle, the Renault 4CV and Dauphine, the Citroën 2CV, etc. As in the US with the rise of GM, the market demanded a broader and more sophisticated product offering. It also became necessary to get serious about sales and service. Thus the franchised dealer concept was borrowed from the US and introduced throughout Western Europe. A marked difference from the US, however, was a somewhat lower degree of competitive intensity. Demand greatly exceeded supply. National manufacturers dominated their national markets – VW, Opel and Ford in Germany; Renault, Peugeot and Citroën in France; Ford, Austin and Morris in the UK; Fiat in Italy; SEAT, Fiat's licencee, in Spain. These companies were national institutions and it was simply taken for granted that they would closely control their routes to market. They could write what they wanted into their contracts with dealers. In a supplier's market, dealers could make good profits anyway, and were not much bothered by potentially inequitable clauses.

Then some cracks began to appear. A Ministry of Finance circular in France, known as the Delors circular (Jacques Delors, later to head the European Commission, being the minister), banned certain excessively one-sided clauses. Questions were raised about vehicle manufacturers' ability to impose themselves as the sole source of spare parts for their dealers, some independent distributors, notably in Germany, finding themselves excluded from this major sector, which they had previously served. There were fights over whether component suppliers could legitimately be prevented from affixing their brands to parts they sold into the OES chains. Last but not least, it became evident that manufacturers' contracts with their dealers were of an exclusive nature and therefore constituted vertical restraints on trade.

The immediate motivation of the founders of a united Europe was political, to prevent a recurrence of the cataclysmic wars which had twice nearly destroyed Europe in the twentieth century. Their ultimate objective was political union, with the example of the thirteen American colonies clearly in mind. Their means was economic union, with an initial emphasis on coal, steel and nuclear power. But the real engine of integration turned out to be the interpenetration of consumer markets, with the automotive industry a leading example. As national monopolies and oligopolies broke down in the face of the rise of intra-European exports and imports, enabled by the Common Market, the defence system for protecting national markets and the dealership system, was bound to come under critical observation.

The Treaty of Rome of 1956, the founding constitutional document of the then European Economic Communities, the precursor of today's European Union, explicitly banned such vertical restraints. However, provision was made for granting individual exemptions for single agreements and block exemptions for whole sectors, where the public interest was thought to justify it. Economic theory (notably the work of Williamson) has long recognised that exclusive agreements can be beneficial, through reducing transaction costs. The proviso, of course, is that they must not then be used to reduce competition to the point at which consumers' interests are seriously damaged. Thus in 1985 the industry negotiated for and was granted a first block exemption, Regulation 123.1985, which made official the status of its distribution system. As European law and regulation takes precedence over national dispositions, except in specific fields such as defence, this enabled the system throughout the Common Market countries, with other non-member states tacitly aligning themselves to it.

The public interest argument for exemption rested on the proposition that road vehicles are complex systems, which require specialist attention for maintenance and repair, without which public safety will be endangered. Furthermore, this should be conducted by the retailer who has sold the vehicle, so that end customers, the owners and operators of the vehicles, may get satisfaction in case of disputes over their quality. Thus the sales–service link became enshrined as an axiom. There was some justification for this, given the level of reliability that prevailed in vehicles at the time. Klaus Stöver, the European Commission lawyer who drafted the regulation, told one of us that one of his prime concerns had been to achieve a balance of equity between the large manufacturers and the small dealers. In retrospect, one may wonder whether his laudable effort did not simply enshrine the manufacturers' ability to divide and conquer. He was also visibly concerned about the manufacturers' propensity to control, feeling very uncomfortable at the idea that they might have knowledge of end transaction prices between dealers and consumers. No-one at the time seems to have realised that that control would be exercised by indirect means, through limiting the discount granted to dealers off list prices, so that they themselves would only discount to a limited extent, by rewarding them not through volume-related discounts but through bonuses linked to the achievement of sales targets – and that this would apply to both new vehicles and spare parts. At the time, though, no serious concern was expressed and all seemed well.

Exemptions, however, are granted for a limited period only, ten years in the case of 123.85. As the time for renewal – or modification, or no renewal – in 1995 drew near, rumblings of discontent were heard: openly, from consumers' associations, led by their European federation, BEUC; from the still frustrated independent parts distributors; and, much more discreetly, from franchised dealers, for whom life had become financially much more difficult, as the European market ran out of growth, consumers started to shop around, and discounting became much more prevalent. However, to the accompaniment of lobbying on an unprecedented scale, the industry got what it wanted, a new Regulation 1475.1995, which essentially repeated the tenets of its predecessor.

But there were some catches, which the industry seems not to have taken too seriously at the time. The Commission's attention had been drawn to some quite large price differences for the same models of new cars between different countries, which it could not rationally explain. The industry was therefore required to keep pre-tax prices within a band of plus or minus 12 per cent. As dealers were still granted exclusive territories, as part of protecting them against excessive manufacturer power, franchise agreements could – and did – ban them from soliciting business outside their allotted territories. As Mahomet could not come to the mountain, the mountain should come to Mahomet – consumers were given the right to purchase freely in any country they chose – a rather weak disposition, one might think, accessible to only the mobile few, but which nevertheless proved a serious problem for the industry. Finally, so-called black clauses were put into the regulation, mainly to protect the rights of the components industry and the independent aftermarket. This time, the new regulation was valid for seven years, to 2002, at which point it would be subject to review.

Trouble was to follow. The industry thought it had got its way and could operate its distribution system untrammelled. The promises were not honoured. Prices continued to move apart, especially in those countries whose currencies were not linked to the Deutschmark. When the Italian lira sharply devalued in the 1990s, national prices for new cars stayed fairly constant in lira, thereby making them instantly attractive to buyers from outside Italy. When German and Austrian customers tried to buy in Italy, VW's importer, on VW's orders, refused their business. This resulted in a fine of €123 million, eventually upheld in the European Court of Appeal. It could have been worse. The Commission has the power to fine an offender up to 10 per cent of its worldwide turnover – enough to cripple almost any company – and to withdraw the exemption from it, thereby destroying its dealer network. Even this sharp warning seemed to go

unheeded, with other companies offending and being fined.

The pound sterling had suffered the same fate as the lira, when the UK was forced to make a humiliating withdrawal from the European Monetary System in 1993. As the pound devalued against other European currencies, so the sterling-denominated price of imported cars had to go up – a natural enough result. In retrospect, this appears to have been manna from heaven for the domestic producers, especially Rover, which was the perpetual sick man of the industry. Given its financial state, it chose to go along with the trend, rather than try to regain share by competing on price. Ford, used to making large profits in the UK, followed suit. This may have given Rover's new owner, BMW, an unjustifiably rosy view of its prospects. Then, in the late 1990s, sterling revalued again sharply. UK car prices did not come down. This time, the imported brands chose not to cut prices.

The UK price trend is shown in figure 6.27. To construct it, we had to go back to base data, behind the European Commission's tracking indices. We compared a UK-market-weighted basket of vehicles, which were continuously in the indices. We compared the UK to Germany, France and Italy, which have similar rates of value-added tax and no other specific sales taxes on cars. We divided the price ratio by the ECU-to-pound exchange rate (the ECU was the predecessor of the euro). The downside 'stickiness' of prices is blatantly clear. The contrast with what happened to wholesale tyre prices (figure 6.28), in which there is a highly competitive market and a similar proportion of imports, is painful.

The growing level of excessive new car prices in the UK drew the attention of consumer bodies and the media. Whereas the custom in continental European countries is for technocrats to fix problems quietly out of the public eye as long as they can, the Anglo-Saxon tradition is more vigorous. Public protests, channelled through the media, are sometimes effective in putting pressure on politicians. The Trade and Industry Select

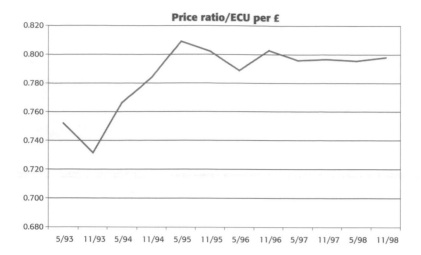

Price ratio/ECU per £

*Source: auto*POLIS calculations from European Commission data

Fig. 6.27 UK vs. Europe price trend

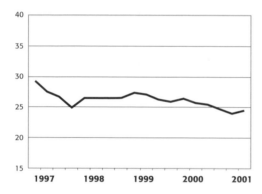

Source: Stapletons, UK Tyre Market 2001, from *Tyre Trender Tracker,* 2002

Fig. 6.28 UK wholesale tyre price trend (£ per unit)

Committee of the House of Commons held a public hearing in October 1998. It was a remarkable performance. Their indignation crossed party lines. They were well briefed; they were courteous to the representatives of the Consumers' Association; they were merciless with the representatives of the industry who produced the trite old arguments about price differences being caused by tax differences and movements in exchange rates. How, they asked, could one reasonably believe that prices could stick for months and years, in a sector where 70 per cent of the products

sold were imported? They were unimpressed that consumers could have recourse to buying abroad: 'Why should my constituents have to drive 100 miles to get a fair deal, let alone travel to the Continent?' asked one indignant member of the committee. They drove a wedge between the representatives of the dealers and those of the manufacturers, getting the former to blame the latter. They lambasted the Office of Fair Trading for its inaction. It was a wonderful day for common sense. Finally, and most importantly, they clearly identified the pricing abuses with the channel control conducted through the vehicle manufacturers' selective and exclusive distribution system.

The Office of Fair Trading duly conducted an investigation. The results and the lack of co-operation on the part of the industry caused them to institute a full-scale enquiry by the Competition Commission. The Commission's report was thorough and detailed, covering virtually every aspect of the subject. The conclusion was unequivocal: there was a complex monopoly in operation; in other words, a number of actors behaving in the same way, thereby producing a situation equivalent in its effects to a monopoly. The selective and exclusive distribution system was what made this

Source: www.eurocarprice.com, in *International Fleet World,* June 2003

Fig. 6.29 Pre tax car price, UK vs. European average

behaviour possible. The industry continued to protest, trotting out its conventional arguments. It even chose to boycott the Commission's public hearing. It was a public relations disaster. The Consumers' Association and the media campaigned against unjustifiable high prices, the former even taking a stand at the 1999 London Motor Show! A consumer boycott of new cars was launched. Parallel imports from other European countries flourished and new car prices fell, as the industry finally caved in – the size of the initial gap and of the subsequent fall is shown in figure 6.29. An unfortunate by-product, inflicted on the industry by itself, is a concertina effect in UK new car sales volumes, which will go on for a long time, similar to that produced by scrappages incentives in France and Italy.

Was this the end of the story? Was it just another storm in an offshore teacup, yet another case of those tiresome Brits being bad Europeans? It was not. To start with, the problem of unjustifiable price differences was limited to neither the UK nor new cars – although it showed up most flagrantly in the combination of those two. Europe had prices in disarray too, for both vehicles and spare parts, as figure 6.30 shows. Vehicle manufacturers claimed that tax differences were a principal

cause of differences in new vehicle prices, but this was because they made it so. True, Denmark imposes a crushing 180 per cent tax on new vehicles, the most extreme of any country in Europe. The manufacturers, importers and dealers tried to make up for this by sacrificing margins – and by making up the loss by very high prices for parts and service.

How, asked the Danish government's competition authority, could this be, when the independent distributors and repairers had no such cross-subsidy to finance and should therefore have out-competed them? Through threatening motorists with the invalidation of their warranties, should their vehicles go into an independent workshop, and by claiming that parts not sourced from the OES sector in manufacturers' boxes were dangerous 'pirate' products. They might have asked why the independents did not attack more vigorously. Perhaps because life was comfortable under the large price umbrella? All in all, though, there was clearly a disfunctioning market. At the other end of the mainstream spectrum of trade-offs, Germans paid more (pre-tax) for new cars but much less for spare parts. The British, and to a lesser extent the Swedes, got caught both ways. No wonder the

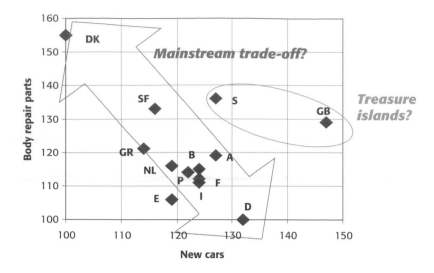

Source: European Commission, Comité Européen de L'Assurance, *auto*POLIS calculations

Fig. 6.30 Pre-tax new car and spare parts prices, 2001

European Commission felt the purposes of the single internal market in Europe had been frustrated.

Furthermore, the whole furore was exquisitely timed as a prelude to the European Commission's own review of how well Regulation 1475.1995 had functioned, conducted during the year 2000. The Commission was very thorough in its review. It had a new and very capable team to undertake it, under a new and very determined Competition Commissioner, Mario Monti. They were impressed by the work of the UK Competition Commission and the rational, economics-based approach taken by the UK Consumers' Association. The industry made two major strategic blunders: first of all, it failed to recognise the quality and seriousness of the new team at the Directorate General for Competition in Brussels; second, it was stuck in such a narcissistic admiration of its own distribution system that it could not imagine that others might have a different view of it.

The Commission published its critical review of Regulation 1475.1995 in September 2000. The overall conclusion was that the regulation had not been effective in implementing the single internal market in Europe in the automotive sector. The industry's selective and exclusive distribution system, mandated by that regulation, was clearly responsible for the industry's continuing ability to treat Europe as a disjointed set of national markets. Consumers were being frustrated in the exercise of their right to buy in other, lower-priced countries, unjustifiable price differences having arisen. To underpin its own assessment, the Commission ordered three independent analyses. One, from *auto*POLIS, critically reviewed the sales–service link, one of the major planks of the existing distribution system, explicitly referred to in Regulation 1475.1995. A second, from a team of academic economists in Louvain and London, looked at the price differences between countries and sought to identify their sources. It concluded that tax differences and exchange rate movements only partly explained them, leaving substantial unexplained residuals. A third study, by a German academic, investigated consumer attitudes to existing and potential alternative retailing and service structures, apparently as a counterweight to a market research study that had been conducted at the behest of the two large French vehicle groups.

Fig. 6.31 EU repossessions (Mario Monti with tow truck)
Source: Automotive News Europe, 20 November 2000

This time around, the Commission was clearly not going to be dictated to. In a speech that shocked the industry, Mario Monti stated that the intention was to put the consumer back behind the steering wheel and no longer to have the car controlled by the back-seat drivers. The spirit is wonderfully captured in the cartoon in figure 6.31, which appeared in *Automotive News Europe* in 2000.

The Commission held a hearing, open to all interested parties, in Brussels in February 2001, at which the authors of the reports were questioned and parties could express their views. It was a landmark event, in that it made clear that the downstream sector of the industry did not consist solely of selling cars but that aftersales service was equally important to the consumer and – in terms of profit contribution – to the industry. It was also made clear for all to see that the franchised dealer sector represented only half of the aftermarket. Even though the front rows of seats were filled with massed ranks of representatives from the vehicle industry and its trade association, ACEA, the independents had their day in court. A second hearing was held, on the fateful day of 11 September 2001, with its impact obviously diluted by the tragic events in the US.

Thereafter, the Commission proceeded to develop a new regulation. Some voices had suggested that the automotive industry no longer needed or deserved a specific exemption of its own and that it should come, like other sectors, under the provisions of Regulation 2341.1999, which applies to all vertical restraint agreements. In the end, it became clear that these were not specific or strong enough, so that a new industry-specific regulation was needed. The Commission ordered an analysis of possible regulatory options from Arthur Andersen Consulting and produced its draft new regulation in July 2001, against a background crescendo of industry lobbying. While the British government quietly sided with the cause of substantive reform, in de facto alliance with the consumers' bodies, the industry spared no effort in trying to oppose it. The French Finance Minister, Laurent Fabius, wrote to Mario Monti, warning of the dire effects of any change in the distribution system on the competitive position of the European automotive industry. So did the Italian Prime Minister, Silvio Berlusconi. Even the German Chancellor, Gerhard Schröder, was mobilised to warn of the terrible economic consequences of intended changes in the franchised dealership system, which would lead to massive job losses in that subsector – a potent political argument in Germany and most of Europe.

That particular argument was pathetically easy to explode. What was under threat, through proposals to allow more competition within the sector and thus the concentration of dealerships, was the sales function. To begin with, the whole of the downstream sales, repair and testing sector creates only about half as much employment as the vehicle production sector, i.e. one-third of the industry as a whole (see figures 2.18 and 2.19). Dealerships constitute about half of that downstream sector employment. Sales represents only a quarter of the total employment within a dealership, with salespersons having a notoriously high turnover: figure 6.32 shows the staffing structure of a dealership. So the bloody shirt was being waved about a sales function that constitutes a volatile one-twenty-fourth of the employment within the industry.

The parts and service functions are the economic heart of the dealership, as shown in a previous section, and – it follows – the major employers. Dealer workshops are well equipped – the manufacturers insist on that. There is a general shortage of qualified automotive mechanics. Those functions are not under threat in any reorganisation of the sector – in fact, the public interest is that they should expand. Dealer workshops are potential tigers – currently caged by the way the dealership system is run, and competitively weakened by having to cross-subsidise sales. There will be more about that in the next section.

Equally easy to explode was the economically infantile argument that the selective and exclusive distribution system is vital to the preservation of consumer choice, as it alone ensures that all of a vehicle manufacturer's products get exposure. To begin with, having an excessive proliferation of products under a regime of de facto maintenance of retail prices set by manufacturers is not genuine consumer choice. Secondly, one of the major functions of the dealer is to shift the less saleable products in the manufacturer's stable – that is what the setting of sales quotas and the bonus system are mainly about. The economic costs of this proliferation are obscured. Many of them are paid for by component suppliers, who don't recognise them or are too afraid of reprisals to protest.

The vehicle industry's approach to dealing with political institutions has not always been brilliant. It tends to be good on technical issues, although it has not always fully presented the longer-term options, in order to make the choices and their implications clear

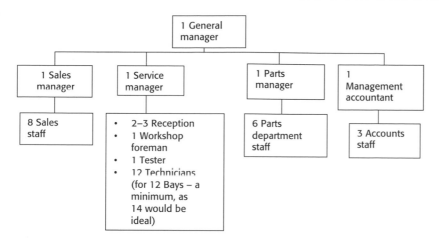

*Source: auto*POLIS, industry sources

Fig. 6.32 Staffing structure of a dealership

to politicians. It is quite good on presenting broader issues, provided there is consensus within the industry about them. But it is hopeless at it when they are controversial. Consequently, it too often comes over as being divided and badly prepared, unable to provide a well-formed and agreed opinion. There are blatant conflicts between manufacturers and their supplier and distributor partners. Particularly in the case of the European Block Exemption review, the vehicle manufacturers appeared to be largely on the defensive, unable to contemplate any alternatives and therefore unwilling to compromise. This can make the industry a difficult partner for governments to negotiate with. There are constant demands for special treatment and hand-outs, particularly incentives to attract new investments or keep threatened plants open.

In the end, the industry lost the argument comprehensively. It had dug itself into the hole of unconditional defence of the existing order, thereby throwing away its opportunities to manoeuvre. Its arguments were threadbare. A leading analyst of the automotive distribution and retailing sector in Europe, who had then moved across into European politics and was familiar with the workings of Europe's institutions, was scathing.

The draft came out and comments were invited from the European Parliament (which has to be consulted on regulations but has no right of co-decision, as it has on directives) and from the industry. In the end, the final document was essentially the draft, with the one concession that the clause on the right of dealers within a selective distribution system to establish themselves in other territories was deferred until 2005: a pretty small concession, considering the importance of the whole regulation. Mario Monti and his team kept their nerve admirably under the heaviest fire that the industry could muster.

So what did we get at the end of this fairly lengthy and acrimonious process? The text of the new Regulation 1470.2002 is not an easy read, as it is written in a legal form. It is, however, worth understanding, as it is in fact a clear exposition, helped by the explanatory notes also published by the Commission. There are many technical and complex aspects to it. We summed up the essential provisions during a speech made to an international aftermarket gathering in Madrid in November 2002 as set out in box 6.2.[7]

[7] John Wormald, 'Main Features and Potential Consequences of the New Automotive Block Exemption Regulation', delivered to the Congreso Internacional FIGIEFA, Madrid, 22 November 2002.

Box 6.2
What kind of a new regulation is this?

Regulation 1475.1995 was framed to enable a system that protected the vehicle industry and the way it managed its distribution channels. This included a system of financial cross-subsidies of new car sales by parts and service activities, which operates within component suppliers, vehicle manufacturers and dealers. Having delved into the functioning (or malfunctioning) of these markets and into their economic structures, the Commission has taken a different approach in devising the new regulation. In the Commission's own words, it is stricter but less prescriptive. It is based on a more economic approach, on understanding relationships within the downstream sector of the industry, and on the principle that economic operators should be allowed to organise distribution according to their needs, within certain limits. The Commission also felt it necessary to address both sales and service, the latter accounting for almost half of the life-cycle cost of vehicles. The new regulation, contrary to the initial urgings of some opponents of selective and exclusive distribution, does not abolish the franchised dealership system, but subjects it to much stricter conditions.

What does it say about sales?

It bans the combination of selectivity and exclusivity in sales, judged to have been a primary means of channel control for the manufacturers. Vehicle manufacturers must choose one system or the other in any country. They cannot have both at once. If a manufacturer chooses to give its dealers exclusive territories, whereby they are forbidden to sell into each other's territories, then those dealers cannot be prevented from selling to unauthorised resellers, who speculatively buy new vehicles for reselling on their own initiative, anywhere in the Union.

If a manufacturer chooses a selective system, it can select its dealers on qualitative criteria (for example, quality of premises) and, if it so wishes, additionally on quantitative criteria (limiting the number it appoints in any given area). In a selective system it can forbid its dealers to sell to resellers but cannot prevent them from pursuing business across the territories of other dealers. From September 2005 it will no longer be able to prevent dealers in such a system from establishing sales outlets in other territories anywhere in the Union. The whole thrust of the new regulation in this respect is to increase intra-brand competition, i.e. between dealers of the same brand. This is intended to counter the manufacturers' policy of reducing the number of sales outlets, which lessens the ability of consumers to shop around.

The new regulation also facilitates multi-branding by obliging manufacturers to allow dealers to display new cars of different brands within the same showroom, as opposed to the separate showrooms that could previously be imposed. Dealers can be made to keep them in distinct areas within the showroom, but one brand is not allowed to crowd out another by forcing the dealer to use all the space to display a particular product. If a brand-specific sales force is required, the manufacturer must pay for it.

Dealers must not be forced to restrict the right of consumers to buy across the Union. The availability clause prevents them or manufacturers from restricting the supply of vehicles to the specification of another national market, or using any other unjustifiable discrimination in prices or delivery times. Sales quotas and bonuses are not allowed to be used to favour sales to customers from within the dealer's territory or country. The right of intermediaries or purchasing agents, who act for a specific individual buyer, are reinforced, although dealers can ask them to identify that buyer, in order to ensure they are not resellers in disguise. Dealers are to be free to conduct leasing business. Leasing companies are considered to be end users (i.e. not resellers), except where a leasing contract provides for transfer of ownership or an option to buy before the end of the leasing contract.

Dealers' contractual rights are significantly strengthened. Contracts must contain the right for either party to appeal to an independent arbitrator in case of a dispute. They can be for an indefinite period, with two years' notice of termination (or one year in the case of network reorganisation with compensation), or for a fixed period of not less than five years, with six months' notice. Dealers are free to sell their business to other dealers of the same brand; authorised repairers can sell to other authorised repairers of the same brand; cross-sales between the two groups are not so covered and can be resisted.

What does it say about service?

The new regulation seeks to maintain consumers' freedom of choice where maintenance and repair are concerned. Dealers can no longer be obliged to perform both sales and service, nor can this be encouraged by cross-business incentives. They must have the option of subcontracting service to repairers authorised by the vehicle manufacturer but can then be required to tell customers where the nearest authorised repairers are located. Manufacturers are allowed to set selection criteria for these but only within carefully specified limits. Provided the authorised network has a level of retention of service for all vehicles of its brand in the national parc not exceeding 30 per cent, dealers can be appointed on an exclusive or on a selective basis, the latter employing both qualitative and quantitative criteria, i.e. the numbers of authorised workshops can be limited. Above this threshold, only qualitative selection is permitted, i.e. all candidates who meet objective criteria must be admitted. As the OES share of the aftermarket averages about 50 per cent across Europe, it is clear that only a minority of brands in a small number of countries will be able to constrain the numbers admitted to their authorised repair networks. Established brands will be exposed to more competition; emerging brands will have easier access to comprehensive repair networks. There can be no location clause for authorised repairers where a selective distribution system has been chosen. Repairers cannot be prevented from having authorisations from different vehicle manufacturers, nor from also operating as independent repairers outside those brands.

What does it say about the independent aftermarket?

The Commission is at particular pains to ensure the survival and capabilities of the independent aftermarket sector, which carries out half of all maintenance and repair activity in Europe. The regulation sets out to ensure that franchised dealers and authorised repairers have more commercial freedom to sell parts to independent repairers, and that authorised repairers are free to buy parts from the independent market.

The regulation also goes to considerable lengths to ensure that the independent sector can have free and fair access to technical information, training and spare parts. The list of organisations having such access is significantly lengthened, and now includes independent parts distributors – this is a major success scored by FIGIEFA – and roadside assistance operators. Safeguards are built in to prevent unauthorised tampering with safety and security settings.

What does it say about spare parts?

Very importantly, it introduces the new term 'original spare part'. This is a part of the same quality as the component used in the assembly of a new vehicle. It is made to the same specifications and production standards, although not necessarily on the same production line. Three categories are recognised within this class of spare parts:

- First, those made by the vehicle manufacturer. The manufacturer can require its authorised repairers to use these for warranty, free servicing and recall work. But it may not prevent its distributors, i.e. dealers, from selling them to independent repairers.
- The second category consists of parts supplied by component suppliers to the manufacturer, which sells them to its dealers. The component supplier cannot be prevented from putting his brand on these parts, on the packaging and on any documentation. The vehicle manufacturer may also affix his brand. Use of these parts can be required for warranty, free service and recall work. The manufacturers' dealers in a selective distribution system cannot be prevented from selling these parts to independent repairers.
- Third are those parts made to a manufacturer's specifications and production standards, although not supplied to it. Again, suppliers have the right to affix their brand. They cannot be prevented from selling them into the independent aftermarket. Authorised repairers cannot be restricted from using them.

'Matching quality spare parts' match the quality of the components used in vehicle assembly but do not have to be made to the original specification. Vehicle manufacturers cannot force their authorised repairers to use original parts supplied to them for normal maintenance and repair, as this would be a restriction on the repairers' freedom. A 30 per cent ceiling is placed on single-sourcing obligations for parts, with no fidelity rebates that might indirectly produce such an obligation. Nor can manufacturers oblige their authorised repairers to inform the consumer of the use of original spare parts from independent sources or of matching quality parts. Invalidation of warranty because either authorised or independent repairers have used parts not supplied by the manufacturer can also lead to the removal of the exemption from that manufacturer's distribution system.

Will it be effective?

While the regulation tries to avoid prescribing one or other distribution or service structure, it does squarely take aim at behaviour patterns that inhibit free competition. The list of hardcore restrictions is a tough one, removing the right to exemption where a vehicle manufacturer imposes any of a long list of restrictions on its distributors or repairers which could reduce fair and open competition.

There are also tough specific conditions, the imposition of which in vertical agreements can also lead to the removal of the right to exemption. They relate to 'non-compete' clauses imposed on distributors or repairers.

Threshold market shares beyond which the exemption will not apply are calculated across all brands for a group and country by country. The threshold is generally 30 per cent, but rises to 40 per cent for quantitative selective distribution of new vehicles and does not apply for qualitative selective distribution. The Commission has the right to withdraw the exemption where similar networks with a combined market share exceeding 50 per cent operate in such a parallel fashion as to exercise undue control over the market, or where there is evidence of abusive behaviour with respect to pricing or other conditions of sale.

The Commission has undertaken to conduct a further review of the functioning of the regulation by 31 May 2008, and to police the system in the meantime. In its own words, 'The Commission will be vigilant in monitoring the implementation of this important Regulation and will not hesitate to take action, where necessary, to ensure that the competition rules are respected and the Regulation operates to the benefit of European consumers.[8]

What consequences will it have for the aftermarket?

This is a carefully devised and tough regulation, which seeks above all to ensure free and open competition in the sales and service of vehicles and which will be enforced. It is a compromise, in that it could not satisfy everyone in every respect. I think the independent aftermarket has got all it could reasonably hope for. I salute all those who fought for change, and particularly FIGIEFA, the one federation that took a really clear position in favour of it.

But it does not prescribe a particular system and therefore does not promise success to any particular category of actors. For you, the independents, therefore, the future will be what you make it. The Commission is holding the door open. You have to walk through it.

These were our words and this was our challenge to one set of actors: those of the independent aftermarket. The events we describe in this section have shifted European vehicle distribution a fair way in the direction of what already exists in the United States (see figure 6.33). There is a slight relaxation on dealers selling to resellers. Dealers are not, however, any better protected against manufacturers bypassing them by selling direct, which remains a major difference from the US. The rules on multi-branding are now much closer to US practice. Dealer protection is strengthened, although still not nearly as strong as in the US. The sales–service link can no longer be imposed.

Under the previous arrangements in Europe, economic rationality in sales and service was given second place to the protection of the vehicle manufacturers' interests. There was a severe imbalance of power in the whole downstream sector of the industry, with the vehicle manufacturers effectively able to dictate the terms they wished to their dealer networks, subject to only weak regulatory constraints. This allowed them to run a fairly watertight and exclusive distribution system, within which they could extend their control to activities which they could get others to invest in. Furthermore, as we saw before, they were able to distort the economics of subsectors and businesses through enforced cross-subsidies. The downstream sector is not efficient today – that is generally the price of protectionism, which is what selective and exclusive distribution was all about. But once the arbitrary constraints are loosened and removed, the laws of the market and of economics will come fully into play in the downstream sector and it will ultimately become competitive.

But what does all this portend for the future? That is what the next section is about.

All power to the distributors – the emergence of countervailing powers

Figure 6.34 shows our view of the inefficiency of the automotive industry's distribution systems, compared to other sectors, induced by its defensive paranoia. Distribution costs vary widely by sector – very high, as a proportion of product costs, for the myriad cans of baked beans put within reach of every consumer everywhere, very low for the very low volumes of very expensive commercial airliners. Car spare parts, new cars and – very probably – new trucks cost too much to distribute because of the redundancy in franchised networks arising from brand

---

[8] Philip Lowe, Director-General for Competition, in the foreword to the Explanatory Brochure to Commission Regulation (EC) no. 1400/2002 of 31 July 2002, 'Distribution and Servicing of Motor Vehicles in the European Union'.

	Europe, old	Europe, new	US
Reselling	Banned	Allowed in exclusive distribution	Allowed
VM direct sales	Allowed	Allowed	Banned
Multi-branding	Strongly restricted	Allowed	Allowed
Dealer protection	Weak	Strengthened	Strong
Sales–service link	Imposed	Not imposed	Not imposed

*Source: auto*POLIS, adapted from Leonardo Volpato, presentation to Fleet News
Conference, Barcelona, 12 March 2002

Fig. 6.33 Closer to the US model

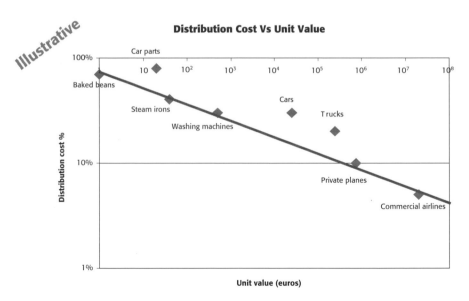

*Source: auto*POLIS

Fig. 6.34 Comparative efficiency of different
distribution sectors

exclusivity, plus disconnections and duplica-
tions in the independent aftermarket. One of
the silliest remarks we ever heard, from an
apologist for the industry, was that new car
distribution 'only cost 30 per cent' and there-

fore was 'more efficient' than the supermarket chains. The former involves 17 million
high-priced transactions a year in Europe. One
single UK supermarket chain, Tesco, handles
almost 50 million customers a year, buying

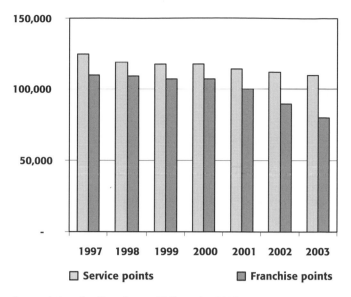

Source: Automotive News Europe, 17 November 2003

Fig. 6.35 Thinning out the networks: franchised dealers in Western Europe

1 billion low-cost items! No wonder it has higher costs of distribution.

It is said that inside every fat man there is a thin man longing to get out. That is exactly the case with the whole downstream sector. We have seen how US dealer networks are already more efficient than European ones because of their greater concentration. They live on even lower gross margins for new cars, even though their service retention is much lower. The costs of distribution are considered to be lower for vehicle manufacturers in the US (although they could be lower still, according to J. D. Power).[9] This is one of the reasons advanced for the higher margins earned there by vehicle manufacturers. It is where the Japanese manufacturers make most of their profits.

In Europe, manufacturers are continuing to rationalise their dealer networks (see figure 6.35. The number of franchise points is coming down fairly fast, as concentration of dealers is encouraged. But this remains a defensive strategy, with no significant concession to multi-branding of sales. The service points are coming down more slowly. Customer con-venience suggests that they should not come down. This was one of the reasons why the European Commission promoted the concept of authorised repairers – to enable the number of service points to stay up. Car sales are infrequent and most consumers are prepared to travel a fair distance, so rationalisation of sales points is acceptable. A cynic would say that making them fewer and farther between within a branded network is also a way to make it more difficult for consumers to play one dealer off against another on price. Some cost will come out of the networks of show-rooms and sales staff through this process but it is not radical change. The process will go on for perhaps three or four more years, leaving Europe with perhaps 60,000 franchise points and showrooms – still way above the US dealer population.

What happens beyond that? We can see two possible scenarios for Europe, shown in figure 6.36. On the left is the starting point, with a modest proportion of what we call

9 J. D. Power, 'Next Exit, the Megastore', Opinion Editorial, *Wall Street Journal*, 28 October 2003.

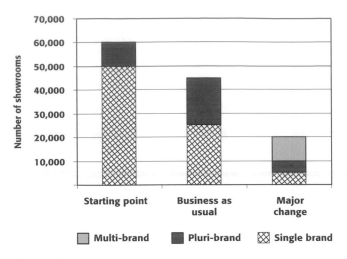

Source: *auto*POLIS

Fig. 6.36 Long-term dealership scenarios for Europe

pluri-brand outlets – pretty much today's mix. In the business-as-usual scenario, we think there will be some further rationalisation, to get Europe a bit closer to the US level of dealer population, with a significant degree of pluri-branding, much of it operated by dealer groups with more than one brand. This will save some additional cost but it will not fundamentally change the crazy economics of distribution. The number of points cannot be taken down much further in a still primarily limited-brand-per-outlet structure or sufficient density of coverage will be lost.

Within this approach, the lean brigade have been pushing what they call the leaning of distribution. But it is a typical partial optimisation of one sub-function. All it does is to centralise stocks, instead of dispersing them throughout the dealer network – entirely sensible, but it only addresses a fraction of distribution costs. They have also been promoting build-to-order (BTO), whereby no vehicle should be assembled unless there is a firm end customer order for it – not just a dealer order for their stock, which they will then have to push to unwilling customers through discounting. It seems to make good sense – just-in-time will be applied right through the supply and distribution chain. Everyone gets

exactly the car they want. No need to discount, so manufacturers' profits improve a good deal. There is a small catch though: not everyone wants a tailor-made suit; most want a cheaper, off-the-peg one. Remember, two-thirds of the car market by sales volume is used cars, in which there is no bespoke. And more and more retail consumers, in Europe at least, are buying second-hand, as fleet buyers take over more and more of the new car market. No-one asked the consumer. BTO is a complete non-flyer in the US market. It is too transparently a ploy to increase prices and take away from the consumer the right to shop around for deals. Not to mention taking the dealer virtually out of the sales loop. All of this is part of an increasingly desperate attempt to tie the consumer to the brand and to short-circuit the emergence of truly strong, truly independent retailers. It is like lean deck-chair distribution on the *Titanic*. Again, it may make sense for upline brands, but it makes less and less sense in the volume market.

All that changes if we accept the need for major structural reform of vehicle distribution and retailing, instead of fiddling around at the margin. That means that the identity of the outlet has to be disconnected from the brand. That is the key assumption behind the

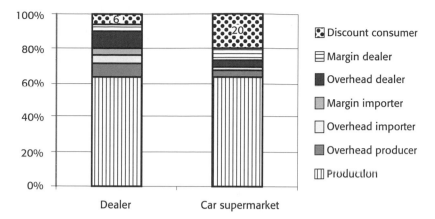

Source: Karel Cardoen, presentation to European Commission, February 2001

Fig. 6.37 Comparative economics of alternative distribution and retailing systems

major change scenario on the right. Its fundamental characteristic is the strong presence of multi-brand sales points. Yes, it is the Wal-Mart scenario, if that is the label you want to use, which is desperately emotive in US dealer circles. It is also the Cardoen scenario, to take a continental European example from Belgium, or the Trade Sales scenario, to take a UK one ('The local dealers don't send us Christmas cards', said a Trade Sales salesperson to us – he was formerly a dealer principal).

This is, of course, heresy in the eyes of the industry. So what could justify such a change? Primarily the economics. Karel Cardoen, the Belgian operators of used car supermarkets, have done the comparison. They are in no doubt about the economics of multi-brand superstores, compared to today's norm of the relatively small, single-brand franchised dealer. The company's comparative analysis is shown in figure 6.37. The car supermarket not only shrinks the internal costs of the dealership, thereby making its sales operations inherently profitable within the existing dealer discount – which would actually be increased, as such powerful operators would extract volume discounts, breaking the traditional fixed discount and sales-related bonus combination – but sales would no longer require cross-subsidising, so

the enforced sales/service bundling would no longer be an economic necessity. More importantly, the car supermarket would take over – much more efficiently – many of the marketing and promotion functions of the vehicle manufacturer and importer, thereby taking out a large proportion of the two-thirds of downstream marketing and distribution costs that are today incurred by the supplier. As much as 3 per cent of the cost of the average vehicle in Europe goes on advertising, most of it product-irrelevant and fatuously uninformative – more than the manufacturers spend on R&D. Another 4–5 per cent goes into running the dealer thought police, who try to micromanage the dealers – which a truly capable independent does not need ('All I want from them is accurate information on products and on delivery dates'). How much goes to pay for the national importers? They become completely superfluous under this scenario. There is a powerful economic case for changing the whole supplier–distributor relationship to a more conventional one (in terms of the great majority of retailing sectors), for at least the more price-sensitive consumer segments, and to let consumers have a choice of channels and formats.

Cardoen do not claim that all car sales should go through such outlets. There will be

• **Official dealers (single brand)**	**20%**
• **Multi-brand dealers**	**20%**
• **Multi-brand superstores (Cardoen)**	**20%**
• **Supermarkets (Tesco, Colruyt)**	**10%**
• **Niche players (only MPV)**	**5%**
• **Internet (Virgin Cars, Jam Jar)**	**10%**
• **Banks/leasing (private/corporate)**	**15%**

Source: As figure 6.37

Fig. 6.38 Possible channel shares of car retailing in 2015

room for more than one format, they say, illustrating this with possible channel shares in 2015 (figure 6.38). All they are asking for is the freedom of distributors to organise themselves as they see fit – a condition which exists in the vast majority of other retailing sectors. The key is to segment the market on the basis of the requirements of consumers, not by supplier brand. Traditionalist consumers will buy food at their local corner shop; the image-conscious at the delicatessen; the no-nonsense buyers at the supermarket; the wholly price-driven at the discount store; those driven by efficiency and time saving direct over the internet. And all of us may exhibit any of these behaviours under different circumstances. The single-brand dealership network is probably just right for Mercedes and BMW, who can afford to put up enough stores for it. The customers expect it as part of the feeling of exclusivity. Service will continue to be bundled in. But what sense does it really make in most of the volume car market? Of course, the whole scenario supposes that the distributor is no longer a conduit into the market for the output of the assembly plants and an adjunct to the product brand but rather an agent on the side of the consumer, a reflector and consolidator of real market demand – which the franchised dealer, however capable and conscientious (and they mostly are), is not, in the last analysis.

Will it happen, or not? It depends on someone stepping into the breach and their being supplied. That already happens to a very

limited degree in Europe, where the small number of all-makes new car supermarkets find their supplies – somehow: through the export sales structures of the manufacturers; via dealers – and even importers – who are desperate to shift excess products. It is much less obvious – curiously – in the US, where vehicle manufacturers' aggressive corporatism has in effect been countered by dealers' defensive corporatism. Just look at the storm of fury and derision provoked by J. D. Power III's suggestions, made in that article in the *Wall Street Journal* in December 2003, that multi-branding might make sense and that automotive distribution might have a thing or two to learn from Wal-Mart. It was regarded as heresy, judging by letters to the trade press with calls for a boycott of his business. But a few voices were raised in his defence, reminding us of what J. D. Power have done for consumers – and for dealers – with their independent appraisals of product quality. They were not loved for it at the beginning but became accepted as a vital component of the industry. There were similar squawks of protest from European vehicle manufacturers when consumer federations and governments launched independent crash tests ten years ago. Now they are proud to receive a high rating from them. It is all about the need for countervailing forces to emerge – the whole thrust of this book.

There are even signs of movement – ever so timid – in Japan, with VT Holding Co. acquiring three Nissan Motor Company sales units. Automakers have nurtured sales affiliates, while keeping them under their control through the manipulation of sales incentives. But amid faltering growth in the new vehicle market, a growing number of sales companies are striving to improve the efficiency of their operations and win more freedom from automakers. In stark contrast is the Beijing Asian Games Village Automotive Exchange: open 365 days a year and displaying more than 500 models sporting 90 different badges.[10] It

---

[10] 'Souk to Supermarket', *Autoasia*, Q3 (2003), p. 10.

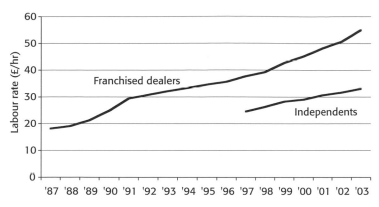

Fig. 6.39 Trends in UK workshop labour charge-out rates (£ per hour)

Source: Chris Oakham, *RMI/Sewells Retail Motor Industry Pay Guide, 2004*

sold over 25,000 cars in the first half of 2003 and was due to move to a new 100,000 square metre site at the end of the year, where service will also be provided. It is a stripped-down, open-air, no-nonsense kind of place – the opposite of the brand temples of conventional dealerships and rather like the UK's Trade Sales site.

Very similar arguments apply to the service and repair aftermarket. Let us look at one aftermarket, the UK, which, as we explained earlier, has structures conveniently somewhere between those of continental Europe and the US. Figure 6.39 shows what has been happening to dealer labour charge-out rates in the UK, as new car business becomes less and less profitable, and as the volume of aftermarket service falls. The dealer's service cash cow is starting to get dangerously overmilked, as the internal cross-subsidy mechanism is driven in an ever higher gear. It is not too different elsewhere. It costs 38 euros an hour for an independent repairer in France, 53 euros an hour for a franchised service dealer and a whopping 80 euros an hour for a main dealer.[11]

But not so whopping as in the UK. Figure 6.40 compares dealer charge-out rates between the UK, France and Germany. They are presented as the rate divided by the general cost of labour in the national economy, and then indexed back to France at 100. Rates are higher in Germany than in France but broadly proportionate to their different levels of general labour costs. The UK is well out of line. Cars, spare parts, labour rates. No wonder it was referred to as Treasure Island by vehicle manufacturers. Of course, it is a bit more difficult to buy a service abroad than to buy a new car from another European country, perhaps with the help of an intermediary. Only in this instance there is no monopoly channel – there is real competition from the independent aftermarket sector. Or there ought to be, if proper structures emerged.

Price is one important factor for consumers. Convenience is another. In the case of service, that means proximity. Figure 6.41 compares how far one has to go on average in the UK to get a job done, with the average duration of that job. Filling one's fuel tank takes 5 to 10 minutes. Provided one does not let the fuel get too low, the proximity of filling stations should not be a great problem. Yet there is, on average, one within 6 miles, even for those who are fussy about their brand. If not, then it is within 2 miles. A tyre or an exhaust job takes an hour or less: no great problem, therefore, waiting while it is done – a great convenience, in fact. So one can afford to drive to the fitting station. With a tyre chain outlet

[11] 'Service Changes in France', *Automotive News Europe*, 20 October 2003.

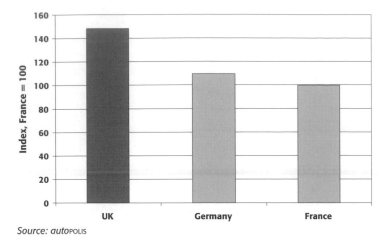

Source: *auto*POLIS

Fig. 6.40 UK vs. French and German service prices

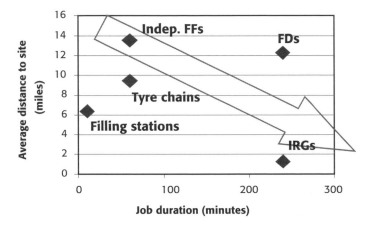

Source: *auto*POLIS
Note: FFs = Fast-fits (Midas Muffler type outlets), FDs = franchised dealers, IRGs = independent repair garages (all makes)

Fig. 6.41 Network density and consumer convenience in the UK

within 10 miles, the UK market is in fact over-served. The fast-fits, led by Kwik-Fit with its 700+ outlets, have the balance about right. A half-day or all-day service job, on the other hand, needs proximity – who is prepared to hang around the shop waiting all that time? It must be close to home or work. The figure shows that, even with 7,000 dealers in the UK, there are too few of their workshops for this purpose. On the other hand, there are

too many small, under-equipped and under-qualified independent repairers. But no wonder they stay in business, when the dealer workshops are so inconveniently located and so over-priced.

It is not actually a problem of there being too few dealer workshops. There are ten times as many as there are Kwik-Fit outlets. It is that they are fragmented between thirty-four different brands. That is the price of brand

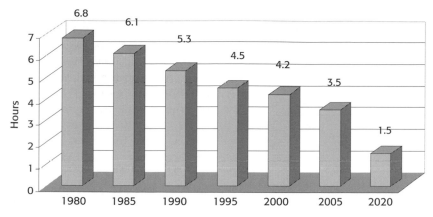

Source: AVAG

Fig. 6.42 Less and less routine service required: maintenance and repair hours per vehicle and year

exclusivity – thorough-going inconvenience for the consumer. In this age of convenience and instant gratification, it is madness. It has only been kept in place by the old regulations. Again, the whole thing is economically inefficient, because of (a) single branding and (b) forced bundling together of sales and service – the latter better managed in the Latin countries of Europe, through the large networks of close-by service sub-dealers.

The last people who seem to have been consulted in the design of the existing arrangements are consumers. So what do they want when it comes to routine service and maintenance? They certainly want convenience, which mainly means proximity. Yet there is too little of this in the franchised sector, too much of it in the independent sector. They also want quality, i.e. getting it right first time and doing it on time. In this case dealers are reasonably good but independents may have more problems, although both sectors are highly variable in this respect. Consumers want a reassuring brand image too – and here the dealers have it, through rub-off from the parent brand, while the independents are just that – they do not belong to any network (but that could change). They want customer relationships – the manufacturers and their dealers invest a fortune in customer relation-

ship management (CRM) systems and call centres, the independents rely on personal contact. (Guess which is more effective?) And, last but certainly not least, consumers want price – with the dealers increasingly out of touch on this, compared to the independents.

So a widening gap is opening up between the two halves of the aftermarket. It is being accentuated by two strong underlying forces, driving them apart. The first is that quality effect. Figure 6.42 shows what is happening to the demand for routine service. It is continuing on a strong downward trend. Service intervals have increased. Service hours have decreased. That puts even more pressure on the dealer cross-subsidy mechanism: fewer hours mean higher hourly rates. That is largely driven by the greater durability of components, an example of which is shown in figure 6.43. It is a triumph for the vehicle manufacturers and especially for their suppliers. But it also means that failure (as opposed to routine wear and tear, as for brake pads or oil filters) now happens so late in the vehicle's life that the repair falls into the lap of the independent repairers. This means fewer cash cows for the dealer, and those that are left have to be milked ever harder.

But we also have an opposing trend, exemplified in figure 6.44. The number of operating

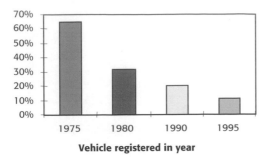

Source: *auto*POLIS client analysis

Fig. 6.43 The shrinking herd of cash cows: probability of master cylinder failure during vehicle's life

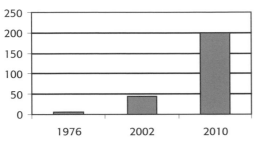

Source: Systems supplier

Fig. 6.44 The rising tide of electronic control systems: number of sensors per new car

parameters in a vehicle that are monitored with the help of sensors is rising exponentially. And behind each sensor now stands a logic circuit and perhaps an actuator to correct the out-of-line condition. And, as we explained on pp. 139–40, they increasingly talk to each other, under software control, through a multiplexed data-bus system. The development of these new systems was not intended as a means of shutting out the independents – we know all too well how far maintenance and repair issues tend to be from the minds of enthusiastic designers. Yet over-enthusiasm for them seems to have helped Mercedes and BMW crash from the top of the heap to the bottom in the J. D. Power quality ratings, and in those of ADAC, the respected German automobile club. ADAC's tracking of 500,000 vehicles showed that electrical and electronic faults were up 23 per cent in 2002

compared to 1998, with failure rates ranging from 5.4 to 36.3 per 1,000 vehicles per year – heading fast into the unaccceptable zone. Moreover, the non-standardisation of systems and their software protocols is a real problem for independent all-makes repairers.

The concerning thing in all this is that the two halves of the aftermarket risk being driven further apart than ever, with consumers left facing more difficult choices and less real competition for their business, especially when it comes to more complex repairs. Look at the comparative ratings of the sectors in figure 6.45, on the five dimensions of convenience, quality, brand image, relationship and cost. A widening split of this kind invites competitive incursion from whomever can put together a better formula. That is exactly what happened in the tyre and exhaust business with the arrival of the fast-fits, which provide drive-in convenience with sufficient proximity, enough of a reputation for quality, their own strong brand images, enough of a relationship in-store, and competitive pricing.

The questions now are not whether and how so much as who and when. Three or four competing national networks of properly equipped and qualified all-makes branded independent service outlets would do the job. That would still leave room for regional and even local operators, or for anyone who chose to specialise in a particular set of functions or kinds of vehicle. As for the distribution and retailing of vehicles, what is needed is freedom to compete and no forced link to vehicle brands, which, again, does not at all preclude voluntary links. What is needed is a set of strong operators, who are in the business of service and repair for its own sake, not as a means to keep customers in the branded dealership and to extort as much money from them as possible to prop up its dubious economics.

Who? Here are some possible candidates:

• Dealer groups could be transformed from their historic structures and roles as

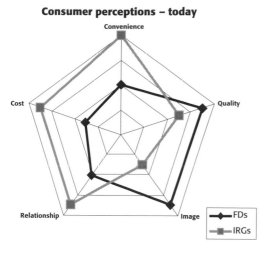

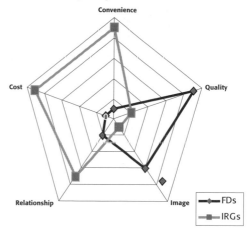

*Source: auto*POLIS

Note: FD – franchised dealer, IRG – independent repair garage

Fig. 6.45 Doing the splits

conglomerates of individual single-brand dealerships into true multi-brand sales and service chains. Today they are still too fragmented, sales-driven and dominated by vehicle manufacturers in most cases – but that could change. Relieved of the burden of cross-subsidising vehicle sales, their workshops could become extremely competitive.

• Parts purchasing/distribution groups are already creating their own all-makes garage chains. But they will have to move fast on garages and change over to co-operating with suppliers in supporting the IAM, rather than simply pressuring them for more discounts.

• Menu service chains/auto centres could achieve national scale, quality and brand image in current service and repair – they start with the priceless assets of knowing how to organise chained formats and of having strong consumer brands, distinct from product brands. But they will need to step up to the new technologies.

• Fast-fit chains could upgrade from de-skilled tasks to full service capabilities – they have the same network and brand strengths as the previous category. But this means a completely new set of skills in the stations,

which may not be easy within their current formats and the capabilities of their existing, de-skilled staff.

• Systems suppliers could create more all-makes specialist referral networks. These are long established in diesel injection systems and are starting to emerge in air conditioning. They could be the specialist back-up tier in diagnostics/electronics, enabling the transformation of other entrants.

• Vehicle manufacturers could get serious about real all-makes service, as opposed to their past and present marginal initiatives, which lack any clear focus or purpose. This would, however, require a considerable change in mentality, from one of protectionism to one of service.

When? Figure 6.46 is a major change scenario for the shares of bay capacity for current service and repair in the seven largest European national aftermarkets (which constitute 85 per cent of demand in Europe). The winners (apart from the consumer) are new all-makes service chains – which barely exist today. The major losers are the traditional independent repair garages; the unqualified will disappear, the qualified will join the chains. The other

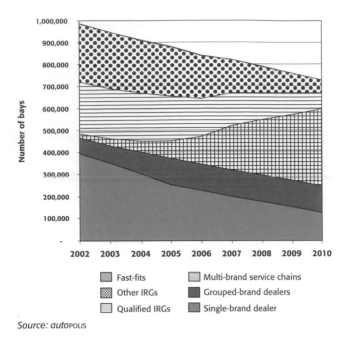

Fig. 6.46 The major change scenario at the workshop level in Europe

loser is the single-brand dealer workshop. The dealers will get doubly hit as this scenario will trigger a massive restructuring of spare parts distribution. Currently, in Europe, there are three times as many local spare parts stores housed by franchised dealers as there are independent parts distributors, for the same old reason – the duplication, nay multiplication, of channels caused by single-branding. Large multi-brand workshop networks are hardly likely to source parts for each brand of vehicle from a different provider. It will play straight into the hands of the independents, who will, however, need to get their act together pretty seriously in terms of building taut, integrated distribution chains.

The economic gains are likely to be formidable. Direct sourcing of vehicles by large multi-brand distribution outlets could cut car prices by 10 per cent. Well-qualified dealer (or ex-dealer) workshops that no longer have to cross-subsidise new car sales could drop their rates 20–30 per cent. Taking out the vehicle manufacturers' monopoly rents on spare parts and rationalising the distri-

bution chains could drop the price of parts by 20 per cent. Everyone gains in this except the vehicle manufacturers – initially, at least. Stripped of their protected proprietary sales channels and their large profits on spare parts, they would come under intense financial pressure. But there is a silver lining. The new distributors would not expect to carry every one of their marginal products: just the opposite, in fact. The resulting shake-out of superfluous product proliferation could take 10–20 per cent out of the product engineering and manufacturing cost base, through all the levels of the supply chain, from manufacturers back to tier 3 suppliers. The new distributors will also take a pretty jaundiced view of manufacturers' attempts to hang more high-margin decorations on the Christmas tree – fitting ever more products that consumers neither want nor need. Navigation systems are ideal examples. Who needs them? Other than taxi drivers and delivery drivers or those trying to get across Tokyo, 95 per cent of personal journeys are along familiar routes. And as for telematics and all the other added gadgetry in the pipeline, excluding government-mandated tolling systems, just how many of us are going to want to convert our cars into mobile offices? And how many of those who do this, or the large number who buy entertainment systems – especially if buying a used car – will want to be tied to the manufacturer's channel and products?

The manufacturers will not make this scenario happen. They will prefer to continue as a bunch of walking wounded, limping along more or less in step. At least the established majors will. The new entrants may take a different view. But we think the big push must come from other parties with enough power to force change. All it needs is vision, aggregated buying power and financial muscle.

In the UK, quirks in personal taxation created a large fleet sector in the new car market years ago. Depending on the definition, it is 50–70 per cent of the new car market. In France it has topped the 40 per cent mark. It is a wonderful dumping ground for surplus production, starting with sales to the short-term rental fleets. Even if the dealers are nominally involved, they only get a small margin on the transaction, the prices being negotiated directly between manufacturer and buyer. A growing proportion of the fleet market is supplied on a lease basis, by leasing companies. Within that, an even faster-growing share is taken by full service leases, in which service and repair are included, as well as the financing of the vehicle. Leasing companies are obviously very interested in new car prices and the residual values at which they can remarket them at the end of the lease period. They extracted from the European Commission the right to be considered end users, as part of the new Block Exemption Regulation. While still relatively fragmented, they are consolidating. In the UK, at least, they are experimenting with non-dealer service. An IBM Consulting survey in the UK, France and Germany reported 85 per cent of fleets and 45 per cent of retail customers being willing to transfer out of the franchised network. The UK fleets voted with their feet on tyre and glass replacement years ago. There is perhaps not quite the same danger in the US, where vehicle manufacturers are banned from direct sales, by-passing their dealers, by the dealer laws. This includes internet direct sales, thanks to a court case in Texas. Fleets make up about 15 per cent of the new car market in the US, compared to up to 50 per cent in Europe. Corporate fleets still take 95 per cent of their vehicles from the Big Three and the situation is similar in Australia, where Holden and Ford (the traditional large domestic manufacturers) also dominate the fleet market. In Europe, fleets are fragmented and the leasing company generally carries the residual value and operating cost risks. In the US, they are cohesive and the corporate customer carries these financial risks.[12]

Banks and consumer finance companies have always been involved in financing vehicle purchases. They are starting to ask questions about manufacturers' attempts to tie their dealers to their captive finance arms. Both manufacturers and dealers are very dependent on finance and insurance (F&I) package sales for profits in the US, a little less so in Europe. The convenience argument is powerful: sign the dealer's loan agreement and get your car fast, as opposed to having to go and talk to your bank or other independent source of finance. No wonder the European automotive industry was worried when the European Commission proposed to impose a fourteen-day cooling-off period on all consumer credit. The system would change if the distributors changed sides from being manufacturers' outlets to acting for the consumer. They could then act as brokers on F&I, or work with independent brokers.

Insurers have the independence, the clout and the access to policyholders to wrest monopoly parts rents from vehicle manufacturers through all-makes purchasing/distribution structures. They will, however, need to make a fundamental change in their attitude towards

12 'Vive la différence', *International Fleet World*, October 2003, p. 12.

the body repair shops, supporting them and taking responsibility for them, instead of merely squeezing their labour charge-out rates. In the UK they are already qualifying alternative sources and distribution channels for body panels. They might lend their authority to helping consumers understand that an original equipment part no longer has to come via a vehicle manufacturer's dealer network and in their boxes.

Once again, we are talking about consolidation in the ranks of the industry's partners and of the need to behave differently towards them in markets which are becoming more transparent and less subject to command-and-control manipulation. A revolution is brewing.

7

When the numbers do not add up

The value destroyers – the rotten financial performance of most vehicle manufacturers

Having painted a picture of an industry which has been filled with mounting troubles for a decade, why was it not more obvious? As Glenn Mercer who heads up the automotive practice with McKinsey in Cleveland puts it, 'the industry is structurally broken'. Why then were we not always reading screaming headlines about the dangers facing this, one of the most important and largest industrial segments in the world, during the late 1990s and beyond, when things became critical?

There is no good answer. Partly, it was because the world's news agencies and news readers are much more interested in stories about the here and now. Partly, it all happened so slowly; it was like a creeping sickness that was difficult to diagnose precisely because it was progressive. Partly, it was because much of the story was covered early on, in dribs and drabs, making it yesterday's news. People got fed up with endless warnings that the sky was falling – and then the business seeming to go on as usual. It sounded like irrelevant doomsaying at a time of booming IT stocks, bubbling house prices and the supposed new paradigm of economic growth.

There was one business sector closely affected by the industry, however, other than those that were direct suppliers and tied distributors being forever trampled on by the carmakers (and consequently afraid to speak out), which identified many years ago exactly what was going on. Some companies within it issued warnings and wrote papers about

the troubles. Almost all reduced their exposure. This sector was the banking and finance industry which long ago understood the severity of the troubles facing the world's automobile business. Progressively, the banks jumped ship. Unlike the suppliers and dealers, who are virtually 100 per cent dependent on the manufacturers, they have alternative sectors to invest in. Deutsche Bank, for example, produces a great many excellent reports on the auto industry and on many other industries. Its extensive 2002 report[1] opens with a still from a Laurel and Hardy movie (figure 7.1). Ollie and Stan sit bewildered and slightly stunned by the wreckage of the automobile that has fallen apart around them. It was an especially good choice, reflecting the feelings of many shareholders and industry watchers about the outlook for the automotive industry today.

In the course of running our consulting and forecasting business, and when chairing or speaking at industry conferences, we have talked to dozens of people in the vehicle and supplier industries, in governments and in the downstream sector. Many have told us stories about the bully-boys at the top, about the financial hardships they face and about the massive fissures opening up in the business. But all their views are essentially soft, qualitative and lacking in that extra something which makes their voices so undeniable. This is why banks, financial information providers and the more thoughtful and responsible academics offer an especially

[1] Deutsche Bank, *The Drivers: How to Navigate the Automotive Industry*, 2002.

Source: Deutsche Bank, *The Drivers*

Fig. 7.1 A jaundiced view?

valuable insight into the industry because their views are reflected quantitatively. They provide the missing hard evidence. In this section we would like to give particular thanks to Deutsche Bank, Citibank, Goldman Sachs and Bloomberg who have provided us not only with data but also with some of the thinking that goes behind our conclusions. The quality of analysis and thinking about the industry within these institutions is, in our view, exceptional and far superior to the typical short-sighted views of the usual buy–sell–hold analysts and single-issue fanatics among the academic community.

The 2002 Deutsche Bank report begins with some startling conclusions:

Over the past 20 years, the [auto] industry has continued to grow in terms of volumes, revenues and employment. However, its relative importance compared to other industry sectors has decreased significantly. Today the industry . . . represents 1.6 per cent of total European market capitalisation, 0.6 per cent of US market capitalisation and 7 per cent of Japan. This compares with 3.6 per cent in Europe, 4 per cent in the US and 4 per cent in Japan 20 years ago.

The Center for Automotive Research at the University of Michigan chimes in: 'How such a large and growing portion of the private sector economy produces such a small return for the value produced is a major question for the researchers involved in this study.'[2] The issues we have discussed in this book so far make us believe that the causes are in fact identifiable. Their financial impact is the subject of this chapter.

As a proportion of the business economy, the automobile sector is valued at less than

---

[2] CAR, 'Estimating the New Automotive Value Chain'.

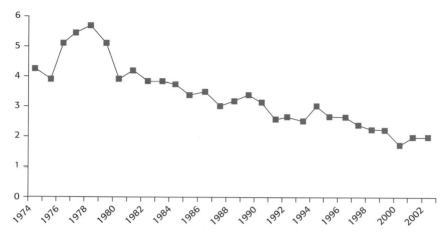

Source: Datastream

Fig. 7.2 Centrality – automotive industry market
cap as percentage of total market cap for Europe,
the US and Japan

a sixth as important as it was in the early
1980s. What a fall from grace! Even that masks
the seriousness of the decline. As we discussed
earlier, the value of the industry to developed-
country economies is more than 10 per cent
of GDP. And yet in the US it is reflected in
a market capitalisation of almost a twentieth
of that. This says that either the industry is
hopelessly undervalued and a colossal buying
opportunity or (do not call your broker just
yet) a basket-case. Sadly it is mostly the latter.

The industry's decline over twenty years is
shown in figure 7.2. For all its social and economic clout it has lost its importance for the
capital markets. It is becoming a sunset industry, a has-been in financial terms – a flagrant
contrast with its continuing social role, its
share of employment and its political influence. What on earth has gone wrong with the
industry of industries?

In the final analysis, it is the financial numbers that count. If an industry makes no profit,
it receives no investment funds. Other than
the regulators, and in the absence of an effective counterweight from the fragmented and
enslaved upstream and downstream sectors of
the industry, only the financial markets (and
to a lesser extent the unions) can exercise

any real power of discipline over the industry's leaders and its direction. Let us therefore
redraw the industry in more financial terms.

The conventional view of the industry is
through the lens of the vehicle manufacturers. They do tend to blot out the rest of the
landscape. 'What's good for General Motors is
good for the rest of America', said Charlie Wil-
son, chairman of GM, to the Senate Committee hearings in 1955. *On a Clear Day You Can
See General Motors* was the title De Lorean gave
his book. And the conventional view of the
manufacturers, and most notably their self-
view, is based on production numbers and
'shifting the iron'. Ask almost any industry
executive, look at almost any industry publication, and it is the production volumes that
stand out. After that come the sales volumes.
To think in terms of sales value or turnover
is simply not something considered by most
people in the business, let alone market capitalisation, as in figure 7.3.

The production perspective could be called
'the view from Detroit'. It means that, in
terms of volume of vehicles sold, the industry
is dominated by the big American firms GM
and Ford, that six groups account for more
than 75 per cent of the market and that the

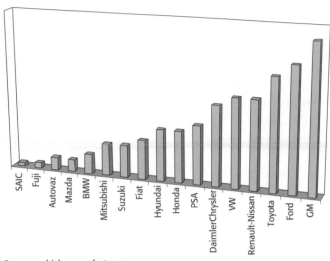

Million units produced

Source: vehicle manufacturers

Fig. 7.3 The view from Detroit

top ten account for almost nine out of ten cars built. Ranked by production volume, the second-biggest producer in 2002, Ford, built 84 per cent of the number of cars produced by the biggest, GM. The tenth-largest, Fiat, built 27 per cent of the number produced by the biggest. There is a fairly smooth downward progression of size, with no-one really outstanding.

Another way to look at the industry is in terms of sales revenues. At first glance the industry looks, perhaps unsurprisingly, little different from the way it looks in terms of output. Yet this angle throws up some interesting anomalies too (see figure 7.4).

Although Toyota ranked third in 2002 in volume terms, it ranked fourth in terms of sales revenues, after DaimlerChrysler. This is because so much of DaimlerChrysler's revenues were from higher value Mercedes cars. Similarly, BMW accounted for 3 per cent of global new car sales revenues but less than 2 per cent of output, while Porsche, with a production volume of just 57,000 cars in 2002, accounted for a share four times that in value terms.

At the other end of the spectrum is Suzuki which made lots of cars, but as most of them were small low-cost vehicles its share of the industry in revenue terms is almost a third of that in output terms. This factor affects Mitsubishi and Nissan too, thanks to their substantial output of 660 cc mini-vehicles, so popular in Japan. The effect of disproportionately higher production volumes of smaller, lower-value cars in Europe also meant that the share in revenue terms of companies like Volkswagen and PSA was lower than might have been expected. Similarly, Hyundai accounted for 5 per cent of global output but less than 2 per cent of global revenues, reflecting a product mix of overwhelmingly cheap cars.

But product mix only very partly accounts for differences in financial performance. Profitability varies in quite a different way from manufacturer to manufacturer. Figure 7.5 is obviously only a snapshot, not a long-term view. And it was taken when some of the heat had gone out of the global industry. It ranks carmakers by their net margin. Porsche, at the top, is the most profitable company, but is something of an anomaly. It is dependent on

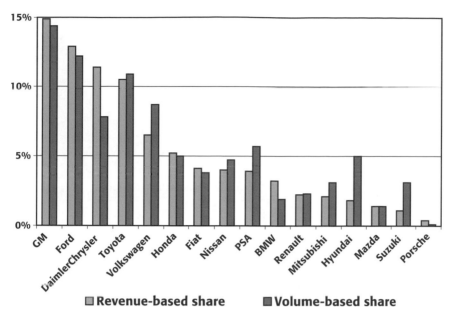

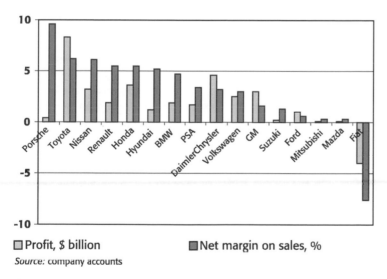

Source: Manufacturers' accounts. Renault and Nissan shown separately, Mitsubishi separately from DaimlerChrysler

Fig. 7.4 The product mix effect: Revenue- and volume-based shares of world market, 2002

Fig. 7.5 Top carmakers ranked by net margin on sales

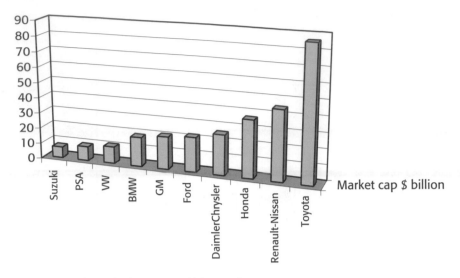

Source: Deutsche Bank, *The Drivers*; vehicle manufacturers

Fig. 7.6 The view from Wall Street

a particular niche which, almost uniquely, it has carved out for itself. Besides, the company would find it hard to survive alone without the assistance of its partnership for product development and assembly with Volkswagen.

Other than the special case of Porsche, then, the most profitable carmakers in the world were the top Japanese firms, Toyota and Nissan, with Honda not far behind. A reflection of their competitive successes? Only partially. Contrary to expectations, the sources of these companies' profits are not uniform. Each uses its domestic market in Japan to provide volume – they typically make little or no margin in Japan. They actually derive the bulk of their financial health from sales in the US. Except where their vehicles are wholly built in the US, this means their margins are highly exchange-rate-dependent. As long as the yen is no stronger than 120 yen to the dollar, these firms are money machines. We shall look at exchange rates again later on. Detroit's Big Three are highly dependent on the US light truck market for profits, which are largely wiped out by losses in other parts of their business. We return to these dependencies and others in a later section.

Hyundai was also highly profitable. Again, though, this was thanks mostly to a weak won

against the then strong US dollar in 2002. Renault and PSA were better performers too, this time because their chic, lower-cost, diesel-engined cars were highly popular in Europe. They were also able to avoid the exchange rate exposure of many other firms thanks to having almost all their sales in one region.

BMW had above average margins mainly thanks to the weak euro and the strong dollar in 2002. This meant US exports were highly lucrative. DaimlerChrysler was a reasonably good performer too, despite the burden of Chrysler – again, though, this was mostly down to advantageous exchange rates and exports to the US.

Towards the right-hand side of the figure we move into the darker side, where margins are thin and liabilities are growing: vast firms with low returns and nearly out-of-control financial discontinuities. These are the giants of the industry like Volkswagen, GM, Ford and Mitsubishi – businesses with huge revenues but tiny returns, struggling on the margin of financial collapse.

Figure 7.6 sees the world from a different angle – that of the capital markets. It is the view from Wall Street (or any other bourse on which the manufacturers are quoted): what the financial markets think the companies

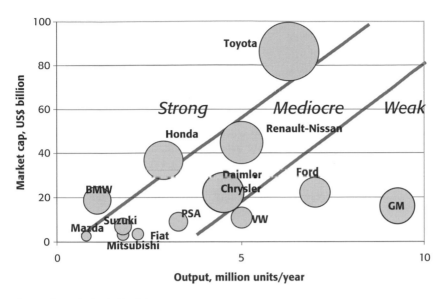

Source: Deutsche Bank, *The Drivers*
Note: Circle size proportionate to market capitalisation

Fig. 7.7 Not firing on all cylinders: market capitalisation and output

are worth. It could also have been called 'the view from Tokyo'. The industry is dominated by one firm, Toyota, with the second-largest barely half its size. The Japanese are clearly on top, allowing for the capitalisation of Renault-Nissan being mainly attributable to the revived Nissan. The tenth-largest company, Suzuki this time, is less than a tenth of the market value of Toyota. Fiat is actually only worth 2.5 per cent or a fortieth of the value of the largest firm, a reflection of its troubles. Even Porsche was worth almost twice as much as Fiat, despite making 57,000 cars in 2002 compared to the Italian group's 2.2 million.

The contrasts are really shown up by combining the two sets of data, as in figure 7.7. The larger the circle, the bigger the market capitalisation, also shown on the y-axis. Production, in millions of units, is shown on the x-axis. In general, you would expect the companies to lie along a line running from the bottom left-hand corner to the top right. That is, the bigger companies should be worth proportionately more than the small ones. Market capitalisation should be a broad reflection of output. Of course there are exceptions for the

specialists and upline manufacturers, which operate to a different price/cost relationship. BMW, for example, should therefore always have a market capitalisation greater than its output would suggest. So should Daimler – without its mismatched partners.

In fact what comes out is a mess: a lack of correlation suggesting something out of order at Laurel and Hardy World Motor Corporation. There is very little relationship between size and value at all: some of the largest companies are worth less than firms half their size in terms of volumes, while some of the smaller companies are worth far more than their output should indicate. There seem to be three broad bands: the strong (top band), the mediocre (middle band) and the weak (lower band).

So, for example, Toyota makes fewer vehicles than GM and Ford, but it is worth more than both of them added together. Similarly, VW and Renault-Nissan make roughly the same number of vehicles each but Renault-Nissan is worth more than four times as much as VW. Honda is worth more than three times as much as VW and 50 per cent more than DaimlerChrysler, despite making a third fewer vehicles than its German-based rivals. Fiat made twice as many cars as BMW in 2002 and yet was worth less than 20 per cent of the German company's value, reflecting the woes afflicting the Italian business.

Our view is that the market capitalisation of these businesses is a much closer reflection of their true competitive positioning in the world than their production volume or sales. So focus on the y-axis, not the x-axis. As we concluded in chapter 4, size for its own sake is no valid objective; nor is global presence necessarily essential.

Yet the industry itself, in traditionally macho style, insists on talking about size – meaning the numbers of vehicles built, which is no reflection of strength. In terms of financial clout, GM has not been the biggest carmaker in the world (as it claims) for years. It is the sixth-largest – and is less than three-quarters of the size of the largest firm in volume terms, Toyota. Similarly, Ford, 'the second biggest carmaker in the world' in most of the press (until Toyota edged it out in 2003), is nothing of the sort. The banks and capital markets have long realised that it is worth 40 per cent less than Honda and a quarter as much as Toyota, despite its volumes.

Toyota had a market capitalisation in 2003 which was greater than GM, Ford, Daimler-Chrysler and Volkswagen *combined*. Not only does this astonishing statistic rarely come out in the press, but much of the coverage might lead you to think the opposite. Why? Because for much of the early 2000s, Toyota's share price was falling steadily and it had to spend billions on a share buy-back programme to try to maintain its own value. Was this because the Japanese market had seen a flaw in Toyota that others had not, a reflection of a company in trouble? Not a bit of it. Paradoxically, Toyota's shares were falling because it was so successful.

Throughout the 1990s, the Japanese economy stagnated and the value of the Nikkei share index dropped progressively, ending up more than 80 per cent down. Many of the banks, which had large chunks of their assets held in company stocks and property, found that the value of both fell faster than they could bear. Commercial property prices fell as rapidly as shares during the 1990s: by as much as 86 per cent in parts of Tokyo and some other cities. An apartment which cost $1 million in 1989, at the property-bubble peak, was worth not much more than $140,000 in 2002. Yet it could have had a mortgage valued at five or six times as great. This was a major cause of the paralysis which afflicted the Japanese economy – that asset prices had fallen so far that people and businesses could not afford to sell their homes or subsidiaries because they were valued so much less than the debt used in purchasing them. To realise the loss meant almost certain bankruptcy. It was better to do nothing. (This is one of the major dangers of a steady deflationary spiral and now afflicts other countries in Asia too, including Singapore and Hong Kong.)

For the banks, this decline in asset values brought an additional problem. By law, banks have to maintain a certain level of liquidity, and a minimum share of total assets must be held in cash or readily convertible assets. So the Japanese banks, like the corporate sector and consumers, could not afford to show the true value of their loans on their books. This meant that their requirements for cash remained largely unchanged while the stagnating economy, zero interest rates and lack of lending meant that their incomes fell. With such problems, the drop in share and property values forced many Japanese banks to close during the late 1990s and early 2000s. Even today many remain in a precarious situation.

To try to stave off bankruptcy and meet their cash requirements, the banks took to selling some of their best assets in an effort to stay afloat. As one of the strongest companies in the Japanese stock market, Toyota's shares were a popular choice of shares to sell. The result was that the banks kept selling Toyota stock to maintain their own liquidity, the supply of its shares in the market rose and the price fell. For Toyota this became a major headache. Between late 2000 and 2003, the

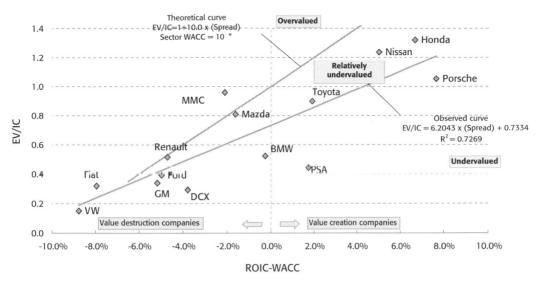

Source: Goldman Sachs Research
Note: ROIC = return on invested capital, WACC = weighted average cost of capital,
EV = economic value, IC = invested capital

Fig. 7.8 Creators and destroyers of value

company produced a series of record results and yet its shares dropped by more than a third – and by more than the overall Japanese stock index.

We used the labels strong, mediocre and weak in figure 7.7 advisedly. Yet it is a reflection of the sad fact that most of the vehicle industry is financially weak, and that it is systematically destroying shareholder value. Figure 7.8, from Goldman Sachs Research in Japan, portrays an analysis of what different vehicle manufacturers have done for their shareholders based on their forecasts of 2003 results. Too many of them are in the value-destruction business. That is why the capital markets are punishing them and why the whole industry has a bad name.

The two key parameters are the return on invested capital (ROIC) (i.e. what the company achieved financially with the money sunk in the business) and the weighted average cost of capital (WACC) (i.e. how much it had to pay to remunerate its financial stakeholders, weighted for the mix between long-term debt and equity). The horizontal axis measures the difference between these two. Any company

placed in the middle of this axis is earning exactly enough to remunerate its stakeholders – but not generating any surplus. One to the left is eating capital. One to the right is adding to it. The vertical axis measures EV/IC, enterprise value divided by invested capital. This is a complex concept developed by Goldman Sachs. The enterprise value consists of the actual value of the business today as measured by the capital markets plus the invested capital. It is then adjusted to account for the future growth of the value of the business.

The detailed explanation of the calculations is as follows,

where EVA = economic value added

$$IC = \text{invested capital}$$
$$= \text{shareholders' equity}$$
$$+ \text{interest-bearing liabilities}$$
$$PV = \text{present value}$$
$$WACC = \text{weighted average cost of capital}$$
$$ROIC = \text{return on invested capital}$$
$$= NOPAT/IC$$

NOPAT = net operating profit after tax.

$$EV = IC + \text{present value of } EVA^{©}$$
$$= IC + \text{present value of}$$
$$\times (NOPAT - IC \times WACC)$$
$$= IC + \text{present value of}$$
$$\times \{(ROIC - WACC) \times IC\}$$
$$= IC + \{(ROIC - WACC) \times IC\}/WACC$$
$$EV/IC = 1 + (ROIC - WACC)/WACC$$
$$= ROIC/WACC.$$

The top line is the theoretical level of EV/IC, i.e. a measure of what the company in the sector ought to be valued at on the equity markets, as a function of its position on the horizontal axis. Any company above that line is overvalued. The second line is the observed trend curve for this set of companies. Any company positioned between the two lines is undervalued relative to its peers in the sector. A company below the bottom line is distinctly undervalued.

The results are telling. All the Japanese manufacturers have been value creators, with the exception of Mazda and MMC (Mitsubishi), which were basket-cases which had to be rescued by Ford and DaimlerChrysler, respectively. Daimler subsequently abandoned MMC, which appears to have been overvalued in the first place. The Japanese Big Three – Toyota, Nissan and Honda – appear relatively undervalued. The only value-creating Europeans have been Porsche and PSA – and both come across as distinctly undervalued. Porsche is fairly clearly positioned in an extreme niche, with very distinctive products, a faithful clientèle and a strong brand, which allows it to charge the high prices that befit really exclusive and distinctive products. The risk to this kind of company is the temptation to overextend. Will, for example, the Cayenne SUV be a worthy addition to its range or a step too far? PSA has also pursued a quite distinctive strategy: a very strictly calculated and limited product range (no SUVs or 4 × 4s, just systematic derivation off a limited range of platforms); two brands (Peugeot and Citroën),

with somewhat different attributes but sharing the same platforms and major components; industry-leading investment in diesel engines (and scale-building in this domain by being willing to share it with other chosen manufacturers, such as Ford, BMW and Toyota); a largely European position, with only very limited overseas ventures. Interesting, too, that PSA is resolutely independent and private-sector, culturally still conservative and a reflection of the prudent virtues of eastern France, its birthplace. BMW has been on the borderline, because of wasting resources on its English patient, Rover – now mercifully consigned to the isolation ward without life-support, where it is not expected to live much longer. (For an entertaining history of that short-lived match and the corporate hubris that led to it, read *BMW and Rover, a Brand too Far – The End of the Road*.[3])

All of the three European national champions – VW, Renault and Fiat – have been major value-destroyers, with VW and Fiat the worst offenders of all, as have the US Big Three. The historical overvaluation of Fiat has since been dramatically corrected. Chrysler has managed to pull the whole of DaimlerChrysler into the destroyers' camp, although not unaided – DaimlerChrysler was also weighed down by its truck business and by its Smart Car venture, even before MMC is added to the scales. It is all a very sorry tale.

In summary? It is grim. At least 60 per cent of the light vehicle industry in the world, based on sales, or 55 per cent based on unit volume, has been value-destroying.

There is also an equally important distinction to be drawn between the quality of the different manoeuvres, specifically mergers and acquisitions, that have taken place in the industry. We take this up in the next section, in which we dig further into how ambitions for global positioning and growth have affected the financial value of manufacturers.

[3] Chris Brady and Andrew Lorenz, *BMW and Rover, a Brand too Far – The End of the Road*, Harlow: FT-Prentice Hall, 2001.

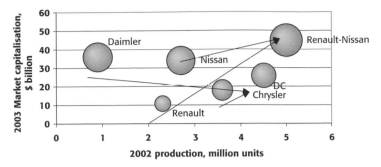

Source: Deutsche Bank, *The Drivers*; autoPOLIS

Fig. 7.9 Pull me up, pull me down

Good growth and bad growth – rational and irrational expansion

Excitement over mega-mergers marked the automotive industry in the late 1990s. Disfigured might be a better term to apply to some of them. Those who do not learn from history are condemned to relive it. Renault had two fiascos in the past: its acquisition of American Motor Corporation and its alliance with Volvo. It seems to have learned the lesson, unlike some others. Figure 7.9 looks at the values and sales volumes of two of the largest recent deals in the industry – Daimler's 'merger of equals' with Chrysler and Renault's capital stake in and alliance with Nissan. All the figures are for 2003, other than the market capitalisations for Daimler and Chrysler, which are shown at the point just before they merged.

What it shows is that Daimler and Chrysler had a combined market capitalisation in 2003 of less than half what they had before. The merger reduced the value of the two businesses by more than $28 billion. Actually, it was worse. Because the value of the combined businesses rose during the stock market boom, the difference between the high and low points was nearer $50 billion. This is, in effect, the destroyed value of the merger at its worst point. Daimler alone is worth almost $9 billion less than it once was.

The process by which Daimler took over Chrysler is entertainingly described in a book by Vlasic and Stertz.[4] The whole adventure comes over as high on thrills and spills but strikingly low on analysis, strategic thinking or real rationale. DaimlerChrysler has subsequently admitted the inadequacy of the due-diligence process. They bought Chrysler at the height of its reputation for product creativity, and just at the point at which the products were seriously ageing, with not enough resources to replace them. Their geographical positioning was about the only thing that was truly complementary. Despite selling its S-Class luxury cars in virtually every country in the world and despite its M-Class assembly plant in Mississippi, Daimler remains a predominantly European car company. Chrysler only sells very limited volumes outside North America. So only some notion of cross-selling into each other's dealer networks might have been entertained.

But that was about it. Their product positionings were vastly different, with upline cars of conservative design the heart of Daimler's business, and vans, light trucks and SUVs the heart of Chrysler's. Their corporate cultures could hardly have been more different, with Daimler the high-tech upline doyen of the European automotive industry and Chrysler the happy-go-lucky twice-rescued-from-bankruptcy folksy feisty American. Their

[4] Bill Vlasic and Bradley A. Stertz, *Taken for a Ride – How Daimler-Benz Drove off with Chrysler*, New York: Harper-Business, 2001.

differing levels of technology and their different market foci meant very little opportunity to share scale in components. A Mercedes V8 in a Chrysler van? You would have to be kidding. In reality, it was *My Fair Lady* in the automotive industry, or the prince marrying the goose girl. Only they did not live happily ever after but ended up in the capital markets' poorhouse.

Just as Chrysler pulled down the arrogant and unheeding Daimler, so Renault pulled up Nissan and Nissan pulled up Renault. Renault's masterly turnaround at Nissan under the charismatic Carlos Ghosn created a subsidiary business worth more than four times the value of its parent. One could even argue that Renault became a drag on its own value. It was a classic take-it-over-and-turn-it-around. Typically, there was lots of scepticism when Renault's stake in Nissan was first announced, although not from us. But 'poor Nissan' was the reaction of much of the Japanese media. Nice Japanese girl forced into marrying a *gaijin*. And not even a German one, for which there might be some grudging respect. But Renault knew what they were doing – which is not to say it was risk-free. They had believed that by pulling out all the stops in every region and market in the world accessible to them they alone could achieve a 4 per cent share of the world market. 'With that, you're driving me into a brick wall', Mr Ghosn reputedly said. So a suitable bride had to be found. Nissan provided a good match.

The results have been dramatic. They were both volume manufacturers, not upline specialists. Coming from the same social background is at least a comfort factor in a marriage. The geographical match was good, with Nissan strong in Japan (although in need of some serious revitalisation there) and in the US, while Renault's strength was in Europe. Renault had design flair, which Nissan lacked: one of the new management team's first actions was to take styling out from under engineering and make it report straight to the top, and to hire a new design chief. Nissan

had a very deep knowledge of how to manage for productivity and quality – its Sunderland, UK, plant became the European productivity and quality leader from its first year. There were heaps of opportunities to rationalise platforms between the two companies, even if that would take time. There were real opportunities to share components, such as putting larger Nissan engines in Renault upline cars. French manufacturers have traditionally not been strong in big engines, partly because of a long history of French vehicle taxes which savagely penalised them. There were also businesses to sell off without too much pain, a components-buying programme to be rationalised, a booming US market, a full new product pipeline and a weak yen. Moreover, the business had in Mr Ghosn a rare leader. The sun shone on Renault-Nissan and Mr Ghosn.

Most importantly, though, both sides took the merger seriously and played the game well. Renault had learned from its disastrous previous alliance with Volvo Cars, where its arrogance had provoked a revolt in Sweden. This time everything was planned meticulously and, above all, planned jointly. Cross-company teams were set up in every major area. Renault put a first-class team into Nissan and Nissan responded to the challenge and to the opportunity. A Nissan engineer now heads engine development at Renault, which is a real proof of reciprocity.

But why did it take outsiders from Renault to turn Nissan around? Did the Japanese company's shareholders simply not notice its deterioration? Or were they unable to force change? Our view, briefly, is that Mr Ghosn and his team proved to be unique. He was not the beginning of a new trend in corporate Japan, whereby the *gaijin* were taking over – and were to be welcomed. He was a rare leader in the industry, or indeed any other.

In a conversation with one of us in Japan he said that his biggest problem had been 'the continuous battle to overcome scepticism'. He talked about how the industry analysts were always too ready to question his and Nissan's abilities to make the necessary changes. He said that he was even able to turn this into a source of motivation – by telling his people that the press and banking analysts thought it could not be done, he made sure they would prove that it could. 'The only strength a company has', he said, 'is the motivation of its people.' A similar attitude exists at Toyota: president Fujio Cho's approach is to 'let the people grow'.

The lesson of it all? It is surely that the industry could do better, very much better, if only it were properly led, on rational grounds, not by accountants or petrol-heads or family appointees as is so often the case. Renault unlocked Nissan's potential. But it is unclear whether it has been as beneficial to Renault, or at least not as quickly. And the last irony? Mr Ghosn is a product of that pillar of the French intellectual, government and business establishment, one of Napoleon's great creations, the Ecole Polytechnique. He is not a typical vehicle manufacturer. He learned his management skills at that other great French and global market and technology leader in its sector, Michelin. He is a blend of French, Lebanese and Brazilian cultures.[5] Some of those in the vehicle industry, which is often so inbred, might do well to ponder these differences.

The initiators of these two mergers (or takeovers – it depends whose viewpoint you take, as in most intercorporate transactions) sought growth by diversification, because their existing operations would not yield enough. One of the simple rules has to do with risk and the ability to control it: diversify into new markets within your existing product range; or diversity into new products within your existing markets. But do not attempt both at once. We suggest that the Renault-Nissan alliance (this is what they officially call it) respected that rule, as their products were broadly similar, including the potential to rationalise underlying components, while maintaining separate brand identities, following the pattern of the VW Group. Daimler-Chrysler simply did not have that product

compatibility and rationalisation potential, so it was a risky double diversification from the start.

Ford's performance in the late 1990s was even more appalling, with even more value lost between the peak of the market and three years later: as much as $70 billion. This was not attributable to misjudged major manufacturer-to-manufacturer deals (although we should be curious to know whether Ford's shareholders will ever see a return on their investment in Jaguar, which Ford indeed saved from death in the late 1980s). But there was an attempt to move the company as a whole radically downstream, in pursuit of the Eldorado of aftermarket revenues. The results were pretty puny: the acquisition of Kwik-Fit in the UK and its European subsidiaries, and attempts to buy up the Ford dealers in the Indianapolis metropolitan area. The sad truth is that Ford never had the spare cash to shift its centre of mass appreciably through diversification. Nor did it have the experience of the new sectors needed to make use of the acquisitions. Lack of attention to the core business of developing and making vehicles also seems to have been caused by the Ford 2000 project. This was an attempt to create world management centres for different parts of the product line, an integrationist approach which we believe to be at the heart of the industry's current problems. It is a subject we shall return to in chapter 8. In passing, many of the troubles Ford got into in the early 2000s and the talk of it having to file for Chapter 11, were not the results of the management of Jac Nasser, although they are often laid at his door. He can perhaps be blamed for some of what went wrong in Europe, but we think the real problems at Ford go back to the relics of a previous era of management, to an excessive preoccupation with finance (which has ironically produced bad financial results) and to a top-down belief in absolute control, stemming from the days of dear Henry.

[5] See Philippe Riès, *Carlos Ghosn, citoyen du monde*, Paris: Editions Grasset, 2003.

What all this says to us is that one really needs to look at vehicle manufacturers more finely than is possible through conventional financial reporting, in order to understand their historical performance properly and to project their future potential with any degree of reliability; and, most particularly, to judge whether a proposed new combination is a good prospect or not. It is plain prudence to look at the industrial and commercial logic of a deal, as well as conducting the conventional financial due-diligence analysis. We continue to be surprised and shocked at how rarely this is done, and to wonder whose interests are being served by many of the transactions in the industry.

The heedless rush to acquire in this industry is also matched by an often considerable reluctance to dispose of, and a pronounced one not to shut down. One of the industry's really major flaws is its endemic over-capacity, which is well documented and has existed for over a decade. It is a chronic major drain on its financial health.

Although capacity is often difficult to measure because factories can work on several shifts, there is generally reckoned to be between 25 per cent and 30 per cent too much in the industry worldwide. Productivity improvements increase this by around 3 per cent a year, which means that in an industry with volume growth that is lower than this (even in the healthy times), the problem is getting progressively worse. The problem is also being made more serious because of the additional capacity which is being laid down in both the developed and the developing markets. North America will have seen a capacity increase of more than 17 per cent between 2000 and 2006, in a market where demand will barely rise at all in that time.

Over-capacity is very much a structural (or perhaps behavioural?) problem for the industry, made worse by the fact that every car-maker sees it as the problem of its rivals. Each lays down additional plant in the hope that the next new model to be made will beat the competition (part of the insane new

product race we talked about in earlier sections). It is something of a pyramid scheme. Only very rarely does a vehicle manufacturer actually close down an assembly plant. There have been some closures in North America. In Europe, only Renault and Ford have followed suit to any significant degree. Renault shut down its original home assembly plant in Boulogne-Billancourt, impossibly located on an island in the River Seine. It also, in the face of a barrage of criticism and insults, had the courage to shut down its uneconomic assembly plant at Vilvoorde in Belgium, a relic of a Europe before the single market. Ford ended vehicle assembly at Dagenham, its oldest major European assembly site, but softened the blow to the local community and the UK balance of payments somewhat by transforming it into a major production centre for diesel engines. Japan has shown extreme reluctance to shut anything at all. National and local governments are characteristically quick to try to prevent closures and job losses through more or less visible subsidies – another endemic plague in this industry. Figure 7.10 provides a global summary of capacity utilisation in vehicle assembly. There seems no prospect of future improvement.

As a rule, rising capacity in a high-fixed-cost business leads to intense price competition and deteriorating profitability, as companies try to hang on to market share. In a market trending downwards, as existed in the US after 11 September 2001, this led to the added insanity of cutting prices as sales declined and costs rose. The tendency to do this 'is what really hurts in this industry', says Deutsche Bank's Oliver Brinkmann in Singapore.

The industry's financial woes are made worse still by its excessively high operational gearing. The degree of operational gearing is a function of a company's level of fixed costs. The higher the fixed costs in a business, the more difficult it is to cut back when times get hard. With so much capacity, fixed costs are already higher than they should be. Most factories in the industry had to run at very high levels of capacity utilisation in the

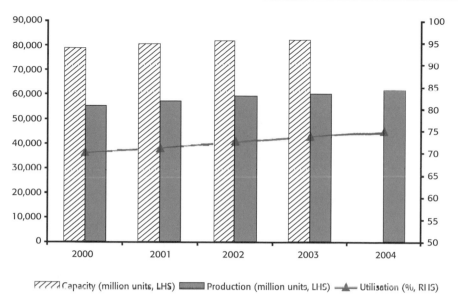

Source: Deutsche Bank, *The Drivers*
Note: This chart is based on a different forecast from other projections on vehicle production provided in this book from a different source, assuming steady but slow growth. If the other, less positive, projections prove more accurate, then the capacity utilisation rate will be lower than indicated here.

Fig. 7.10 The global over-capacity problem

1990s – usually more than 80 per cent – to make any money at all. Yet running at these rates was only marginally profitable when the markets were at their peak. Even one of the top performers, PSA, could still only make a halfway decent return, compared with many other industries, at more than 100 per cent capacity utilisation (it made a 5 per cent return on 101 per cent capacity utilisation in 2001). This is because at that level of output it had already moved into the zone of spiralling costs, as the industrial system was driven past its comfortable operating range.

When we looked at VW in the late 1980s, it could only break even with 95 per cent capacity utilisation and a 10 per cent market price premium for the Golf in Germany. The situation has improved since then but the underlying problem has not gone away. This remains a brutally high-cost, low-margin business, with substantial downside risks when the model goes only slightly awry.

Deutsche Bank estimates that the fixed costs in the industry are as high as 30 per cent of sales. This means that for as little as a 3 per cent decline in sales revenues (when the market drops back), the industry experiences a 24 per cent drop in operating profit. A 3 per cent drop in prices, however, with volumes staying the same, hits the bottom line by as much as 60 per cent. This is what is meant by operational gearing. The results of their calculations are shown in figure 7.11.

For most of the 1990s and early 2000s, then, the auto industry was running at the very edges of the flywheel and yet few understood it – and shockingly few within the industry itself. The cyclical earnings problems were commonly seen as a result of changes in sales volumes but it was much more the result of this operational gearing. When volumes fell, the manufacturers struggled to cover their fixed costs. This made them try to stimulate demand by cutting prices – which resulted in a double whammy – negative volumes and negative pricing – which explains why so many carmakers got into such a serious financial pickle so soon, when times got hard. As Jeff

	Basic financial structure	**If sales decline 3%**	**If prices are cut 3%**
Sales revenues	100	97	97
Variable costs	60	58.2	60
Fixed costs	35	35	35
Profit (EBIT)	5	3.8	2
Change in profits		−24%	−60%

Source: Deutsche Bank

Fig. 7.11 The risky downside of high operational gearing

Ng of Citigroup in New York says, 'It is easy to get into a death spiral, which just gets worse.'

The effect of the operational gearing problem is multiplied on the component suppliers, as they are often forced to bear the brunt of the carmakers' woes through cost-cutting efforts. Moreover, this gearing affects the upside too, but not positively. As volumes grow, the financial benefits are usually offset by higher costs, to run extra shifts, pay overtime, etc., which explains why even PSA could make little more than an unexciting return at the best of times.

Over-capacity, poor operational gearing, a lack of product differentiation in most instances, coupled with a deluded belief that it can be achieved (sorry, Mr Carmaker, it is true), intense price competition and an inability to cover the costs of capital during the sales cycle are the main reasons why the auto sector became so undervalued. Steve Allen, a partner with BearingPoint in Singapore, puts it simply, 'It is a failed industry.'

The insanity of the incentives which were introduced in the US after the terrorist attacks in New York took time to show their full impact. But if you drop the whole market price level by as much as $3,500 per vehicle through incentives, then of course you can 'stimulate the market'. Consumers were happily persuaded to buy their originally intended product for less and some even traded up to better vehicles. Yet this also created a fantastic glut of used vehicles which are still being fed through to the market, crash-ing residual values. There will be a horrible concertina effect in terms of sales volumes, future prices and second-hand values for years to come, just as happened when incentives were offered to scrap older cars in France and Italy in the early 1990s. Furthermore, incentives become institutionalised in the minds of consumers, making a nonsense of manufacturers' obsession with maintaining list prices. In passing, one of the major benefits that would accrue from the emergence of truly independent large retailers would be their disappearance anyway.

Partly, of course, this structural mess has been caused by the inflexibility of the industry's cost structure. But that is to be kind. Mostly it is down to managers who are too keen to keep the factories running, too scared to lose share for a while and too foolish to understand the economics of their own industry adequately. Carlos Ghosn said to us that this insane desire to maintain share was one of the things he changed first when he took the helm at Nissan. It was profit that mattered; share gains came from having cars that people wanted. It was not down to giving cars away. 'When you are obsessed with market share, you end up buying market share', he said. The whole concept of the quality of earnings seemed to have become almost alien to the industry.

By the early 2000s, these structural difficulties had become increasingly clear to some working around the industry, notably the banks and the capital markets. They were increasingly reflected in availability of funds to the sector. The banks and the capital markets began to punish the firms that had a weak financial position in several ways. First, they downgraded their credit and debt ratings, in some cases to 'junk' status. This meant that financiers charged more for lending to these companies. While a typical blue-chip business might borrow at 150 basis points (thousandths of a percentage point) above treasury bill rates, companies like Ford and GM were forced to pay as much as 400–500 basis points over in 2003, reflecting their low 'near junk' status.

Banks and financial institutions also demanded higher spreads when things looked bad. They forced companies into borrowing against their assets, rather than against their creditworthiness. And they securitised any loans given to these firms immediately to keep them off their balance sheets. That way, if things went wrong, it would be the holders of the securities – those people who bought Ford or GM bonds, for example – who would suffer the loss, not the banks that originally lent the companies the money.

Deutsche Bank thinks that 'only strong premium brand players stand any chance of generating full economic value'. Perhaps so. But that means very few of the current players. Brand hype and premium pricing are a recourse for the very few, not the many. There need to be major structural changes in the volume vehicle industry if it is to return to financial viability. There also needs to be a different attitude towards their partners on the part of the manufacturers. The perilous consequences of the present poor relationships are addressed in the next section.

Killing the geese that lay the golden eggs – how poor relationships with key partners help make the industry unattractive to the financial markets

The vehicle manufacturers tend to think – and to encourage everyone else to think – of themselves as the industry. This is very far from being the case, as we have demonstrated in previous chapters. While they are the architects of the business and of the vehicle, they need to work ever more closely with an indispensable set of partners and stakeholders. These include:

- government agencies (the need for them to manage the negative by-products of motorised mobility was emphasised in chapter 2);
- systems and components suppliers, who increasingly make development and production possible (the poor quality of relationships with this sector was described in chapter 5);
- distributors and service providers, who make the product useable by consumers, private and public (the emerging threat of a major transfer of power to them was discussed in chapter 6);
- the financial markets (discussed in this chapter);
- their other stakeholders – their workforce and buyers of vehicles;
- their customers.

One of the first questions a vehicle manufacturer asks about a potential supplier is whether they have the financial viability to stay the course. The reasons are obvious – being let down by a bankrupted supplier can bring the whole production system to a standstill in this interdependent industry. This is ironic, given how suppliers are treated. They are being pillaged for short-term gain, on the Viking-like assumption that they always have hidden reserves, which can be raided again next year. This is not what the financial results show, except where a supplier has the courage – or is in the unique position – to be able to refuse to pay the Danegeld demanded by Harald Costdown and his friendly purchasing people. Pay up once and those low fast boats will be back next season. Ask any gathering of suppliers and you will hear the same refrain. It is also a guaranteed stimulus for cheating. We know of one small but highly profitable tier 2 manufacturing business that actually takes on extra staff when the tier 1 customers come to inspect it. The relationship between insurers and crash repairers is all too often similar, involving indiscriminate pressure on prices and margins, recourse to cheating, and lack of investment in real productivity and quality. In Australia they have apparently even taken to burning insurance assessors' cars.

The financial impact on the supplier industry has been frankly deplorable. The CAR study of the automotive value chain[6] constitutes a devastating critique of the relationship with suppliers. To quote a key finding,

OE value *(i.e. that achieved by the vehicle manufacturers)* increased by an impressive 79.8 per cent *(from 1990 to 2000)*, although labour compensation increased by only 23.8 per cent. Materials increased by 42.5 per cent in constant dollars, or far less than the change in OE value netted for labour compensation – which increased by 110.4 per cent. Clearly, the vehicle firms as opposed to labor or other types of suppliers captured a larger portion of the overall increase in automotive value during 1990–2000 (emphasis in original).

In making forecasts, the report uses two different assumptions for the future split of the upstream value of assembled vehicles between OE value added and the value of materials and other purchases produced by suppliers. It quotes the Bureau of the Census report that the motor vehicle assembly industry took 28 per cent of the value of manufacturers' shipments in 1990 but 33 per cent in 1997. It goes on to say,

The difference in the ratios seems counter-intuitive because it is generally thought that vehicle firms reduced their share of shipments value during the 1990 to 1997 period. This subject is thought to be important because of the perilous business conditions of the independent supplier sector in 1997 and certainly today. Is it possible that vehicle producers shifted much of the work of manufacturing the vehicle to the supplier sector in the 1990s but not the net value of performing this work? Did the OE firms somehow keep this value in the form of increased monopsony rents and higher labour (and perhaps executive) compensation?

Is the Pope a Catholic?

The same report quotes the S&P Automotive Supplier Index on an 18 per cent decline in return on assets at suppliers between 1994 and 2000. *World Automotive Manufacturing* quotes a survey[7] of 126 global automotive suppliers and nineteen manufacturers by Alix Partners LLC, which it describes as an international investment firm that specialises in turning around financially troubled companies. The survey painted a bleak picture for many suppliers:

Through the downward price pressure created by over-capacity and extreme competition, suppliers can expect lower profits and thinner margins . . . fiscal health is also a major contributor, with 47 per cent of North American companies, 26 per cent of European suppliers and 36 per cent of Asian suppliers in fiscal danger . . . suppliers and manufacturers in good fiscal shape are getting stronger, while weaker companies are continually falling further behind . . . companies with high debt and other financial problems will find it more expensive and difficult to borrow money.

The survey said that the over-capacity problem in the industry was also expected to worsen dramatically, from 32.1 million units in 2003 to 42.1 million in 2010.

It is the same story in France. A survey of profitability in 2000 showed the industry earning a 3.8 per cent return on sales but Tier 1 component makers generating –0.04 per cent and their suppliers 1.8 per cent, whereas PSA and Renault earned 3.1 per cent and 5.4 per cent, respectively, in 2002. The same survey source shows exactly the same transfer of value from suppliers to manufacturers as the CAR analysis (see figure 7.12).

Foie gras is obtained by feeding geese, not starving them to death. The vehicle manufacturers risk being left with the beaks and feet. It is simply suicidal behaviour.

The industry's record of managing its workforce has also been a mixed one. In the early 2000s, Toyota's Georgetown plant in

---

[6] CAR, 'Estimating the New Automotive Value Chain'.
[7] 'Investment Firm Sees Bleak Future for Suppliers', *World Automotive Manufacturing*, July 2003.

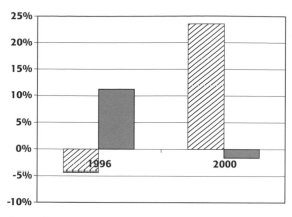

☑**Manufacturers**
■**Suppliers**

Source: SESSI, 'Les 4 pages de statistiques industrielles', no. 164, Paris: Ministry of Economics, Finance and Industry, 2002

Fig. 7.12 Sectoral financial results: net profit/value added in the French automotive industry

	GM	Toyota	Differential
Total wages	$37.39	$22.03	$15.36
Other benefits	$25.39	$14.69	$10.70
Total labour Costs/hour	$62.78	$36.72	$26.06
Hours to make a vehicle	39.34	31.63	7.71
Labour cost per vehicle	$2,469.77	$1,161.45	$1,308.31

Source: Deutsche Bank, *The Drivers*; Harbor Associates

Fig. 7.13 Comparative labour costs in North American vehicle production, 2002

Kentucky had 900 employees and produced up to 436,000 vehicles a year on two lines. In contrast, a typical Big Three plant had 2,000 people and produced just over 250,000 units a year. As the American firms typically paid more to their line workers, who were in turn less productive, labour costs could be as much as $1,300 more per vehicle. The sources of this difference are analysed in figure 7.13.

As well as lower labour costs and higher productivity, the Japanese had three other pro-

duction advantages in the US. First, they were capable of ramping up new products faster and could change from making one model to another within a day, with no time lost. Ford and GM often had to shut down plants for weeks for a major model changeover. After a changeover, the Japanese were also able to ramp up to full production within 24 days – something that took the Big Three as long as three months. This provided additional cost advantages, by maximising their capacity

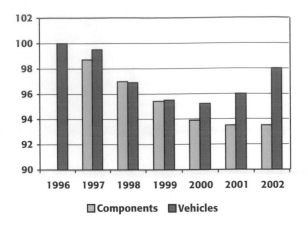

Source: Quoted in Algoé, 'Adaptation structurclle'

Fig. 7.14 A widening gap: index of industrial selling prices, France

utilisation of an assembly plant worth more than $1 billion for longer.

Second, the Japanese plants were more flexible – they could produce one and a half times as many models as a Big Three plant, on average. This meant that they could respond faster to changes in demand and produce a wider range of models, better meeting the market's needs. This had another advantage. It meant that the Japanese could offer lower sales incentives, because they were more likely to be able to build what the consumer actually wanted and was willing to pay for. Unlike the more rigid production approach of the Big Three, they were less likely to simply have to 'shift' product. Third, as Deutsche Bank points out, the Japanese had an attitude advantage too – the levels of staff enthusiasm at their plants offered tangible benefits. This not only meant fewer faults, lower warranty costs and better residuals but also better attendance and so higher productivity. Toyota North America says that as many as 60 per cent of their employees have a perfect attendance record while some of the Big Three plants report as much as 10 per cent daily absenteeism.[8]

By 2003, GM and Ford were effectively owned by their workers. GM had shareholders' equity of just less than $7 billion and a market capitalisation of $20 billion. Yet it also had healthcare liabilities for existing and ex-employees of $41 billion and pension liabilities of nearly $20 billion (these rose and fell with the value of stocks and shares). Similarly, Ford had shareholders' equity of just under $6 billion and a market capitalisation of $22 billion in 2003. But it had $14 billion worth of healthcare liabilities and $9 billion in pension liabilities too.

GM had to spend $1,300 per car in paying the health and welfare costs of ex-employees and Ford had to spend more than $700. At the same time, they had less efficient car plants, higher labour costs and poorer residuals than their Japanese rivals and yet they still saw fit to offer incentives of $3,500 or more per vehicle, despite these dire financial straits. Why did they do this? The answer, of course, is that they had little choice. With such high fixed costs, they had to keep the factories running, even if each car made a loss. That strategy could only last for long, however.

Throughout 2002 and 2003, when Ford and GM's problems with healthcare and pensions liabilities became most serious, they claimed that this was an unfair burden on them, which did not affect their Japanese rivals. Superficially, this was true. But it was also a sleight of hand. First, Toyota, Honda and the others with transplant factories in the US had smaller pension liabilities because they had simply been around for less time. They had few retired workers. Their liabilities will eventually grow. Second, and more importantly, GM and Ford had much higher pension and welfare liabilities because they had been forced to downsize, because they had lost share, and because they had not been as successful. GM had 2.5 retirees for every active worker and it cannot get out of this bind until at least 2007, depending on death rates. Ford and Chrysler were slightly better off, but still had more liability workers than real ones.

---

[8] For a hilarious but penetrating account of life on the assembly line in Detroit, read Ben Hamper, *Rivethead, Tales from the Assembly Line*: New York: Warner Books, 1992.

Towards the end of 2003, after a bond issue and some recovery in share prices in the US, GM made an announcement that its pensions shortfall had been addressed: a seemingly successful outcome for what had become an urgent and essential financial repair. Yet such troubles may still resurface if stock prices take another tumble or its fund fails to achieve the expected growth targets. There remain its healthcare liabilities too – a thorny issue because they are growing so rapidly.

In passing, it is worth looking at the power of the United Auto Workers (UAW) union which has a role to play in both of these issues and others. The power of the UAW is unique in the industry, only partly rivalled by the South Korean unions and, once upon a time, the hold exercised by the Confédération Générale du Travail (CGT), the communist-affiliated union, upon Renault in France. The UAW is a very strong union, well organised, well informed, well financed, well led and with a strong discipline amongst its members. It plays the Big Three off against each other with consummate skill. Its cohesion is surely a natural reaction to the anti-union abuses of the 1930s, described earlier. For once, a partner group to the vehicle manufacturers has consolidated and learned how to exercise collective strength. Whether the scale of the demands serves the longer-term interests of American auto industry workers is another matter. The 40 per cent penetration of the US market by foreign makes (Chrysler being still taken as American in this calculation) suggests a problem. Foreign penetration of Europe, taken as a single market, by non-European brands is under 15 per cent. Imports take under 5 per cent of the Japanese market. Detroit and the UAW, locked in a kind of timeless conflict, have done everything to ensure that their home market is increasingly handed over to foreigners. The financial results are there to be seen.

Much of what happens with the supplier community also applies to the downstream sector. Dealers in the UK had a record year for new vehicle volumes in 2003. They also had lower net margins than ever: a perfect microcosm of the manufacturers trying to pump up growth at the expense of others. All this may help relieve financial pressures on them in the short term, but it creates a terrible long-term threat, especially given what may be looming in the downstream sector in Europe.

A more subtle relationship problem is that of consumer finance. Financing vehicle sales is another area of dangerous dependency and potential future conflict. Figure 7.15 shows a historical time series of how dependent the US Big Three are on profits from their financial arms. The situation at Ford and GM in 2002 and 2003 deserves some particular attention. These companies had become banks, in effect, rather than carmakers, and not very good ones at that. In 2002, GM Acceptance Corp. (GMAC), the auto finance arm of the company, accounted for half the parent's total profits. A further 29 per cent of GM's profits came from offering mortgages. Ford Credit accounted for 142 per cent of Ford's profits that year. Worse, these shares were rising.

Ford and GM were not terribly good banks. They lent mostly on assets that they themselves sold and had to discount which, in turn, affected the residual values of the products on which the loans were secured. Because of the operational gearing, the finance arms of these firms were running high risks. The lease financing they offered provides an example of how both companies allowed the needs of their financing businesses to become secondary to their sales volume goals. Ford and GM were eventually forced to cut back on lease financing, precisely because they had created such a destructive downward spiral for themselves.

The profitability of leasing businesses is based on a number of critical factors, one of which is the residual value of the car. Although there is no way to independently verify the residual value assumptions the two firms made, there is enough suspicion to suggest that they were optimistic, especially in the light of a falling market. The impact of this can be devastating. According to Deutsche

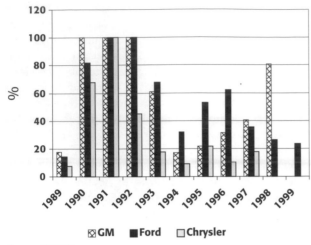

Source: GERPISA

Fig. 7.15 The US Big Three's dependency on vehicle finance profits

Bank, a 1 per cent decline in residual values in 2003 effectively cut Ford's profits by more than $205 million and GM's by $160 million. Moreover, Ford and GM's residuals were much worse than Toyota's, creating a further disadvantage. (The extent of these problems and their outcome is a little opaque, however. In one of our conversations with GM, they claimed that they had now managed to accrue all of their leasing liabilities and so were clean in this respect.)

An average three-year-old Toyota was worth 48 per cent of its initial purchase price, while the average Ford was worth much less, just 38 per cent. This meant that Toyota could offer a three-year lease on a $25,000 car for $361 a month while the same-priced Ford cost $431 a month. To maintain share, Ford had to match prices, which cut straight through to its bottom line. Every time Ford chose to match Toyota it cost $2,500 per vehicle before even a dollar of dealer incentives had been paid.

Almost all car and truck residual values dropped throughout 2002 and 2003. Again, the US manufacturers suffered most, because the bulk of their revenues and margins were coming from the light truck sector where values were falling fastest.

As the market softened in 2002, the tendency to offer longer terms on the loans increased the risks further still. As sales declined, it became common for the Big Three to offer five-year loans at zero per cent. These loans had two downsides. First, the car buyer had negative equity for longer – that is, it would typically take more than four years of payments before the costs of providing the financing were recovered – before the payments exceeded the cost of the loan. This increased the risk and amount of any default. Second, because the buyer was tied to payments for longer, he tended to replace his vehicle less frequently, lowering annual demand.

Ford and GM also took the risky step of increasing the amounts of the loans on offer and offering loans to people with poorer and poorer credit ratings at a time when prices were falling, unemployment was rising and personal bankruptcies had reached their highest level for more than a decade. The effects of this decision will last for years, leading to a further rise in the number of accounts that 'go bad' and larger individual account losses for these two companies. Ford's credit losses had already risen by 41 per cent between early 2000 and late 2002, while the amount it lost on each bad transaction grew by 19 per cent in the same time to more than $7,500 per loan. Similarly, GM's credit loss provisions rose almost four and a half times, from $404 million in 1999 to $1,789 million in 2002.

As Deutsche Bank pointed out, the Big Three faced a 'bad mix', with the prospect of rising interest rates, falling market shares, low and falling residuals and a weak economy. It is easy to see why the US industry was on the brink of a crisis. Yet few in the media or the industry could see it or believed it. At the same time, GM and Ford were increasing the number of vehicles on which they lent, partly, it seems fair to assume, because this was the main source of their profitability by this time. It was also an easier way to push product for them to maintain output and cover fixed costs. GM almost doubled its financing share of retail sales from 28 per cent in 1996 to 50 per cent in 2001.

Ford Credit and GMAC had another side, of course. They had to borrow to finance the car loans. Seeing what was coming, the main ratings agencies kept downgrading their debt ratings, increasing their costs. Ford and GM had to pay more for their money. In March 2002 both were rated so as to have to pay around 200 basis points more than US Treasuries for their ten-year debt. By the end of the year this had risen to between 450 and 500 basis points, with Ford worse off. They were being forced to pay more because the pricing of their debt was directly linked to the probability of default. Borrowers were worried that these were captive banks and they were concerned about a conflict of interest. They saw that Ford and GM were squeezing their finance arms for profit while using them to maintain volumes. Lenders saw a rising probability that the businesses would have to sell or spin-off assets to maintain liquidity. With over-capacity, anything they sold would fetch fire-sale prices.

As credit ratings tumbled and the situation deteriorated, Ford was forced to shift from unsecured to secured debt. In 2000, 22 per cent of Ford Credit's financing came from unsecured commercial paper. By 2002 this had dropped to just 2 per cent. Ford was effectively closed out of the unsecured debt market. As a result, it had to increase the share of money it raised against its own assets from zero in 2000 to 23 per cent in 2003. In effect, both firms were in a hole and simply kept digging ever deeper. (Chrysler was in exactly the same pickle at the time, but its figures were not available for us to review separately.)

For years they had all lost money on their primary businesses: making cars. Now they had become banks. But because they were lending on cars that were not profitable in the first place, it all went even more awry. The growth in revenues in the financial services businesses became directly linked to the growth in car sales as well as the share of sales financed by these captive banks. Revenue growth was also affected by the companies' access to capital, which was deteriorating. At the same time, expenses were rising. Credit provisions and repossessions were growing while used car prices were falling, reducing the value of the assets being lent against. It all became a terrible downward spiral, where keeping the factories running and offering higher and higher discounts became like a treadmill – a path to nowhere.

US dealers also rely heavily on F&I, as well as service and parts, as figure 7.16 demonstrates. Protected by state dealership laws, they are at least free to shop around for the best deal. European manufacturers also depend on revenues from their captive finance houses, although not as much as the US Big Three (see figure 7.17). And it is absolutely clear which operations have the most attractive profit margins (figure 7.18).

In true European style, however, they put considerable pressure on their dealers not to use non-captive sources of finance (see figure 7.19). The dealer can quite easily put pressure on the customer, making only the captive finance instantly available at the point and time of sale of the vehicle. If customers want another option, they have to locate and

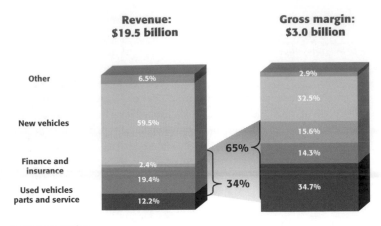

Source: AutoNation

Fig. 7.16 US dealer reliance on F&I

Breakdown of sales and operating margins, PSA group, 2000

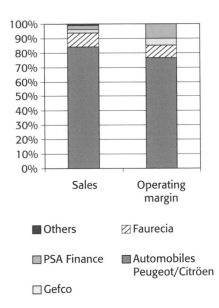

■ Others   ▨ Faurecia

▨ PSA Finance   ■ Automobiles Peugeot/Citröen

□ Gefco

Fig. 7.17 French manufacturers' dependence on financing profits

Breakdown of sales and operating margins, Renault group, 2000

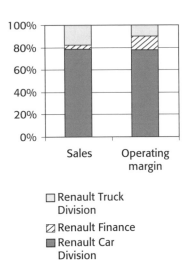

□ Renault Truck Division

▨ Renault Finance

■ Renault Car Division

Source: Comité des Constructeurs Français d'Automobiles, 2001 report

negotiate it 'off line', which is much less convenient for them. This is yet another case of forced bundling that was not addressed by the European Commission in the new Block Exemption Regulation, but which could all too easily attract their interest. There was a panic in the industry when the Commission's Directorate General for Consumer Affairs proposed a fourteen-day cooling-off period on all consumer loans, including auto loans.

Vehicle finance is a huge market, worth €20 billion per year in France alone. Some 60 per cent of sales there are financed on some form of credit. Banks capture just over

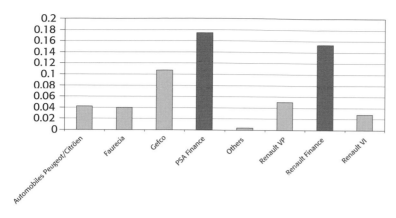

Source: As figure 7.17

Fig. 7.18 French vehicle manufacturers' operating margins by division

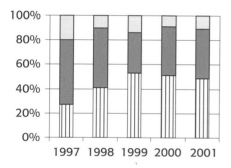

☐ Three sources or more

■ Two sources

▥ One source

Source: Autos Infos, December 2001

Fig. 7.19 Pressure on French dealers to single-source finance

50 per cent of this, finance houses, including the vehicle manufacturers' captive arms, just under 50 per cent. There is a fierce battle for market share, liable to lead to some of the same errors as in the US. As the company car and fleet market sectors continue to grow, so does the penetration of leasing within them, with the fastest growth expected in operational leases: those in which not only the vehicle but full aftersales service support is provided (see figure 7.20).

Again, a fight is shaping up between leasing companies belonging to the vehicle manufacturers and the independents. Figure 7.21

shows the largest leasing companies in France. Here the vehicle manufacturers are strong players, with Renault and PSA in second and third places, but the situation is different in each European country. The vehicle manufacturers persistently use the short-term rental fleets, the long-term rental or lease companies, direct sales to fleets and even their own employees as ways of shifting cars into the market and boosting their market share. The question, of course, has to be: at what price? What residual values have they built into these deals? What discounts are they giving? There is a major lack of transparency around these dealings, as there is around the common practice of manufacturers and dealers pre-registering cars, so that they can be sold on the second-hand market at a steep discount from list – without those list prices having to be adjusted. It is, once again, very unhealthy economics. While it may boost sales, turnover and short-term margins, it assuredly builds up trouble for the future, when those cars come back into the second-hand market, depress its price structure, and ultimately that of the new car market, by offering a very credible alternative to private buyers, and even to the more canny fleet operators.

The independent leasing sector is still very fragmented in Europe, as figure 7.22 shows. It will surely consolidate, under the usual competitive and economic pressures. Then the

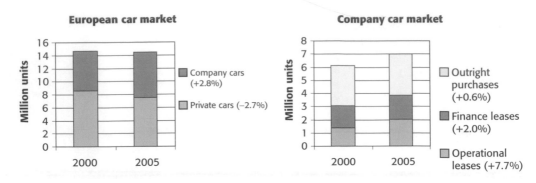

Sources: *autoPOLIS* forecasts

Fig. 7.20 Growth prospects for leasing in Europe

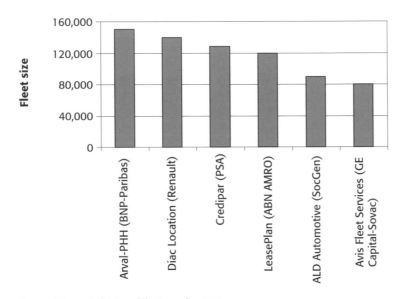

Source: *L'Argus de l'Automobile,* November 2001

Fig. 7.21 Leading leasing company fleets in France

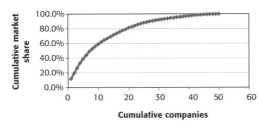

Source: Datamonitor, *autoPOLIS*

Fig. 7.22 The fragmented European vehicle leasing industry: top 50 leasing companies, Europe (based on operating leases)

battle will sharpen in intensity. Major financial institutions not already in this sector are taking an active interest in it. Retail leasing has never really taken off in Europe but is dominated by the vehicle manufacturers' captive arms, for the reasons of convenience and bundling described above.

The relatively small US automotive retail lease market is also dominated by the vehicle manufacturers' captive leasing arms, as figure 7.23 shows. The top four retail lessors are manufacturers' captive finance companies.

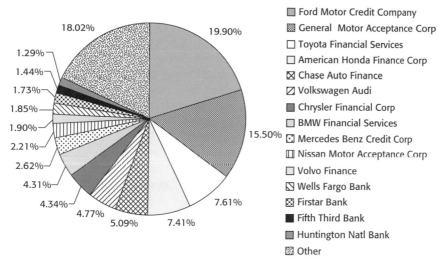

- ▨ Ford Motor Credit Company
- ▨ General Motor Acceptance Corp
- ☐ Toyota Financial Services
- ☐ American Honda Finance Corp
- ⊠ Chase Auto Finance
- ▨ Volkswagen Audi
- ▨ Chrysler Financial Corp
- ▨ BMW Financial Services
- ⊡ Mercedes Benz Credit Corp
- ▥ Nissan Motor Acceptance Corp
- ☐ Volvo Finance
- ▨ Wells Fargo Bank
- ⊠ Firstar Bank
- ■ Fifth Third Bank
- ▨ Huntington Natl Bank
- ▨ Other

Source: NADA

Fig. 7.23 US automotive retail lease market shares for banks and captives, 2001 (total volume 2.8 million)

Of the top ten retail bank lease funders, all are captives but Chase, which booked nearly three times as many leases as Wells, its nearest rival. Toyota and Honda have made effective use of leasing to increase market share. Retail leasing is a much more common phenomenon in the upline import market, which tends to serve sophisticated high-income and high-net-worth individuals, than in the mass Big Three market. In the latter retail leasing has regressed, as cash incentives have taken over.

The universality of the sales finance and leasing phenomenon, at least in Western developed countries, is further demonstrated by the penetration of leasing in Australia, shown in figure 7.24.

Wherever one looks, the industry is desperately pursuing volume and market share. It uses financing to boost sales, which is entirely legitimate. One of the major problems of emerging markets, such as China, is the absence of such a financing sector, often inhibited by state regulation. Where things start to come apart is when captive proprietary finance is sold at uncompetitive rates through

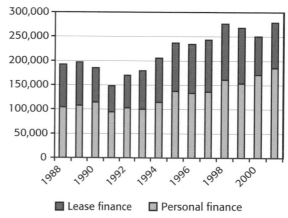

■ Lease finance   ☐ Personal finance

Source: Australian Automotive Intelligence Yearbook: www.aaintelligence.com.au; *auto*POLIS

Fig. 7.24 Growth of personal and lease finance in Australia

forced bundling and misleading information and used to cross-subsidise vehicle production operations, or when leasing and buy-back commitment are made on a non-transparent and uneconomic basis. Once again, all this creates enormous exposures and vulnerabilities. We shall look at them in the next section.

A fractured industry – the fault lines and the financial exposures

So far, this chapter has revealed the financial fragility of the global automotive industry. We have identified its endemically poor profitability and the resulting lack of affection for it on the part of the capital markets. We have explored the sources of weakness, notably the way in which vehicle manufacturers all too often – although there are honourable exceptions – abuse their various partners, who are also stakeholders in the great enterprise of motorised mobility, and how they are still acting out fantasies of global growth in what is essentially a mature and pluri-regional industry.

We believe that over the long term the automotive industry will destroy value. The auto industry is mature, so the long-term growth potential of the sector is below average. The industry is characterised by over-capacity and commoditised product offerings, which means that price competition is very tough and ROCE (return on capital employed) is poor. Over the last cycle, auto companies did not (on average) cover their cost of capital and we see little evidence of this changing in the near future. In our view, only strong premium brand players stand a chance of generating economic value over a full cycle.

We are still a long way from reaching equilibrium of demand and supply. For the industry to reach demand–supply equilibrium would require a structural shift in auto companies' policy to cutting back on capex, downsizing their businesses and releasing cashflow to shareholders. However, we are probably still a long way from such a shift in attitude.[9]

Deutsche Bank firmly puts the finger on the structural and behavioural deficiencies that are at the root of the automotive industry's financial weakness (see the above quotation). We share this view, except that we add two more factors: product proliferation and the misuse of branding. In chapter 5, we described how manufacturers are incurring huge development and manufacturing cost penalties for themselves and the whole industry by introducing far too many new products, in the vain hope of gaining market share in a saturated market, in which everyone is playing the same game. With the exception of a very limited number of brands, whose positioning and image correspond to real physical differentiation in performance and value to their owners, the branding and product differentiation game is being grossly overplayed by the majority of the industry. The failure of most volume manufacturers to accept that they are purveyors of a commodity product in a mature and very competitive market is at the root of most of the problems. Their unwillingness or inability to understand and face up to the economic realities of their business is damaging the whole industry. Their use of one-sided power in relationships with their upstream and downstream partners, in an attempt to deflect the financial heat away from themselves, only causes further damage to the infrastructure of the industry, which risks becoming irreversible.

We go farther than that. Let us pull together some of the threads which emerged in earlier chapters:

- There is no significant growth left and the industry can no longer escape the consequences of its own maturity (chapter 1).
- There are no new places to run to and the emerging markets are already breeding new competition (chapters 2 and 4).
- The industry faces a need for accelerated investment, in order to deploy the new technologies, for pressing geo-political, economic, environmental and societal reasons (chapter 3).
- The competitive structure of the industry is not yet fully rational (chapter 4).
- There are far too many platforms, models, derivatives and major components on offer – far more than are needed to provide an adequate level of choice and competition. The excessive costs of these are to a large extent extorted from the systems and components suppliers under duress (chapter 5).

---

[9] Deutsche Bank, *The Drivers*.

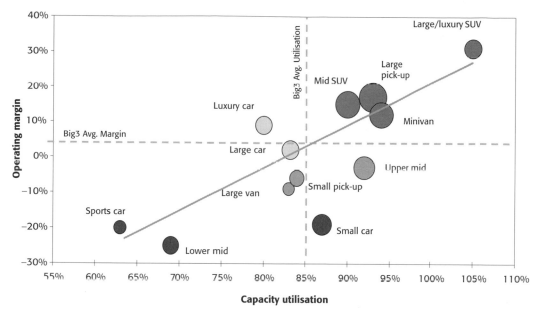

Source: Goldman Sachs

Fig. 7.25 US Big Three's earnings structure, 2002

- The downstream sector is unnecessarily complicated by the prevalence of proprietary retail outlets, which are financially propped up by excessive profits on dealer service and parts, and which have been kept in place by protectionist regulation and practices at the behest of the manufacturers (chapter 6).
- The industry's relationship to the capital markets – the providers of funds – is very badly degraded. There is not much sign of most of the industry having understood this. Indeed, its already weak profitability is under threat, as relationships become increasingly abusive (chapter 7).

Most of the vehicle manufacturers face real threats. The US Big Three, having already lost effective control of the passenger car market in North America to Asian competitors, face a new threat from them in the shape of light trucks in their domestic market – their profit engine (see figure 7.25). There is also a risk – minor today but possibly very serious in the future – of Americans becoming

serious about the economic, environmental and (yes) political consequences of their heavy consumption of oil-based fuels in the transport sector. The Big Three have little chance of re-establishing Europe as a major source of profits. They have virtually none of making a major showing in Asia, despite their acquisitions and investments there. They are not helped by the intransigent attitudes of the UAW, which cannot, however, be blamed for playing their own power game.

Figure 7.26 breaks down Chrysler's North American operating profit in the good old days of 1998, when it was still profitable. It is very clear. Chrysler made all its money in three product groups: the minivans, which it pioneered (Voyager, Caravan and especially Town & Country); SUVs (Jeep, especially Grand Cherokee); and the large pick-ups (especially Ram). The rest, including all the cars, contributed nothing financially.

The US Big Three have become hugely dependent on the profits they make on light trucks in North America: Chrysler totally so, Ford highly and GM relatively less – we saw

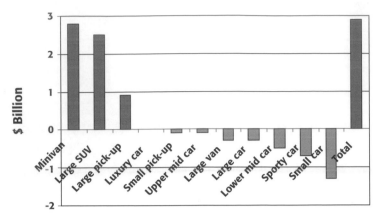

Source: Accounts

Fig. 7.26 The good old days: Chrysler North American operating profit, 1998

their positions by product group in chapter 4. This is a risk exposure, given that the Japanese are starting to move in on this sector. But there is another very important lesson to be drawn from the figure: unless you are very large, you cannot be good at every product and you make money only from the ones at which you are good.

So why do vehicle manufacturers not simply specialise in what they are good at? Given that Chrysler is so good at non-car light passenger vehicles, why does it bother with cars, which only lose it money? Renault is brilliant at innovative European small and medium car packages. Look at the succession of clever products: the Renault 5, the first car explicitly aimed at women drivers; the Renault 16, the first family-sized hatchback, in the age when hypermarkets developed in France; the Twingo, the first of the attractive small city cars; the Scenic, the vehicle that pioneered the minivan, European style, and was a runaway success, achieving three times the volume initially estimated. But has it ever managed to produce a plausible upline car? Its innovative styling simply does not work for these. Its cars just look odd to the more conservative buyers of upline cars. Conversely, what on earth does the A-Class do for the well-grounded product positioning, the brand image and the solid

earnings of Mercedes-Benz? It is a Class A diluter of them, in our opinion. Not to mention Chrysler. And why does PSA not major on being the supplier of diesel engines to the gentry?

The answer is: because every vehicle manufacturer, other than the niche specialists, is still obsessed with providing a full range and a vehicle in every class, so that consumers can move up the range as they go through their motoring lives. But the Second Revolution was long ago and the world has moved on. Being a GM or VW or Ford or Fiat owner all one's life no longer exists as a concept in the minds of most consumers. They have too much choice in all other walks of life to fall for that any more. Brand loyalty has all but gone out the window in the volume car market.

Part of the answer is also because every vehicle manufacturer feels obliged to drag along a huge family of more or less unruly children that bear its name: the traditional dealer network. It is just like the belief in the pre-industrial age that having many children was a guarantee of security in old age. In this case, it is just a guarantee of a very expensive route to market which creates massive redundancy in the whole distribution and service chain.

The mindset is also fixed because every vehicle manufacturer, other than the smallest, and with a few exceptions for particular products, feels obliged to develop and build its own engines and transmissions, whereas these are really generic items with no real specific link to vehicle brands, except perhaps in the upline car sectors. We saw the vast degree of redundancy this produces earlier, with the eighty-three engine families in Europe.

The thinking is also rigid because they have all embraced the Third Revolution, based on lean thinking, believing that leanness defeats scale and removes the costs of diversity. In fact, they have embraced 'lean' but not 'thinking'. Why make the physical distribution of new vehicles lean but not the distribution system itself? Because that requires diversity of formats and networks, rather than Soviet-age uniformity, including the acceptance of large Wal-Mart-style, Cardoen-style, and Trade Sales-style all-makes outlets. Why make engineering and production lean but not the vastly over-proliferated product lines? Because that means abandoning cherished and wholly outdated illusions of completeness and brand loyalty. Why go on trying to be a Comecon-era Kombinat when you could be a profitable specialist in a freely competitive market? Because that would require thinking the unthinkable, challenging the current economics of the madhouse. Why pursue globalisation when the real recipe is ABB's old slogan, 'Being Local Everywhere'? Because that might require learning from other industries (yes, there are some other quite big mature ones, which have undergone radical change, such as electrical engineering or chemicals).

So the real exposure of the US automotive industry may be to too little change, rather than too much. Is it worth anyone other than GM trying to fight the Japanese on cars? Or is GM going to trump everyone else by making its revolutionary hydrogen-fuelled, fuel-cell-powered skateboard concept tomorrow's industry standard? Are its European operations really worth sustaining? Who will control the central nervous system of the vehicle, i.e. should there be different proprietary standards, or one common one? Should change be

sought in the distribution system? Can a better accommodation be found with the UAW?

Similar hard questions need to be asked and answered in Europe, although for different reasons. For example, are manufacturers trying to be too clever with some of the new technologies, notably all-singing, all-communicating electronics, in pursuit of differentiation and premium pricing? Are they not laying themselves open to an attack by the Japanese, by handing them back their old trump card of superior passive quality? Is it good enough to tell Toyota not to attack Mercedes-Benz and BMW on these grounds because comparative advertising is banned in Europe? That has been challenged successfully in other sectors. Worse, it exists, in non-partisan form, through two sets of mass-membership organisations: the automobile clubs and the consumer federations. Are we going to continue to get the same kinds of answer that J. D. Power got from a major manufacturer when it first set its sights on running comparative car quality surveys in Europe? 'If you land, we'll drive you back into the sea', it was told.

Is the European industry willing to learn the lessons from what happened to it over block exemption? Surely it must have better answers than that made by one of its representatives to the charge of political ineptitude: 'We're not understood'? Is it prepared to faced up to the costs of the product proliferation race and bring them under control? There remains plenty of opportunity to reduce costs, to everyone's benefit.

Let us look into what goes into the pre-tax retail price of an average European car – in the current state of proliferation of products and distribution channels, and after a de-proliferation to a more reasonable level of offerings. We have adapted today's price and cost structure from the Deutsche Bank report, introducing cost categories that fit more closely with the organisation of the new vehicle business than theirs, for today's structure in a proliferated industry (the left-hand column of figures in figure 7.27) in euros per

	Proliferated (euro/vehicle)	Deproliferation factor	Deproliferated (euro/vehicle)	Gain (euro/vehicle)	Industry gain (billion euros)
Average selling price	**19,000**	**90%**	**17,100**	**1,900**	**29**
Dealer gross margin	1,500				
Incentives	1,200				
Price of retail distribution	2,700	75%	2,025	675	10
VM's net price	**16,300**	**92%**	**15,075**		
Transportation	350	100%	350	-	
Warranty costs	350	60%	210	140	2
VM's marketing and sales overhead	1,900	50%	950	950	14
Cost of wholesale distribution	**2,600**	**58%**	**1,510**	**1,090**	**16**
Cost of distribution	**5,300**	**75%**	**3,975**	**1,325**	**20**
Price of bought-in materials	**8,150**	**95%**	**7,743**	**408**	**6**
VM's manufacturing labour	2,200	90%	1,980	220	3
Manufacturing overhead	500	110%	550	50	1
Depreciation	800	75%	600	200	3
VM's internal manufacturing cost	**3,500**	**89%**	**3,130**	**370**	**6**
Product development	**950**	**70%**	**665**	**285**	**4**
General and administrative overhead	**450**	**50%**	**225**	**225**	**3**
Total VM's costs	**15,650**	**85%**	**13,273**	**2,378**	**36**
VM's EBIT	*650%*	*277%*	*1,803*	*1,153*	*17*

Source: *auto*POLIS, adapted from Deutsche Bank *The Drivers*, table 6, p. 23.

Fig. 7.27 Breakdown of the price of an average car in Europe

vehicle. We then apply a de-proliferation factor, based on our experience and some of the analyses in the previous chapters and sections, to arrive at the de-proliferated price and cost structure per vehicle. The difference is shown in the fourth column of figure 7.27 and the European industry's potential gain, in billions of euros per year, in the fifth column. This can be viewed as the current level of waste induced by product and channel proliferation:

- As with Deutsche Bank, we assume an average pre-tax selling price of €19,000. The dealer makes a gross margin of €1,500, i.e. 8 per cent after he has granted his own discounts from list price to his customers, plus another €1,200 in a posteriori incentives, so that the price paid by the manufacturer for the retail dealer's services is €2,700 per unit, or 14 per cent of the selling price.
- After de-proliferation, we assume that selling prices drop by 10 per cent. This is an

assumption which is validated by the results further down, which show that the industry can easily afford it. The annual gain to European consumers is €29 billion a year. It would be up to governments to decide whether they simply let this be passed on, which will lower their value added and special sales tax receipts by some €9 billion, recoup just the lost €9 billion, or take some more to pump into auto-related research or infrastructural spending. An additional €20 billion a year would pay for a great deal of intelligent highway implementation, for example. The vehicle manufacturer would sell the vehicle to the dealer for an effective net price of €16,300, falling to €15,075 in the de-proliferated scenario.

- Transportation costs would remain the same – we assume the same volume of cars going to the same places. Warranty costs should go down significantly. We have assumed a 50 per cent slowing down in the new product introduction rate, so that a product lives twice as long on average. Thus the cost of wholesale distribution (undertaken by vehicle manufacturers and their national importers in each country, who are mainly their own subsidiaries) is similar to that of the retail level. It is the absence of an independent wholesale level that has caused so many of the distribution and pricing problems in Europe.

- In the de-proliferated scenario, large national and international retail chains emerge, which integrate wholesaling as well, both on an all-makes basis. As the Cardoen analysis in chapter 6 shows, they can do both the wholesaling and the retailing of new cars for much less cost, the total price of distribution (costs + margins) dropping from some 28 per cent to 23 per cent of a lower selling price. Very importantly, it is the emergence of these large independent groups that causes the de-proliferation of product lines, as they start to exercise major influence upon the product planning process. Unlike today's tied franchised dealers, they cannot be forced to shift hard-to-sell product. They will buy direct from the factory, in full knowledge of costs. As they assume most of the responsibilities of the manufacturer's importer and many of those now carried out by the manufacturer (network development and policing), the manufacturer's internal marketing and sales overheads can be dramatically cut. So €20 billion a year can be saved on distribution in total.
- We have dropped the price paid by the manufacturer for bought-in materials by a prudent 5 per cent. In reality, a 50 per cent de-proliferation will cut suppliers' engineering and manufacturing costs by anywhere up to 15–20 per cent.
- De-proliferation saves the vehicle manufacturer 5 per cent and restores an additional 10 per cent or more of margin to the beleaguered components industry – which will also need to accelerate its technological investments sharply, in order to apply and deploy the new technologies. The manufac-

turers save €6 billion and another €12 billion can be pumped back into the components industry.

- Manufacturing labour costs are estimated to fall by about 10 per cent, because of learning effects and reduced complexity in plants. We have allowed a slightly increased manufacturing overhead to cope with the greater strain placed on equipment kept in service longer. Depreciation is reduced for the same reason.
- The vehicle manufacturer's internal manufacturing cost falls by some 10 per cent.
- Deutsche Bank estimates product development spend at close to €1,000 per vehicle per year, with 60 per cent spent on platforms and 40 per cent on adapting platforms for models.
- We have assumed a 25 per cent reduction, which already allows for applying some of the new technologies.
- As a result of all this, the vehicle manufacturer's EBIT per vehicle almost triple, despite a 10 per cent fall in the price to the consumer. The annual gain to the vehicle industry is €17 billion: enough to restore its deficient profits (which would otherwise be hit by the decoupling of sales from service and the consequent loss of their monopoly rents on parts distribution) and allow a massive investment in the new-technology vehicles.

Interestingly, this is the same conclusion that Arthur Andersen came to in their report evaluating regulatory options for the European Commission in 2002. Unfortunately it was buried in an appendix on page 326 of the report, behind mountains of bizarre diagrams and verbiage. Their mass retailer scenario assumed just this double de-proliferation of channels and products and produced similar gains in costs and margins all round. Perhaps the Commission found the implications too hot to put up front, for they require the abandonment on a large scale of the traditional franchised dealership system and a massive transfer of power from manufacturers to independent distributors.

There is another huge knock-on benefit. With service decoupled from sales and no longer forced to subsidise it within the traditional dealership structure, the charge-out rates for service labour of the ex-dealer shops could drop by 25–30 per cent. There would be a unified aftermarket with true competition, in the place of one artificially divided into two camps by an iron curtain. Again, not of all this need be handed straight over to the car owner or operator. There needs to be a general raising of standards and margins in the whole downstream service sector.

And what about the Japanese? What are the opportunities and risks they face? They are clearly on a roll in North America. We believe the block exemption changes in Europe play strongly in their favour. Difficulties in establishing distribution have held them back in the past. They no longer need do so now. Their main risk is a rather special one: going too slowly. They succeeded with standard products with very little regional adaptation in the US market, but lost their initial impetus in Europe by sticking to that strategy there. They need to move much more radically towards regional decentralisation of responsibility. This obviously affects products; it also affects production. They will have to reduce their dependence on Japan as a volume-driving (but not very profitable) home base. Within the worldwide automotive pattern of production and consumption, Japan remains an anomaly, producing almost twice as many vehicles as it registers domestically, and with only marginal imports.

So if there is this new Eldorado of an unbundled and reconstituted industry, with production in the right places and the right relationships with strong independent suppliers and equally strong and independent distributors, why are we not there already? What has held us up? In a word, control – the manufacturers' obsession with control beyond their normal boundaries. This control has prevented the full accomplishment of the structural revolution in the systems and components indus-try and kept in place massive duplication of development effort, as the CAR study[10] indicates. It has prevented the supplier industry from having its full say about the costs of product proliferation. Above all, the tight control over single-brand channels has completely stifled the growth of strong distributors who could bring the proliferation of products and channels under some control.

What is most damaging is the lack of restructuring within the industry as a whole. Yet we believe that many of the conventional historical constraints can be loosened if the industry unbundles itself and reaggregates into economically more viable units working with each other on an equitable basis. It has not happened because the large vehicle manufacturer conglomerates remain largely in charge of resource allocation. In the absence of external monitoring and control, this has become distinctly sub-optimal, with a strong predilection for preserving the status quo. The bundling and conglomeration have made it extremely difficult for the capital markets to play their role in stimulating the reallocation of funds from mature to growing sectors in the industry, and from unsuccessful to successful businesses. There is a desperate lack of transparency about the industrial, commercial and consequently financial justification for intercorporate transactions. The situation is just as bad for large projects. Would it not be salutary if astute outside analysts pored over major vehicle developments, or intended additions to world capacity in emerging markets?

We believe that the industry is at a historic turning point, where it can choose between two alternative futures. One is to try to continue the present system of command–control–confuse, which has led it into increasing problems with the financial community. The other is to face up to restructuring and openness. We discuss these alternative futures in the last two chapters.

[10] CAR, 'Estimating the New Automotive Value Chain'.

8

Choosing a future for the automotive industry

If nothing changes – Graceless Degradation

In this book we have systematically reviewed many of the different facets of the world's auto industry, looking at the sector not as a business but as an 'economic phenomenon'. We wanted to look at the industry as a business too, of course, but also at the car as a source of mobility, at the industry's impact within society as a whole, and at the auto sector in a much more holistic way than has been done before.

Where does it take us?

The answer is inevitably mixed. On the positive side, there is the increase in mobility the car has brought us: a colossal economic and social benefit for mankind. On the positive side, too, the industry has done much to address the environmental damage it once caused. Although there are still pollutants from cars, and the volume of carbon dioxide emissions is still rising, the damage vehicles cause through other emissions has been dramatically reduced and will fall much further in the years to come. This has been the result of much effort by the industry and by governments. Cars are also safer, and although the number of road deaths has risen substantially, much of this is a result of a lack of economic development – that is, it is a tragic phenomenon facing the developing world but also one that will eventually be fixed. There are options open to governments and drivers to reduce the carnage today, of course, which should be widely adopted. The vehicle industry has mostly acted responsibly in the face of these challenges, although too often with an initial resistance. It can

scarcely be blamed for inadequate road infrastructures or driver education. It might, however, do well to tone down some of its advertising, which continues to appeal too much to the boy racer hidden in some of us. It would also do well to think about how it works with legislators, to find a more constructive approach.

What else? We know that eventually, and probably some time relatively soon, oil availability will become a problem. We know too that the industry is responding to this challenge. But we can say with certainty that the emergence of a widely used fleet of differently powered vehicles is still many years away and that the traditional gasoline and diesel engines will dominate the roads for the foreseeable future.

The value of the increase in mobility is almost impossible to estimate but it is clearly very high. We can travel and work in so many different places, we can communicate more easily and we have many more opportunities to meet our personal goals and objectives thanks to the car. Cars have transformed the lives of most people in the developed world and this has created huge economic wealth, faster growth and much greater individual freedom. These are immensely valuable benefits.

What about the other side of the equation? Clearly there is congestion and this is getting worse. Moreover it is eating into the primary benefit, mobility. But even congestion can be tackled and its costs still come nowhere near the benefits cars bring. There is also a growing number of deaths and injuries on the roads, although again these can be greatly reduced.

The responsibility here lies almost entirely with legislators.

The main problems brought about by the car industry which have been identified through our analysis are of a different sort altogether. They focus much more on the business itself, and on the providers of the machines that generate all these mobility benefits. The industry is in deep trouble and facing years of difficulties ahead. Worse, many of the troubles that lie in front are self-inflicted. For an industry which accounts for 10 per cent of the GDP of developed economies and brings millions of jobs, this is an issue for us all.

What will happen if a better model is not found; what will happen if the industry carries on its current path?

First, let us review the situation. There are really two main elements to the troubles facing the 'industry of industries'. The first, as we highlighted at the very beginning of this book, is that growth has come to a halt. Global sales slowed dramatically after the oil shocks of the 1970s and came to a stop after 1999. Although there are some places that might provide growth in the future they are too small, too slow-growing or too volatile to make them sufficiently attractive – they will not make up the necessary shortfall. To make matters worse, the few really major new markets such as China are going to be extremely difficult to access.

In the longer term, perhaps a decade from now, as some of the emerging markets become more substantial, this situation may change. The growth in these places may be sufficient to push the industry back into expansion. In the meantime, however, there is a problem.

This problem is and never was going to cause a catharsis, however. There is very little chance of an explosive collapse as a result of it. It is not likely to cause a sudden collapse of the world's top vehicle makers. Indeed the industry has, seemingly, carried on quite happily with low rates of growth for more than thirty years.

Yet managing through these years of low growth has come at a price. To counter the low rates of the expansion since the 1970s, to make up the shortfall, the vehicle manufacturers have responded by increasing the 'content' of their vehicles and raising the real price. There are lots more features and goodies in cars and carmakers have charged us for these. More recently, they have vastly increased the range of models available, in the hope of enticing more buyers, regardless of the added economic cost. They have extracted revenues through the aftermarket, by charging us ever more for spare parts and dealer repairs, especially in Europe. The big vehicle makers have increasingly turned to financing vehicle sales as a source of revenue. In Europe, they have tried another route, which has resulted in them being accused of an abuse of monopoly power, by restricting sales across borders in an effort to maintain different price levels in different countries.

None of this was, to be frank, very good. Moreover, by the early 2000s, it was coming to an end. The competitive pressures after 1999 when the rate of global growth fell to zero resulted in most carmakers cutting the prices of their cars in real terms. So the higher-price revenue stream dried up. In Europe, the Brussels authorities heavily fined carmakers who restricted cross-border sales. So that avenue was being shut off too. The new Block Exemption Regulation means that the unjustified price differences for new cars have started to level out, while the over-pricing for parts and repairs has begun to come under threat, by law. The banks have finally woken up to the lending risks, cutting the credit status of carmakers to levels that have clipped the wings of their financing businesses to difficult-to-sustain levels.

So in the late 1990s and early 2000s the carmakers were using more and more desperate means to get out of the bind of the lack of growth. But these means were ending. The result was that most vehicle manufacturers started to destroy value. They also started to exert even greater pressure on the components industry and the downstream sector as times got harder. These sectors came under enormous pressure and were effectively starved of margins by most of the vehicle makers.

The effects of all of these actions were manifest in the second major element of the troubles facing the industry – its financial problems, as they came to a head.

Throughout the boom years, carmakers were making rotten returns and had few ways left to improve their margins quickly. Some, like Fiat and Daewoo, faced collapse. Others sat on the edge of the financial abyss. There were exceptions such as Toyota, Porsche and Peugeot, but they were few. And even those firms feared a trade or market backlash as their more troubled rivals fell ever faster down the financial hole they had dug for themselves.

In effect, the industry had built a giant pressure cooker for itself, which had been rising in temperature for three decades. It had seen low growth or no growth throughout this time, but instead of addressing this problem properly it had squeezed revenue from every possible source, even if this was beyond its proper economic remit. Now that strategy was reaching its limits and the financial structure of the industry was the most obvious symptom of what this meant.

The effects of these woes were made worse by the stubbornness of many of the industry's managers. They might try to excuse their behaviour because the pressure took so long to build up. But it seems to us that the implications could have been much less severe had it not been for a head-in-the-sand attitude which made many in the business almost blind to the situation they were in. Their businesses had had problems which had lasted for many years, but because they had found other ways to address the lack of growth, the real roots of the troubles were ignored. Much of this is down to the confrontational attitude adopted by vehicle manufacturers to the market, to rivals and to suppliers, and it was far from productive. Squeeze those around you before looking to yourself, seemed to be the motto. It stems, in our view, from the very earliest days

of the industry, and the Fordist approach subsequently adopted by many others which gave managers an almost imperial attitude to those around them.

There are other reasons for this myopia of course. The situation was a little like the endless debates that seem to have taken place over how to save Venice from the floods which may one day consume it. No one can quite decide what to do there either, especially while the interim solutions seem to provide at least some relief and the impression of action. For the managers of some of the big car companies this was the case too. Why not milk the suppliers and the aftermarket rather than face the reality of the situation? Besides, by the time the industry floods come, most of these managers would have moved on or retired.

So what exactly were the industry's managers so afraid of? What were the hard decisions they should have been taking? How could they have fixed the financial discontinuities that they faced before they became so serious?

The answers are inevitably hard.

They would have had to have gone back to basics, to accept that the growth was over and that industry maturity had arrived (for at least a generation), and act accordingly. But who wants to do that? Who wants to work for a mature business?

They should have cut capacity. They should have redesigned their businesses to make money out of making cars again. They should have reduced the number of models and platforms instead of increasing them. They should have avoided painful follies like those of building so many plants in so-called developing markets. They should have shut them down when it became clear that the volumes in these places were not going to meet expectations. They should have laid people off, stopped milking the aftermarket, not exploited cross-border price differentials in Europe, stopped restricting access to the market in Japan and freed up their dealers almost everywhere to promote the creation of a rational economic business.

Those would have been the tough decisions and the right ones for the industry but no-one wanted to take them. Each individual firm certainly feared losing ground through any retraction. But more of a problem, we think, was that most could not see the reality of their position; they lacked the necessary understanding of their long-term economic position.

Moreover, there was and is an alternative route for the industry. Instead of avoiding these hard decisions, the carmakers could have looked at an entirely new model for their businesses, such as the one we discuss in chapter 9. But the direction actually taken by most firms will have implications for some time to come.

So what will that mean? What will the policy of squeezing partners and suppliers, of resisting the correct decisions, do? Eventually, the laws of economics will prevail, although they are likely to be applied in a skewed form and in ways which are far from ideal. This is why we have called this section, this future for the industry, Graceless Degradation. Without any positive movement, however painful that may have been in the short term, the industry faces many years of rumbling pain, with a gradual slide downwards for most firms. It could have been so much easier.

What will happen? An indication is provided through an analysis of figure 8.1. The pressures on the industry will be felt at many levels simultaneously, both within the business and outside, by governments, consumers and financiers.

Looking first from the industry's viewpoint, the financial pain will become ever more acute for all parts of the value chain. Some will feel it more than others. As a general rule, those that are adding value in figure 8.1 will prevail; those destroying value will suffer most. That is, after all, the effect of economics.

In the top left-hand corner of the diagram Porsche is unlikely to feel too much pain. Although the market for its cars is likely to suffer in the ups and downs of Western economies (and the company's sales volumes can fluctuate wildly during downturns), Porsche has a strong, flexible and unique market position. It is profitable, has manufacturing which it can switch off at little cost, a defensible market niche position and massive brand loyalty. Whether or not its foray into the off-road sector with the Cayenne proves to have been a success remains to be seen – the jury is still out. But the company has a strong position and few immediate threats. We have few worries about the future of Porsche.

Unfortunately, Porsche's position is rare. Close by on the diagram are BMW and Mercedes, two of Germany's most powerful brands. For BMW the outlook should be good. Again, the company seems to have found a strong and defensible market position, mostly in Europe and the US. It has a history of successfully building on this, of developing new models, of maintaining quality levels and of staying at the cutting edge of the sportily designed high-end segment of the market. The only real question over BMW's future is not to do with its size, even though it is comparatively small by global standards, but over its growth prospects. The company is mining a finite niche and one that will eventually face the prospects of demographic stagnation in Europe and slow, highly competitive expansion in the US. Although there are plans to develop the brand in China, we think that this will be far from easy, especially given the company's approach.[1] For BMW, though, the unhappy years facing the industry are unlikely to bring too much damage.

For Mercedes the story is very different. Mercedes itself is a powerful brand with an unrivalled reputation. It is, arguably, the father of the industry. And were the company still a stand-alone business, we would have far fewer concerns. But it is not. Thanks to a strategy driven by a desire to join the big-boy league,

---

[1] For more details see Graeme Maxton, 'China: Fools Drive In', *Business China* (Economic Intelligence Unit), 31 March 2003.

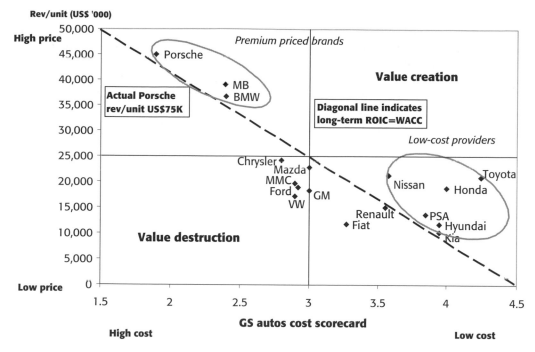

Rev/unit (US$ '000)

Source: Goldman Sachs Japan

Fig. 8.1 Where the degradation comes

and for that purpose alone, it seems, the company built a shaky new position for itself in the late 1990s. The acquisition of Chrysler is still likely to prove very costly. The link with Mitsubishi was a disaster and it could be seen as such for more than a year before Daimler eventually withdrew. The truck business is highly cyclical and barely profitable, despite being the biggest in the world outside China. The Smart business is struggling. The Maybach risks being an expensive irrelevance. And throughout the late 1990s and early 2000s the strategies for growth through alliance and acquisition have proved expensive in management time. They have been a source of distraction, leading to a thinning of attention elsewhere. This began to affect the quality levels of the main brand in 2003 too.

In late 2003 Mercedes began (reportedly) discussing the possibility of selling Chrysler to its management, a little like BMW sold off Rover – in that case for a £10 payment and a handsome cash handout to the ailing British company. This was a brave and sensible decision for BMW, despite the price paid. If Mercedes can pull off the same stunt, it would do well. But the costs will be high and the prospects for a stand-alone Chrysler are not good. Mercedes will have to pay a great deal to off-load its sick American patient.

If it does not do this, though, the risks could be greater still. Chrysler could easily get into a downward spiral where it cannot compete, cannot fund on-going model development and haemorrhages cash. This is the risk that could prove fatal to its German-based parent. To avoid this, Mercedes may be forced to downsize its American affiliate substantially or even close it. Either option would have significant implications for Mercedes' brand image in the US and for sales. There would also be something of a backlash against the Germans if they were seen to be cutting back a major US company after promising so much. After all, the post-acquisition travails with some disgruntled shareholders quickly became acrimonious, a sign that further troubles with Chrysler would not be well received. So Mercedes faces a future which could be much harder than for its German upline rival, BMW.

We now move towards the centre of the figure, to those firms that have a middle market position in terms of price but, according to Goldman Sachs, are all value destroyers. These firms include the two largest firms ranked by sales – GM and Ford – as well as Chrysler, Mazda, Mitsubishi (MMC) and Volkswagen. All risk moving further towards the bottom left-hand corner. That is, they risk falling into a situation where the prices for their vehicles are further eroded at the same time as their costs rise, thanks to lower or stable volumes and more models. They are also likely to have to ramp up their marketing and advertising spending as well as boosting discounts in the short term to stave off decline. So prices will fall and costs will rise.

Of all these firms, GM is perhaps in the best position, and perhaps surprisingly. Although we have criticised GM greatly for its products, market position in many places and its economics, recent conversations with the firm suggest that an important change has been taking place. Turning around a car company that is sliding like this is inevitably a long drawn-out process. So any of the fruits of this change in thinking will take time. But we have found that the latest generation of top managers in GM are all too aware of some of the longer-term difficulties the company faces. It seems ready to consider some very radical options in an effort to fix its underlying economics. More of this in chapter 9. But we have a sense that GM is more aware of the dangers that the industry faces than most of its rivals. While many see the broader picture, they are often too focused on the immediate cash needs, and for good reason. GM seems to have found the inner strength to consider the bigger picture too.

Still, without some radical thinking it will be hard for GM to move itself to the right of where it lay on the diagram in 2003. In Europe it is losing money and there is little chance of it moving back into profit quickly. In the US, the steady erosion of prices after 2001 and the prospects for sales during the next five years will make life hard for the firm. It has lost share progressively, is still burdened with healthcare and pensions liabilities, and is flying at the edge of financial sense with its sales incentives. It has a stake in a ragbag of companies in Japan and South Korea. Some of these could prove good, such as Suzuki in Japan. Others, such as Isuzu or Daewoo in South Korea, could prove troublesome. One option could be for GM to sell its stakes in these companies in the event of it getting into more serious trouble. Its stakes in Suzuki and Subaru could be valuable, its shares of Daewoo and Isuzu less so.

For GM there is also the possibility of China. The company has achieved a great deal there with its local partner Shanghai Automotive and the market is, of course, likely to grow rapidly, even if it will be very volatile. But, as we have also made clear, China will not be easy. The Chinese want to develop their own auto industry and they are, culturally at least, unlikely to let it be controlled by a foreign firm, especially an American one. It would be very easy for the Chinese, at some point, to crank the handle of nationalism and stifle GM's plans. There is also the issue of counterfeits, which GM has already had to contend with. So it would be folly for GM to count on China as the solution to its long-term growth problems.

There are few other places for GM to go. The company's plant in South-East Asia – in Thailand – is a model of how not to establish a business in the region. It may find some opportunities in Latin America or even in Eastern and Central Europe, but these will be small. So unless the company acts more radically, it risks drifting to the lower left of the Goldman Sachs chart, where the real prices of its vehicles decline at the same time as its costs rise. The effect? The same as for all the others in this predicament: a deteriorating financial situation as well as greater and greater pressure on suppliers to cut costs. Eventually the model will become unsustainable. Then, depending on what the competition is doing, GM will have to make some hard decisions. It will have to cut costs more and build revenues. That will mean that the prices of its vehicles will have to rise, plants will have to close, the model range will have to be reduced and subsidiaries will have to be sold off. How severe these measures will have to be is difficult to guess. But without any other option, they will be painful and prolonged.

For Ford, the second-largest firm in terms of sales, the prospects are even less rosy. There was much speculation in 2002 and 2003 that the company could get itself into a financial mess sufficiently serious to force it into Chapter 11 and file for administrative bankruptcy. This may still happen. But it is our view that Bill Ford, the current chairman, will avoid that at all costs. That is, he will not see the company founded by his great-grandfather forced from family control under his watch. He will do everything possible to avoid the ignominy of losing the ties of history.

This is by no means a foregone conclusion, however. Family influence in Motorola, Hewlett Packard and several other firms was lost in the early 2000s after several generations. And Ford needs some radical surgery which may only be possible with an entirely different style of leadership.

Either way, the outlook for Ford is difficult. It is losing share in its main markets, has had a troubled position in Europe for more than a decade, and has a comparatively weak position in the emerging markets. Prices are falling and costs are rising. The firm is drifting towards the bottom left-hand corner of the Goldman Sachs chart. It is also being progressively cut off from the capital markets and has substantial long-term healthcare and pensions liabilities.

These troubles will mean much the same for Ford as for GM, only worse. More plants will have to be shut, more people will need to be laid off, and even more pressure will be put on suppliers. New model plans will have to be trimmed. Ford will accelerate down the death spiral mentioned before by Jeff Ng at Citigroup. Eventually, there will come a crunch. Then the company will have to unbundle and reassemble its businesses more rationally.

Given the situation, this is likely to need some deep and invasive surgery. Ford may have to sell off many prized assets, such as Jaguar, Land Rover, Mazda and Volvo. Even then, these are not likely to raise much. Few of these businesses are making decent returns – quite the opposite, apart from Volvo – and their market valuations are low. There are also likely to be few buyers, even at fire-sale prices. Jaguar is probably in the worst situation. It cost Ford a great deal to acquire in the late 1980s, the company has spent a fortune trying to turn it around and it has not returned even a tiny fraction of this investment. It is a valuable brand, perhaps, but a company which is also not worth much. The story is similar with Land Rover, although as well as having a good brand this company also has some good technology. For Mazda, again the value is likely to be low. The company was only valued by the capital markets at around $2.5 billion in 2003, a drop in the ocean of Ford's financial woes. Although Volvo might be the most easily saleable (perhaps to Bosch, one of our interviewees speculated), few of Ford's subsidiaries will raise the money required for the broader business to survive. So Ford may have to consider even more radical changes, such as withdrawal from the market in Europe and a retreat to its original home market – where it might then risk turning into a second Chrysler, trapped between GM and the Japanese: a graceless and perhaps terminal degradation for one of the fathers of the industry.

For Chrysler, the prospects are dependent on the decisions of Mercedes. If it stays within the German-controlled group, then the outlook is difficult, as we have discussed. If it is spun off in some way, then the prospects may be rosier for a time – especially if it is given a large farewell bonus. At the end of the day, though, the company on its own might be as fragile as MG Rover. To rank number four or five in a highly competitive, price-driven market is likely to be hard. It might be able to survive for some time as a purely North American niche player, focused on light trucks, at the price of some further downsizing. There may be a partial analogy here with Peugeot's concentration on Europe and careful economy of style. Chrysler has certainly shown a remarkable talent for recovery from the brink on more than one previous occasion – with some help from Uncle Sam. How long this position would be tenable in the face of the Japanese incursion into the US light truck market is another matter.

For Chrysler's one-time partner and arm's length affiliate Mitsubishi the options are even harder. When Mercedes took management control, the financial position within the Japanese company was extremely weak and the product pipeline nearly empty. Mercedes made substantial changes to improve the situation, and with cutbacks which reduced the company's debts. There were also a series of facelifts to the company's cars which provided some life to the product line-up for a while. But the strategy of easing credit availability to maintain sales in the US backfired. Although volumes were boosted for a while, the banks eventually cut off the funds available to the company and sales dropped back.

Despite the positive changes, Mitsubishi still had a chasm to jump, to develop completely new products and to restore its reputation, financial foundations and image. This is why Daimler eventually abandoned Mitsubishi in 2004, when it refused to invest further in the ailing business. What the Japanese company can do next is hard to predict. It certainly seems unlikely that it will find (or even want) another foreign investor after such a debacle. It is now in a very weak position, having suffered a series of setbacks through a combination of bad luck, poor management and being spurned. Radical restructuring will be essential. Even then, there may be little the

company can do to avoid falling further into the abyss.

The final company in the middle part of the Goldman Sachs chart is Volkswagen, the largest European carmaker and the dominant one in the region for the last fifteen years. Despite its size, VW has always suffered from a significant financial weakness – too high a cost base. This means that the company has to operate at very high levels of capacity utilisation to make a profit. With the prospects for a stagnant European market, this will be hard. Like the others in the middle group, the company faces lower price realisation as competitive intensity and costs rise. It is likely to have to boost marketing and advertising spend to protect its position.

Volkswagen also has a strong position in China and in parts of South America, as well as a healthy although comparatively stable position in the US. All will help, although none will be sufficient to counter the wider problems the company faces. But VW is likely to benefit from the degradation of some of its rivals in Europe. It gained substantial share in Italy as Fiat declined and is likely to gain from the woes afflicting both GM and Ford in Europe too. On balance, then, we think that VW should be able to remain in its current strategic position and may even strengthen a little. VW is not vulnerable to a takeover. For now, at least, it is partially protected by its ownership structure – the government of the state of Lower Saxony, where its headquarters are located, has partial ownership and additional rights of refusal. The EU authorities have challenged this, saying it is a barrier to competition, so this protection may not last.

In the lower right-hand quadrant of Goldman Sachs's chart sit a mixed bag of mostly healthy firms, with one especially weak exception. The weak firm is Fiat, which at the time of writing is in a state of accelerated decline which looks hard to reverse. We see the company gradually dropping out of the European big league and perhaps being broken up. Alfa Romeo would make a tasty bite for VW, while

Ferrari would add to the stables of any number of companies.

For the others in the group, the prospects are generally pretty good – unless there is the sort of radical change in the structure of the industry that we shall propose in chapter 9.

But without any such radical overhaul in the industry, these remaining firms should prosper. Renault, thanks greatly to its tie-up with Nissan, should be able to withstand the storms. Its cost base should improve and its price realisation should increase, thanks greatly to the Nissan side of the business. Nissan has been able to transform its models with Renault's help, and this should help it gain further market share both in Japan and elsewhere. Renault also appears to have effectively protected itself from a possible takeover, through its capital structure.

PSA (Peugeot-Citroën) should remain much as now, we think, making good returns (certainly for this industry) by virtue of a strong position in the European market. Much will depend on the company maintaining its lead in diesel engines and small cars. But its tie-up with Toyota in very small cars and the likely decline facing rivals Ford and GM in the region are likely to bring additional share and sales to the French group.

For Hyundai, the prospects are not so healthy, certainly in the long term. In the short term, the company should be able to grow thanks to its low-cost position and its consequent ability to compete in the US and Europe, where price competition will intensify for a while. In the medium and longer term, however, it faces several challenges. The first is the growing maturity and increasing competition in its domestic market, South Korea. Sales have reached a peak, mostly for demographic reasons, and local rivals – notably Samsung (controlled by Renault) and GM-owned Daewoo – are providing a challenge that has not existed for Hyundai for a while. In the longer term, the company will face a new threat to its overseas sales from emergent Chinese firms. These will specifically target its low-cost segment first and are likely to offer even lower prices. In the end, Hyundai risks being squeezed between the Chinese on one side and the better-branded, higher-technology providers from Japan and Europe on the other. This is why we said earlier on that there was a risk that South Korea's foray into the auto industry could end up being a thirty-year fireworks display. They are unlikely to have created any companies that are sustainable in the long term.

Finally, for the last two firms, Honda and Toyota, the prospects are good. Both have a strong position and are likely to benefit from the decline of many of their rivals. They are the most globally balanced of all vehicle manufacturers in terms of their market footprints, other than Renault-Nissan, once this alliance has achieved its platform and components rationalisation – the US and European arms of both GM and Ford having little in common in terms of product. Both have a healthy financial position too, although both could do more perhaps to sharpen their product designs for Europe and make their businesses more profitable in Japan.

So for the vehicle manufacturers, then, there will be a mixture of consolidation and more fragmentation as some of the big companies are forced to sell subsidiaries and some of the newer rivals in China and India expand. For many companies there will be a Graceless Degradation and for all there will be a period of dog-eat-dog change: a sub-optimal evolution thanks to the still semi-feudal mentality prevailing within most vehicle makers.

In the end, there will be fewer large vehicle makers, many of the top firms will be a fraction of their former selves, and many jobs, much experience and a great deal of value will be lost. To have taken a different course would have been so much more efficient, but it would also have been beyond the mindset such change requires within most firms.

Eventually, the number of car models on offer will decline (in that some firms will be knocked out of the market while others will continue to proliferate), the choice available to consumers will decline and prices will gradually rise.

Collateral damage – the effect on the vehicle manufacturers' partners

On the way down, during the Graceless Degradation facing the industry unless it reforms, the worst-placed carmakers will inadvertently crush their suppliers, squeezing many to the point of bankruptcy in order to extract more savings. The world's car parts makers will suffer horribly during this time, and this will have several knock-on consequences.

For those firms that supply one of the losers and which are heavily dependent on one product for their livelihoods the outlook is very bad. Many will be forced out of business with potentially serious effects for their customers and sub-suppliers. It is possible, for example, that a weaker vehicle manufacturer could sow the seeds of its own destruction by crushing one of its own critical suppliers out of business.

For those that supply a wider range of products to the weaker carmakers the prospect is disintegration. For companies such as Delphi, still heavily dependent on GM, and Visteon, which still counts Ford as its major customer, or Valeo, which is a conglomerate of mainly tier 2 product lines, there is a substantial risk of downsizing and fragmentation. There is, after all, little strategic logic to these businesses, now that the systems and components industry is well into its transition from country-based to global. They simply sell a wide range of car parts, mostly to one company in the case of the first two. Moreover, there is little physical integration of most of the parts they sell and few technological synergies between them, although that may be less true of Delphi than the others. So they face being forced to cut back, to sell off their saleable businesses to rivals and becoming a shadow of what they once were. Of course, they could try to manage

to diversify their customer bases quickly but this is almost impossible too. Supply contracts are often decided years in advance, locking customers to their suppliers for the life of a model. Under this scenario, Toyota is expected to prosper and so then will Denso.

For the remainder – companies that sell single or multiple products to a range of vehicle makers – the choices are plain. As we know from our discussions, many of the firms in this situation are already a long way down the road in thinking about this and have come to the same conclusions we have. They will have to choose their customers with care. This means that they will progressively abandon the weaker vehicle makers, especially as these customers increase the pressure on prices, hastening the process of some carmakers' decline.

Again, at the end of the day, there will be many fewer parts makers, prices for components will generally rise and choice will decline. All of this is good and right. But at the same time a great deal of capability will be lost from the industry and a great many jobs. This change could have been achieved so much better.

During this degradation process, there are likely to be other consequences too. Many of the auto industry's components manufacturers are increasingly vocal about how tired they are at the way they are treated by many of the vehicle manufacturers. But they have had little power to fight back. When forced into a corner, however, they might. Some have already spoken to us about how they might mount a campaign aimed at legislators. They feel a need to have their story heard. Most feel that they have been unfairly brutalised by their customers already, that many carmakers have been using their monopsonist power unfairly and that it is time that this changed. So expect a different kind of news story from the components manufacturers in the newspapers.

Further down the supply chain the effects will be similar. Smaller sub-suppliers are at the mercy of who their customers are. If they have backed a winner they will survive and maybe prosper. If not, they face a tough time. Most tier 2 suppliers will need to decide whether they are going to be global specialists, investing in product technology and development, mastering manufacturing processes and costs, and putting in capacity wherever in the world their customers call for it; or whether they are going to act as local capacity providers, with all the risks of competitive displacement by suppliers from lower-cost countries that that entails. Again, the necessary consolidation and geographical redeployment of assets is not likely to be optimal in an environment of simple, brutal, undifferentiated pressure on prices. Many of the good suppliers will disappear with the bad.

At the other end of the supply chain, there is likely to be an equally messy time. The dealers and distributors of cars made by the winning carmakers will do better, although even here they risk the loss of their servicing businesses in Europe and they will see all sorts of new competitors springing up. For those who sell the cars made by the firms set to suffer most, for those supplying cars made by Ford, Fiat or GM for example, there are considerable uncertainties. They could easily find themselves having to retail a diminishing model line-up with ever lower margins. Moreover they would be expected to sell cars with declining residual values – which customers feel uneasy about buying. Again, some of these companies will be powerless to respond to these pressures; they will be at the mercy of the fate of their suppliers, the carmakers. This is the price of slavish adherence to the concept of single-brand proprietary distribution, in which dealers have to a large extent been used as conduits into the market for the output of the assembly plants. Once again, the good will get dragged down with the bad, unable to control their own fate, because they have not been able or willing to become truly independent businesses and strong enough to act as a counterweight to their domineering masters.

The process of Graceless Degradation is likely to take as long as a decade, although for some firms the serious implications will come much sooner. Overall, though, it will be a long drawn-out and nasty business where the tussles between the unions, the suppliers, the legislators and the dealers will become more heated and more intense. Even those with a strong position are likely to find that the choppy waters surrounding the industry will impact upon them too. If dealers and suppliers around the world are being squeezed, if margins across the industry are under pressure, if there is a climate of fear among the unions, everyone's nerves will become frayed.

Investment in new technology will be cut back too, meaning that solutions to today's emissions problems will be shelved. Even without having to spend on cutting-edge fuel cells or lower emission engines, Deutsche Bank thinks that the industry will have to increase R&D spending on existing technologies by 20 per cent to meet coming legislative and competitive demands. How can this be funded? It will certainly mean that blue-sky spending will go to hell – and it may fatally compromise the industry's ability to respond to social and environmental challenges.

Governments will come under pressure during this time to intervene too. They will be asked to raise trade barriers perhaps, to bail out weaker firms and to support dying sectors within the industry. Some governments will probably respond to these calls, making the whole process less economically efficient and even more sub-optimal. Some nations will be left without an industry – large chunks of their economy will go – as is happening in Italy with Fiat. Public sector resources will be diverted from where they should be applied – ensuring sustainable mobility of acceptable quality – in all regions of the world. The worst sufferers will be the emerging markets, which will not receive the needed transfer of experience in emissions, safety and traffic management that they need from those regions which have preceded them down the route of motorisation.

And what will be left? An industry looking as if it has gone through a war: some victors with difficult tales to tell, many injured, weakened perhaps irretrievably, and a number of major casualties; an end-game that is not the best possible one. There will a be lot of lost jobs, lost brands and models, lost products, a lot of economic discontinuities remaining and a lot of bad blood between suppliers, customers, unions and legislators. The prices of cars will be higher, the choice given to consumers will be less. Yet fewer models will be economically efficient to manufacture. Choice will go down in an arbitrary manner – the industry will lose good products along with the bad. It is likely to lose, for example, a large part of the Italian styling industry, which would be a tragedy. A colossal waste of automotive talent and experience will occur. A few big firms will dominate the industry but they are unlikely to be those that dominate it today. For a while the sector will be profitable again. But schisms will remain, problems will be unresolved. Eventually these will return to haunt the industry again: in ten years, perhaps, when the Chinese become strong.

This process is not elegant. Instead of having a rational business, there will simply be a different, higher-cost one. Rick Wagonner, the chairman of GM, has argued that the loss of a few companies is a solution to the industry's problems. This might be so, were the industry rational in its economics and behaviour. We simply do not believe the outcome will be so clean and simple, given the deep instincts for command-and-control within the industry and the protectionist reactions that surround it.

So another decade of trouble for the industry beckons, in a business that has shown a grotesque inability to reform itself.

There is, inevitably, a better way – a solution to these problems – and it is one we are about to review. But it will need a radical change in the mindset of the industry and the adoption of a entirely new business model. That will be extremely hard, conceptually as well as practically. And, as we shall see, it is often the strongest companies in the industry today that are least prepared or likely to make the necessary leap of imagination. It could all be very different.

9

Time for a model change

A way out of the impasse – the Fourth automotive Revolution

In the course of this book, we have identified three major transitions that the industry has gone through in the first hundred years of its existence. Each of them was a revolution, in that it involved a major discontinuity in the organisation of the industry and enabled a leap forward in productivity and cost. In each instance, the manufacturer that provoked the change benefited disproportionately. It changed the rules of the game, upset the competitive equilibrium and leapt ahead of its less perceptive and innovative competitors.

The first three great automotive revolutions are portrayed in figure 9.1. The first huge transition was the epoch-making work of Henry Ford. He leap-frogged over all his craft-based competitors by applying mass-production techniques. The price paid was total standardisation of the product, perhaps even the line worker. In his turn, Sloan leap-frogged over Ford by reintroducing a controlled level of customisation, coupled with divisionalisation and a rational distribution of roles between specialised entities. Then Toyota leap-frogged over the customised mass-producers with lean production. Its competitors stayed in the game by semi-successfully copying leanness and by pushing yet further down the customisation road. Our belief, our argument, is that this further customisation is now well into the zone of diminishing returns, as the industry fails to understand the cost penalties of product proliferation. This is why there is both the need and the opportunity for what we have called the Fourth Revolution.

Our analysis of the underlying economics of the industry leads us to believe that it can be structured and run in a far more cost-effective manner. There are enormous structural redundancies at virtually all levels of the business today, which are the result of an outmoded definition of roles, held together by forced, power-based relationships. There is a better way to tackle the enormous and deepening problems of this industry than to be reactive and tinker at the margins, while allowing oneself to be eventually overwhelmed by circumstances.

Our message is that the industry is at the edge of another potentially great transition. It needs to revisit the other lesson of Sloan, the one about roles. It needs to re-cut its economics along different lines. It needs to unbundle and reconstitute itself in order to achieve the optimal balance between scale (which favours a good cost position) and diversity (which favours market penetration and better prices) at each level of the long chain that leads from primary materials producers through the vehicle manufacturer to the service garage – and even into recycling.

The Fourth Revolution we are proposing is simple in concept and radical in what it will mean. It means that companies will have to take an entirely different look at their businesses; they will have to redefine them. They will have to re-cut them along new and much more economically attractive lines.

Should a carmaker actually make cars? Should it make engines? Should it sell or even brand cars? Could a carmaker retreat to a

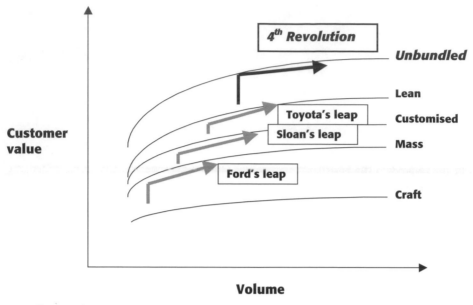

*Source: auto*POLIS

Fig. 9.1 The four automotive revolutions

position where it does not actually manufacture cars or develop their underlying technologies at all? Could a carmaker establish a sustainable business buying these sorts of services in, defining the vehicle, branding it and selling it – a carmaker with a good reputation for model innovation, a healthy dealer network and not enough money to make everything in-house? Could another carmaker specialise in the underlying technologies or the process of assembly? Could it relinquish its business in the rest of the industry and build cars to order for someone else? Could it sell platforms and engines to companies that today would be regarded as rivals? Could it assemble cars that have been designed by entirely different companies, that are sold in separate multi-brand outlets or that are branded by firms that have never even been in the automotive industry before? Could some car companies just focus on engines, on the electronics architecture of a car or bolting the parts together?

The potential gains at all levels of the value chain from a radical change in thinking like this are immense, as shown on pp. 241–4,

which is why we repeat them in summary here. In Europe alone:

- End customers pay 10 per cent less for the equivalent new car, saving themselves $29 billion per year.
- Distribution and retailing cost 25 per cent less, saving $20 billion, while the mass retailers who take over these functions are able to have a normal commercial relationship with their suppliers and to earn normal returns on their investments. As part of this, manufacturers save a huge amount on their own distribution and marketing costs.
- Manufacturers pay 5 per cent less for their bought-in parts and materials, saving $6 billion per year. But suppliers gain two to three times as much on their own costs, as product proliferation is no longer forced on them. There is no further need for the brutal pressures on them to cut prices. Again, the commercial relationship becomes a normal one. Suppliers' margins are restored to the point at which they can really fulfil their expanded roles in product development and production.

- Vehicle manufacturers' margins are tripled, restoring their financial health and enabling them to invest in the various new technologies required to keep them in business in an increasingly demanding social and regulatory environment.

That is the scale of the potential gains, as we can grasp them today. They are in all probability even greater, once the new industry model is properly adopted and perfected.

There are heavy requirements on the industry if it is to achieve this new stage of economic perfection. First of all, individual manufacturers must abandon their old industry model and its comforting pseudo-certainties:

- Each must, as a function of its own circumstances and possibilities, redefine what its future core business must be. Should it be an integrated developer of platforms, major driveline components and complete vehicles? Or could it survive better in the role of designer and packager – the virtual manufacturer concept – at the limit? Similar fundamental questions need to be asked about manufacturing. What should stay in-house; what could be more effectively bought in?
- Each must define the extent of that core business. What customer segments will they target? What do these customers want; what are they prepared to pay for it? Must each manufacturer offer a full line-up of products or could they specialise? Does the achievement of competitive scale and cost position require a regional or a global position? Will this enable them to differentiate themselves from competitors, as opposed to competing head-on?
- Each must decide on its optimal channels to market, as a function of the real requirements and preferences of customers in its chosen market segments. Should these channels be brand proprietary or common? What functions should be incorporated? Which partners should be selected to carry out these roles?

Every current and potential actor in the huge systems, components, materials and services supply industry needs to be asking itself similar questions:

- How will the existing tiering pyramid evolve? What new roles could emerge, notably independent developers and producers of platforms but also independent providers of novel-technology powertrains and – very critically – of the systems architecture or central nervous system of the vehicle?
- Which role should each actor choose? Will the one equipped with the technology, R&D capabilities, manufacturing skills and ability to interface with the vehicle manufacturers be a true systems supplier? Should another be a technology-based tier 2 component supplier? Is another's best prospect to provide flexible manufacturing capacity?
- For each player in their chosen role, what is the minimum rational extent of their future business for it to be sustainable and defensible? Must all conceivable applications be covered, or is specialisation in a sub-set viable? Are the applications homogeneous across the globe or is a regional presence feasible?

The same kinds of issues must be dealt with in the downstream sector:

- In what circumstances does the traditional bundled dealership, closely linked to one vehicle brand, have a future?
- What is the scope for other formats, from pluri-branded dealerships to hard sales-only discounters? Aiming at what customer segments in which countries and regions?
- What is the opportunity for properly constituted and resourced all-makes routine service chains? What services must they offer? What are the future roles for deskilled chains? For technical specialists?
- What roles can be played in parts distribution? Can independent distribution groups take over a significant part of supplying current and ex-franchise dealers? Is it best for

them to control their own chains of branded workshops, or to deal at arm's length? How can these workshops be supported with technical and marketing information and assistance?

Supporting services will also need to revisit their business definitions:

- What are the legitimate roles of sales financing and leasing in developing and stabilising new vehicle markets? At what point do they tip over into becoming unwitting tools of volume-hungry manufacturers or of insolvent and unreliable consumers? Should a bank exploit its customer relationships and database to sell cars?
- How can insurers ensure that the crash repair industry, of which they are the largest customers, is structured and functions effectively?
- What role can contract engineering suppliers play in the new dispensation, or systems houses? How should they define their fields, in terms of services, applications, customers and geographical coverage?

The capital markets may play new roles too:

- How can they exercise much more effective control a priori, instead of discovering the results a posteriori? What kind of information should they seek from the industry? Should it not be much more segmented, for example identifying the promised and achieved economic results of major projects, whether new vehicles, new systems, new production facilities or new distribution and service networks?
- What financial instruments could be used in different circumstances? Should, for example, finance be raised for specific major projects, as opposed to funding the balance sheets of large corporate entities, with little or no internal transparency?

Governments need to revisit their roles, be better informed and more pro-active, and interface with the industry more effectively:

- How can they encourage the industry to experiment with new technologies that make better use of fuel resources and limit environmental damage?
- How can they best get a grip on traffic congestion and road safety in the advanced countries?
- How can they best ensure the transfer of learning to developing countries, in order to help them limit the negative environmental and social impact of their inevitable motorisation?
- How can they ensure the right balance between competition and collaboration between the different levels and players in and around the industry?

The above requirements are necessarily generic. The plot gets a lot more vivid and exciting if we allow ourselves to speculate a bit about individual players. As in all revolutions, there will be major upsets, i.e. major winners and major losers. The fact that the economic model of the industry is due to change so much means that the competitive rules of the game will also be greatly modified. Those who appear almost invincible today may emerge seriously weakened. Unexpected players, from both inside and outside the industry, may rise to prominence. Let us look a few examples.

We believe that a Fourth Revolution model will allow less sameness and more role differentiation between vehicle manufacturers:

- Of all vehicle manufacturers Toyota plays the current automotive system closest to perfection. It has gone to immense trouble to eliminate waste and inefficiency from the current system. But so did Henry Ford in his time – only to be leap-frogged over by the infant GM's superior new approach. We do see it as a major gainer in the medium term, again, within the current system, eating away at the US and European heartlands. It has immense financial, technological and manufacturing strengths. But it also tends to the conservative. It is a steam-roller, heading down a clear path. What if that path changes? What if it is outflanked by one or more competitors who 'lean' the whole structure of their business, as opposed to just its operating practices?

- GM may be in a favourable position to exploit its continuing large size and the scale of its cashflow. It has always maintained a large commitment to real R&D, as opposed to applied engineering within product development. If any player does, it should be able to maintain proprietary control over propulsion technologies, vehicle systems integration (the central nervous system) and at least some platforms – within the new dispensation. It also seems to have become more aware of the limits of its current path and more open to the ideas of a radical solution. Could it find another Alfred Sloan within itself, to instigate the new revolution?

- Fourth Revolution thinking should also be a natural concept for Daimler-Benz, across cars as well as light and heavy vehicles – it is the world's largest manufacturer of trucks and buses outside China. Its more limited volume in passenger cars, compared to the volume giants, is compensated for by its upline price positioning. It has played a pioneering role in the new technologies, from fuel cell cars to telematics. But its ability to sustain and finance this investment for the long term risks being fatally compromised by the drain imposed by its American and Swiss patients – Chrysler and Smart. It has also been weakened in many ways through its link with Mitsubishi. Daimler really needs to redefine what will be its future core businesses if it is to prosper. Perhaps that might bring the company sufficient impetus for change. We hope so.

- Chrysler could in theory play the exact opposite strategy, reverting to its historical positioning as a regional low-integration innovator, relying on other people's scale and buying in much of its technology, including its engines and model platforms, for example. These are the scale-driven parts of developing a vehicle. If Chrysler let others do this, it could develop a strong role in using these

to develop specialist vehicles for specialist niches: something it has shown an enduring ability to do. This assumes that it survives its present financial debacle and the Japanese attack on its US home market.

- Ford should have the scale and resources to play a similar role to GM. However, its toing and froing between centralisation and decentralisation, exemplified by the Ford 2000 project, its attempted entry into and retreat from the downstream sector, and the general rigidity of its management do not suggest openness to imaginative strategies. The company still remains marked by the legacy of Fordism and a finance-driven approach to business. The unbundling revolution may not come in time to save it, and it risks not understanding how to play by the Fourth Revolution's rules. In the meantime Ford in Europe is at serious risk, in the context of Ford's US troubles and the apparent difficulty in overcoming them. GM Europe should be better placed in the new paradigm, thanks to its generally greater autonomy from its parent.

- Renault-Nissan has shown the ability to execute major turnarounds. Above all, it is prepared to make a fundamental analysis of a situation and to explore radical alternatives. With enough internal rationalisation – which needs to go well beyond the original objective of ten common platforms by 2010 – it could remain a large, integrated group. It arguably has the broadest overview of world markets of any competitor, with major positions in all three major automotive regions. It is another potential early adopter of the concept, especially given the flair of its leaders.

- PSA Peugeot-Citroën has shown the willingness to seek joint scale with other vehicle manufacturers, notably through the sharing of its second-generation diesel engine technology. Its care in husbanding its development resources to support a carefully delimited product line, together with its focus on Europe as its principal market, shows how it defines its core business. But it is also a fairly conservative group, successful within the existing norms of the industry. This may cause it some of the same adaptation problems as Toyota. It could also have some real problems if the driveline technology base of the industry changes substantially.

- There is every prospect of Fiat disappearing as a corporate entity within the near to medium term. Under present industry arrangements, Italy will be devastated. Unbundling might, however, reduce the misery, allowing specific units to be salvaged. These could include engineering, specialised facilities and a limited number of the more up-to-date assembly plants. Why could Italy not offer assembly operations for new vehicle integrators, for those who have chosen to focus their core businesses on other parts of the value chain and for those who want to unbundle vehicle production? The styling sector in Italy could find a new lease of life too.

- VW is perhaps the hardest to call. It is furthest along the platform rationalisation road today but has been showing ominous signs of excess product proliferation and brand confusion of late. Would its management have the breadth of vision and foresight to offer its platforms to others, in order to maintain scale, as PSA has done in diesel engines? To succeed, it needs to unbundle and rebundle in search of the optimal scale/diversity balance at each level, given its high fixed costs and persistent low profitability. That will require some radical thinking.

- Honda might need to go down the PSA route, perhaps becoming a gasoline engine expert, sharing these products with others. Whether it has the flexibility to do so is another question. It faces some of the same risks as Toyota and VW.

- BMW appears secure in a Fourth Revolution, provided it can sustain its hitherto very successful product development strategy (with a fairly limited offering) and premium quality image. It is vulnerable to a major shift in driveline technology, however, as its concept of hydrogen-fuelled piston engines is not particularly convincing. BMW might have to consider unbundling its engines, perhaps, and that may be a difficult step for it to take for many reasons.

- The smaller manufacturers from the developed regions are now all under the control of larger groups. Their best chance, as with Chrysler, might be to decouple from them and act as virtual manufacturers, selling into niche markets. Whether this leaves room for all of them is questionable. Volvo might survive but not Saab. Jaguar and Land Rover do not start with favourable circumstances, nor does MG Rover – even though the latter has started down this road to a limited degree with India's Tata.

- The peripheral Asian players seem unlikely to survive a Fourth Revolution. South Korea may not be able to support even one major carmaker. Daewoo, Samsung, Kia and Ssangyong have already been absorbed. Proton is an entirely artificial creation, living behind protectionist walls. Hyundai risks being squeezed between competitive pressures, a mature domestic market and the emerging power of the Chinese.

- As discussed earlier, two or more Chinese majors may emerge, plus one Indian, Tata. All of these would be able, in our opinion, to adapt to a new model. Indeed all are well placed to exploit it. Russia may want to support its own independent manufacturers but their ability to keep up technologically is getting weaker and weaker, as Russia continues to stagnate politically and economically. We see less potential there.

In the end, we are likely to end up with a very small club of integrated majors – probably three or four of today's set plus a couple of Chinese. These would be the big firms and some of those familiar to us today. These companies would provide a full range of automotive products and technologies; they would be scale driven. They would also brand and sell the products they build and provide much of their base technology to companies regarded as rivals today.

Who might these big firms be? GM, perhaps. Renault-Nissan, maybe. Both have the greatest chances, along with First Auto Works, Shanghai Auto and Tata, of being in the new big league. Others with the potential to play at this level are less obvious. As we have already said, Toyota's potential role in a Fourth Revolution remains unclear to us. That is a big gap. The remaining integrated majors may come as a result of acquisitions, orchestrated by those outside the industry perhaps, with the concept and the drive to push it through. They may be large component and systems makers today. But these companies could include entirely new entrants to the industry – broad-based engineering companies, banking and finance houses, those developing new engine technologies, even oil companies – businesses with the vision to push through a Fourth Revolution and with a role to play.

We are also likely to be left with a couple of upline specialists, of which BMW looks likely to be one. There would also be space for a few local assemblers serving niches, such as Chrysler. This group might also include Porsche as well as Peugeot and Honda perhaps. There are also likely to be a number of entirely new businesses within the industry, playing entirely different roles from those defined today. Chemicals and electronics companies, plastics businesses and even fashion designers could find completely new business opportunities. These will be people who can cut out a role for themselves, outsource what they cannot provide and build sustainable new business models in a changed industry.

The unbundling of the automotive business would mean that there might only be a dozen platforms in each region, with an overlap between those used for passenger cars in the US and Japan. That compares with more than 200 around the world today. Just imagine how much saving this would generate for the components sector through proper standardisation. Just imagine how much easier it would make the assembly and repairs business.

Much will depend on the systems and components industry. This has already made a considerable start on rationalisation around the world but it has a good deal further to go along this road. Survival is going to be a matter of forcing the pace of investment in new technologies, products and manufacturing processes, while achieving the sales revenues, margins and cashflow to support it all. As in vehicle manufacturing, the unbundling scenario supports a more rational allocation of resources, as individual actors are forced to adopt more clearly defined and economically rational roles. Remaining national or regional champions will no longer be protected, either by vehicle manufacturers or by governments, except in some markets such as China and India.

Within any given business in this new model for the industry – and a business is defined by a clearly related set of technologies, applications and accessible volumes – we expect to see three or four competitors. The geographical scope of the different businesses will continue to vary, as explained in chapter 5. Standardisation of componentry in pursuit of scale-derived cost gains may extend the supply radius for some of the intermediate categories of product somewhat. The remaining Japanese *keiretsu* structures will be forced open, a trend which has already begun. Conglomeration of unrelated systems and components will cease to have much attraction. Bosch, Denso and Delphi are prospective large survivors, with the latter forced to accelerate its redeployment from its GM-related base of activities to more focused sets with a wider customer base. Visteon, well behind it in this process, may face some difficulties, as will Valeo, unless it goes through an accelerated redeployment of its portfolio. Magneti Marelli is already facing dissolution.

Tier 2 suppliers will be very substantially rationalised and forced to make clear choices of positioning. We can expect to see the emergence of some real global players, based on specialised technologies and capabilities. For many others, the prospects are grim. That is, unfortunately, a cost of the new model – although it is a cost of any model for the future of the industry. There are simply too many sub-scale companies at this level of the business today.

The most radical area of change will be in the downstream sector, simply because it is still so far from the future unbundled Fourth Revolution model. A very few upline vehicle manufacturers and their customers will continue to be able to afford the traditional close-coupled, fully bundled, brand-exclusive retailing system. The volume middle ground will be occupied by powerful independent multi-makes sales chains, following more general retail practices. The same will happen in routine service and repair. Major outlet brands will be reduced from thirty or forty to three or four, with some local chains and independents still co-existing with them, as will networks of technical service and repair specialists, controlled by Tier 1 systems suppliers. Major restructuring will also happen in the crash repair sector, as insurers give up on half-hearted approval schemes, accept more normal trading relationships and concentrate their powers of economic persuasion on the supply of parts and paint.

The downstream changes will take some time to happen. They will be bitterly resisted by vested interests – the vehicle manufacturers everywhere and entrenched dealer bodies in the US. The UK and perhaps some Belgian dealer groups are the likely early leaders in Europe, with other countries following suit later. Reform of protective dealer laws is an extremely difficult subject in the US. The critical factor will be control of emergent true service networks. This is because service is the fount of aftermarket revenues, for dealers as well as manufacturers, as described in chapter 6. Nothing will accelerate the shake-out of sales channels and of product lines as effectively as the removal of monopoly rents in service and parts. Similar arguments apply in vehicle-related financial services.

A Fourth Revolution in the automotive industry would be just as radical as all the previous revolutions. It would change the eco-nomics of the business, change the rules of the game and allow new companies to move the industry, the technology and the car as a social phenomenon forward. With a Fourth Revolution we can look forward to a much leaner, more efficient and more profitable industry. It would be lean in all its structures and functions, not just in the manufacturing ones affected by the lean production movement. The Fourth Revolution would unleash a vast amount of intellectual energy, offer a wide variety of new directions and generate an array of new ideas from which huge gains in performance could be expected. It will not be a short or easy road. There will be much resistance. But in the end economic rationality will prevail.

There is a choice, then, and it is the industry that has to choose. Does it want the Graceless Degradation that will be the outcome of its refusal, its failure to act? Or does it have the courage to think about orderly, but revolutionary, reform once again. As in the past, with the other three revolutions, the benefits of positive change will be much greater. A planned revolution is infinitely preferable.

One final point. The options facing the world's automotive industry – a Graceless Degradation or a Fourth Revolution – are not mutually exclusive. Nor are they absolutes. A situation in which there is no change in direction will be more likely to lead to a messy series of compromises. The degradation is likely to be a little more graceful, a little less messy, than we have postulated. Similarly, a Fourth Revolution will take time to have any radical effect. It may not seem to be much of a revolution for a while.

We have detailed the options in this way to show the range of possibilities – the extremes. At one end, this 'industry of industries' could face a rather unhappy decade for reasons that many in the business will find hard to understand. At the other, there is the possibility of radical change, of positive change: change of the sort the industry has been famous for in the past. Our challenge, our intention with this book, is very simple. In some very small way we would like to help make that change possible.

Last words – lessons from history

There are many theories about the structures of economic sectors and why some actors and nations within them are more or less successful. Much academic research has been expended on theories of competition. Much is written about corporate culture, quite a lot of it pretty woolly. All these subjects are treated largely separately. Their intersections and interactions have not been much explored.

Within the confines of this short book, we have sought to explore the structures, relationships and behaviour patterns within one of the world's greatest industries – an industry which, because of the complexity of its final products, is particularly marked by inevitable interdependencies between its various levels and actors; one in which the cultures and behaviour of its architects and leaders, the vehicle manufacturers, have a very real effect on all the other actors who have to work with or against them. As we have worked in this industry over the years, and as we have thought about how we would describe the industry in this book, the persistence of cultural and behavioural patterns over long periods of time has struck us very forcefully.

Revolutions happen because the present state of affairs becomes intolerable for a significant proportion of the actors involved in it. The system as a whole has simply become dysfunctional. A change of paradigm is required. A revolution – unlike a coup d'état – is something that has been brewing for a while, as the forces for change gather their strength, until the historic moment comes, while the existing masters cling obstinately to power by every protective and repressive means at their disposal. They no longer lead, they micro-

manage, terrified of truly delegating power. The longer they oppose the change, the more graceless the degradation and the greater the risk of destructive conflagration. They are ultimately unable to micro-manage in enough scope and detail and lose control.

We believe this to be the situation of much of the automotive industry today, at the start of its second century, even though we are talking about an oligarchy and not a single ruling power. All the signs are there:

- self-importance and obsession with power – the firmly held belief, for example, that the industry is unique and owed a special deal;
- lack of trust in partners – we have detailed this extensively, with respect to both the upstream and downstream sectors of the industry;
- compulsive command-and-control behaviour – the very costly and ultimately ineffective policing and micro-managing of franchised dealers is a good example of this;
- reluctance to relinquish territory, clinging on to close supervision of suppliers, and the failure to accept real delegation of responsibility to them;
- contempt for legal authority – one can hardly find a better example than the whole sorry saga of the European automotive industry's approach to the 2002 renewal of the Block Exemption Regulation;
- squandering resources – the product proliferation race, which vies with the 1970s horsepower race in the US for unproductive absurdity;
- bribing the masses with bread and circuses – look no further than the auto shows, the ludicrous advertising, motor 'sport', all designed to feed infantile fantasies rather than meet any real needs;
- blind faith in outmoded dogmas – the obsession with branding, even unrelated to any real product attributes, and in branded proprietary distribution channels;
- irrational responses to legitimate criticism – the head-in-the sand attitude taken by the

vehicle industry to the flagrant pricing abuses to which UK consumers were subjected, and their exposure by consumer groups and the media.

Our Fourth Revolution is the most profound of them all, for it affects not just the production function, as did the first three revolutions, but the whole system of relationships in the industry. Once the industry moved out of the phase of the pure entrepreneur, the polymath who had to and could do everything more or less for himself, relationships with partners became steadily more important. Only their quality never kept up with this. It has generally been – with some honourable exceptions – at least one step behind the times. Micro-management is not the same thing as empowerment. It is the transition from the former to the latter that the automotive industry has yet to complete.

Karl Marx believed and taught that if the structures of production and wealth creation were put in the right hands the state and its set of relationships would wither away. The tragedy of the communist adventure in the Soviet Union was that exactly the opposite happened. The founding fathers of the American republic believed the opposite. The US constitution secures the relationships, checks and balances of the government, while economic actors are left to devise their roles and structures as freely as possible. This is exactly the transition in the management of the downstream sector of the industry that the European Commission has undertaken, from the previous two Block Exemption Regulations to the latest. The key to the efficient and equitable functioning of the sector lies, they saw, in proper relationships, within a framework of checks and balances. Structures of networks were not to be prescribed but left to the economic actors, within the framework of the regulation. It is an enormous philosophical and practical change. We believe that few in the industry have really understood its importance and potential impact. They need to.

The challenge to each and every actor in this vast industry is to move from micro-management and cross-border poaching to leadership and real collaboration.

What is our role in all this; why have we written this book? Quite simply because we want to help promote positive change. A velvet revolution, of the sort that happened in Portugal, is infinitely preferable to the revolution that happened in Yugoslavia. Apart from writing this book, in helping to identify the roots of this revolution – which has applications in a great many other business sectors too, we believe – we also try to work in more practical ways. Through our work in the industry, with governments and with universities, we have consistently found that those that lead the industry, in major corporations and minor, often need a push, a voice from the outside to help promote new thinking. Much of our work is in this area and will continue to be.

So what do you need to do, how should you take your business and think about it differently? How can you decide whether or not you need to behave differently, approach the market in a new way? After all, you may not need to change at all. But you should periodically ask the pertinent questions. We have several suggestions of steps you can take without calling in people like us.

1 First, understand the legitimate best limits of your core business, and concentrate on that. Do not squander resources by straying outside its limits. Be very clear about what you need to hold on to, what you can and should share, and what you should delegate to more competent partners. Think about it from the ground up on occasion.

2 Get to grips with its economics. Know when to invest and when not to. Do not over-egg the pudding, for example by pouring in more and more products when that only leads to a negative-sum game. Do not pour money into emerging markets just because your competitors do. See if it really makes

sense and think about the best time to enter.

3 Know your competitors. Do not get into a head-on clash of imitation and sterile rivalry, which only leads to value-destroying price wars. Seek a real differentiation in your products and market positioning, which will in turn support a valid brand image, to which consumers can really relate.

4 Nurture your selected partners and help them grow in competence. Share the benefits generously.

5 Welcome variety and experimentation, particularly in the downstream sector and its channels. Do not seek to impose uniformity and conformity.

These precepts apply to all companies in this and other industries. In the automotive industry they apply to vehicle designers and assemblers; suppliers of every description and in every tier of the supply chain; distributors and retailers; service and repair providers; financial institutions, working with every level of the industry; government agencies; consumer groups; and political institutions.

For governments there are similar questions as well as those about emissions, road safety and the transfer of knowledge to others.

The Fourth Revolution is as much a way of thinking as a way of organising this or any other industry. It is just like any other revolution.

Index

DATE DUE